1 John, 2 John, 3 John

Pentecostal Commentary Series

General Editor

John Christopher Thomas

Deo Publishing

1 JOHN
2 JOHN
3 JOHN

John Christopher Thomas

BLANDFORD FORUM

Pentecostal Commentary Series

First published by T&T Clark International, 2004
and in the USA and Canada by The Pilgrim Press, 2004
This edition copyright © 2011 Deo Publishing
P.O. Box 6284, Blandford Forum, Dorset DT11 1AQ, UK

All rights reserved. No part of this publication may be reproduced, translated, stored in a retrieval system, or transmitted in any form or by any means, electronic, mechanical, photocopying, recording or otherwise, without prior written permission from the publisher.

Adapted from an edition typeset by TMW Typesetting, Sheffield
Printed by Henry Ling Ltd, at the Dorset Press, Dorchester, DT1 1HD, UK

British Library Cataloguing-in-Publication data
A catalogue record for this book is available from the British Library

ISBN 978-1-905679-21-8

For my Sweetheart

Contents

Editor's Preface	ix
Author's Preface	xiii
Abbreviations	xvi
Introduction	1

Part I

3 John	16

Part II

2 John	38

Part III

1 John	54
1 John 1.1-4	61
1 John 1.5–2.2	71
1 John 2.3-17	92
1 John 2.18-27	123
1 John 2.28–3.10	142
1 John 3.11-17	171
1 John 3.18-24	184
1 John 4.1-6	197
1 John 4.7–5.5	214
1 John 5.6-12	249
1 John 5.13-21	264
Bibliography	283

Editor's Preface

The purpose of this commentary series is to provide reasonably priced commentaries written from a distinctively Pentecostal perspective primarily for pastors, lay persons, and Bible students. Therefore, while the works are based upon the best of scholarship, they are written in popular language. The aim is to communicate the meaning of the text, with minimal technical distractions.

In order to explain the need for such an attempt to read the biblical text, it is necessary to understand something of the ethos of Pentecostalism.

Pentecostalism is a relatively recent phenomenon in comparison to its Christian siblings, given that its formal origins go back about a hundred years. By any means of calculation it continues to grow very rapidly in many places around the globe and accounts for a not insignificant percentage of the world's Christians. Current estimates of those who would identify themselves as part of the Pentecostal-Charismatic movements range from 380,000,000 to 500,000,000. According to David Barrett, the global profile of Pentecostalism is as follows:

> Some 29 percent of all members worldwide are white, 71 percent are nonwhite. Members are more urban than rural, more female than male, more children (under eighteen years) than adults, more third-world (66 per cent) than western world (32 per cent), more living in poverty (87 per cent) than affluence (13 per cent), more family-related than individualist.[1]

Yet, despite its demographic significance, Pentecostalism continues to be largely misunderstood by many outside the movement. For example, there are those who 'see Pentecostalism as essentially fundamentalist Christianity with a doctrine of Spirit baptism and gifts added on' and others who view it 'as an experience which fits equally well in any spirituality or theological system – perhaps adding some needed zest or interest'.[2] Yet, those who know the tradition well are aware how far from

---

1 D. Barrett, 'Statistics, Global', in S.M. Burgess and G.B. McGee (eds.), *Dictionary of the Pentecostal and Charismatic Movements* (Grand Rapids: Zondervan, 1988), pp. 810-29 (811).
2 Steven J. Land, *Pentecostal Spirituality: A Passion for the Kingdom* (JPTSup, 1; Sheffield: Sheffield Academic Press, 1993), p. 29.

the truth such assessments are. As Donald W. Dayton[3] and Steven J. Land[4] have demonstrated, standing at the theological heart of Pentecostalism is the message of the fivefold gospel: Jesus is Savior, Sanctifier, Holy Spirit Baptizer, Healer, and Coming King. This paradigm not only identifies the theological heart of the tradition, but also immediately reveals the ways in which Pentecostalism as a movement is both similar to and dissimilar from others within Christendom. When the fivefold gospel paradigm is used as the main point of reference Pentecostalism's near kinship to the holiness tradition is obvious, as is the fundamental difference from many of those within the more reformed Evangelical tradition. It also reveals the surprising similarities between Pentecostalism and the Roman Catholic and Orthodox traditions.

Therefore, the production of a Pentecostal Commentary Series representative of the tradition's ethos requires more than simply selecting contributors who have had a glossolalic experience. Rather, the process of composition as well as the physical format of the commentary should be in keeping with the ethos and spirituality of the tradition.

In the attempt to insure a writing process representative of the tradition, each contributor has been urged to incorporate the following disciplines in the writing of the commentary on a particular biblical book. Writers have been encouraged to engage in prayer for this project, both as individuals and as members of a community of believers. Specifically, the guidance of the Holy Spirit has been sought in these times of prayer, for the leadership of the Spirit in interpretation is essential. Specific times of prayer where the body intercedes on the writer's behalf and seeks to hear from the Lord have been encouraged.

Given the Pentecostal commitment to body ministry, where various members of the body have specific calls and responsibilities, writers have been asked to explore ways in which their scholarship might be contextualized within their own local church body and thereby be strengthened by the dynamic interaction between the Holy Spirit, the body of Christ, and the Word of God. Writers were encouraged to covenant with their churches concerning this writing project in order to seek out their spiritual support. Where possible, writers were asked to explore the possibility of leading a group Bible study on the given biblical book. Ideally, such groups included representatives from each group of the target readership.

Writers were also encouraged to seek out the advice and critique of gifted colleagues who would join with them in this project so as not to

---

3   Donald W. Dayton, *The Theological Roots of Pentecostalism* (Peabody, MA: Hendrickson, 1991).
4   Land, *Pentecostal Spirituality*.

work in isolation. This endeavor was conceived as too difficult and far-reaching to go alone. Rather it is conceived of as part of the ministry of the body of Christ, for the glory of God.

The commentary attempts to be in keeping with the ethos and spirituality of the tradition in its physical format as well. Specifically, the commentaries seek to reflect the dialogical way in which the tradition tends to approach the biblical text. Thus, each commentary begins with a series of questions designed to lift up corporate and individual issues that are illuminated in the biblical book under examination. This section identifies those key issues that are taken up in the commentary that follows. This section invites the reader to interpret his or her life context in a confessional-critical manner, as a hermeneutical task, revealing the need(s) to be addressed by the text. Such an opening serves to contextualize the commentary in the life of the Church from the very beginning and serves to teach the reader how the Bible can legitimately be used in contemporary life.

Flowing out of this initial section, the introduction proper seeks to inform the reader as to the need, process, purpose, time, and place of composition. As a trajectory of the initial section, the introduction proper seeks to be a necessary part of the commentary for the reader, and attempts to avoid the strange and irrelevant discussions that introductions often pursue. The introductions normally include topics of special interest to Pentecostals along with the usual introductory matters of authorship, place of composition, destination, audience, date, and theological emphases. A rather detailed discussion of the genre and structure of the book forms the basis of organization for the exposition that follows the introduction. In addition, a section devoted to the book's teaching about the Holy Spirit is included in the introduction.

The commentary proper provides a running exposition on the text, provides extended comments on texts of special significance for Pentecostals, and acknowledges and interacts with major options in interpreting individual passages. It also provides periodic opportunities for reflection upon and personal response to the biblical text. The reflection and response components normally occur at the end of a major section of the book. Here, a theme prominent in a specific passage is summarized in the light of the reading offered in the commentary. Next, the readers encounter a series of questions designed to lead them in corporate and personal reflection about this dimension of the text. Finally, the readers are encouraged to respond to the biblical text in specific ways. Such reflection and response is consistent with the tradition's practice of not simply hearing the words of Scripture but responding to them in concrete ways. It is the literary equivalent to the altar call.

In the attempt not to overtax the popular reader, footnotes have been used *carefully and sparingly*. However, when additional, more technical discussions are deemed necessary, they are placed in the footnotes. In addition, Greek and Hebrew words are found only within parentheses or in the footnotes.

Every attempt has been made to insure that the constituency of the movement is represented in some way among the contributors. It is my hope and prayer that the work of these women and men, from a variety of continents, races, and communities, will aid the Pentecostal community (and other interested individuals and communities) in hearing the biblical text in new and authentic ways.

John Christopher Thomas

Author's Preface

The completion of a writing project is cause for a variety of emotions. There is the joy and satisfaction of knowing that the time devoted to such a task has not been in vain. There is the humility of knowing full well one's limitations and weaknesses; limitations and weaknesses that invariably are reflected in one's work. And there is gratitude; the gratitude felt for all those who played some role in the project's successful completion.

Over a decade ago David J.A. Clines and Philip R. Davies responded enthusiastically to a proposal for Sheffield Academic Press to undertake the publication of a series of academic monographs devoted to Pentecostal Theology. Included in their response was an invitation for me and my colleagues, Rick Moore and Steve Land, to edit a journal as well. Thus was born the *Journal of Pentecostal Theology* and its accompanying supplement series of monographs. Owing to the vision and courage of these scholars and publishers, formal voice was given to Pentecostal scholars working in a variety of theological disciplines, literally from around the world. These ventures led to others, including a commitment to undertake the publication of the Pentecostal Commentary Series. Without the trust, vision, patience, and support of Philip and David, it is doubtful whether these projects would have found the place that they have in the academic community. This volume, then, is a kind of first fruits of what I hope will be a fruitful harvest for the Pentecostal Commentary Series and Sheffield Academic Press. I am honored to have worked so closely with these scholars and am happy to thank them publicly at this time for all they have done for me and my colleagues in the Pentecostal movement. I should also like to thank Sarah Norman for her detailed editing of the manuscript.

One does not write a commentary without the aid of those interpreters who have gone before. My debt to a variety of writers on the Johannine Epistles should be evident in the pages of the commentary itself.

This commentary was produced over the course of the last seven years. Some sections of it were written while in England as a Visiting Scholar at the University of Gloucestershire, Visiting Fellow at Wolfson College, Cambridge, and Visiting Fellow at Tyndale House, Cambridge.

I should like to thank Fred Hughes and Andrew Lincoln (Cheltenham), Principal Gordon Johnson (Wolfson College), and Bruce Winter (Tyndale House) for making these short stays possible.

However, the bulk of this volume was written in the midst of my teaching and other duties at the Church of God Theological Seminary, where it has been my happy privilege to serve full-time since 1982. Needless to say, the Seminary's contributions to this project have been enormous. During exploratory discussions about the nature and shape of a Pentecostal commentary, Rick D. Moore and Cheryl Bridges Johns were my constant dialogue partners. The active participation of a variety of students from numerous countries around the world in my yearly Seminar on the Johannine Epistles greatly aided this work. I offer my thanks to these students for their comments, observations, questions, and constructive criticisms. Specific mention should be made of Heather Landrus who read a draft of the manuscript and offered numerous helpful comments about it and to my graduate assistant Richard Hicks, who read the proofs of this manuscript. Thanks also are due my colleagues at the Seminary who make it a creative, constructive, and enriching environment in which to pursue numerous issues of theological, spiritual, and academic significance. Kimberly Ervin Alexander and Lee Roy Martin have been especially close colleagues to me during the writing of this commentary and have offered a variety of supports and encouragements at most every step of the way. Thanks should also be given to members of the Postgrad Seminar for offering valuable comments on the reading of 1 Jn 2.18-27. This project would not have been completed at this time without the generous grant of a study leave by the Seminary during the Autumn Term, 2001. I should very much like to offer my heartfelt thanks to the Seminary Board of Directors, former President Donald M. Walker, and current President Steven J. Land, for the gracious provision of this study leave.

The other community that has played a significant role in the production of this commentary is the Woodward Ave. Church of God in Athens, TN, where it has been my privilege to serve as part-time Associate Pastor since 1981. This thriving community represents the best of the Pentecostal tradition in its dynamic living out of the faith, its unfailing openness to the poor and others on society's margins, and its commitment to community life in the Spirit. This community has contributed to the production of this commentary in a variety of small group settings, as well as in response to periodic sermons on 1 John. But the community's contributions go far beyond discussions, reflection, and dialogue about the text of the Johannine Epistles. It includes the spiritual support of brothers and sisters whose lives have been forever altered owing to the reception of the gospel and the work of the Spirit. To have had my academic work undergirded by the love, concern, and prayers of those often forgotten by society has informed the commentary in deep and powerful ways. The earnest intercession on my behalf by those formerly enslaved by alcohol, drugs, prostitution, sexual addictions, as well as by ex-convicts, the mentally and physically challenged, immigrants (both legal and illegal), and the working poor is both a humbling and strengthening experience. My thanks to this group of believers cannot be conveyed in mere words. I hope that my own participation in this community's life conveys something of the depth of my gratitude and affection. Specific mention should be made of my parents and pastors, Wayne and Betty Fritts, whose support of me and my work know no boundaries. I would be remiss not to offer my deepest thanks to Vincent Castellani and Kevin Wallace, who joined with me in this ministry at my weakest moments and shouldered more than their share of pastoral responsibilities in order that I could take advantage of the study leave granted me by the seminary to complete the writing of this commentary.

Finally, I should like to thank my wife, Barbara, and daughters, Paige and Lori, whose love, support, and enthusiasm make all that I do possible. To Barbara I say thanks for the gift of a life that is far too often arranged around my writing and research schedule. To Paige and Lori I join with the Elder in saying, 'I have no greater joy than hearing that my children walk in the Truth' (3 Jn 4).

May the Lord use this reading of 1 John, 2 John, and 3 John as pleases him.

ABBREVIATIONS

ACCS	G. Bray (ed.), *Ancient Christian Commentary in Scripture*, XI (Downers Grove, IL: InterVarsity Press, 2000)
ANF	Anti-Nicene Fathers
BibSac	*Bibliotheca Sacra*
EDNT	*Exegetical Dictionary of the New Testament*
EvQ	*Evangelical Quarterly*
JBL	*Journal of Biblical Literature*
JSNT	*Journal for the Study of the New Testament*
NovT	*Novum Testamentum*
NTS	*New Testament Studies*

Introduction

What happens when leaders within the Church disagree? How can one be open to the leading of the Holy Spirit and, at the same time, not go beyond the teaching of Scripture? Since believers have an anointing from God and do not need anyone to teach them (1 Jn 2.27), what role, if any, should teachers play within the Church? What should be the attitude of believers to those who proclaim a teaching that is not in accord with Scripture? What is a believer's responsibility when a brother or sister sins? What should a believer do when he or she sins? Is it possible to sin a sin unto death and what would that mean? Who is the antichrist and what does he believe? Is there more than one antichrist and, if so, how may they be detected? What can be known about the Lord's return and how can a believer prepare for it? How can a believer know that he or she is walking in the light and that he or she is a child of God? How can one overcome the world? And finally, what is the significance of love within the Church?

Questions such as these are of vital importance to individual believers and Christian congregations alike. These and many other issues are addressed in the three works commonly known as the Johannine Epistles. However, it is not always easy to cull answers to questions like these from the Scripture. For the Bible is more than just a collection of proof-texts to be used to satisfy curiosity, however honest such inquiries may be. Rather, the Bible is a collection of dynamic documents, each coming from a particular historical situation and having its own unique reason for being. In order to make best use of what the Johannine Epistles have to say about the issues raised above, it is necessary to gain some understanding of why they were written in the first place. Therefore, before approaching the text of the Epistles itself, some time will be spent in an attempt to determine what situation called these writings forth, who composed them, when they were written, where they were written, and for whom they were composed. Each of these components should make any explorations of the text all the richer.

The Johannine Epistles and the Fourth Gospel

A comparison of the Johannine Epistles with the Gospel of John reveals a good number of similarities. In fact, the similarities are so great in terms of vocabulary, style, and theology that the vast majority of scholars believe that these documents come from the same community if not from the same author. While it is indeed possible to interpret the Epistles on their own terms with no reference to other biblical books, it is much more advantageous to interpret them in the light of their relationship with the Fourth Gospel. But what is the exact nature of this relationship and what are its implications?

There is reason to believe that the Gospel of John existed at least in some form prior to the composition of the Epistles.[1] The primary evidence for this belief is the fact that the Epistles, especially 1 John, seem to presuppose the existence of the Fourth Gospel. While no passage from the Fourth Gospel is directly quoted in the Epistles, several passages in the latter appear to build on those in the former.[2] Another piece of evidence for this chronological order is that 1 John reflects a different kind of life situation than that of the Fourth Gospel. More specifically, the Epistles appear to have been written when the community had been torn by strife, a situation not suggested by the Fourth Gospel. Another piece of evidence, which suggests that the Epistles presuppose the Gospel, is that even the opponents in 1 John seem to have based their beliefs on the teaching found in the Fourth Gospel.

The major implication of all this is that the Epistles should be read with one eye on the Fourth Gospel.

The Johannine Community

If the Fourth Gospel and the Epistles come from the same hand and/or community and if the churches addressed in the Epistles are under the oversight and influence of the Elder, a title the author of 2 and 3 John uses for himself, then it is legitimate to speak of a community of disciples and churches: the Johannine community.

It is clear from the Fourth Gospel that standing at the heart of the

---

1   It appears that the Fourth Gospel was composed over a long period of time. It is possible that the bulk of the Gospel was complete but had not been published in its final form when the Epistles were written.

2   Cf., e.g., the way in which the prologue in 1 Jn 1.1-4 seems to build off its counterpart in Jn 1.1-18. More detailed attention is given to these similarities in the commentary proper.

community's life was the Beloved Disciple. According to the Fourth Gospel the Beloved Disciple was an eyewitness to the earthly ministry of Jesus and his testimony formed the basis of the community's belief in Jesus (cf. esp. Jn 19.35 and 21.24). It may be deduced from the evidence in the Fourth Gospel that the Beloved Disciple was a prominent teacher and that his role as an eyewitness had attracted several disciples around him. Thus, in one sense, to speak of the Johannine community is simply to identify the Beloved Disciple and his followers as constituting a clearly defined group. However, the Epistles demonstrate that this community was larger than just the one group gathered around the Beloved Disciple. It appears that several churches were part of this community and that they all came under the influence of the Beloved Disciple in one way or another.[3]

The History of the Johannine Community

A provisional outline of the history of the Johannine community, divided into four phases or periods, may be set forth as follows.[4] *The earliest period in the history of the community* is the point at which the Beloved Disciple, an eyewitness to Jesus' ministry, left Palestine (perhaps Jerusalem) and took up residence in or around Ephesus in Asia Minor. This migration probably occurred sometime in the mid to late 60s of the first century CE. The Beloved Disciple's departure was in all likelihood related to the turmoil prior to or at the beginning of the First Jewish War against Rome (66–70 CE). The Beloved Disciple was no doubt accompanied by other believers. *The second phase in the community's history* was the establishment of the community proper and its initial growth. During this period, the Fourth Gospel began to take shape through the preaching and teaching of the Beloved Disciple. As he was one of the few remaining eyewitnesses of Jesus' ministry, the Beloved Disciple's testimony was especially cherished. From c. 70 to 90 CE, the Fourth Gospel continued to develop, perhaps taking the form of two editions. *Phase three in the community's history* saw the disruption of the community, possibly owing to the absence of the Beloved Disciple, who may have been imprisoned on Patmos. The community appears to have split into at least two parts. The Elder (who is most likely the Beloved Disciple) wrote the Epistles in an attempt to solidify those still loyal to the truth, and to defend the gospel as it was rightly to be understood. In all likelihood these works were written c. 100 CE. *The final phase in the*

---

3   The extent of the community is taken up in the commentary below.
4   For a similar but more exhaustive treatment of this topic cf. M. Hengel, *The Johannine Question* (Philadelphia: Trinity Press International, 1989).

community's history witnessed the death of the Beloved Disciple, the publication of the Fourth Gospel in its final form, and the absorption of the community into the great Church and the following of the path that led to Gnosticism on the part of the opponents.

Consequently, the Johannine Epistles were written at a crucial point in the history of the community and their proper interpretation depends in part upon an appreciation of their context. The student of the Johannine Epistles is well advised to read the Epistles with a constant focus upon the community's history.

Authorship

As is the case with many New Testament documents, the author of these Epistles is unnamed. Although such anonymity makes the task of identifying the author difficult, the Epistles give us several clues as to who may have written them. First, the similarity in style to the Fourth Gospel may suggest that the same person who wrote the Gospel is the author of the Epistles as well. Second, John is named in the title of these Epistles in all extant manuscripts. Third, the author identifies himself as the Elder in 2 Jn 1 and 3 Jn 1.

The Author of the Fourth Gospel and the Authorship of the Johannine Epistles

A careful reading of both the Fourth Gospel and the Johannine Epistles reveals that these documents are very similar in expression. One of the leading experts on the Johannine literature goes so far as to say that no two New Testament works are more similar in expression than 1 John and the Fourth Gospel, not even Luke and Acts.[5] Despite such similarities, a number of scholars believe that different writers are responsible for the Gospel and the Epistles. Although a variety of arguments are offered in support of this opinion,[6] one of the primary reasons so many scholars follow this course is the current dominance of the opinion that several hands were involved in the composition of the Fourth Gospel. However, a major problem with such hypotheses is that the more hands one discovers in the composition process of the Johannine literature, the more difficult it becomes to explain the essential unity of style found in the Fourth Gospel and 1 John.[7] The simplest explanation for such literary affinity is to attribute these works to the same hand. If the Johannine

---

5   R.E. Brown, *The Epistles of John* (Garden City, NY: Doubleday, 1982), p. 21.
6   Cf. the discussion in I.H. Marshall, *The Epistles of John* (Grand Rapids: Eerdmans, 1978), pp. 31-48, for an assessment of these arguments.
7   Cf. Hengel, *The Johannine Question*, pp. 88-94.

documents were written in the general order described earlier, most differences in thought are rather easily explicable.

Therefore, if the Beloved Disciple is primarily responsible for the composition of the Fourth Gospel (a claim made in Jn 21.24), then perhaps he was involved in the writing of the Epistles as well.

The Titles of the Johannine Epistles

The titles of the Epistles may also have some bearing on the identity of the author. Of all the manuscripts that contain one or more of the Johannine Epistles, the name John appears in the title. It is commonly noted that since titles were not originally part of the text of a given work, they are not to be relied upon for determining the identity of the author. However, such an assessment does not give adequate attention to how or why New Testament documents were given titles in the first place. An examination of this issue reveals that titles of New Testament documents emerged for some of the following reasons.[8]

First, it was the custom of the earliest Church to read letters in worship (1 Thess. 5.27) and to exchange correspondence for reading (Col. 4.16). By the middle of the second century CE there were already collections of Christian literature which were regularly read in the context of worship.[9] As soon as a community had more than one Epistle or gospel, there would be a need to distinguish between them by use of titles.

Second, there is some evidence that the early Church collected the works of a given writer (i.e. the letters of Paul, Ignatius, and Dionysius). Many times these collections were stored in what might be called a community archive or church library, perhaps located in the home of the individual who hosted the 'house church'. Such collections would make necessary the assigning of titles to distinguish between individual works by the same author.

Third, the physical characteristics of the earliest manuscripts and the patterns of the scribes who produced them appear to have been remarkably uniform from the beginning. Such consistency implies that titles were part of these documents from early in the process of assembly.

With regard to the Johannine Epistles in particular, it is conceivable

---

8   Much of what follows is dependent upon a discussion of the emergence of titles for New Testament documents by M. Hengel, *Studies in the Gospel of Mark* (trans. J. Bowden; Philadelphia: Fortress Press, 1985), pp. 64-84.

9   For example, Justin Martyr, *Apology* 1.67.3, can write, 'And on the day called Sunday there is a meeting in one place of those who live in the cities or the country, and the memoirs of the apostles or the writings of the prophets are read as long as time permits.'

that titles were given to the individual works at the time they were collected in the community. At the very least it may be assumed that these titles were assigned at the time the Fourth Gospel was 'published' and the letters began to circulate in the Church at large.

The significance of this evidence is that the name contained in the title of these Epistles, John, may very well be that of the person who wrote or caused these Epistles to have been written.

The Elder

The clearest hint about the identity of the author of the Epistles comes within the text of 2 and 3 John. In the first verse of each document the author identifies himself as 'the Elder'. Although much ambiguity surrounds such a use of this title, several things may safely be deduced from it.

First, it would seem obvious that although modern readers do not know who this Elder is, the recipients of 2 and 3 John would know his identity. The Elder in the Johannine community would be as well known as a contemporary Christian leader who signed a letter to a parishioner with the words 'Your Pastor'. Second, in contrast to the usage of the term 'elder' in other New Testament documents, where there appear to have been several elders in each community, the author of 2 and 3 John refers to himself as *the* Elder. Such a designation implies a distinct position for this Elder. Whether there were other elders in the community or not, clearly the author of these Epistles had a special authority. Third, again in contrast to the use of elder in other New Testament documents, where an elder's ministry was apparently restricted to a specific local community, the author of 2 and 3 John exercises an authority over several churches. Such influence distinguishes *the* Elder from others who bear that title in the New Testament.

The Greek term for elder (πρεσβύτερος), from which the English word 'Presbyter' comes, could mean either (a) a man advanced in years or (b) a leader of a community. Often these two dimensions of the meaning were combined in that ordinarily leaders in a specific community would be men of some years. The Elder here mentioned, no doubt, combines these two aspects.

A tentative assessment of the evidence suggests that the author of the Epistles (1) was regarded as the Elder (or leader) of the community, (2) was associated with the name John, and (3) was perhaps involved in the composition of the Fourth Gospel.

Options Concerning Authorship

Two candidates merit special consideration as the author in the light of the conclusions drawn above: the well-known John the son of Zebedee and the more elusive figure John the Elder.[10]

John the Son of Zebedee

Several arguments might be offered in support of John the son of Zebedee as the author of the Johannine Epistles. First, if John the son of Zebedee wrote the Epistles it would explain the Epistles' titles. Second, this John has often been identified as the Beloved Disciple, which would explain the many similarities between the Epistles and the Fourth Gospel. Third, the son of Zebedee was an eyewitness to Jesus' ministry, which would account for the eyewitness claims in the Fourth Gospel and the Epistles. Fourth, as early as the latter part of the second century CE one or more of the Epistles were attributed to John the Apostle.[11] Fifth, there is some early evidence that apostles could be referred to as elders (cf. 1 Pet. 5.1).[12]

However, there are several problems in identifying the author of the Johannine Epistles with the son of Zebedee.[13] Perhaps the most serious problem is the fact that there is no evidence until the latter half of the second century CE that the Apostle John was ever in or near Ephesus. The closest the New Testament comes to making such a claim is found in Rev. 1.9 where a certain John is located on the Isle of Patmos. Ignatius, who wrote to the church at Ephesus c. 110-115 CE, makes no mention of John but goes to great lengths to demonstrate his close relationship to Paul. Although others claim that both Polycarp and Papias had a personal relationship with the son of Zebedee, neither Polycarp nor Papias makes such a claim.

A second problem with this approach to the authorship of the Epistles is that some evidence exists which suggests that John the son of Zebedee

---

10   It is, of course, possible that the Elder of 2 and 3 John is simply an anonymous leader in the Johannine community, but his singular stature and influence make such an identification unlikely. For arguments in favor of such a view cf. Brown, *The Epistles of John*, pp. 650-51.

11   Early references include: the Muratorian Canon, Irenaeus (*Against Heresies* 1.16.3), Tertullian (*Against Marcion* 4.2), Clement of Alexandria (Eusebius, *Ecclesiastical History* 3.23.3-19; 6.14.5), and Dionysius (Eusebius, *Ecclesiastical History* 7.25.7-8.11).

12   Cf. the remarks of Papias in Eusebius, *Ecclesiastical History* 3.39.3-4.

13   The following objections draw upon the works of C.K. Barrett, *The Gospel According to St. John* (Philadelphia: Westminster Press, 1978), pp. 102-105, and P. Parker, 'John the Son of Zebedee and the Fourth Gospel', *JBL* 81 (1962), pp. 35-43.

was martyred early in the Church's history. In Mk 10.39, Jesus appears to prophesy the martyrdom of both James and John. Papias, as quoted by Philip of Side (c. 430 CE), states that both James and John were killed by the Jews.[14]

Other difficulties include the following: (a) while the son of Zebedee was from Galilee, the Fourth Gospel concentrates on Jerusalem; (b) although John exhibits a good deal of interest in exorcism (Lk. 7.39-40), the Fourth Gospel ignores the topic; and (c) the son of Zebedee was a fisherman from Galilee who was treated as a stranger at the court of the high priest in Acts 4.5-23, yet Jn 18.15-16 notes that the Beloved Disciple was known to the high priest. Consequently, while complications of this nature do not disqualify the son of Zebedee as the author of the Epistles, they do make such an identification problematic.

John the Elder

Interestingly enough, there is evidence for the existence of an individual known as John the Elder. Eusebius, the so-called first Church historian (c. 260-340 CE), preserves the testimony of an early Christian figure named Papias, who had written a five-volume work on 'The Oracles of Jesus'. According to Papias there was an elder named John who had been a disciple of the Lord, whom Papias had interviewed. In fact this John appears to be the basis of much of Papias's testimony. Papias, who wrote c. 120-130 CE, investigated the origins of Christianity, consulting any who had spoken with the apostles. In particular, Papias was interested in the elders' words:

> but if ever anyone came who had followed the presbyters [elders], I inquired into the words of the presbyters [elders], what Andrew or Peter or Philip or Thomas or James or John or Matthew, or any other of the Lord's disciples, had said, and what Aristion and the presbyter [elder] John, the Lord's disciples, were saying.[15]

Several things are interesting about this quotation. First, it is obvious that Papias had investigated (ἀνέκρινον) some time before he wrote. Second, it is apparent that the apostles had spoken in the past (εἶπεν). Third, Aristion and John the Elder were quite clearly alive at the time of Papias's interview (λέγουσιν). Fourth, it seems obvious that the Elder was an eyewitness of Jesus' ministry. Fifth, the elders seem to constitute

---

14   The statement of Papias is also recorded by Georgius Monachus (in the ninth century) and is supported by Syriac and African martyrologies.
15   Cited according to the translation of K. Lake, *Eusebius: Ecclesiastical History*, I (London: Heinemann, 1926), p. 293.

a group of leaders who knew the apostles personally. In the case of Aristion and John the Elder, they were themselves witnesses to Jesus' ministry. Sixth, the list of disciples in Papias is remarkably close to the lists of the disciples in the Fourth Gospel (1.40, 44-45; 21.2) as the following comparison makes clear.

Papias's list of the disciples	Fourth Gospel's list of the disciples
Andrew	Andrew
Peter	Peter
Philip	Philip
Thomas	Thomas
James	Sons of Zebedee
John	
Matthew	Nathaniel
Aristion	Two Other Disicples
John the Elder	

When John the Elder is regarded as the author of the Epistles, it clears up the following points. (1) It explains the similarity in the lists of the disciples in the Fourth Gospel and in Papias, because Papias's list would have come from the Elder. (2) It explains why the technical use of the word 'apostle' is missing from the Fourth Gospel and the Johannine Epistles, as the author was an eyewitness but not an apostle. (3) It explains why there is no mention of John the Apostle by, for example, Ignatius and Polycarp, as being in Ephesus, because John the Elder was in Ephesus not the son of Zebedee. (4) It explains the anonymity of the Fourth Gospel. (5) The use of the title 'the Elder' in 2 and 3 John is better understood. (6) The Fourth Gospel suggests that the Beloved Disciple lived to be quite old (cf. Jn 21.20-23). The Elder would be an accurate designation for the Beloved Disciple near the end of the first century.

Assuming that John the Elder is the author of the Epistles what might be known about him? It is possible to deduce several things about this figure.[16] He was born c. 15 CE as a member of the priestly aristocracy. Becoming interested as a young man in the ministry of John the Baptist, he ultimately became a follower of Jesus, witnessing his fate firsthand in Jerusalem. Perhaps he had close contact with both John the son of Zebedee and Philip the Evangelist. Just before the Jewish War (c. 62 CE) he migrated to Ephesus, where near the age of 50 he founded a community which flourished for about 35 years. As he outlived the other eyewitnesses of Jesus' ministry, he became the Beloved Disciple to his community, the grand old man, 'the Elder'. His preaching and teaching

---

16   Cf. Hengel, *The Johannine Question*, pp. 133-34.

became the basis of the Fourth Gospel, which grew during his ministry. He was exiled near the end of his life on Patmos, during which time the community began to be torn apart. Upon his return from exile he wrote the Epistles.

Provenance and Date

Despite arguments in favor of Syria and Alexandria as the place of composition, the uniform testimony of the early Church favors Ephesus. Not only does the external testimony of a variety of early Christian writers support this position, but the unrivaled influence of the Johannine literature in Asia Minor makes other locations difficult to defend.

As indicated earlier, the date of composition is probably somewhere between 97–103 CE, near the end of the Beloved Disciple's life.

Order of Composition and the Life Setting of the Epistles

The order in which this commentary examines the Johannine Epistles is the reverse of their appearance in the canon. This means that 3 John is the first letter to be examined, followed by 2 John, and finally 1 John. Two reasons may be offered for this non-traditional approach. First, it makes better pedagogical sense to begin the study with 3 John so as to insure that it is read on its own terms, rather than trying to force an interpretation on it based in part upon a reading of 1 and 2 John. Reading 2 John before 1 John ensures that this short letter receives adequate attention in its own right, rather than treating it as a mere appendage to, or summary of, 1 John.

Second, although it is difficult to discern with any degree of certainty the chronological order in which the Epistles were written, several things suggest that these letters may have been written in the reverse order of their canonical standing.[17] It should, of course, be remembered that the canonical order of New Testament Epistles was determined by length. Letters written by the same individual were arranged in descending order, with the longest letter standing first and the shortest letter standing last. Therefore, canonical order tells us little about the date of an Epistle's composition.

When 3 John is studied on its own terms, without the benefit or hindrance of reading it through the lens of 1 and 2 John, it becomes immediately apparent that 3 John has absolutely nothing to do with the

---

17 For a more extended treatment cf. J.C. Thomas, 'The Order of the Composition of the Johannine Epistles', *NovT* 37 (1995), pp. 68–75.

false teaching which 1 and 2 John identify and combat. The absence of a reference to such false teaching implies one of four things: (1) either 3 John was written shortly before the outbreak of the false teaching described in 1 and 2 John; (2) 3 John was written after the outbreak of the false teaching to a congregation within the community which had not yet been made aware of the theological deviation; (3) 3 John was written after the outbreak of the false teaching but the Elder chooses to make only extraordinarily subtle references to the false teaching; (4) 3 John was written long after the theological controversy had passed.

The last option would appear to be ruled out owing to the several similarities between 2 and 3 John. Such similarities seem to suggest that these two letters are not separated by a long interval of time. Concerning the second and third options, it is simply too difficult to believe that the same author who is so quick to discuss the dangers of false teaching in 1 and 2 John would write to a community and/or individual and not make the slightest reference to such false teaching. Even if the dominant theme in 3 John is hospitality, one would expect the Elder at least to mention the threat of the false teachers as an additional reason for Gaius to render support to the emissaries from the Elder. If, as most scholars believe, the problem with Diotrephes is unrelated to the false teaching, then a tension such as the one that exists between the Elder and Diotrephes could have arisen at any time. If Diotrephes' exclusion of the Elder's emissaries was the result of the advice given in 2 Jn 10 to refuse those who would bring false teaching, surely the Elder would have drawn attention to his earlier instructions or reminded Gaius that such a course of action was to be taken because of heretical teaching. In addition, it would be wrong to conclude that it was the emergence of false teaching that prompted the initiation of sending emissaries from one congregation to another within the Johannine community. The mobility that existed in early Christianity generally argues against this idea, as does the fact that the Fourth Gospel itself contains mandates for missionary activity (cf. Jn 4.31-38; 20.19-23).

When approached on *its* own terms, 2 John reads very much like an initial attempt to warn a particular community, at some distance from the Elder, of the impending visit of false teachers. This short letter makes two basic points: (1) it warns the readers about the inevitable arrival of the deceivers and (2) it instructs the readers to take swift and decisive action if and when these deceivers arrive. The strict instructions given in vv. 10-11 read more like an initial emergency measure than the 'final' answer to the problem of false teachers, owing to the fact that the Elder's approach in 3 John is much less drastic. There, he goes to extraordinary lengths to dialogue with and respond to his 'opponent' Diotrephes. It appears that the threat of deceivers dividing the community in 2 John calls for far more severe measures. In all likelihood, the Elder wrote several other letters of warning to surrounding communities at the outbreak of this deception that no longer survive.

In contrast, 1 John gives clear evidence that some time had elapsed since the first appearance of the deceivers. This assessment is based, in part, on the fact that by the time 1 John was written the false teachers had left the Johannine community (1 Jn 2.18-27; 4.1-6) and had established an alternative community with its own distinctive interpretation of the Johannine Jesus traditions. But before these opponents left the Johannine community they had apparently caused such serious problems that a more comprehensive response was needed than that given in 2 Jn 10-11. It would appear that 1 John represents the result of the theological reflection generated within the community over the teaching of the opponents. This document, then, was written as a response to the opponents in order to expose their deviant theology and to encourage those within the community to remain loyal to that which was received from the beginning.

It might of course be objected that the non-epistolary form of 1 John indicates that it was a sermon designed for those congregations in close proximity to the Elder, implying that 2 John was written later for those congregations at some distance from the Elder. However, this proposal fails to convince for several reasons. First, as has already been noted, when 1 and 2 John are approached independently, it is 1 John, not 2 John, which shows signs of being the later of the two. Second, if 1 John was intended for those in close proximity to the Elder, one wonders why the document would have been written in the first place, as the Elder would have been able to address these congregations firsthand. Third, this proposal fails to take into adequate account the similarities between 1 John and other 'sermons' intended to function in some ways as an Epistle (e.g. Hebrews). In all likelihood, 1 John circulated among various congregations in the Johannine community with variable prescripts and greetings or several short personal notes to the different principals of the house church congregations.[18]

In the light of the preceding discussions, the order of examination of the Johannine Epistles proposed in this commentary would appear to be justified.

---

18 Hengel, *The Johannine Question*, p. 48.

The Holy Spirit in 1 John

The attention given to the Holy Spirit in 1 John shows signs of continuity and discontinuity with that found in the Fourth Gospel. On the one hand, a number of activities attributed to the Spirit in the Fourth Gospel find application in 1 John. On the other hand, one of the dominant titles given to the Spirit in the Fourth Gospel, the Paraclete, never has reference to the Spirit in 1 John. Thus, the voice of 1 John makes a distinct contribution to the New Testament view of the Holy Spirit. As there are no explicit references to the Spirit in 3 and 2 John, the following overview is based on 1 John.

There appear to be four dimensions of the Spirit's role in 1 John, all of which are related in one way or another to knowledge or knowing. The first reference to the Spirit in 1 John takes the form of a Greek term (χρῖσμα) often translated 'anointing'. This word, which appears twice in 1 John (2.20, 27), has reference to an 'anointing' received from 'the Holy One', enabling the believers to know 'all things'. This anointing makes the need for human teachers unnecessary, for it teaches the believers all things and is constantly available to them as it 'remains in you'. Emphasis is placed upon the veracity of the 'anointing', as opposed to the deception of the antichrists' false teaching, a topic of great importance in the passage in which this discussion takes place (2.18-27).

This first allusion to the Spirit is matched by the last allusion to the Spirit in 1 John (5.20). Very near the book's conclusion the readers are told that they have been given 'the ability to understand'. The Greek word translated by the phrase 'the ability to understand' (διάνοιαν) conveys more the idea of the means by which one understands, than understanding itself. As with the discussion of 'anointing', emphasis is placed upon the relationship between the Spirit's work and the authentic teaching about God and his Son Jesus Christ. Thus, one dimension of the Spirit's work in 1 John is as trustworthy teacher, especially as it relates to knowing God and his Son.

A second dimension of the Spirit's work in 1 John is the role the Spirit plays in assuring the believers of their relationship with God. On two occasions (3.24; 4.13), near identical statements occur that contain reference to the fact that believers can know of their mutual indwelling with God by means of the Spirit. Both passages underscore the importance of the Spirit in this process by inclusion of the phrase 'out of the Spirit [which] he has given us'. This activity of the Spirit is not spelled out in the text but appears to include prophetic activity through human spokespersons. It also appears that this activity of the Spirit is connected with witness (4.14). Again, knowing is very much at the heart of this activity.

A third aspect of the Spirit's work in 1 John concerns the Spirit's role in distinguishing between 'the Spirit of Truth' and 'the spirit of deception'. In this passage (4.1-6) a spirit's confession (or lack of confession) of 'Jesus Christ having come in the flesh' reveals whether or not 'the Spirit of Truth' inspires such activity. In contrast to the activity of 'the Spirit of Truth' is 'that of the antichrist' (v. 3) and 'the spirit of deception' (v. 6), which inspires a lack of confession of Jesus and keeps the world from hearing the witness of the community, respectively. It appears that the S/spirit works through human spokespersons, so that this dimension of the Spirit's activity is especially connected to the process of discernment. It is through the Spirit of Truth that the believers 'know' this.

In the final explicit references to the Spirit in 1 John, emphasis is placed upon the Spirit's role as witness to Jesus. In this text (5.6, 8), full of interpretive challenges, the multifaceted elements of the intimate relationship between the Spirit and Jesus converge. Not only is the intimate nature of their relationship very much in view, but also the relationship of the Spirit with God, and the two other witnesses, the water and the blood. In some ways, the other emphases come together in the Spirit's work as witness. For despite the claims of the false teachers, the Spirit's work as witness makes clear to the community that they are indeed of God, 'know' the truth, and stand in continuity with this true witness when they themselves engage in witness.

Part I

3 JOHN

The letter entitled 3 John is the shortest book in the New Testament, consisting of 219 words in the Greek text. Its brevity, more than any other factor, is the reason for its location in the canon behind 1 and 2 John, as New Testament documents by the same authors were commonly arranged by length, in descending order.[1] As such, 3 John would have rather easily fit on a single sheet of papyrus, the normal length of Greco-Roman letters of the day.[2]

The Literary Genre of 3 John

Not only does 3 John resemble a number of secular Greco-Roman letters in its brevity, but it also shares a number of structural and literary features. The broad outline of such letters may be delineated as follows:

I.   An A (author) to B (recipient) Greeting
II. A Wish for Health
III. Expressions of Thanks for the Receipt of Good News
IV. Body (Opening) — Occasion
V.   Body (Closing) — Recapitulation and Promise of Visit
VI. Closing Formula — Greetings of Mutual Friends.[3]

In order to demonstrate 3 John's similarities to other letters of the time, two examples will be cited. The first is a letter from one brother to another:

> Irenaeus to Apollinarius his dearest brother many greetings. I pray continually for your health, and I myself am well. I wish you to know that I reached land on the sixth of the month Epeiph and we unloaded our cargo on the eighteenth of the same month. I went up to Rome, on the

---

[1] Although 3 John is divided into 15 verses compared to 2 John's 13, 3 John is some 26 words shorter.

[2] Hengel, *The Johannine Question*, p. 29, suggests that the length of 2 and 3 John would be equivalent to the modern-day postcard.

[3] J. Lieu, *The Second and Third Epistles of John* (Edinburgh: T. & T. Clark, 1986), pp. 38-39. Cf. also the discussion in Brown, *The Epistles of John*, pp. 788-95.

twenty-fifth of the same month and the place welcomed us as the god willed, and we are daily expecting our discharge, it so being that up till today nobody in the corn fleet has been released. Many salutations to your wife and to Serenus and to all who love you, each by name. Goodbye. Mesore 9. [Addressed] To Apollinarius from his brother Irenaeus.[4]

Another example comes from an Egyptian soldier in the Roman navy to his father:

> Apion to Epimachus his father and lord many greetings. Before all things I pray that thou art in health, and that thou dost prosper and fare well continually together with my sister and her daughter and my brother. I thank the lord Serapis that, when I was in peril in the sea, he saved me immediately. When I came to Miseni I received as viaticum (journey-money) from the Caesar three pieces of gold. And it is well with me. I beseech thee therefore, my lord father, write unto me a little letter, firstly of thy health, secondly of that of my brother and sister, thirdly that I may do obeisance to thy hand because thou hast taught me well and I therefore hope to advance quickly, if the gods will. Salute Capito much and my brother and sister and Serenilla and my friends. I sent [or 'am sending'] thee by Euctemon a little picture of me. Moreover my name is Antonis Maximus. Fare thee well, I pray. Centura Athenonica. There saluteth thee Serenus the son of Agathus Daemon, and...the son of...and Turbo the son of Gallonius and D[...]sen [...]...[5]

The similarities between these two letters and 3 John are difficult to miss. They demonstrate that one is dealing with an authentically private piece of correspondence in 3 John.

3 John offers to the reader the first and most intriguing glimpse into the Johannine community. It reveals a complex of congregations tied together by a series of messengers/emissaries. This letter also reveals a rift in the community particularly between the Elder and Diotrephes. If one relies upon 1 and 2 John in order to determine the cause of the rift, the conclusion would in all likelihood involve false teaching, which is so prominently discussed in these other Johannine Epistles. However, one searches 3 John in vain for the slightest hint of heresy. In point of fact, no one would even suspect that false teaching was at issue if 3 John existed on its own. Such arguments from silence are all the more difficult in the light of the Elder's willingness to condemn false teaching and his eagerness to combat it at every point in 1 and 2 John.

In order to understand the purpose of 3 John, the roles of the only

---

4   Cited according to the translation found in C.K. Barrett, *The New Testament Background: Selected Documents* (New York: Harper & Row, 1987), p. 30.

5   Cited according to the translation in A. Deissmann, *Light from the Ancient East* (trans. L.R.M. Strachan; Grand Rapids: Baker Book House, 1978), p. 180.

three members of the Johannine community whose names are known (Gaius, Diotrephes and Demetrius) must be explored. While many theories surround the purpose of 3 John and the persons named, it seems that the following minimal information may be assumed about each.

Very simply put, Gaius is the person to whom the letter is written; Diotrephes is an antagonist/opponent of the Elder; while Demetrius is being commended by the Elder to Gaius. But a closer examination reveals a host of questions at most every turn. First, what is the relationship of Gaius to the Elder and exactly who is Gaius and what is his position? Second, what is the relationship of Diotrephes to the Elder, why does he oppose the Elder, and what is his position or authority? Third, exactly what is Demetrius' function and why, if Gaius has offered hospitality to emissaries of the Elder, would the Elder be so worried about Demetrius' reception and that Gaius would withdraw such support?

Rather than trying to argue out every point of the various hypotheses offered as answers to these questions, it would seem most advantageous to become acquainted generally with the options, but then to concentrate on the text of 3 John itself. Each of the following options focuses to one extent or another on Diotrephes and his opposition to the Elder.

1. One view is that Diotrephes is the first person known to have striven to be a monarchical bishop, anticipating the stance of Ignatius by a few years.[6] The Elder, who comes from a less structured, more charismatic background, disdains such love of prominence.

2. Another approach simply inverts the role of Diotrephes and the Elder. On this view, Diotrephes is the charismatic, led by the Spirit, who is out of step with most of the other leaders, while the Elder represents a position often associated with the emergence of Early Catholicism.

3. Another view identifies Diotrephes as a wealthy member of the Johannine community who hosts one particular Johannine congregation (house church) in his home.[7] On this view, Diotrephes is beginning to exert undue control over the congregation.

4. It has been rather common to assume that Diotrephes was one of the heretics/false teachers so severely condemned in 1 and 2 John. The obvious problem here is that 3 John gives no hint that such is the case.

5. One proposal goes so far as to argue that Diotrephes is an orthodox

---

6   Cf. Ignatius, *Ephesians* 6.1; *Magnesians* 6.1; 7.1; 13.2; *Trallians* 2.1-3; 3.1; 7.2; 12.2; *Smyrnaens* 8.1-9.1.

7   Wealthier members of early Christian communities often hosted the house church for the simple reason that their homes could ordinarily accommodate more people.

church leader while the Elder is an excommunicated heretic.

6. Another hypothesis asserts that the Elder and Diotrephes are on the same side against false teaching but disagree over the best way to handle the false teachers. The Elder advocates discernment, while Diotrephes refuses to admit any traveling teachers.

7. Finally, it has been proposed that the tension between the Elder and Diotrephes was simply the result of a misunderstanding.[8] (a) An anonymous teacher receives a revelation in the Spirit which deviates from the Elder, but this teacher begins to travel in the name of the Elder. (b) Diotrephes discerns the heretical content of the teaching and decides that if the Elder stands for this position he (Diotrephes) will have nothing else to do with the Elder or his emissaries. (c) The Elder pens 3 John as a rebuke, not knowing the full story. (d) The letter is followed up by a visit, which was threatened in 3 Jn 10. (e) The Elder and Diotrephes discover what has happened. (f) Finally, the Elder agrees with Diotrephes' strategy in combating false teachers (2 John 10-11).

The strengths and weaknesses of each of these proposals should be revealed in the examination of the text of 3 John which follows.

The Literary Structure of 3 John

The following outline of 3 John helps to identify the Epistle's literary structure and flow of thought:

I. Greeting (1)
II. Wish for Health (2)
III. Expression of Joy: Thanksgiving (3-4)
IV. Body Opening: General Petition/Desire (5-8)
V. Body Middle: Occasion (9-10)
VI. Body Middle: Specific Desire (11-12)
VII. Body Closing (13-14)
VIII. Concluding Formula (15)

In addition to identifying the letter's major points and flow of thought, the outline demonstrates just how much 3 John resembles secular letters of the day.

---

8   R. Price, 'The *Sitz-im-Leben* of Third John: A New Reconstruction', *EvQ* 61 (1989), pp. 109-19.

Significant Words and Themes

A quick read of 3 John reveals a number of terms and/or themes that are remarkably prominent in a book of 219 words. Some of the more important words are:

English Term	Greek Term	Occurrences	Location	Percentage
Truth	ἀλήθεια	7 uses	1, 3(b,c), 4, 8, 12(a,b)	3.1%
Love	ἀγαπάω	6 uses	1(a,b), 2, 5, 6, 11	2.7%
Witness	μαρτυρέω	5 uses	3, 6, 12(a,b,c)	2.28%
Brother	ἀδελφός	3 uses	3, 5, 10	1.36%
Church	ἐκκλησία	3 uses	6, 9, 10	1.36%
Write	γράφω	3 uses	9, 13(a,b)	1.36%
Work	ἔργον	3 uses	5, 8, 10	1.36%
Walk	περιπατέω	2 uses	3, 4	0.9%
Receive	λαμβάνω	2 uses	7, 8	0.9%
Receive	ἐπιδέχομαι	2 uses	9, 10	0.9%

As might be expected, the three most frequently used words (ἀλήθεια, ἀγαπάω, μαρτυρέω) are quite common in the Fourth Gospel as well.

The Text

Verse 1: The Greeting

The letter begins with the greeting typical of Greco-Roman letters, an A (author) to B (recipient) greeting. Although similar in many ways to secular letters, one distinctive aspect of 3 John is the use of a title rather than a name for the author.

The writer introduces himself as the Elder, a title which conveys special authority and lays claim to a certain position. In the Introduction, it was suggested that the Elder is to be identified with John the Elder, whom Papias mentions as a disciple of the Lord. It appears that this elder had been an eyewitness to Jesus' ministry, had founded a community in or around Ephesus in the 60s, was regarded as the Beloved Disciple by his followers, and was in effect the grand old man of the community. While the Elder speaks with authority, he does not come across as dictatorial. In fact, given the threat that Diotrephes posed it is remarkable that the Elder does not refer to any special authority, as Paul does when his role as an apostle had been challenged.

The letter is addressed to a certain Gaius. This very common name is given to three other individuals in the New Testament: (1) Gaius, who had served as Paul's host in Corinth (Rom. 16.23); (2) Gaius of Macedonia who was a companion of Paul (Acts 19.29); and (3) Gaius of Derbe who was appointed to carry the collection to Jerusalem (Acts 20.4). Owing, in part, to the widespread use of the name,[9] there is little reason to identify the Gaius mentioned in 3 John 1 with any of these individuals.

It is indeed difficult to determine much about this particular Gaius. Several items in the letter suggest that he was not only part of the Johannine community, but also may have been one of the Elder's disciples. Beloved ('Ἀγαπητέ) is a favorite designation of John for those under his care.[10] Since this term rarely occurs outside the New Testament[11] and since this word and its cognates take on special meaning in the Johannine literature, it is likely that such a use here conveys not only the Elder's desire to endear Gaius to himself but also his genuine affection for Gaius.

Although the phrase 'whom I love in truth' is paralleled to a certain extent in secular letters of this era, the Elder does not appear simply to be following convention, even though a similar formula is used in 2 John 1. The use of the personal pronoun 'I' (ἐγώ) suggests that the Elder is emphasizing his own personal affection for Gaius. For the Elder to express his love for this individual indicates that Gaius lives in accord with the command to 'love one another' given in 1 Jn 4.7. While 'in truth' (ἐν ἀληθείᾳ) could mean 'truly' or 'really', owing to its distinct place in Johannine thought it probably expresses more than simply that Gaius is recognized as part of the Johannine community.[12] Granted the use of 'truth' in 1 or 2 John, as well as its seven occurrences in 3 John, signifies that much, its place in the Fourth Gospel suggests that for John 'in (the) truth' comes very close to Paul's use of 'in Christ' or 'in the Lord'.[13] In the Fourth Gospel Jesus is not only full of truth (Jn 1.14), but is himself the truth (Jn 14.6). In other words, 'in truth' designates that John recognizes Gaius to be in the way of truth (the Johannine community) and that the Elder's love for him is 'in the Lord'.

---

9   F.F. Bruce, *The Epistles of John* (Grand Rapids: Eerdmans, 1970), p. 147, notes that Gaius was one of the 18 names a Roman parent could choose as a first name for a son.
10   Of the 61 New Testament occurrences of ἀγαπητέ 10 are in the Johannine Epistles: 1 Jn 2.7; 3.2, 21; 4.1, 7, 11; 3 Jn 1, 2, 5, 11.
11   D.E. Hiebert, 'An Exposition of 3 John 1-4', *BibSac* 144 (1987), pp. 53-65 (59).
12   Contra Lieu, *The Second and Third Epistles of John*, p. 102. Cf. S.S. Smalley, *1, 2, 3 John* (Waco, TX: Word Books, 1984), p. 343, who notes that, 'John's use of "truth" in his letters is never casual'.
13   Cf. Hengel, *The Johannine Question*, p. 35.

Verse 2: The Wish for Health

Two surprises are contained in v. 2. First, there is no greeting as commonly occurs in both Christian and secular letters. Such an omission is quite unusual. Second, 3 John contains a wish for health strikingly similar to secular letters of the day. The health wish in the letter from Apion to his father Epimachus is particularly noteworthy: 'Before all things I pray that thou art in health, and that thou do'st prosper and fare well continually...'[14]

John begins v. 2 by once again referring to Gaius as Beloved as he continues his attempt to identify with his reader, using this term at the beginning of his expression of a health wish for Gaius. Such a term of endearment would perhaps make this wish sound less formalistic, but it is difficult to believe that this addition alone would cause Gaius to interpret the health wish in any other fashion than most readers (both secular and Christian) would have, as a polite good wish for health and prosperity.[15]

A lack of attention to the similarity between this health wish and its secular counterparts has produced some odd interpretations of this verse. On the one hand, some scholars have interpreted John's words to mean that Gaius was ill and in need of special intercession. However, such an interpretation would of necessity imply the same interpretation in secular letters where similar words are found. On the other hand, some contemporary preachers have used this verse as part of a rather elaborate doctrine of prosperity and health. But again, consistency would demand that one attribute a similar theology to all those secular writers who used a similar formula. However, conclusions of this nature appear to be unfounded. Therefore, one should be careful not to use 3 John 2 in such an uncritical fashion.

But having made these qualifications, one must still determine the Elder's intent. Several things may be deduced. First, John desires[16] Gaius' health and prosperity in every way. The desire for health is obviously in accord with much New Testament thought (e.g. Jas 5.14-18). Yet, the wish for prosperity seems at first glance to be at odds with the preponderance of New Testament admonitions which advocate a rather neutral attitude toward wealth (cf. Mk 10.17-31). In all likelihood, the

---

14   πρὸ μὲν πάντων εὔχομαί σε ὑγιαίνειν καὶ διὰ παντὸς ἐρωμένον ἐτυχεῖν. As cited in Deissmann, *Light from the Ancient East*, pp. 179-80.
15   Brown, *The Epistles of John*, p. 703.
16   It is possible to translate εὔχομαι as 'pray' or 'wish'. Cf. J.C. Thomas, 'ευχη', in T. Gilbrant (ed.), *The Complete Bible Library: The New Testament Greek–English Dictionary – Delta-Episilon* (Springfield: Complete Bible Library, 1990), pp. 658-59.

Elder's prayer for Gaius is directly connected to his ministry of hospitality to the traveling Johannine emissaries.

It is possible to take the phrase 'just as your soul prospers' as a reference to spiritual prosperity, balancing the reference to physical prosperity in v. 2a. However, this interpretation is not likely in the light of John's use of soul (ψυχή) elsewhere. The majority of occurrences of the word (ψυχή) in Johannine literature denote life which one may lay down, not simply the spiritual side of the human being. On this view, the Elder prays for prosperity and health in the light of Gaius' life generally. The prayer is not for some docetic spirituality but the sum total of Gaius' life, which no doubt includes his actions such as hospitality. In this verse, the connection between Gaius' material prosperity and his missionary support is very much the point.

Verses 3 and 4: Expression of Joy (Thanksgiving)

The Elder now expresses his joy at the reports various brothers have brought concerning the action of Gaius. It could very well be that these two verses function as the thanksgiving found in many secular letters of the time. As the Epistles will reveal, Gaius has befriended certain Johannine brothers by offering them hospitality at the very time that Diotrephes has refused such service. This ministry on Gaius' part appears to have taken place recently, as both 'coming' (ἐρχομένων) and 'testifying' (μαρτυρούντων) are present participles, implying that brothers were habitually coming to the Elder with word about Gaius. Such activity is enough to ensure that Gaius is in the truth. The connection between the truth and proper action is a close one in the Johannine literature. For John, the way one shows that he or she is in the truth is to love one another in deed (cf. 1 Jn 4.20-21; 3.18-19). Conversely, no truth is in the one who does not keep the commands (1 Jn 2.4).

It may be that the brothers who brought word to the Elder were the same as those brothers mentioned in vv. 5-10, Johannine missionaries. Whether such ones originate from the Elder's congregation or were traveling to his congregation via Gaius' house, it is obvious that they are respected representatives of the Johannine community. The giving of hospitality demonstrates that Gaius walks in truth.

It is difficult to determine if the word 'as' (καθὼς) is used to reflect the Elder's own thoughts concerning Gaius' action or if it is a sign of indirect discourse indicating that 'you walk in truth' is the report brought by the brothers. In either case, Gaius is highly commended by this phrase.

'To walk' is a familiar metaphor in the Epistles occurring in 1 Jn 1.6, 7;

2.11; 2 Jn 4, 6. Three ideas are present in its use. First, walking is tied to fellowship both positively (1 Jn 1.7) and negatively (1 Jn 1.6). That is to say that 'to walk' is paramount to having fellowship with. Second, walking in truth is to live according to the commands of God/Jesus (2 Jn 6). Third, since the greatest command in the Johannine community was to love one another (1 Jn 3.11), one's love toward the brothers and sisters was a sign of his or her walking in the truth, whereas it is impossible to walk in the truth if one hates a brother or sister (1 Jn 2.11). Therefore, for the Elder to state that Gaius walks in the truth is to acknowledge that he has fellowship with Jesus as evidenced by the fact that he loves the brothers and sisters, which most recently has been typified by his generous hospitality toward them.

In v. 4 the Elder makes clear that his earlier expression of joy (v. 3) was no mere formality, as some have deduced owing to the similar phrase in 2 John 4. In point of fact, nothing in all of life brings him the joy and satisfaction that does hearing that his children walk in truth. To make this point, the Elder uses a double comparative. The word used here (μειζοτέραν) is the comparative form of the normal comparative (μείζων), meaning 'more greater'.[17] That his children walk in the fellowship of the love command means that his ministry has been successful and his life fulfilled. His reference to Gaius and others as 'my children' could perhaps mean that they were his converts, as the term tends to mean in Paul (1 Cor. 4.14; Gal. 4.19; Phil. 2.22). But more than likely 'children' designates all those under the Elder's spiritual oversight. The use of children (τέκνα) in 2 John demonstrates that members of individual congregations could be referred to as children (2 Jn 1, 13).

Verse 5-8: Body Opening — General Petition/Desire

With v. 5 the body of the letter commences. Here the Elder reveals the purpose and/or occasion of the letter. He both commends Gaius for his hospitality and encourages him to continue in this support. Such support is all the more significant since Diotrephes has refused to receive the Johannine missionaries. However, before examining these verses in detail a word should be said about the importance of hospitality in the early Church.

The New Testament documents suggest that there was a high degree of mobility in early Christianity. Such travel was indicative of the frequency with which people from various strata of society journeyed, but was particularly consistent with the habit of many of those within

---

17   Brown, *The Epistles of John*, p. 706.

the Jewish community, who would strive to make numerous pilgrimages in their lifetimes. However, travel was not easy either in terms of the physical energies required or in accommodations along the way. Most inns of the time were quite unreliable and notorious for vices repugnant to Christians. Consequently, believers were often hard-pressed to find suitable accommodations. People who knew folks along the way would ordinarily attempt to establish their own network of places to stay.[18]

Therefore, the rendering of hospitality generally became part of standard Christian practice in many segments of the early Church (cf. Rom. 16.1, 2: Acts 16.15; and *Did.* 12.1-5). But the rendering of hospitality came to have a special place in the early Church: 'because successful evangelization efforts by itinerant prophets and ministers were dependent upon such support (Mt. 10.11-15; Rom. 16.1. 2; Acts 16.15; 3 Jn 5-8; Did. 11.1-6)'.[19]

Verse 5. For the third time Gaius is called 'Beloved', as the Elder commends him for his hospitable activity. In the performance of these tasks Gaius is acting faithfully (lit. 'doing faithfulness'). The expression 'when you do' is a subjunctive expression which suggests that 'Gaius had welcomed the "brothers", and helped them, on a number of occasions'.[20] The Greek word translated 'do' (ἐργάζομαι) carries with it the idea of work, perhaps even difficult labor.[21] Paul uses the word and its cognates to convey an idea similar to that expressed here (cf. Gal. 6.10; Col. 3.23; and esp. Tit. 3.13-14). Such hard work on behalf of the brethren is laudable, but particularly so when the brethren are strangers to the one giving hospitality. Apparently, some of the brothers who bore witness to John on behalf of Gaius had been strangers at the time of their reception. Obviously, Demetrius, who will be recommended to Gaius by the Elder in v. 12, is a stranger.

Verse 6. In v. 3 it was revealed that brothers were habitually coming and testifying how Gaius walked in the truth. This verse informs that these brothers (that is 'Those who testified') did so before the whole church. The Elder perhaps makes reference to testimonies of one particular act of hospitality or more probably to a whole series of testimonies.[22]

---

18 Cf. the discussion in Lieu, *The Second and Third Epistles of John*, p. 126.
19 J.C. Thomas, *Footwashing in John 13 and the Johannine Community* (JSNTSup, 61; Sheffield: Sheffield Academic Press, 1991), p. 135.
20 Smalley, *1, 2, 3 John*, p. 349.
21 D.E. Hiebert, 'An Exposition of 3 John 5-10', *BibSac* 144 (1987), pp. 194-207 (196).
22 As the aorist verb ἐμαρτύρησαν implies. Brown, *The Epistles of John*, p. 709.

Apparently, upon the return of the brothers the church would be gathered together to hear the report of the missionaries, as is described in Acts 14.26-27. More than likely 'church' denotes a local house-church, as the only other occurrences of 'church' (ἐκκλησία) in the Johannine Epistles, all found in 3 John (6, 9, 10), indicate such a use for the word. The Elder's mention of Gaius's love is both a reference to his concrete acts of hospitality, as well as an equivalent for walking in the truth.

It is in the second phrase of the sentence that the Elder makes his request known. 'You do well' (Καλῶς ποιήσεις) is an idiomatic form of making a request. 'You would do well' might better be translated, 'would you please continue to do well' (cf. Jas 2.8 and Ignatius, *Symrn.* 10.1). The specifics of the request are that Gaius might send off the brother(s) in a manner worthy of God. 'To send along' (προπέμψας) is used here in a rather technical way to designate specific aid given to missionaries in the early Church (cf. Acts 15.3; Rom. 15.24; 1 Cor. 16.6, 11; 2 Cor. 1.16; Tit. 3.13; Polycarp, *Phil.* 1.1). The kind of support offered would not only include provision during their stay, but also appropriate supplies for their journey (food, money, washing their clothes, etc.).[23] Such an undertaking was no small affair and would require both means and will. Gaius is urged to aid them in a manner worthy of God. This (genitive) construction would mean either that his action should be of such a nature that it could have been rendered to God himself, or that it would result in the glory of God. Perhaps the Elder is intentional in this ambiguity, as is the author of the Fourth Gospel on various occasions. The Elder's request for support of the brothers is made despite the fact that problems and resultant criteria for determining who may or may not receive support were arising at this time in other areas of the Church (cf. *Did.* 11.1-7).

That the Elder is asking Gaius to continue in his ministry of hospitality is clear enough. What is not so clear is why, if Gaius had been faithful in this support, would the Elder appear to be urging him on this point? Three ways of answering this question may be cited. Perhaps the Elder's tortured language is a sign that the Elder is advancing his case very cautiously, meaning that Gaius had not yet been won over to the Elder's position.[24] Or perhaps another reconstruction is nearer the mark. It is argued that Gaius, who was known for his hospitality, had stepped in to offer support as a result of the emergency created by Diotrephes. In this case, the Elder's request is an attempt to secure Gaius's home as a regular stopping off point for the Johannine missionaries in the future. In

---

23   Marshall, *The Epistles of John*, p. 86.
24   Lieu, *The Second and Third Epistles of John*, p. 106.

any event, it would appear certain that the Diotrephes incident had occasioned the letter and that the Elder was attempting to head off any problem that might be developing. While this proposal might be correct, it may be that the Elder writes simply to reassure Gaius and to counter any misinformation or influence that might be coming to individuals like Gaius from Diotrephes. In any event, the Elder's appeal to Gaius is direct. It could very well be the case that Gaius hosts a house church.

Verse 7. The Elder now gives the motivation for the brothers' mission, 'it was for the sake of the name'. These emissaries traveled for no reason other than to evangelize and spread the story of salvation. The expression 'the name' (τοῦ ὀνόματος) is a bit puzzling in that it is not completely clear whether the Elder intends in it a reference to God, which would be consistent with Jewish practice and would follow the last three words of v. 6 well (ἀξίως τοῦ θεοῦ), or to Jesus, which would be common in the early Church (cf. Acts 4.12; 5.41; 9.16, 21; Rom. 1.5; 1 Jn 2.12; Ignatius, *Eph.* 7; *Phil.* 10). If 'the name' has reference to Jesus, then perhaps the reference owes its origins to Jesus' words in Mk 9.37 about 'welcoming one in my name' and to the gradual substitution of Jesus' name for Yahweh, as the transference of the title 'Lord' (κύριος) might imply. As Brown suggests, perhaps the use of the name should be related 'to the custom of being baptized in(to) the name of Jesus (Acts 8.16; 1 Cor 1.13, 15) or to the partial Johannine equivalent of believing in(to) the name of Jesus (John 1.12, 3.18)'.[25] It is only natural that those who go out for the sake of the name should receive support and assistance from others who also identify with the name.

In the other Johannine Epistles, the term (ἐξῆλθον) is used of those secessionists who went out from the community into false teaching (i.e. they withdrew from the community). There is no way of gauging whether the Elder intends any contrast between the missionaries and the secessionists by the use of this verb.

Part of the motivation to support these brothers is owing to the fact that they have determined not to take help from the pagans.[26] The only other occurrences in the New Testament of the word used here for pagan (ἐθνικός) confirms that the Elder has in mind non-believing Gentiles (cf. Mt. 5.47; 6.7; and especially 18.17 where both church [ἐκκλησία] and pagan [ἐθνικός] occur in close proximity). The reason for this decision may be twofold. First, Jesus had instructed his disciples to take nothing

---

25 Brown, *The Epistles of John*, p. 712.
26 Which the use of μηδὲν with the non-indicative implies. Brown, *The Epistles of John*, p. 713.

with them on their journey (Mt. 10.10), an instruction which seems to have lived on in sections of the early Church (*Did.* 11.6). Second, religious beggars were plentiful in antiquity. To avoid offense, Paul on occasion refused support.[27]

Verse 8. In the light of the fact that these brothers go out for the sake of the name and will accept nothing from unbelievers, Christians are under a special obligation to support such missionaries. 'Therefore' (οὖν) indicates that what follows is a plan of action based upon the preceding statement. The Elder makes emphatic the point that 'we' Johannine believers must receive (ὑπολαμβάνειν) those who receive (λαμβάνοντες) nothing from unbelievers. The emphatic personal pronoun 'we' (ἡμεῖς), contrasts the Johannine Christians from unbelievers. Another means by which the Elder emphasizes the believers' obligation is by use of 'we are obligated' (ὀφείλομεν). The Greek word used here (ὀφείλω), many times translated 'ought' or 'should', conveys much more of an obligation than such translations suggest. Each occurrence of this term in the Johannine literature makes clear that a moral obligation is being enjoined, not simply a suggestion that one might follow. [See, e.g. Jn 13.14 'you also ought (ὀφείλετε) to wash one another's feet'; 1 Jn 2.6 'The one who claims to abide in him ought (ὀφείλει) to walk just as that one himself also walked'; 1 Jn 3.16 'we also ought (ὀφείλομεν) to lay down our life in behalf of the brothers'; 1 Jn 4.11 'Beloved, if God loved us truly, we also ought (ὀφείλομεν) to love one another'.] The Elder's emphasis would hardly have been lost on Gaius.[28]

To receive the brothers means that they should be supported. The idea is similar to that expressed in v. 6. In using the words 'such ones as these' (τοὺς τοιούτους), 'The author is referring to the missionaries who are so generous as to set out for the sake of the name without accepting anything'.[29]

One of the results of such support of the Johannine missionaries is that we might be 'coworkers in the truth' (συνεργοὶ τῇ ἀληθείᾳ). Through their actions Gaius and others can demonstrate that they are fellow-workers with the truth. If, as 2 Jn 11 states, one who befriends a false teacher fellowships in his evil works, then one who befriends such ones as these, works in cooperation with the truth. As noted in v. 1, the word

---

27 As an example of such activities cf. Deissmann, *Light from the Ancient East*, pp. 108-110.
28 Cf. the discussion in Thomas, *Footwashing in John 13 and the Johannine Community*, p. 109.
29 Brown, *The Epistles of John*, p. 714.

'truth', has a christological dimension and may here signify being a coworker with Jesus.

Verses 9-10: Body Middle—Occasion

Although the Elder has already made his petition known to Gaius, he now seems to reveal the occasion of the letter itself, which concerns the actions of Diotrephes, his authority in the church and his relationship with the Elder.

These two verses reveal that Diotrephes is guilty of five things: (1) he would not receive the Elder's letter; (2) he slanders the Elder and the brothers with evil words; (3) he does not receive the brothers; (4) he stops those who desire to receive them; and (5) he throws out of the church anyone who aids the brothers.

Verse 9. Apparently the Elder had written a short letter to the church.[30] Obviously, the church mentioned here and in v. 10 is not the same congregation mentioned earlier in v. 6. Although the letter here described no longer exists, it is likely that it was a commendation of a missionary/traveler. However, 'the one who loves to be first among them', Diotrephes, refused the Elder by refusing the letter. The word translated 'the one who loves to be first' (φιλοπρωτεύων) is unique in the New Testament. The charge is that Diotrephes loves prominence in the community. Perhaps there is a contrast between Gaius' love (for the Johannine emissaries) and Diotrephes' love of prominence. However, further details about the meaning of the phrase are difficult to come by.

It could be that Diotrephes has become or aspires to become a bishop. In this case the Elder, who either opposes institutionalization as such or the elevation of Diotrephes in particular, is against such a move. Another view is to identify Diotrephes with false teaching so that his rejection of the Elder is the result of theological differences. Perhaps it is more reasonable to view Diotrephes as a zealous member of the community whose leadership skills have resulted in a position of authority in the church (he certainly appears to have a variety of powers according to v. 10).

Unfortunately, Diotrephes has a moral flaw, in contrast to the command to love one another, *he* loves to be first. Such an attitude must have been difficult to understand in a community that was accustomed to the example of John the Baptist, among others, who exemplified humility in terms of self-estimation. The fact that 'the one who loves to

---

30 Attempts to identify this composition with either 1 or 2 John both fail.

be first among them' (ὁ φιλοπρωτεύων αὐτῶν) precedes Diotrephes' name heightens the force of this accusation. This moral flaw manifests itself in a constant refusal to receive (οὐκ ἐπιδέχεται) the Elder's authority. It is possible that 'of them' should be taken to imply that Gaius is not a part of Diotrephes' congregation, as 'of them' rather than 'of us' appears.

While it might be correct to conclude that, 'There is nothing to indicate that Diotrephes held false opinions', it is only half true to conclude 'his ambition only is blamed'. Diotrephes' actions demonstrate that he has broken fellowship with the Elder and the broader community and as a result does not obey the command of love.

Verse 10. Owing to the fact that Diotrephes would not receive the Johannine emissaries, the Elder announces that he plans a trip to make clear what Diotrephes does and says, a course of action not unlike that proposed by Paul in 2 Cor. 12.14 and 13.1. Such a visit would allow the Elder to make known everything that had transpired. This verse suggests that John has the authority to act in this situation.[31]

Although some may desire to defend Diotrephes as a pastor concerned about his congregation and those who visit it, v. 10 makes clear that the love of prominence is not Diotrephes' only fault. He habitually babbled foolishly about the Elder attempting to slander him, and thereby ruin his reputation.

Not only did Diotrephes refuse to receive the Elder *et al.*, and slander him, but he also refused to receive the brothers. By stressing that Diotrephes was not content with actions directed toward him alone, the Elder suggests that the treatment of others was determined in part by the way they related to John. Diotrephes habitually refused to receive the Johannine missionaries. This refusal not only implies a rejection of the Elder's authority, but also effectively puts an end to the missionary work as manifest in that community. What is more, Diotrephes feels such strong opposition to the Elder that he habitually forbids any who desire to receive emissaries from doing so. Again it appears that the connection between the Elder and those who desire to receive the missionaries may be partial motivation for Diotrephes' action.

---

31   The Venerable Bede, *On 3 John, ACCS*, XI, p. 242, explains the Elder's actions as follows: 'It is true that we must do nothing to stir up the tongues of the accusers, lest they should perish on our account. Likewise we must patiently endure those who attack us because of their own wickedness, so that we may become better people. Nevertheless there are times when we have to protest, because those who spread evil stories about us may corrupt the minds of innocent people who otherwise would have heard nothing but good about us.'

But Diotrephes does not stop with such hostile actions. He goes so far as to throw any sympathizers out of the church. While formal excommunication likely is not meant, the exclusion of these believers may have been based loosely upon the action advocated by Jesus (Mt. 18.15-17) and Paul (1 Cor. 5.1-13). It suddenly becomes obvious that to stand with the Elder entails opposing Diotrephes. It also becomes obvious that any attempt to withstand Diotrephes will be met with dangerous hostility.[32]

The thrust of vv. 9-10 makes clear the purpose for the letter, that Gaius' hospitality is all the more important owing to Diotrephes' actions and it suggests that Gaius' walking in the truth might be severely tested.

Verses 11-12: Body Middle — Specific Petition/Desire

Verse 11. For the third time the Elder refers to Gaius as 'Beloved'. Coming on the heels of such an intense section as vv. 9-10, the use of this term of endearment marks a change in the tone of the letter as well as in its content. It might be best to regard vv. 9-10 as a parenthetical statement, interrupting the thought of vv. 5-8 and 11-12. Yet, at the same time, v. 11 functions as a transition between the evil actions of Diotrephes and the good example of Demetrius.

Although Gaius has taken the appropriate actions up to this point and although the Elder appears to expect him to continue in the truth, John drives home the point that the rendering of hospitality is not a neutral issue but goes to the very heart of the faith. For in the offer of hospitality a believer is doing good, a sign that he or she is of God. He also makes the point that conforming to the influence of Diotrephes is an extremely serious matter. Only here does the verb 'imitate' (μιμεῖσθαι) appear in the Johannine literature. Hiebert asserts that the term, 'conveys the picture of observing a course of action and then repeating it'.[33]

The basic idea expressed in this verse is not unlike that of 1 Jn 3.4-10, where a very clear line of demarcation is drawn between those who sin and those who do righteousness. The following observation seems very much to the point:

> On no account is he (Gaius) to be led astray by the bad example of Diotrephes and to follow him (v. 11). His practical behavior shows whether he comes from God... Anyone who (like Diotrephes) rejects the brethren and breaks off communion with the elder and his community 'has not seen

---

32 In this case, Gaius must either not be a member of Diotrephes' church or he has been absent from it for a while.

33 D.E. Hiebert, 'An Exposition of 3 John 11-14', *BibSac* 144 (1987), pp. 293-304 (294-95).

God' (cf. 1 John 3.6). The elder describes this clear either/or in the language of Johannine dualism as 'doing good' or 'evil'; faith and action are inseparably connected in the specific situation of conflict. For him, the human individual is a unity; faith and personal behavior cannot be torn apart. So for the elder, how one behaves towards a Christian brother at one's own front door is the deciding factor over faith and unbelief, life or death, light and darkness.[34]

The word used here for evil (κακός) gives a bit more emphasis to that which is harmful than does the other Greek word for bad (πονηρός). In the Shepherd of Hermas (*Man.* 8.10) 'doing good' is manifested in showing hospitality.[35]

To see God is to be admitted into his presence, to acknowledge him, and to experience him (cf. Jn 3.3). Seeing the Father is only possible through seeing Jesus (Jn 14.9). Those who practise evil have no hope of seeing God.

Verse 12. A third individual is now named, Demetrius. The name itself means 'belonging to Demeter' which indicates that Demetrius came from a pagan background.[36] Despite the fact that Demetrius was quite a common Roman name, many commentators attempt to identify him with (1) Demetrius the silversmith of Ephesus mentioned in Acts 19.24, 38; (2) Demas (a shortened form of Demetrius) one of Paul's fellow-workers (Col. 4.14 and Phlm. 24) who eventually forsook Paul owing to his love of this present world (2 Tim. 4.10); or (3) the Bishop Demetrius said to have been ordained by the Apostle John (*Apostolic Constitutions* 7.46.9). Although the first two suggestions explain the strong recommendation by the Elder, owing to Demetrius' life which left much to be desired, it is much more likely that all we know of this Demetrius is what is recorded in 3 John.

Despite the fact that it is possible to treat the mention of Demetrius as if he has nothing to do with the missionary activity the Elder advocates,[37] it is very difficult to account for his mention otherwise. The following conclusion appears close to the mark:

> It can be taken as virtually certain that he was the bearer of the letter (cf. Rom. 16.1f.) and as highly probable that he was a traveling missionary,

---

34   Hengel, *The Johannine Question*, p. 36.
35   'For in hospitality may be found the practice of good' (ἐν γὰρ τῃ φιλοξενιᾳ εὑπίσκεται ἀγαθοποίησίς ποτε).
36   However, it should be observed that Christians did not choose Old Testament names for their children until the third century. For example, Origen, who was reared in a Christian home, bears a pagan name.
37   As does Lieu, *The Second and Third Epistles of John*, p. 119.

possibly one of the group which had been made unwelcome by Diotrephes. He was however a stranger to Gaius.[38]

If these conclusions are valid, then the mention of Demetrius makes sense as do the recommendations.

In v. 12, three witnesses are offered on Demetrius' behalf, as prescribed in the Torah (Deut. 19.15). First, everyone (in the Johannine community) knows of and has testified to Demetrius. The tense of the Greek verb (μεμαρτύρηται) is perfect, which indicates that such testimony had been accumulating over a period of time. Paradoxically, though his reputation is widespread, apparently Gaius does not know him. Second, the truth itself testifies of Demetrius. Although a case can be made for taking 'truth' as a reference to Jesus or truth as a body of teaching, it seems likely that here truth should be understood in the same way it was in v. 3. That is to say, his fellowship, his keeping the commands and his loving the brothers and sisters testify of him. Third, the Elder places his own testimony in support of Demetrius, speaking with the authority of the community. This final phrase, 'and you know that our testimony is true', is reminiscent of Jn 19.35 and 21.24 (cf. also 5.31-32) and suggests that this phrase was one that the Elder may have used and could explain why it appears in the Fourth Gospel.

Verses 13-14: Body Closing

The Elder closes his Epistles with a formula that may have been a standard one for him. The first phrase 'many other things I have to write you' is perhaps an explanation for the brevity of the Epistles, although its length is not distinctive in comparison with other first-century letters. Hengel takes these two verses as evidence of the Elder's aversion to letter-writing and shows that he is a master of the spoken word and oral teaching, but was not a well-trained rhetorical writer.[39] The word translated 'ink' (μέλανος) literally means 'black', and came to mean ink. It was a combination of powdered charcoal, lamp black or soot mixed with gum and water.[40]

No doubt the Elder had many sensitive issues to discuss with Gaius, but these matters would be best handled face to face, literally 'mouth to mouth' (στόμα πρὸς στόμα). His promise to visit, mentioned earlier in v. 10, is paralleled in the closing sections of many of the letters of the

---

38 Marshall, *The Epistles of John*, p. 93.
39 Hengel, *The Johannine Question*, p. 37.
40 Hiebert, 'An Exposition of 3 John 11-14', p. 301.

day. However, the mention of 'immediately', which does not appear in 2 John, may suggest a special urgency on the Elder's part.

Verse 15 — Concluding Formula

Several aspects of this final verse are significant. First, the use of 'peace' as a final greeting is a departure from the epistolary norm. This Semitic formula was common enough in the New Testament (Gal. 6.16; Eph. 6.23; 1 Pet. 5.14), but almost certainly came to have a special significance in the Johannine community owing to Jesus' use of 'peace'. First, in Jn 14.27 Jesus promises to give the disciples peace; then in Jn 20.19, 26 he gives peace to them and to Thomas. This same peace is being spoken to the 'troubled' Gaius as it was to the original disciples, one of whom was the Beloved Disciple.

Second, the greetings sent from one church to another constitute the Elder's 'reminder that *koinonia* is an essential part of Johannine life (1 John 1.3, 7). Diotrephes has done more than cut himself off from the Presbyter; he has endangered the relationship of one church to another'.[41] 'The friends' (οἱ φίλοι) must have reference to Johannine Christians meeting in a house church with or near the Elder. In the Fourth Gospel (15.14) Jesus reveals that his disciples are no longer called slaves but friends for they do what he asks and know that he has heard from the Father. The use of 'friends' in 3 John 15 is understood to be informed by the usage by Jesus in the Fourth Gospel.

Third, his final words to 'greet the friends by name' (ἀσπάζου τοὺς φίλους κατ' ὄνομα) was a normal part of the concluding formula in many first-century letters.[42] However, this note may also reflect the Elder's desire to make sure all the believers stood with him in the dispute with Diotrephes. This greeting may also be a very subtle request that Gaius share the contents of this letter with the other Christians, in contrast to Diotrephes' refusal to do so.

Reflection and Response — Part One

Having completed a very careful reading of 3 John, we are now in a better position to reflect upon its significance for today and respond to the words which the Lord desires to speak to our own hearts personally and corporately.

---

41 Brown, *The Epistles of John*, p. 750.
42 Cf. Deissmann, *Light from the Ancient East*, p. 193.

Reflection

One of the several aspects of 3 John worthy of intentional reflection is the love of prominence. According to 3 John, Diotrephes' fundamental problem was his desire to be first in the community. This attitude led Diotrephes to a variety of hostile actions, to cut himself off from those with whom he differed, to keep others silent and in line with his own thought, and to use threats and manipulation to secure his desired goal.

In order to facilitate our reflection upon this aspect of the text, a series of questions will be raised. Are there leaders in the church today who act in a fashion similar to Diotrephes? In your opinion, how widespread is this leadership model? Have you ever known personally leaders in the Church who remind you of Diotrephes? If so, what actions triggered this identification? How does it feel to be led by a leader like Diotrephes? In what ways does such leadership impair the ministry of the body?

It is, of course, easier to remove the speck from the eye of a brother or sister than it is to remove the beam from our own. But no reflection on the biblical text is adequate until the light of Scripture is turned upon our own hearts. Therefore, several additional questions must be raised of a more personal nature beginning with, Do I love to be first among those in the community? Or perhaps a better way to construct this question is, in what ways do I love to be first and why? How would I act and relate to others if I did not have this desire for such prominence? More specifically, how are the results of this desire manifest in my life? Have I followed the evil example of Diotrephes, convincing myself that one must be prepared to act thus in order to 'get ahead'? When confronted with challenges to my authority have I sought to malign my challenger and destroy his or her influence through slander or so-called 'sharing'? Am I prone to make attempts to control such situations by demanding absolute conformity to my strategy of dealing with the situation? Do I attempt to alienate and isolate those with whom I disagree, thereby demeaning them and treating with contempt their personhood through my actions and attitudes? Have I been tempted to mistreat or punish others because they are closely associated with a 'political opponent'?

Response

Of course, it does little good simply to identify such discouraging attitudes and actions in our hearts and lives. There must be a response to the issues raised by the Scripture. Among the appropriate responses that might be given, the following steps would appear to merit serious consideration.

First, it is absolutely necessary that our sinful activities and/or shortcomings be acknowledged honestly. Therefore, it might be advisable to go back through the reflection questions in order to ensure that they are answered. Perhaps writing down the answers would prove helpful.

Second, find a faithful and trusted brother or sister to whom these faults may be confessed for the purpose of intercession.

Third, earnestly seek God, confessing these specific sins. Make sure that such times of prayer focus, in an intentional way, upon these areas of failure.

Fourth, in consultation with other members of the body, commit to action that helps you live out a more faithful life, as it relates to these matters, accountable to the body of Christ.

Part II

2 JOHN

Next to 3 John, 2 John is the shortest book in the New Testament totaling 245 words in the Greek text. It functions as a link between 3 John and 1 John in that it is both similar to and dissimilar from each of the other Johannine Epistles. On the one hand, 2 John is like 3 John in that it is a short note easily contained on a single sheet of papyrus. It is from the Elder and uses a certain number of words common to both Epistles. Another similarity to 3 John is the way in which 2 John resembles secular letters of the day, although not nearly to the extent that does 3 John.

On the other hand, the occasion and purpose of 2 John have much more in common with 1 John than 3 John, in that like 1 John it deals with false teaching. More specifically, 2 John introduces the readers to a theological rift in the community and allows them to see how such a problem is handled by the Elder. Some of the vocabulary of 2 John is much more like that of 1 John with its emphasis on children, antichrist, the beginning, teaching, commandment, and the prominence given to God the Father, and Jesus Christ the Son who has come in the flesh.

Therefore, as the shift is made from 3 John to 2 John the reader moves a long way toward understanding a different aspect of the community's history.

The Literary Structure of 2 John

The following outline of 2 John helps to identify the Epistle's literary structure and flow of thought:

I. Greeting (1-3)
II. Expression of Joy: Thanksgiving (4)
III. Body Opening: Petition (5-6)
IV. Body Middle: Occasion (7)
V. Body Middle: Petition/Admonition (8-11)
VI. Body Closing (12)
VII. Concluding Formula (13)

Significant Words and Themes

A quick read of 2 John reveals a number of terms and themes that are remarkably prominent in a book of 245 words. Some of the more important words are:

English Term	Greek Term	Occurrences	Location	Percentage
Truth	ἀλήθεια	5 uses	1(a, b), 2, 3, 4	2.04%
Love	ἀγαπάω	4 uses	1, 3, 5, 6	1.63%
Command	ἐντολή	4 uses	4, 5, 6(a, b)	1.63%
Father	πατρός	4 uses	3(a, b), 4, 9	1.63%
Children	τέκνα	3 uses	1, 4, 13	1.22%
Walk	περιπατέω	3 uses	4, 6(a, c)	1.22%
Teaching	διδαχή	3 uses	9(a, b), 10	1.22%

Of the other significant terms in 2 John the following deserve special notice: 'receive' (λαμβάνω), 'beginning' (ἀρχή), 'son' (υἱός), 'greet' (χαίρειν), 'God' (θεός), 'Jesus' (Ἰησοῦς), 'Christ' (Χριστός), and 'our' (ἡμῶν).

Not only is the frequency of a given word significant, but the way in which the Elder groups them together in different parts of the Epistle is also important and helps to identify the purpose of the author.[1]

The Text

Verses 1-3: Greeting

Verse 1. This Epistle begins, as most letters of the time, with the typical A (author) to B (recipient) greeting. Its major departure from this form is that neither the author nor the recipient is named. As in 3 John, the writer identifies himself as *the* Elder, a title which conveys special authority and lays claim to a certain position. As noted in the Introduction, this elder had been an eyewitness to Jesus' ministry, had founded a community in or around Ephesus in the 60s, was regarded as the Beloved Disciple by his followers, and was in effect the grand old man of the community.

The letter is addressed to the Elect Lady (ἐκλεκτῇ κυρίᾳ). At first sight it appears that 2 John is addressed to a woman and her children,[2] as 'Lady' (κυρία) is used frequently in the papyri, but usually qualified in some way.[3] From early on there have been attempts to identify this lady.

---

1 O. Artus, 'La Seconde Epître de Jean', *Foi et Vie* 86 (1987), pp. 27-34.
2 B.F. Westcott, *The Epistles of St. John* (Grand Rapids: Eerdmans, 1966), p. 224, notes that this is most natural reading of the text.
3 Cf. the examples in Deissmann, *Light from the Ancient East*, pp. 167, 192-93.

Near the end of the second century CE Clement of Alexandria concluded that 2 John was written to virgins, in particular to a Babylonian lady named Electa.[4] It is possible that the Elder is addressing this letter to an esteemed Christian woman and the house church which she hosts. Several women in the early Church provided such a service (e.g. Acts 12.12). Added to this is the fact that women seem to figure prominently in the Johannine community. However, as attractive as this interpretive option is, the impersonal nature of the Epistles, as well as the greeting from the children of her sister, make it unlikely.

For these and other reasons it seems best to take 'Lady' (κυρία) as having reference to a local congregation within the Johannine community.[5] It was not unusual in the ancient world for a nation, city or church to be personified as a woman. In the second century Hermas (*Vis.* 3.1.3) records that an old lady, who is identified as the church, is called 'Lady' (κυρία). By using this form of address the Elder may be emphasizing the great value of the community.[6] If this conclusion is sound, the children are to be identified as members of the congregation. Such a use of 'children' is a bit of a departure from how the term is used in 3 John, where it appears to designate believers over which the Elder has oversight. The use in 2 John 1, 4, and 13 suggests that these 'children' are members of individual congregations.

Although the phrase 'whom I love in truth' is paralleled to a certain extent in some contemporary secular letters,[7] the Elder does not appear simply to be following convention, even though a similar formula is used in 3 John 1. The use of the personal pronoun I (ἐγὼ) suggests that the Elder is emphasizing his own personal affection for the Lady. For the Elder to express his love in this fashion demonstrates that the church lives in accord with the command to 'love one another' given in Jn 13.34 and 15.12, 17. While 'in truth' (ἐν ἀληθείᾳ) could mean 'truly' or 'really', owing to its distinct place in Johannine thought it probably expresses more than simply that this church is recognized as part of the Johannine community.[8] Granted, the use of truth in 1 or 2 John, as well as its seven

---

4 Clement of Alexandria, 'Stromata I 4: Comments on the Second Epistle of John', ANF, II, p. 576.
5 An interpretation that goes back at least to Hilary of Arles (*Introductory Commentary on 2 John*, ACCS, XI, p. 231).
6 A suggestion made by Hengel, *The Johannine Question*, p. 29.
7 L. Bellenus Gemellus, a war veteran who wrote between 94–110 CE, uses the formula 'who loves us (thee) according to truth' [τοὺς φιλοῦντες ἡμᾶς (σὲ) πρὸς ἀληθιαν]. Cf. Deissmann, *Light from the Ancient East*, p. 248 n. 4.
8 Contra Lieu, *The Second and Third Epistles of John*, p. 102. Cf. Smalley, *1, 2, 3 John*, p. 343, who notes that, 'John's use of "truth" in his letters is never casual'.

occurrences in 3 John, signifies that much, but its place in the Fourth Gospel suggests that for John 'in (the) truth' comes very close to Paul's use of 'in the Lord' (ἐν κυρίῳ) or 'in Christ' (ἐν χριστῷ).[9] In the Fourth Gospel, Jesus is not only full of truth (Jn 1.14), but is himself the truth (Jn 14.6). In other words, 'in truth' (ἐν ἀληθείᾳ) designates that John recognizes the Lady to be in the way of truth (the Johannine community) and that the Elder's love for her is 'in the Lord'. It should be noted that 'whom' (οὓς) most likely is used to include both the church and its individual members.

Such love is not confined to the Elder but exists throughout the Johannine community. This statement suggests that the church's reputation for walking in the truth is well known, but perhaps more importantly, the church is in fellowship with those who for some time have known Jesus.

Verse 2. The Elder's emphasis on the truth continues in this verse. In addition to what has already been observed regarding truth, the concentration of the terminology in these four verses shows that truth is a special concern for the Elder and talk about truth may even have a polemical character to it.[10] At the very least it prepares the reader for the following controversy surrounding the false teaching.

The Elder notes that both his love and that of the rest of the community is the result of the truth which abides in them. Previously it was noted that truth has a specific christological dimension to it in the Johannine literature. Now a close tie is implied with the Spirit of Truth of whom Jesus said, 'You know him because he abides with you and is in you' (Jn 14.17b).[11] The tie between love and truth exemplified here is frequent in the Johannine literature. The verse ends with a promise that as long as truth exists, which will be forever, love will exist.

Verse 3. It is customary to follow the A to B form of address with some sort of greeting. Not only does John follow other Christian letters in Christianizing the standard greeting, but he also makes it distinctively Johannine.

One peculiarity is the way his blessing of 'grace, mercy, and peace' becomes not a wish but a statement of fact. These *will* be with the believers. It is also made distinctive by the way in which the Elder

---

9   Cf. Hengel, *The Johannine Question*, p. 35.
10 Artus, 'La Seconde Epître de Jean', p. 30.
11 As Lieu, *The Second and Third Epistles of John*, p. 69, observes, 'it would seem to be preeminently that which can characterise the community and its members'.

includes himself in the blessing. This specific formula (grace, mercy, peace) is found in two other New Testament documents (1 Tim. 1.2; 2 Tim. 1.2), while 'grace' occurs four times in the Fourth Gospel (all in the prologue 1.14, 16, 17) and 'peace' occurs six times (all in the Book of Glory 14.27, 16.33; 20.19, 21, 26). As in 3 John 15, the mention of peace would remind the readers of the peace that Jesus brings to the disciples.

The rest of the greeting is distinctively Johannine. Note how 'from' (παρά) is used before both the Father and the Son, emphasizing the (equal?) role of each in relationship to human beings. In contrast to 3 John, where 'concerning the name' (ὑπὲρ γὰρ τοῦ ὀνόματος) is as close as one gets to the naming of God, the Elder prominently mentions God the Father and both names Jesus and identifies him as Son of God.[12] The Fourth Gospel, as well as 1 John, places a great deal of emphasis upon the role of the Father and upon Jesus' unique sonship. Without an explicit statement of fact, by the mention of Jesus Christ the readers are being prepared for the issue around which the false teaching revolves.

The greeting is rounded out by the phrase 'in truth and love'. But, does this phrase modify the way in which grace, mercy and peace indwell? Are truth and love the condition for God's gift of grace, mercy and peace? Or are grace, mercy and peace exercises of truth and love?[13] Perhaps John is again being intentionally ambiguous so that the reader must contemplate the richness of the expression and its many possible meanings.

Verse 4: Expression of Joy—Thanksgiving

Unlike 3 John, the Elder does not here include a wish for health but instead moves to a thanksgiving section. In this verse the Elder elicits for himself the audience's attention, their receptivity and their goodwill by expressing his personal joy at their behavior.[14]

The reason for his joy is what he found, apparently when some members of this congregation had visited the Elder's church. The fact that 'I rejoiced' (ἐχάρην) occurs in the aorist tense suggests that the Elder's encounter had taken place in the past, but the context clearly conveys the idea that their behavior, or at least the Elder's impression of it, has continued to the present. In 3 John 4 the Elder states that he could have no greater joy than to hear that his children are walking in the truth. Here he demonstrates that he has genuine joy when other

---

12   2 John 3 is the only place where it occurs.
13   Brown, *The Epistles of John*, p. 659.
14   D.F. Watson, 'A Rhetorical Analysis of 2 John', *NTS* 35 (1989), pp. 104-30 (111), calls this section an *exordium*.

'children' are found walking in the truth. It is difficult to determine whether or not 'some of your children' (ἐκ τῶν τέκνων σου) implies that some of the Lady's children do not walk in the truth. Intentionally or not, the phrase *does* prepare the reader for a divided community.

The Elder begins to define this walking in the truth by referring to the commandment received from the Father. 'Command' (ἐντολή) is one of the most frequent nouns in 2 John (occurring four times), which equals almost half the usage in the entire Fourth Gospel.[15] This commandment is identified in v. 5, 'love one another'. The attribution of this commandment to the Father rather than Jesus is in keeping with the Johannine view that the Father is 'the ultimate source of the message declared by Jesus (Jn 7.16-17) and by his followers (1 Jn 1.5)'.[16]

Verses 5-6: Body Opening—Petition (General)

Verse 5. The body of the Epistles begins with v. 5, where the Elder makes his general petition known. He employs three devices to endear himself to the readers ensuring the best possible reception. First, following standard epistolary practice he uses a complementary term (κυρία) to address his audience. Second, the Elder uses a standard word for making a request (ἐρωτάω) in his appeal to the church. Third, he includes himself throughout this verse by use of the first person plural, 'we/us'.

The Elder also makes use of two references to time in vv. 5-6. In the phrase, 'And now I ask you', the author places emphasis upon the current situation of the church he addresses. This use of 'now' (νῦν) contrasts their present context with the immediate past, implied by 'I rejoiced' (Ἐχάρην) in v. 4, and with the distant past, the beginning of the community implied by 'from the beginning' (ἀπ' ἀρχῆς) which occurs in both v. 5 and v. 6. The Elder's request concerns a commandment. Three things are said about this command: (1) it is received from the Father, (2) it is not new, and (3) the community has possessed it from the beginning.[17] This command is no recent innovation, as was the teaching of the opponents (v. 9), but is established in the bedrock of the community. If the Beloved Disciple is to be identified with the Elder, then the emphasis upon 'from the beginning' may be a subtle contrast between the legitimacy of his message as over against that of the false teachers. In one sense the command is no longer new, for it was given over half a century before by Jesus himself (Jn 13.34; 15.12, 17).

---

15   Brown, *The Epistles of John*, pp. 662-63.
16   Marshall, *The Epistles of John*, p. 66.
17   Brown, *The Epistles of John*, p. 684.

This commandment is expressed in the phrase 'in order that we might love one another' (ἵνα ἀγαπῶμεν ἀλλήλους), which is syntactically and logically related to the primary verb in the verse, 'I request' (ἐρωτῶ). In other words, 'I make this request of you...that you love one another'.[18] The command to love one another is foundational for John's church, for this love is to be the pattern and motive for Christian living and it serves to set the Church off from the world. This commandment:

> is constitutive for the community in two senses: a) because loyalty to that which has belonged to the community 'from the beginning' is essential for continuing in genuine 'Christian' life against the dangers of innovation (2.24), and b) because love is still a principle of unity — no-one can fail to love his brother and still be a member of the community (2.9f.).[19]

For the Elder, love is a practical, costly caring for the needs of others to the point of giving one's life for another believer (1 Jn 3.16-18). This love also includes affection for brothers and sisters.[20] One writer goes so far as to say that:

> In this v the elder asks his readers to practice something with which all three persons of the Trinity are concerned. For love comes from the Father (1 John 4.7), it is manifested by the Son (3.16), and it is made available by the life-giving Spirit (4.13-16).[21]

Verse 6. The Elder now seeks to refine and emphasize that which he has said earlier. Two definitions are contained in this verse both of which begin with 'this' (αὕτη), a purpose (ἵνα) clause, and a form of 'walk' (περιπατέω).[22]

The phrase 'and this is' (καὶ αὕτη ἐστὶν) is often used by John to explain something which has just been stated. The author appears to be intentionally repetitious so as to drive home the point about the interelationship of love and command in Johannine thought. One of the ways he drives home this point is by the chiastic structure of v. 6, where the sentence mirrors itself to a certain extent: love, command — command, love. Another way this is done is by the clear-cut but brief definitions which are offered. Finally, the Elder's amplification by repetition emphasizes the nature of love.[23] It would seem safe to conclude that 'walking in the truth', 'walking in love' and 'walking in the com-

---

18 Brown, *The Epistles of John*, p. 684.
19 Lieu, *The Second and Third Epistles of John*, p. 75.
20 Marshall, *The Epistles of John*, p. 67.
21 Smalley, *1, 2, 3 John*, p. 325.
22 Watson, 'A Rhetorical Analysis of 2 John', p. 120.
23 Watson, 'A Rhetorical Analysis of 2 John', p. 121.

mands' are different ways to say the same thing. All of these phrases emphasize fellowship and proper action, and are grounded in the origin of the community.

Verse 7: Body Middle—Occasion

The Elder now makes the purpose of this Epistles clear in a verse that stands near the middle of the letter. Loosely connecting this verse with the preceding one by the use of 'because' (ὅτι), John shows that the urgency of his request for walking in the command of love is intertwined with the occasion of the Epistles.

This verse, which begins and ends with a form of the word 'deceiver' (πλάνος), introduces an apocalyptic/eschatological element into the letter. Many deceivers have gone out. This word (πλάνος) and its cognates appear only in 1 Jn 2.26; 3.7; 4.6 and here in the Johannine literature, where it is associated with the description of antichrist and it is used as a contrast to the Spirit of Truth (cf. also Jn 7.12, 47; Rev. 2.20; 12.9; 13.14; 19.20; 20.3, 8, 10).

The Elder says that these deceivers 'have gone out' (ἐξῆλθον) into the world. Several things should be noted about this phrase. First, such language is reminiscent of the going out of Judas after Satan entered him (Jn 13.27, 30). Second, the language implies that the deceivers were at one time part of the community from which they left and entered the world. Third, 'to go out' in Johannine language may well be missionary terminology (3 Jn 7; cf. also Jn 17.18; 20.21), suggesting that the deceivers are engaging in missionary activity. Although nothing in 2 John gives evidence that such missionaries had already been active in this particular congregation, vv. 8-11 make explicit that the Elder expects that they would arrive sooner than later. Fourth, the use of 'many' (πολλοί) may indicate in contrast to 'some' of the children found walking in truth in v. 4, that there were now more deceivers engaged in missionary activity than members loyal to the community. Having gone out into the world (a neutral term here) these missionaries will seek to deceive everyone they can, including members of the community.

The middle phrase of v. 7 is as close to a description of the content of the deceivers' teaching as the Elder gives.[24] In the Johannine literature, except on one occasion, (public) confession has a christological content.[25]

---

24   As Hengel, *The Johannine Question*, p. 41, observes: 'One of the riddles of Jewish and early Christian polemic is that it hardly ever really names its opponents, but tends to use derogatory paraphrases.'
25   Brown, *The Epistles of John*, p. 669.

Here, it is interesting that the Elder describes the deception by citing that which the deceivers do not confess. Unfortunately, the precise nature of the confession is difficult to determine, for not only is there very meager evidence from which to draw, but there is also some ambiguity in the slogan itself. In 1 Jn 4.2 the test of faith is 'Jesus Christ having come in the flesh', no doubt a reference to the Incarnation. However, in v. 7 the slogan is 'Jesus Christ coming (ἐρχόμενον) in the flesh'. On the one hand, if the Elder had simply wanted to identify the denial of the Incarnation here, the statement found in 1 Jn 4.2 is probably to be preferred. On the other hand, while it is impossible to dismiss the idea that the return of Jesus is here at issue,[26] there is little or no evidence of this problem in the Johannine literature. It is likely that the present participle is used by the Elder to identify the deceptive teaching as involving one specific part of the Incarnation. Apparently, some in the early Church felt that at the crucifixion/resurrection Jesus gave up the flesh. The Elder's statement would make clear that Jesus was always in the flesh, something the deceivers could not affirm.

Such false teaching is clearly to be identified as representing that of the deceiver and the antichrist. In fact, the Elder can say that the one who practices such deception is none other than the antichrist. The word 'antichrist' is unique to the Johannine Epistles and (1) comes to signify the beginning of the last days (1 Jn 2.18); (2) is associated with the denial of Father and Son (1 Jn 2.22); and (3) is associated with denying an aspect of the Incarnation (1 Jn 4.2-3). In some ways the antichrist is the archenemy of Jesus, but in other ways he represents an attitude or belief about Jesus. Those who have gone out from the community with false teaching may be identified as antichrists. According to 1 John 2.18 'many' (πολλοί) antichrists have gone out, so in 2 John 7 'many deceivers' (πολλοὶ πλάνοι) have gone out.

The Elder in v. 7 very subtly brings the last days into view and heightens the importance of proper action on behalf of the believers by bringing apocalyptic expectation to bear. At the very least, the specific petitions and admonitions found in 2 John 8-11 are better understood against this backdrop.

Verses 8-11: Body Middle – Petition/Admonition

That these four verses form one section in the letter is apparent from the way in which the word 'work' appears at the beginning of the section, as

---

26 An interpretation offered by Oecumenius among others (*Commentary on 2 John*, ACCS, XI, p. 236).

a verb in v. 8, and at the close of the section, as a noun in v. 11. In addition, the multiple use of the word 'teaching' (διδαχῇ) in vv. 9 and 10 suggests that the Elder is intentionally calling attention to the content of these verses.[27] The section as a whole is devoted to warning the readers about the consequences of association with the false teaching and advising them as to how they should respond to it when it comes.

Verse 8. The Elder continues the thought of the previous verse by using a warning that occurs in several eschatological passages in the New Testament. The readers are admonished to watch themselves. Personal vigilance is the appropriate response to the approaching false teaching. The admonition to watch is found in other apocalyptic contexts in the New Testament (cf. Eph. 5.15; Col. 2.8; Heb. 10.25). The nearest parallel is found in the so-called 'little apocalypse' in Mark 13, where Jesus instructs the disciples to watch out for false christs and false prophets.[28] The reason for such vigilance is indicated in the Greek text by a purpose (ἵνα) clause. The purpose is expressed both positively and negatively, 'in order that you might not lose' and that 'you might receive a full reward'. In the Fourth Gospel 'to lose' (ἀπόλλυμι) occurs about ten times usually in the context of 'not losing those who belong to Jesus' (Jn 3.16; 6.39; 10.28; 17.12; 18.9). The closest parallel is found in 6.27 which reads, 'You should not be working for the food which is subject to loss but for food that lasts for eternal life'. In the immediate context (v. 29) Jesus says, 'This is the work of God: Have faith in him whom he sent.'[29] The implication of 2 John 8, in the light of John 6, is that the readers were in danger of losing the work of God (eternal life) if they followed those who deny 'Jesus coming in the flesh'.

Rather than losing they are to gain the full reward. Despite the fact that some are disturbed by any mention of reward in 2 John, it should be noted that in the New Testament rewards are spoken of often. The idea and word for reward appears in Jn 4.35-36. This passage suggests that the laborer receives the reward of the harvest itself. The 'full' reward implies that a partial reward is already available but that it will be granted in full one day. Such an emphasis is reminiscent of the eschatological balance in the Fourth Gospel itself. It appears that the reward in 2 John 8 is eternal life (for other meanings of reward in the New Testament cf. Mk 9.41; 1 Cor. 3.8-9; Rev. 11.18; 22.12).

---

27 Cf. Artus, 'La Seconde Epître de Jean', p. 29.
28 Brown, *The Epistles of John*, p. 671.
29 Brown, *The Epistles of John*, p. 672.

Verse 9. The Elder continues his warning by means of an antithesis, whereby he contrasts the effects of not remaining in the teaching of Christ with that of remaining in the teaching of Christ.

Apparently, the deceivers were making claims to go beyond the community's teaching as a result of the Paraclete's activity. After all the Fourth Gospel makes clear that the disciples did not always understand the meaning of Jesus' teaching until after the resurrection (cf. Jn 2.22; 7.39; 12.16) and that the Paraclete will lead and guide into all truth (Jn 16.12-15). However, the Elder argues that such 'teaching' goes beyond the teaching of Christ. Since the Paraclete would only speak that which the Father and/or Son reveals, their claim is illegitimate inasmuch as it involves the denial of Jesus Christ coming in the flesh and it results in not having either the Father or the Son. So while some of the Elect Lady's children walk in the truth by remaining in the teaching of Christ (and fulfill the command of Jesus in Jn 8.31), the deceivers walk in darkness because they do not remain (dwell) in the truth.

It is possible to understand the phrase 'the teaching of Christ' (τῇ διδαχῇ τοῦ Χριστοῦ) in one of two ways. If the words are taken as an objective genitive it means the teaching about Christ, in other words, the community's doctrine. The doctrinal nature of v. 7 might be offered in support of this interpretation.

If the phrase is taken as a subjective genitive it means the content of Jesus' teaching. Support for this interpretation comes from the fact that such a construction appears in Rev. 2.14, 15 ('the teaching of Balaam/the Nicolaitans') and that the Fourth Gospel emphasizes Jesus' own teaching (7.16, 17). Perhaps there is even a reference here to Jesus' command that 'they love one another'. If the teaching (διδαχή) has reference to Jesus' teaching, this emphasis is not unlike that found in 1 Jn 2.23-24, where that which was heard comes from the beginning.

Those who go beyond this teaching 'do not have God'. By this phrase, which echoes covenantal language, the Elder notes a personal relationship with God. According to the Fourth Gospel such a relationship is possible only through Jesus. In contrast, the one who remains in the teaching (of him) walks in the truth and has both Father and Son.[30] As in 1 Jn 2.23, 24, there is no knowledge, fellowship or remaining in the Son without the Father and vice versa. This emphasis on Father and Son, along with that in vv. 3 and 7, suggests that the Elder sees the christological controversy in broad terms.

---

30   Hengel, *The Johannine Question*, p. 42, suggests that such Father and Son language is at least binitarian and perhaps even trinitarian, noting the Son's elevation to a role equal to that of the Father.

The implicit warning of the verse is that unless the readers 'watch (βλέπετε) themselves' they may lose their relationship with God, the very ground of their salvation.

Verse 10. The Elder now moves to his specific request which is phrased in very practical, if not altogether clear, terms. The phrase 'if anyone comes' (εἴ τις ἔρχεται) expresses that the Elder expects individual missionaries to arrive at their door, not that this is merely possible. This certainty of expectancy is not only additional evidence for the frequency with which a church would receive visitors from other congregations (cf. 3 John), but may also suggest that the secession has only recently occurred and that deceivers were on their way to the churches. The factor that determines whether or not the emissary will find a reception is the nature of the teaching (διδαχή) which one bears. If the teaching is not in accord with the love command or the proper christological orientation, an emissary is not to be received.

Although 'house' (οἰκίαν) is without the article (anarthrous) and may have reference to a house church, in several other New Testament references to house churches another Greek term (οἶκος) appears, not the one used here (οἰκία) (cf. Rom. 16.5; 1 Cor. 16.19; Col. 4.15; Phlm. 2). Therefore, the Elder may very well be restricting the hospitality any Christian might offer to such a one who brings the teaching of Christ. It must be remembered that hospitality was essential to missionary activity. The reception here described is, no doubt, a missionary reception that would carry with it various kinds of supports. If given to a false teacher it would end up enabling such a false teacher to continue with this evil work. Even the greeting of peace, which itself creates community, is to be withheld.[31]

This harsh admonition sounds very cold and knee-jerk in character. However, in reality it is likely that various members of the community would have offered some form of hospitality during the process of determining whether one was orthodox or not. The test mentioned in 1 Jn 4.1-3, where the spirits are examined, does not seem to have been carried out on the doorstep, but perhaps in the context of worship, or at the least during a time of dialogue with the prospective host. Revelation 2.2 testifies to the testing of would-be apostles within the community.

Rather than regarding the Elder's comments as overly harsh, one must remember the drastic situation that called them forth. Paul (1 Cor. 5.9, 11), the *Didache* (10, 11) and Ignatius (*Eph.* 7.1; *Symrn.* 4.1) among others advocate rather harsh actions and/or struggled with how to handle the

---

31 Hengel, *The Johannine Question*, p. 43.

emerging false teachers. Clement of Alexandria is surely correct when he notes that such action is advocated in order to prevent those who are weak in the faith from being seduced by evil teachers.[32]

Verse 11. The reason for such extreme action is explained in v. 11. Greeting again is at issue. If the greeting mentioned here is connected to the offer of hospitality to missionaries, then the Elder is singling out the effects of such support. The welcome implies solidarity and at the least furthers the aims of these false teachers. Anyone who 'greets' these false teachers fellowships with evil deeds rather than God, the Elder or the community. Evil works is defined in the Johannine literature by its use in Fourth Gospel 3.19; 7.7. But in 1 Jn 2.13-14 'the evil one' is Satan and in 1 Jn 3.12 Cain, who belonged to the evil one, killed Abel because his works were evil. Obviously, the threat of a share in terrible deeds was a stirring warning to the reader about the danger of any contact with false teachers. Absolute avoidance of this type is the only way to ensure protection from contamination.

Verse 12: Body Closing

The Elder closes this letter in a way very similar to the close of 3 John. The first phrase 'many other things I have to write you' is perhaps an explanation for the brevity of the Epistles, although as with 3 John its length is not distinctive in comparison with other first-century letters. While the same word is used for 'ink' (μέλανος) as in 3 John 13, here reference is made to the substance upon which writing is inscribed, papyrus, not the instrument of the writing.

Given the urgency of the occasion the other matters about which the Elder would like to speak would have to be handled face to face, literally 'mouth to mouth' (στόμα πρὸς στόμα). This implied promise to visit is found in the closing sections of many of the letters of the day. The addition of 'in order that our joy might be made complete' (ἵνα ἡ χαρὰ ἡμῶν πεπληρωμένη ᾖ) forms an inclusio with v. 4. The idea itself is rich in Johannine thought (1 Jn 1.1-4 and Fourth Gospel 15.11; 16.24; 17.13) and that makes its appearance here hardly trivial, rather it expresses genuine emotions.

Verse 13: Concluding Formula

The Elder brings this short Epistle to a close by creatively crafting a concluding formula that contains a couple of important features. First,

---

32   Clement, 'Stromata I 4: Comments on the Second Epistle of John', p. 577.

an inclusio is created by his reference to the children of the Elect Lady's sister. If his earlier mention of the Elect Lady and her children has reference to a specific congregation and its members (v. 1), then mention of the children of the Elect Lady's sister no doubt has reference to another congregation and its members. In all likelihood this congregation is that of the Elder himself. Second, by utilizing a corporate greeting the Elder underscores the importance of community and implicitly reminds the readers about the danger of receiving deceivers into their midst, as such action would ultimately cause them to lose their reward. At the same time, this communal emphasis serves to encourage these Johannine believers that despite the dangers they face, they are not alone.

Reflection and Response—Part Two

Reflection

One of the more prominent themes found in 2 John is that of deceivers and false teaching. The readers are warned of the imminent arrival of those who deny Jesus' coming in the flesh. These deceivers are not content to remain in the teaching of Christ, but go beyond it, perhaps under the guise of the Paraclete leading them into new 'truths'. However, there should be no mistaking the extraordinarily dangerous nature of their teaching. Those who embrace it will ultimately lose their relationship with the Father and their reward of eternal life.

The Elder even goes so far as to indicate that offering such deceivers missionary support, even uttering the greeting of peace, will result in the contamination of believers by the false teachers' evil works. Despite the Elder's general teaching on love in 2 John, these false teachers and their teaching are to be avoided at all costs, for indeed, they are deceivers and antichrists. Clearly, the Elder's words are relevant to the contemporary Church. To facilitate reflection a series of questions are here raised.

If an antichrist, as defined in 2 John, is one who is involved in false teaching about Jesus, are there individuals or groups today who might be deemed to be antichrists? What are the signs that prompted this identification? How extensive is the presence of such false teachers? Are they active outside the Christian community or are false teachers present even within the Church itself? In what way does their presence affect the Church and its ministry? Is the Church making an adequate attempt to protect its children from such deceivers?

While most of us are quite prepared to give assent to the fact that false teaching poses some threat to the welfare of the Church, we are not always conscious of our own possible involvement in false teaching.

Thus, several additional questions are now raised of a more personal nature. Have I ever been involved in a group or church whose teaching deviated in significant ways from the teaching of Christ? What has been my attitude to those whom I know to be missionaries of false teaching? Have I supported, or am I supporting, ministries that promote teachings that go beyond the teaching of Christ? In what ways am I accountable to others for the teaching which I receive and endorse by my financial support? Have I considered sufficiently the negative consequences of my ministry support of those who go beyond the 'teaching of Christ' both personally and corporately? In what ways do I need to re-examine my acceptance and support of certain ministries?

Response

How may one respond to this issue raised by the text?

First, it is important to examine the ministries with which you are connected (including TV, Internet and radio ministries) to determine whether they are faithful to the teaching of Christ. An intentional examination may reveal more about the theological strengths and weaknesses of a particular ministry. Listen and read carefully in order to discern these matters for yourself.

Second, consult with members of the body of Christ with regard to your examination. The counsel of trusted teachers and ministers within the community may prove especially helpful in determining your next course of action. Prayerfully reflect together about your discoveries.

Third, after personal examination and consultation with those in the body, sever any supportive relationship you may have with a person or ministry that goes beyond the teaching of Christ. Such a step is not an appropriate one for any and all minor differences of opinion, but rather should be taken when it is clear that the ministry in question deviates from the teaching of Christ on the scale of that described in 2 John. It is very important not to support and, consequently, fellowship with such 'missionary' activity. Good and discerning stewardship is very much the issue here.

Finally, commit to and take concrete steps to begin a systematic study of the Scripture in order to be in a better position to discern the truth from deception. Making yourself accountable in this step to other members of the body may prove to be a great source of encouragement as you make this long-term commitment.

PART III

1 John

Several things may be assumed regarding 1 John in the light of 2 and 3 John. First, it appears that the same author who wrote 2 and 3 John is responsible for 1 John as well. As noted earlier the most likely candidates are John the Elder or John the son of Zebedee. This individual was an eyewitness to the ministry of Jesus and founded a community in or near Ephesus around 66 CE. As he was one of the few remaining eyewitnesses his testimony was cherished and he became the Beloved Disciple of the community. As the grand old man of the Church (the Elder), he held a position of authority unrivaled in his circle.

The examination of 2 John revealed that the Johannine community faced a situation which could threaten its very existence. This threat came from certain false teachers who were challenging several basic tenets of the faith as understood by the community. From 2 John it may be deduced that these teachers: (1) were many (πολλοί); (2) were not obeying the love command which was fundamental to the community; (3) were innovative in their teaching, perhaps attributing such departures from the community's teaching to the ministry of the Paraclete; (4) were denying certain aspects of the Incarnation; (5) were not in a right relationship with God, in part because of their denial of the Son; (6) and, any who followed their teaching were in danger of losing eternal life.

It appears that 2 John preceded 1 John chronologically. On this view, 2 John would be a quick note dashed off to a particular congregation within the community, putting them on notice that they should expect to encounter some of the false teachers who have left the community for the world. While the Elder fully expects these deceivers to approach the church (2 Jn 10), it appears as though the false teachers have yet to make an entry into the community addressed in 2 John.

The situation as evidenced in 1 John is quite different. The impression left there is that not only had many false teachers left the faith, but also that the community was having to battle them. In other words, the probability of 2 John has become a reality in 1 John. Not only does 1 John confirm most of what has been revealed about the deceivers in 2 John, but it also adds a great deal of information about them and the situation that the Church faced. One of the things which becomes even more apparent is the way in which the teaching found in the Fourth Gospel underlies and may account for the false teaching itself. In other words, the false teaching appears to have resulted from inappropriate conclusions reached about the teaching of Jesus as found in the Fourth Gospel.

Before examining the text of 1 John, the literary genre and structure of the work should be identified.

The Literary Genre of 1 John

Having given careful consideration to the literary genre of 2 and 3 John, the lack of epistolary characteristics in 1 John becomes easily recognizable. On the one hand, absent are the identity of the author and the addressees, the wish for health, the greeting and the occasion around which the petitions, both general and specific, are located. On the other hand, the author uses the verb 'to write' some 13 times and the second person pronoun ('you') often. Such practices demonstrate that while the author may not have been comfortable with writing, preferring the spoken word, he has adopted a form of communication which obviously was intended for an audience to hear.

As becomes obvious, 1 John exists to make clear the position of the Elder with regard to Christology and its resulting implications, especially love and eternal life. Although a variety of literary genres have been proposed as most like that of 1 John, it appears that this composition is in reality a commentary of sorts. 'His was not a commentary in a systematic or verse-by-verse style but an attempt to expound GJohn ideas misinterpreted by the secessionists.'[1] As such, 1 John represents a more deliberative attempt to address the deceivers than does 2 John. It may be that 1 John was addressed to the many house churches in and around Ephesus and required no other epistolary markings. Or perhaps it served as a sermon circulated to those areas in which the deceivers had moved but which the Elder was unable to visit personally and was accompanied by a trustworthy representative of the Elder and required no further identification. It is also possible that the identifying characteristics were omitted when the document was copied for the church archives.

The Literary Structure and Major Themes of 1 John

Identifying the structure of 1 John is a most difficult interpretive challenge for the student of this book. The nature of this challenge is reflected by the lack of any sort of consensus among scholars with regard to the structure of 1 John and by the fact that some interpreters have given up altogether on the possibility of ever being able to identify a

---

1   Brown, *The Epistles of John*, p. 90.

clear structure in the book. But, by paying careful attention to the literary patterns contained in the work and allowing the text to reveal its own shape, a structure of 1 John may be identified.[2]

A variety of literary indicators in the work reveal certain dimensions of the text's structure. Several literary patterns in the text of 1 John have been identified which may serve as markers identifying specific literary units within the book. These include: (1) three occurrences of 'if we say' (ἐὰν εἴπωμεν) in 1.6–2.2; (2) three sentences that use the formula 'the one who says' (ὁ λέγων) in 2.4-11; (3) seven clauses in 2.29–3.10 where the construction 'each one who' (πᾶς ὁ) is followed by a participle; (4) and the use of 'we know' (οἴδαμεν) as the lead verb three times at the conclusion of the book (5.18-20). In addition to these textual markers, there are a few portions of the text that interpreters never break up owing to their subject matter: 2.12-14; 2.15-17; and 4.1-6.[3] Such clues, while not solving the puzzle of the structure of 1 John as a whole, do reveal something of the nature of the book's microstructure if not its macrostructure. To ignore clues like these would seem to ensure that the interpreter has little chance of identifying the broader structure of 1 John.

In addition to these hints, a careful reading of the content of the individual passages reveals broader indicators in the text, such as the book's flow and development of thought and especially its repetition of theme and vocabulary, which point to the work's structure. Specifically, it appears that 1 John has a concentric or chiastic structure. That is to say, the text seems to mirror itself, with the most important section standing at the center of the work. By the use of similar catchwords and phrases and sections which parallel one another in terms of content, the author indicates a desire for the reader to reflect upon the connections between different portions of the text.

The basic structure of 1 John may be set forth as follows:

A 1.1-4: Prologue – Eternal Life
  B 1.5–2.2: Making Him a Liar (Walking)
    C 2.3-17: New Commandment (Love)
      D 2.18-27: Antichrists
        E 2.28–3.10: Confidence – Do Not Sin
          F 3.11-17: Love One Another
        E' 3.18-24: Confidence – Keep the Commands
      D' 4.1-6: Antichrists
    C' 4.7–5.5: God's Love and Ours
  B' 5.6-12: Making Him a Liar (Testimony)
A' 5.13-21: Conclusion – Eternal Life

---

2   For a more complete discussion cf. J.C. Thomas, 'The Literary Structure of 1 John', *NovT* 40 (1998), pp. 369-81.
3   Brown, *The Epistles of John*, p. 118.

This structure should become clear as the reader makes his or her way through the text of 1 John. In what follows, brief comment is offered on several of the prominent features of the structure of 1 John, with attention first being given to the structure's center.

Love One Another (3.11-17)

At the center of the book (section F) stands a discussion of what is the most important commandment for the Johannine community, to love one another. The supreme love of Jesus and the corresponding love that believers are to have for one another are contrasted with the hatred of evildoers, the biblical example of Cain illustrating the point. The writer makes clear that this kind of love is closely connected to eternal life, while those who do not love remain in death. The kind of love advocated is one which is expressed not only in word but in deed – helping those who are in need, even to the point of laying down one's life. This passage then contains three ideas that are very important in 1 John: love, eternal life and remaining (μένω). The emphasis on love is also developed in sections C and C' and is mentioned in two other parts of the book (sections E and E').

Confidence before God (2.28-3.10 and 3.18-24)

Standing on either side of this central pericope are passages that are connected to one another in several ways but most clearly by the use of the phrase 'confidence before God'. Section E (2.28-3.10) is marked off as a literary unit by the pericope's frequent use of the term 'children' (τέκνα) and the contrasting of those who are born of God with those born of the Devil. Additionally, there are seven occurrences of the construction 'each one who' (πᾶς ὁ) followed by a participle. There is also an emphasis in this text upon remaining (2.28; 3.6, 9). Clearly, one of the most important emphases of this passage is the correlation between confidence before God and moral purity. Specifically, in order to be confident before God one must purify oneself as he (Jesus) is pure, practice righteousness, and not remain in sin. The pericope concludes by noting that the one who does not love his brother is not of God.

Although articulated somewhat differently, Section E' (3.18-24) is also concerned with confidence before God. Again, moral purity is very much in evidence, although this time the emphasis is upon whether or not the believer's heart condemns him or her. In this case confidence before God leads to the believer's asking for whatever is needed. The heart does not condemn the one who keeps the commands, especially the commands to believe in the name of his son Jesus Christ and *to love one another*. Whereas moral purity indicates whether or not one is a child of God in section E, here keeping the commands indicates that one remains in God and God remains in him or her. In the former passage, the seed (σπέρμα) of God remains in the believer (3.9), in the latter it is 'out of the Spirit' that has been given (3.24b).

Antichrists (2.18-27 and 4.1-6)

The two passages that border those devoted to confidence before God have a number of thematic similarities. The first of the two texts, section D (2.18-27), opens with a discussion of the last hour and the arrival of the antichrists, who were formerly part of the community. It continues by emphasizing the way in which the 'anointing' (χρῖσμα) they have received from the Holy One ensures that they know all things, the implication being that they should be able to discern the difference between truth and lies. The liar denies that Jesus is the Christ; the antichrist denies the Father and the Son; those who deny the Son do not have the Father. Proper confession indicates that one has the Father and remains in that which was heard from the beginning. Such remaining is the promise: eternal life. In a final admonition the readers are warned about the deceivers and reminded that if they remain in the 'anointing' (χρῖσμα) they have received, they will need no teacher, for this 'anointing' (χρῖσμα) will teach them the truth. There they are to remain.

The parallel to this pericope, section D' (4.1-6), is equally concerned about false teaching and begins with an admonition to test every spirit to determine its origin. Section D had indicated that many antichrists had gone out, now in section D' it is noted that many false prophets have gone out into the world. Like its parallel passage, this text also indicates that confession is an important aspect in discerning/testing the spirits. The one who confesses Jesus having come in the flesh is of God. The one who does otherwise is not only 'not of God', but is identified as the antichrist. Because the readers are 'of God', they hear him; whereas those who are not of God do not hear him. Discerning between the Spirit of God and the spirit of deception is made possible, in part, by the confession one does or does not make.

The New Commandment/God's Love and Ours (2.3-17 and 4.7–5.5)

The two texts that stand on either side of the antichrist passages are devoted to the command to love. In section C (2.3-17) there is a very close connection between keeping the commands and loving as one ought. The text begins by asserting that the evidence (knowledge) of knowing God is the keeping of the commands. In contrast to the one who does not keep the commands and is a liar, the one who keeps his word is assured that the love of God has been perfected, which is itself evidence of knowing God. The keeping of the new commandment, to love one's brother (or sister), indicates that one walks in the light—for hating one's brother (or sister) reveals that one walks in darkness. In vv. 12-14 are found six declarations (divided into two poetic sections), about forgiveness of sin, knowledge of the one from the beginning, and victory over the evil one for the young men, in whom the word of God remains. The writer closes this section by returning to a discussion of love, indicating the diametric opposition between love of the world and love of the father. The things of the world, which is fading, are contrasted with doing God's will, which remains forever.

Two things stand out about section C' (4.7-5.5). First, the number of points of contact between this passage and section C are astonishingly high. Second, as 1 John nears its end, several terms that have appeared earlier in the book reappear in this passage. The primary theme of this section is love. The text contains a number of elements which make clear its major emphasis, beginning with a form of the word love (Ἀγαπητοί) to address the readers. Following this are affirmations that God is (the origin of) love (vv. 7, 8, 16) and that he first loved us (vv. 10, 19), which resulted in the sending of his son into the world (vv. 9, 10, 14). The command to 'love one another' is never far from view, nor is the connection between loving God and loving one's brother (and sister). In point of fact, the evidence of knowing, remaining in and being born of God is love for one's brother. Whereas in section C (2.4), the one who claimed to know God but did not keep his commands is called a liar, so in C' (4.20) the one who claims to love God but hates his brother (or sister) is a liar. In the former section (2.5) the love of God has been perfected in the one who keeps his word, while in the latter the love of God has been perfected in those who love one another (v. 12) and remain in God (v. 17). Such perfect love casts out all fear of (the) judgment, while those who fear reveal a lack of such perfected love (v. 18). As in section C, there is a close tie between love and keeping his commands (5.2, 3).

But such parallels do not exhaust the ways in which these texts are intertwined. One finds an affirmation about the forgiveness of sins not only in section C (2.12), but also in section C' (4.10). In addition both passages contain declarations about 'overcoming'. In 2.13, 14, it is said that the young men have overcome (νενικήκατε) the evil one, while in 5.4, 5 'our faith' is identified as the 'victory that overcomes' (ἡ νίκη ἡ νικήσασα). In section C (2.14) the children 'have known the Father', while in C' (4.7) 'the one who loves knows God'. In 2.14, the word of God 'remains' in the 'young men', while in 4.12, 13, 16 God 'remains' in us. Another point of literary affinity between these passages is found in the statements that concern the one who hates his or her brother or sister (2.11 and 4.20). Both of these sections underscore clearly the fundamental connection between proper claims (belief) and proper conduct (actions).

Along with section F, these two parallel passages make clear that the command to love one another is an extremely important aspect of this work's message.

Making Him a Liar (1.5–2.2 and 5.6-12)

At first glance the texts that stand on either side of the passages devoted to the love command do not appear to be connected in any fashion. However, despite first impressions, there are several ways in which these texts are related. The most impressive similarity is the catchphrase to 'make him a liar'. God is the object in both occurrences of this phrase. This statement is made as a result of an improper claim regarding sinlessness in 1.10 and a lack of belief in God in 5.10. In both cases the veracity of God is being challenged: implicitly in the former, explicitly in the latter. It might not be going too far to say that in section B (1.5–2.2) God is made a liar by an improper claim regarding one's walk, while in section B' God is made a liar by improper belief with regard to God's testimony.

In addition to the appearance of this catchphrase, each of these sections stresses the blood of Jesus. Although the Greek term for blood (αἷμα) appears only once in section B (1.7), it clearly exerts a significant influence on the rest of the passage. The relationship of Jesus' blood to sin is that it cleanses the individual from all sin and/or unrighteousness. In section B', the double mention of the blood qualifies the way in which Jesus had come and is identified as one of three witnesses (to Jesus). For the reader of 1 John, the appearance of 'blood' (αἷμα) in B' would scarcely be understood in any other fashion than as connected to the cleansing and forgiveness of sin as in section B.

A final point of contact is that both passages begin with similar statements: 'And this is the message' in 1.5 and 'This is the one who comes' in 5.6. Near the end of section B' (5.11), a similar phrase appears: 'And this is the testimony'.

Eternal Life (1.1-4 and 5.13-21)

As might be expected, the beginning and conclusion of 1 John differ significantly in that they serve different purposes. Section A introduces the readers to what follows, while section A' appears to offer a conclusion which in some ways builds upon several themes that have appeared before and develops them further. Yet, despite such divergent aims, they too have something in common. Eternal life is identified in both sections as being central to the purpose of the work. Standing at the heart of section A (1.2-3) is a discussion of eternal life, which here appears to be a reference to Jesus, and, consequently, the reason for writing. In the first verse of section A', the purpose of the writing is so that the readers would know they have eternal life (5.13). The final portion of this section (5.20) also makes a last reference to eternal life. Given the prominent positioning of eternal life in sections A and A', it comes as no surprise to find the reappearance of this topic in sections D, F and B'.

Four aspects of this outline should be emphasized. First, standing at the center of the book is a discussion of what is the most important commandment for the Johannine community, to love one another. This emphasis is also developed in two other parts of the book (cf. sections C and C'). Second, this outline also makes clear the crucial role the issue of eternal life plays in this document. References to eternal life stand at the beginning, middle and end of 1 John, implying that it figures prominently in John's purpose for writing. This topic is also mentioned in other parts of the book (cf. sections D and B'). Third, a fair amount of attention is given to deceivers and antichrists, who oppose the community and its beliefs. Fourth, the way one lives and acts (one's walk or testimony) reflects upon the character of God. To use John's language, if one walks outside the light, it makes God a liar.

A final observation should be made about one of the major themes in 1 John before the text is examined. Given the fact that the term 'remain' (μένω) occurs frequently throughout the work and appears in almost every section of 1 John (2.6, 10, 14, 17, 19, 24, 27, 28; 3.6, 9, 14, 15, 17, 24; 4.12, 13, 15, 16), it appears safe to assume that this term is quite significant for the author.

The Text

1 John 1.1-4

One of the first things evident when reading the prologue of 1 John is its similarity to the prologue of the Fourth Gospel. Numerous terms familiar from the Fourth Gospel reappear here in creative ways. It is also apparent that not every portion of the Fourth Gospel's prologue is the subject of comment in 1 John. This fact suggests that 1 John functions as a commentary on those specific parts of the Fourth Gospel which were the focus of attention in the struggle between the community and the secessionists. As with the prologue of the Fourth Gospel, 1 Jn 1.1-4 shows some signs of being a self-contained literary unit.[4]

At least two grammatical problems are encountered in these first four verses.[5] First, these four verses constitute one long sentence in the Greek text. This problem is made all the more difficult by the fact that on two occasions the long sentence is interrupted by parenthetical phrases ('about the word of life' at the end of v. 1 and the whole of v. 2). Grammatically then, v. 3a follows v. 1e. Second, similar to some German constructions, the main verb in these verses does not appear until near the end of the sentence (v. 3b, 'we *proclaim* also to you'), which causes numerous translation problems.[6]

Verse 1. Four times in v. 1 John uses a construction that begins with 'that which' (ὅ). Not only does the writer place the object first in each of these constructions but he also withholds the identity of these objects until the end of v. 1 and the beginning of v. 2. In this way John builds the readers' anticipation with each use of 'that which' (ὅ). John's initial use of this construction begins the work. Here reference is made to 'That which was from the beginning' ("Ο ἦν ἀπ' ἀρχῆς). There are, of course, a variety of ways in which this phrase might be understood in the light of the Fourth Gospel. For example, the most immediate parallel is that found in the prologue of the Fourth Gospel where 'beginning' (ἀρχή) has reference to a period before the creation of the world. Additional support for this interpretation might be found in the following verse, Jn 1.2, as well as in Jn 8.44, where Jesus charges that the Devil has been a murderer from the beginning. However, the Fourth Gospel also uses this term (ἀρχή) with reference to various aspects of the beginning of Jesus' ministry (cf. 2.11; 6.64; 8.25; 15.27; 16.4; cf. also 2 Jn 6) and it seems likely that the beginning of Jesus' ministry is meant here as well. The significance of this beginning for the Elder can hardly be missed, for in these his opening words, he calls the readers' attention to the importance of first things as he takes them back to the ministry of Jesus and its significance for the community.[7] Such reference implies that Jesus' ministry has a certain priority over other experiences or claims.

---

4   Smalley, *1, 2, 3 John*, p. 4.
5   Brown, *The Epistles of John*, p. 153.
6   Brown, *The Epistles of John*, p. 153. In addition to these two grammatical problems Brown observes, 'There is a puzzling alteration of tenses in the many "we" verbal forms, especially of the aorist and the perfect.'
7   Bede, *ACCS*, XI, p. 167, notes, 'The disciples were with Jesus from the beginning, and so they could preach what they had seen and heard in his presence without any ambiguity' (*Homilies on the Gospels* 2.16).

That which was from the beginning is also that which 'we have heard'. This first of four sensory verbs employed by the Elder has appeared already in 2 Jn 6 as having taken place in the beginning. On that occasion the love command is described as that which was heard from the beginning. Clearly, reference is made to that which was heard in the ministry of Jesus. Although including the love command, here the scope of that which was heard is likely to be much wider, for in the Fourth Gospel hearing is an especially prominent concept and is closely connected to the idea of belief. On the negative side, the community knows from the Fourth Gospel that unless one 'hears' it is impossible to believe Jesus, the Father, or those who bear witness (5.37; 8.43, 47; 9.27). At the same time, the reader knows that it is possible to hear but to be scandalized by what is heard (6.60) or it is possible not to be able to receive it (12.47). But perhaps the worst indictment of all is that those who oppose Jesus hear from their father the Devil (8.38).

On the positive side, those who hear Jesus believe in him (1.37, 40; 4.42; 14.28), belong to God (8.47), have eternal life (5.24), show that they are his sheep (10.3, 8, 16, 27), will rise from their graves (5.25, 28), and hear from the Father (6.45, 14.24). Not only do the disciples hear in the Fourth Gospel, but Jesus himself also hears. Jesus bears witness (3.32; 8.26, 40; 15.15) and renders judgment on the basis of what he hears (5.30). When Jesus hears he acts with concern (9.35; 11.4, 6). Furthermore, God hears Jesus (11.41-42), while the coming Paraclete says what he hears as well (16.13). It is not insignificant that the first and last mention of 'hearing' in the Fourth Gospel have reference to the testimony regarding Jesus; that of John the Baptist (1.37, 40) and the Beloved Disciple (21.7) respectively. For the Elder to lay claim to having heard, then, should not be easily passed over but is a way in which he aligns himself (and those who stand with him) with the kind of authentic faith and response that characterized those whom the community had come to know as examples of belief. The fact that the verb occurs in the perfect tense may indicate that for the writer the effects of that which was heard in the past continue to be felt in the present. Such language underscores John's qualification to address his readers.

Not only does John claim to have heard that which was from the beginning, but he also stresses that he has 'seen' that which was from the beginning 'with his (our) eyes'. As with hearing, seeing has a rich background in the Fourth Gospel and John appears to be drawing upon the readers' knowledge again at this point. Although there are five words used in the Fourth Gospel for seeing, and the meanings of these terms overlap, the primary focus at this point is upon the term that occurs here in the text (ὁράω). Consistently, John seems to use this term for 'see' to denote a specific kind of vision. It is this sort of seeing that forms the basis of John the Baptist's testimony (1.34). Such sight enables those who have seen Jesus to see the Father (14.7, 9), for Jesus has seen the Father (6.46). The possibility of this seeing is affirmed even though the prologue of the Fourth Gospel states that no one has seen God at any time (1.18). This term is used especially by Jesus as a challenge (1.39) and promise to would-be disciples with regard to what they will experience owing to their relationship with him. Such seeing would include 'greater things' than supernatural knowledge (1.50), 'the opening of the heavens' (1.51) and the manifestation of 'the glory of God' (11.40). But, John's use of this term (ὁράω) seems to reach its culmination when it describes the seeing of Jesus as the Son of Man (9.37), eschatological agent (16.16-22), the suffering lamb on the cross (19.35) and the resurrected Lord (20.18, 25, 29). Often such seeing of Jesus is closely connected with testimony and/or proclamation (cf. 1.34; 19.35; 20.18, 25). It is in this latter sense that the word is used here in 1 Jn 1.1. By laying claim to this term the author once again utilizes very powerful Johannine imagery to emphasize his authority and the importance of the testimony which he bears. The Beloved Disciple's appearance at the cross (and the explicit statements made regarding the validity of his witness), the use of this term in the resurrection appearances and the stress which John places upon seeing 'with our eyes' make it likely that the emphasis here is upon eyewitness testimony.[8] The reference to eyes may also highlight the accuracy of that which was seen. As with the previous verb, this verb also appears in the perfect tense indicating that the effects of the past seeing are still felt in the present.

Oddly enough, this phrase is followed by another that emphasizes seeing, only in this case a different Greek verb is used (θεάομαι). In all likelihood, this verb for 'see' and the one used previously are not intended to designate different types of sight, but appear to function as synonyms in this verse. But why would the writer use two such synonyms at this point? A couple of observations should be made in responding to this question. First, whenever clear repetition occurs in such close proximity in ancient texts the intention of the writer is emphasis. This device was a favorite of ancient authors particularly in predominantly oral cultures. In this case, the use of repetition allows John to underscore his previous point about what he (and others) had seen. Such emphasis makes explicit the importance of his earlier claim. Second, perhaps even more significant than the repetition itself is the specific term utilized. For here, the parallel with the prologue of the

---

8   The use of eyes in the Fourth Gospel stresses the aspect of physical sight.

Fourth Gospel is most obvious. This same verb occurs in the great incarnational passage (1.14), where the emphasis is upon seeing the glory of God in the flesh which the Word (λόγος) becomes. In fact, the same exact form of the verb occurs in both verses (ἐθεασάμεθα). Such identical usage is more than coincidence; this obviously draws on the readers' knowledge of the Fourth Gospel in utilizing the incarnational language par excellence of the Johannine church. Perhaps the use of the (aorist) past tense in this case appears owing to its occurrence in Jn 1.14, in which case the entire incarnation is described as one event.

The fourth sensory verb used in the prologue of 1 John does not appear at all in the Fourth Gospel. Despite this fact, some assistance in interpretation may be rendered by the use of 'hands' in this phrase. There are only two places in the Fourth Gospel that mention the hands of the disciples. In 13.9 Peter requests that Jesus wash his hands. However, the most relevant passage for this verse is found in 20.27, where Jesus instructs Thomas to place his hand in Jesus' side. Such a reference suggests that the readers of 1 John would most likely think of this resurrection story. That reference is made to the resurrection might also be supported by the use of the term for handle (ψηλαφάω) in Lk. 24.39, one of its four New Testament occurrences, where Jesus seeks to demonstrate to the startled and frightened disciples that he is alive. The (aorist) past tense may also support this line of interpretation, implying that John has in mind a particular 'handling' of Jesus. Clearly, with each of these phrases the author underscores the importance of eyewitness testimony to the life, ministry and resurrection of Jesus.

At this point the author seems to stop his train of thought long enough to mention the object of his reflection, the word of life. Again John picks up on an idea from the Fourth Gospel's prologue. One of the most prominent features of that section is the teaching about the Logos. This Word was with the Father before creation and was the agent of creation. This same Word is described as having within himself, life. This same Word became flesh and dwelt among the disciples. Such a description of the Word fits in well with what has been said thus far in the prologue of 1 John. Not only is the Word said to give life in Jn 1.4, but on two occasions he is said to *be* life (11.25; 14.6). This Word of Life offers eternal life on numerous occasions in the Fourth Gospel. While it is possible to take this phrase as the message about life or as the life-giving message,[9] the background of the Fourth Gospel suggests that John is repeating a certain aspect of the Fourth Gospel's prologue in a creative new fashion. The following conclusion seems close to the mark: 'So the "word of life"

---

9   So Brown, *The Epistles of John*, pp. 165-66.

is at once a reference to Jesus the Word who is the origin of life and an allusion to the preaching about him.'[10]

It is difficult to avoid the conclusion that through this first verse John seeks to draw out the implications of Jn 1.14, which states that the Word became flesh, and to emphasize the importance of the true humanity of Jesus. It should be noted that such an emphasis is not wholly unexpected, in that 2 John 7 reveals the existence of those who are unable to confess 'Jesus Christ coming in the flesh'. This verse also makes very clear John's own place as witness and his personal relationship with the 'Word of Life'.

Verse 2. This verse makes clear that the Word of Life has reference to the person of Jesus, for here 'the Life' (ἡ ζωὴ) appears in place of the name Jesus. Perhaps this substitution is employed to preserve a parallel with the Fourth Gospel's prologue, where Jesus is unnamed until 1.17. At any rate, there can be little doubt that the Fourth Gospel's prologue forms the backdrop against which this phrase is to be understood. In 1 Jn 1.2 the author makes explicit what was implicit in Jn 1.1-4. As noted earlier, the Word is identified as the source of life (Jn 1.4) and on two occasions, Jesus is identified as Life (11.25; 14.6). Throughout the Fourth Gospel Jesus either promises and/or confers life (3.15-16, 36; 4.14, 36; 5.24, 26, 29, 39-40; 6.27, 40, 47, 54; 12.25, 50; 17.2) or identifies himself (or is identified) as the origin of (eternal) life (6.33, 35, 48, 51, 53, 63, 68; 8.12; 10.10, 28; 17.3; 20.31). Not only can Jesus be identified as Life in the Fourth Gospel, his word, that is his message, might also legitimately be referred to as 'the word of life'. The overwhelming majority of uses of 'word' (λόγος) in the Fourth Gospel have the meaning of message.[11] However, given the prominence of Logos in the prologue of the Fourth Gospel it is difficult to dismiss this dimension of the phrase. Consequently, it is perhaps safest to take this phrase as an example of Johannine ambiguity.

John remarks that the Life 'was manifest'. In the Fourth Gospel, this verb (φανερόω) has an especially close tie to the unfolding (revelatory) purposes of God. Various events take place in order that Jesus and his mission might be manifested (1.31; 9.3). Jesus' first sign in Cana (2.11) results in the manifestation of his glory to the disciples, just as part of his mission was the manifestation of his Father's name before men and

---

[10] D.M. Smith, *First, Second, and Third John* (Louisville, KY: John Knox Press, 1991), p. 36.
[11] Brown, *The Epistles of John*, p. 164, notes that λόγος appears some 25 times in the Fourth Gospel with that meaning.

women (17.6). The use of this term culminates in the resurrection accounts where it appears three times in describing Jesus' resurrection appearances to the disciples (21.1, 14). By appealing to the manifestation of the Life, John not only continues his emphasis upon the incarnational dimension of Jesus' life and mission but he also continues to underscore the authoritative nature of his own testimony owing to his status as eyewitness. Equally clear is the fact that there is a growing emphasis upon the resurrection of Jesus.

The reappearance of the (perfect) past tense of the first verb used, meaning 'to see' (ὁράω), suggests that the ground of the community's witness and proclamation is that which was seen in the past, but the effects of which are still with them. On the basis of what had been seen, John (and his community) bears witness. The verb 'to witness' or 'testify' (μαρτυρέω) and the noun 'witness' or 'testimony' (μαρτύριον) appear 43 times and 21 times respectively in the Fourth Gospel and Johannine Epistles. This is equal to about one-half their occurrences in the New Testament. Such a major theme suggests that John's use of the term here builds upon its use in the Fourth Gospel. There these terms are used to describe the Baptist's testimony about Jesus (1.7, 8, 15, 19, 32, 34; 3.26, 28; 5.33), the unneeded testimony of 'men' (2.25), the testimony of the Samaritan woman (4.39), the testimony of the Scriptures (5.39), the testimony of the Father (5.39; 8.18), the testimony of Jesus' works (10.25) given from the Father (5.36), the charge that Jesus' testimony is false (8.13), the testimony of the crowds (12.17), Jesus' own testimony (3.11, 32, 33; 4.44; 5.31-33, 37; 7.7; 8.13, 14, 17, 18; 13.21; 18.23, 37), the testimony of the Paraclete (15.26), the testimony of the disciples (15.27) and the testimony of the Beloved Disciple (19.35; 21.24). As revealed in 3 John, testimony is a prominent concept there, designating the brothers' testimony about Gaius (3 Jn 3, 6) and the testimony about Demetrius by all those in the community, the truth itself, and the Elder *et al.* (3 Jn 12). Witness terminology also figures prominently in Revelation (1.2, 5, 9; 2.13; 3.14; 11.3; 12.11, 17; 15.5; 17.6; 19.10; 22.16, 18, 20).

Clearly the idea of testimony was prominent in the Johannine community and conveys the notion that the community itself was conscious of trial imagery. In 1 Jn 1.2, John's testimony identifies him with those who faithfully aligned themselves with Jesus and the work he accomplished on behalf of the one who sent him. Just as he has seen and witnessed, so John has seen and witnessed. Near the end of 1 John it becomes clear that such testimony comes via the Spirit/God (5.6, 8, 10) and one's relationship to Jesus/God (5.10). In the light of what John will go on to say about the deceivers later in 1 John, there may also be present in this statement a conscious hearkening back to Jesus' words to

Nicodemus in 3.11, 'Truly, truly I say to you, "That which we know we are speaking and that which we have seen we are testifying, and you would not receive our testimony".' In doing so, John not only demonstrates his own solidarity with Jesus, but he also shows that the notion of a rejected testimony was not without precedent in the community's history. Such a warning would also serve to remind the community about the consequences of responding to the testimony of Jesus and now to that of John in an inappropriate manner, as had the deceivers. The use of the verb in the present tense implies that John's testimony is an ongoing dimension of his life's ministry.

At the same time, John introduces the idea of proclamation. The word translated 'we proclaim' (ἀπαγγέλλομεν) and the other associated terms in its word family are used in the Fourth Gospel primarily to describe what will be revealed in the future by Jesus (4.25) and the Paraclete (16.13-15) and how it will be revealed (16.25). One form of the word is used by the man healed at the pool to 'proclaim' Jesus to the Jews (5.15). One of the terms is also used to describe Mary Magdalene's resurrection proclamation, 'I have seen the Lord' (20.18). The Johannine background of this term allows John both to lay claim to the continuity of his own proclamation with the revelatory work of Jesus and the Paraclete and to continue his emphasis upon the resurrection of Jesus. As with the verb 'to witness', 'proclaim' also appears in the present tense implying that John is currently in the process of proclamation as he writes. Therefore, in utilizing this term John conveys the sense that he is in the process of making known to his readers information of extraordinary value.

The content of John's proclamation to the community is Eternal Life, a prominent theme in the Fourth Gospel. In point of fact, the reason that the Fourth Gospel was written was to ensure that its readers might receive or continue in eternal life (20.31). Two of the metaphors Jesus used for eternal life are living water and bread from heaven. Those who eat or drink of such will never be hungry or thirsty again. For John eternal life comes as a result of the exaltation of Jesus (3.15) and belief in him (3.36; 5.24). It comes because the Father sent the Son in order that those who believe would not be destroyed (3.16, 36). It is life which is characteristic of another age. But on this occasion in 1 John it seems that eternal life has reference to the person of Jesus. Such a use of Eternal Life is not surprising in light of the fact that the Fourth Gospel identifies Jesus as Life as well as the origin of life (cf. the discussion of 1 Jn 1.2 above). Specifically, John says that this Eternal Life was with the Father.

By introducing 'the Father' into the discussion at this point, John accomplishes several things. First, it is clear that the author is once again directing the readers' attention to their knowledge of the Fourth Gospel, for God is often referred to as Father in that book. Such a reference reaffirms the close connection between this document (1 John) and the community's foundational document (the Fourth Gospel). Second, John wastes little time in revealing the absolute unity of the Father and the Life. Such a view would be natural for those with a knowledge of the Fourth Gospel, for there the unity between Father and Son is emphasized on a number of occasions and in many ways (e.g. Jn 10.38; 14.6, 9-11, 20; 15.23-24; 16.3; 17.21). Neither is this emphasis an altogether unexpected one in that 2 John has already disclosed the existence of those who were denying the absolutely essential nature of this relationship. Such a mention here is an indication of the problem to which John will return later in the work. Third, despite the fact that on several occasions the Fourth Gospel recounts Jesus' words about returning to the Father (16.10, 17, 28; 20.17), it seems likely that the intended parallel to the statement in 1 Jn 1.2 is found in the prologue of the Fourth Gospel (Jn 1.1), where John writes, 'In the beginning was the Word and the Word was with God and the Word was God'. Two points suggest that reference is here being made to the thought of Jn 1.1. In stating that Eternal Life was with the Father, John makes use of the same preposition for 'with' (πρός) in both verses. In addition to this similarity, John uses the same verb to indicate that Eternal Life 'was' (ἦν) with the Father, an expression which in its Gospel context describes the relationship between the Word and God as a pre-existent one. In light of this parallel, it is difficult to avoid the conclusion that in 1 Jn 1.2 the author is affirming the pre-existence of Jesus. Before closing his parenthetical statement, John seeks to make clear what had earlier been implied in his description of the Life being manifested. Here he underscores the fact that these revelatory events had involved them, that is to say that they had been 'manifested to us'. Eternal Life had not simply been manifested generally, but the manifestation was specifically for John and those with him. This reaffirmation of the Incarnation also serves to emphasize the authority of John's message.

Verse 3. After the parenthetical statement of v. 2, the author now resumes his main train of thought. In order to ensure continuity of logic John makes use of two terms that have appeared already in v. 1. In addition to preserving continuity, such repetition refuses to allow the reader to miss the emphasis John places upon the origin of his message and its incarnational dimension. It is only at this point, after two full verses, that the main verb is finally introduced. By so delaying the introduction of the main verb, a greater expectancy is created within the reader than would otherwise have occurred. It is that which was seen (perfect tense) and that which was heard (perfect tense) that is now being proclaimed by John. To be more precise, the continuing powerful effects of what was seen and heard (and no doubt handled) have resulted in John's present proclamation to his readers ('you').

By means of a purpose (ἵνα) clause John reveals the purpose of his proclamation. It is in order that his readers might (continue to) have fellowship with him. Although the term does not appear in the Fourth Gospel, the concept of fellowship is quite close to the Johannine understanding of 'abiding', 'remaining' or 'having'. In the Johannine literature, fellowship (κοινωνία) denotes 'participation with' or 'sharing in'. Part of this definition is revealed in 2 John 11, where the Elect Lady and her children are warned that if they welcome the deceivers, they would be in fellowship or communion with the deceivers' evil works. The basis of such negative fellowship was the reception of emissaries who were not confessing 'Jesus coming in the flesh'. Such ones had gone beyond the teaching of Christ and as a result did not have God. In his previous words in 1 Jn 1.1-3, the author makes very clear that he (and those with him) stand in extraordinarily close proximity to the Eternal Life of whom he has an intimate knowledge. In this light, it is significant that not only is John's relationship to Eternal Life emphasized, but Eternal Life's relationship to the Father as well. Clearly, one implication of the fellowship (κοινωνία) about which John speaks is that he and his readers might (continue to) remain together in the reality of that which he proclaims, that which was from the beginning. Therefore, it appears that the basis of the readers' fellowship with John is dependent, at least in part, upon their own identification with his proclamation.

Significantly, John does not allow his readers to misunderstand his words regarding fellowship. In the second portion of v. 3 the author makes explicit the precise nature of his fellowship: it is with both the Father and his Son Jesus Christ. The mention of the Father and his Son Jesus Christ at this point in 1 John accomplishes two things. (1) It indicates to the reader that John is assuming an awareness on the reader's part that in the Fourth Gospel Jesus is identified as God's Son or the Son of the Father on numerous occasions (1.18, 34, 49; 3.16-18, 35; 5.25; 10.36; 11.4, 27; 19.7; 20.31) and that their essential unity is often affirmed (4.34; 5.19-21, 23-24, 26, 30; 6.38-39, 44; 7.16, 18, 28; 14.13; 17.1 and numerous other passages regarding 'the one who sent me'). (2) This mention alerts the reader that just as in 2 John, one's relationship to the Father *and* the Son is very significant. Such language suggests that maintaining fellowship with both the Father and Son will prove to be crucial in the exposition that follows.

Verse 4. Now John states the reason for writing 'these things' by use of another purpose (ἵνα) clause, 'in order that our joy might be complete'. While mention of 'these things' no doubt includes the preceding verses, it in all likelihood has reference to the entire work. The use of the plural 'we' and the fact that this statement follows the emphasis upon 'our' fellowship implies that the completed joy is dependent upon one's relationship to the community. In the Fourth Gospel, John the Baptist likened his completed joy to that of the friend of the bridegroom who hears the voice of the bridegroom (3.29). But the nearest parallel is to the words of Jesus when on two occasions he explains that the reason for his words are in order that the disciples' joy might be complete (15.11; 17.13). Jesus also tells the disciples to ask (the Father) and receive in order that their joy might be complete (16.24). The use of such traditional Johannine language indicates that the writer is purposely drawing a parallel between the importance of Jesus' words for complete joy in the Fourth Gospel and their importance now through his own mediation of them. This language also hearkens back to the idea expressed in 2 John 12, that such joy is produced by shared fellowship. The point seems to be that the writer's joy would be made complete if what he writes results in the readers' (continued) fellowship with him.

1 John 1.5–2.2

The first major section of 1 John following the prologue opens by identifying the message which was heard and is proclaimed (1.5); it continues with the refutation of three erroneous claims (vv. 6-10) and concludes with a statement regarding sin (a topic introduced in the discussion of erroneous claims) and its remedy (2.1-2). This passage develops certain themes of the previous section while taking up additional Johannine ones, which include: 'light' and 'darkness', 'fellowship', 'walking', 'truth' and 'lies', 'sin', 'confession', 'cleansing' and 'Jesus Christ'. It also includes a phrase that will appear later in a parallel passage, 'we make him (God) a liar'.

Verse 5. Following its prologue the Fourth Gospel states, 'And this is the witness' to introduce the ministry of John the Baptist as well as to begin its major emphasis on witness/testimony. In 1 Jn 1.5 a similar formula is used which seems to parallel the opening of the Fourth Gospel in an intentional way. Here the formula is 'And this is the message'. Just as the phrase in the Fourth Gospel picked up on the witness motif which preceded it in the Gospel's prologue and introduces the emphasis that follows, so in 1 Jn 1.5 the term 'message' picks up on the references to proclamation in its prologue and introduces the following major discussion. As will become clear later, this sort of formula appears frequently in the Epistles (cf. 1 Jn 2.25; 3.23; 5.4; 5.11, 14; 2 Jn 6; cf. also 1 Jn 3.11; 5.3; 5.9).

The term translated message (ἀγγελία) occurs only twice in the New Testament, here and in 1 Jn 3.11. That it has reference to Jesus' message as proclaimed in the Fourth Gospel is indicated by the fact that the message 'has been heard', no doubt to be understood as that heard from the beginning (of Jesus' ministry), and by the fact that Jesus Christ is almost certainly the antecedent in the phrase 'from him' which follows in v. 5. It is this message, which has been heard in the past but remains in our ears, that is now being proclaimed to you. In describing this process of proclamation, the author employs a term (ἀναγγέλλομεν) which, in the Fourth Gospel, is used to describe the activity of the Messiah (4.25) and the Paraclete (16.13, 14, 15), as well as the proclamation of the man at the pool that Jesus is the one who had made him whole (5.15).[12] The appropriation of this language indicates that the author sees himself as standing in the line of those who are able to offer authoritative proclamation. Appeal to such language may also be a subtle hint that what John proclaims is that which the Paraclete has proclaimed, which in turn owes its origins to the proclamation of Jesus. In this way, the author leaves little doubt that what he writes stands in continuity with 'that which was from the beginning'.

The content of Jesus' message, which John now proclaims, is that 'God is Light and in him is no darkness at all'. Although this statement might at first sound abstract and in some ways undefined, readers of the Fourth Gospel understand the phrase in a more concrete fashion. First, the reader knows that when similar statements are made in the Fourth Gospel (i.e. 'God is Spirit'; 4.24), there are ethical and/or moral obligations that follow ('it is necessary for those who worship him to worship in spirit and truth'; 4.24). Not only does the statement 'God is Light' have such implications for the reader in 1 Jn 1.6-7, but the statement 'God is Love', which occurs later in 1 John (4.8), is also accompanied by concrete implications (4.11-12). Second, the reader would be aware of the way in which the opening of 1 John continues to parallel the prologue of the Fourth Gospel, as significant terms found in the Gospel reappear in the Epistles (in the same order!).[13] Thus, despite the fact that 1.5 begins a

---

12   For this interpretation cf. the discussion in J.C. Thomas, ' "Stop Sinning Lest Something Worse Come Upon You": The Man at the Pool in John 5', *JSNT* 59 (1995), pp. 3-20 (18).
13   A. Plummer, *The Epistles of S. John* (Cambridge: Cambridge University Press,

new section of the Epistles, some degree of continuity with the previous section is preserved by the parallels with the Fourth Gospel's prologue.

The reader is not completely unprepared for the appearance of the word 'light' in 1.5 since the term (φῶς) figures prominently in the Fourth Gospel and was a familiar metaphor throughout the ancient world. In the Gospel several aspects of the meaning of 'light' are revealed. First, there is a clear identification between Jesus and the Light. Not only does the prologue describe the Logos as the Light (1.4, 5, 7-9), but Jesus himself also explicitly claims to be the Light later in the Fourth Gospel (8.12; 9.5; 12.46). He is the true/genuine Light that shines on every person. Second, the Fourth Gospel reveals a clear line of demarcation between light and darkness. The mission of the Light is to shine in the darkness, illuminating that which is dark. One result of the Light shining in the darkness (1.5) is that individuals are forced to accept (love) or reject (hate) the Light (3.19-21). Third, those who do the truth are identified as those who come to the Light (3.21) and those who walk and believe in the Light (12.35-36) are identified as 'sons (υἱοί) of light' (12.36). Such ones as these have left the darkness of unbelief and come to know the Light of salvation. Therefore, the reader of 1 John is prepared for the distinction between light and darkness made in v. 5 and the ethical implications which follow.

However, given this impressive backdrop,[14] it comes as some surprise that in 1.5 *God*, not Jesus, is identified as Light. What accounts for this unexpected shift? The reader has already learned that an extraordinarily close connection exists between the Father and the Son (2 Jn 3, 9; 1 Jn 1.3). The intimate nature of this relationship is explored more fully later in 1 John. From the Fourth Gospel (3.32; 5.30; 8.26, 40; 15.15) the reader understands that the Son acts and speaks on behalf of the Father and that those who have seen the Son have seen the Father (14.8-14). Therefore, Jesus' proclamation and revelation of himself ('I am the Light of the World') is a proclamation and revelation of the Father. In this light, for the writer to begin with the statement 'God is Light' indicates that he is taking the reader back to the ultimate source of revelation and illumination (the Father) and at the same time underscores the essential unity between God (the Father) and Jesus.[15]

1896), p. 24, observes that the four terms, 'word, life, light, and darkness' appear in both documents in the same order.
14   Nearly half of the occurrences of φῶs in the New Testament are found in the Johannine literature.
15   Origen, *ACCS*, XI, p. 170, offers the following observation on this relationship, 'God is light, according to John. The only-begotten Son therefore is the brightness of that light, proceeding from God without separation, as brightness from light, and

This positive statement ('God is Light') is followed by a negative one ('and in him there is no darkness at all'), the first of many examples of such parallelism in 1 John. This strong contrast (note the two negatives in the Greek text—οὐκ and οὐδεμία) makes clear that there is absolutely no possibility that light and darkness exist together in God. Their functions are antithetical. But exactly what does darkness mean in this context? In the Fourth Gospel a close connection exists between darkness and night. Generally, these terms convey the idea of a realm hidden from light, in which one's walk is uncertain (e.g. Jn 12.35). However, it is revealed early on (3.19) that there is a fundamental tie between darkness and evil works. Given the Fourth Gospel's symbolism and its intentional use of ambiguity it appears that even its references to 'night' as a temporal indicator are not devoid of symbolic meaning (3.2; 13.30; 19.39; 21.3).[16]

What should be underscored at this point is that there is no connection between God and darkness. The need for such a statement alerts the reader that a major issue is the claim(s) being made with regard to light and darkness and it prepares the reader for the following discussion about moral obligation.

The remainder of this section (1.6-2.2) is structured around six 'if' (ἐάν) clauses, which are divided into three pairs of positive and negative statements. Each pair begins with a (false) claim, which John anticipates being made, and is followed by a statement through which he seeks to inform his readers of their proper course of action. In all likelihood, each of the false claims was being made by those who had left the community. For John to make reference to such claims at the outset of the work indicates that he expects some of these ideas are still present and might resurface within the ranks of the community. A final general observation about the remainder of this section concerns the possibility that there is some sort of progression in the severity of the claims, in that the first claim results in making the speaker a liar, while the final claim results in making God a liar.

Verses 6-7
The first pair of 'if' clauses are found in vv. 6-7. Each of the false claims begins with the phrase 'If we claim'. In raising these issues the author uses the first person plural 'we' and so (theoretically) identifies with the claim. By utilizing this approach he reveals a pastoral concern in

lightening the whole creation' (*On First Principles* 1.2.7).
16   Cf. esp. C.R. Koester, *Symbolism in the Fourth Gospel: Meaning, Mystery, Community* (Minneapolis, MN: Fortress Press, 1995), pp. 123-52.

addressing issues which he considers to be patently false. He also demonstrates an expectation that such views might be voiced in the community from time to time (no doubt through the lingering influence of those who had left the community).

Verse 6. The first false claim is to have fellowship with God while walking in darkness. Earlier (v. 3) John made reference to the importance of fellowship, identifying it as one of the reasons for this writing. At that point he made clear that it was essential for his readers to have (or maintain) fellowship with him (and those who stand with him), owing to his (their) unique relationship to and knowledge of Eternal Life. The implications of such fellowship are clarified further by the statement that his (their) fellowship is with both the Father and his Son, Jesus Christ. The reader would scarcely have forgotten the words of v. 3 when reading those in v. 6 regarding fellowship.

It is clear in the Greek text that John has placed the emphasis in v. 6 on the fellowship claimed (as κοινωνίαν stands first in the sentence). Such emphasis indicates that John regards this claim to have fellowship with God as a rival (and illegitimate) one. When read against the backdrop of v. 3, this claim to fellowship with God is noticably different. While John makes clear his fellowship is with both God and his son Jesus Christ, in the rival claim of v. 6, there is no mention of the Son. Although it is possible to take this omission as inconsequential, 2 John has already revealed that part of the Elder's dispute with the secessionists involved the latter's apparent disregard of the significance of Jesus Christ as God's Son, which resulted in a variety of christological problems.

If the mention of fellowship with God apart from the Son hints that something might be wrong with this claim, the rest of the phrase ('and walks in darkness') makes clear that something is amiss. As revealed in 3 and 2 John, to walk is a familiar metaphor in the Johannine literature. From Jn 6.66, one discovers that not walking with Jesus is a way to describe those who, owing to the hardness of his teaching, stopped following him. This usage implies that in the Johannine world, walking with Jesus might be synonymous with following him and is not far removed from the idea of fellowship. The reader also knows of Jesus' teaching, from the Fourth Gospel (8.12), that 'the one who follows me will never walk in darkness, but will have the Light of Life' and that walking in the light ensures one will not stumble (11.9, 10), while walking in darkness is a sign of not knowing where one is going (12.35). In the Fourth Gospel, then, walking in darkness is viewed as diametrically opposed to following Jesus, walking in the light.

In 1 Jn 1.6, the present tense of the verb 'walk' suggests that those who make the claim to have fellowship with God, habitually walk in darkness. This language indicates that the abode of such a person is a realm characterized by stumbling, uncertainty and evil works. Even before reading the second half of v. 6, the reader understands that one cannot make valid claims to have fellowship with God and walk in darkness, for it has just been made clear in v. 5 that there is no darkness in God at all.

'If we claim...we lie.' John now states what should already be obvious to the readers. To claim fellowship with God while walking in darkness is false. By the use of 'we' the author emphasizes that even if we, the bearers of the tradition, were to make such claims while habitually walking in darkness, *we* would be lying! But the reader is likely to read more into the charge of lying than simply telling something that is not true, for Jesus has said in the Fourth Gospel (8.44) that those who lie reveal their origin.[17] They are children of the Devil! For when the liar (your father) lies, he speaks his native tongue! Later in 1 John, it will become clear that those who lie lead others astray.[18] Therefore, to charge that those who make the claim to have fellowship with God while walking in darkness are lying indicates that such ones belong to the sphere of the Devil, the realm of darkness.

To live in such a way is described by John as, 'we do not do the truth'. According to Jesus' teaching in Jn 3.21, 'The one who does the truth comes to the Light'. Here the adverse is true, the one who walks in darkness does not do the truth. The connections between evil works, darkness, lies and deception converge at this point. Not to do the truth reveals that one does not live according to the commands of God/Jesus (2 Jn 6), identifies with the realm of darkness, and is far from having fellowship with Jesus, who is full of truth (Jn 1.14) and is the Truth (Jn 14.6). 1 John 1.6 testifies to the fact that, as revealed in 3 and 2 John, for the Johannine community there is to be no division between doctrine (claims) and ethics (doing).

Verse 7. Since John is not content simply to identify the false teaching of his opponents, he balances each of these three false claims with a declaration about appropriate conduct and belief. Verse 7 contains the first such declaration and is also introduced by an 'if' (ἐάν) clause. In v. 6 John points out that the 'words' (claims) of the deceivers are invalidated by their 'actions' (walk). Here, he contrasts the 'words' (claims) of the

---

17 Brown, *The Epistles of John*, p. 236.
18 R. Schnackenburg, *The Johannine Epistles* (trans. R. Fuller and S. Fuller; New York: Crossroad, 1992), p. 77.

deceivers with the 'actions' (walk) of those in the community; a walk which is a sign of one's fellowship with others and of one's purity through Jesus.

The words 'in the light' stand first in the Greek text, indicating that emphasis is placed upon this particular aspect of this statement. By placing such emphasis here, at least two things are accomplished. First, a contrast is drawn between the domain where the opponents walk (darkness) and the domain where those in the community walk (light). Second, the readers would appreciate the subtle connection made between the character of the readers (who walk in the light) and the character of God (who is the light), a connection which will be made more explicit with the next phrase.

As noted in the comment on v. 6, in the Fourth Gospel walking serves as a metaphor for following. Those who walk in the light conform to Jesus' command (Jn 12.35) to walk while they (the disciples) have the light. It is perhaps not without significance that here the verb 'walk' is used in the present tense, implying that such walking in the light is habitual, characteristic of the believer's life.

John now makes explicit the connection between God (who is light) and his readers (who walk in the light) by stating that their walk is in conformity to God, who is himself in the Light. In v. 5, John has said, 'God is Light', while in v. 7 God is said to be 'in the light'. The author may intend this subtle shift to convey the idea that not only can light be used to describe the essence of God's nature, but also to indicate that the standard against which the believer is to evaluate his or her walk (conduct) is God himself. That John is unafraid of using God or the Son of God as the standard of the believer's conduct is confirmed later in the book (1 Jn 3.3), where he encourages the reader to purify his or her own life using Jesus as the standard of purity.

Two things may be known about those who walk in the light. First, they have fellowship. However, John does not say that this fellowship is with God, as the opponents claimed, but rather John says that this fellowship is with 'one another'. Although this statement seems to be an abrupt change in thought, it is not quite as unexpected as it first appears. Earlier (1.3), John had indicated the purpose for his proclamation was that his readers might have fellowship with him (and the community – 'us'). In that verse he revealed that such fellowship was, at the same time, fellowship with the Father and his Son Jesus Christ. In a very subtle way then, John *does* claim that one who walks in the light has fellowship with God (both the Father and Son). However, his somewhat unexpected shift underscores the fact that for John salvation is not some individualistic, pietistic experience, but must be rooted and grounded in community.

One who walks in the light finds himself or herself accompanied by others on this journey. It would appear that for John, one's walking in the light can be judged on the basis of one's relationships in the community. In contrast to the opponents, who claimed a 'transcendent' fellowship with God while walking in darkness, those who walk in the light demonstrate their fellowship with God by means of their concrete fellowship with one another.[19] This idea is not unrelated to the relationship between love for one's brother or sister and love for God that will reappear later in the book (4.20).

A second thing known about those who walk in the light is that 'the blood of Jesus his Son cleanses us from every sin'. This statement introduces a number of ideas that are new to the argument of 1 John: Jesus' atoning death, sin and cleansing in particular. The Fourth Gospel gives two hints with regard to the efficacious nature of Jesus' shed blood. In Jn 1.29, the Baptist says, 'Behold, the lamb of God who takes away the sin of the world'. While not altogether clear as to the meaning of this declaration, the readers' suspicions are that this lamb is somehow related to the paschal lamb. Such suspicions are confirmed later in the Fourth Gospel (19.33-34), when Jesus dies at the very time the passover lambs are slain. Although the Fourth Gospel indicates that the blood of Jesus is essential for eternal life (6.53-57; 19.34), John's statement here in 1 John builds upon and makes explicit that theme in a way the Fourth Gospel does not. Therefore, the explicit mention of Jesus' blood as that which takes away sin makes clear that the basis of one's forgiveness from all sin (salvation itself) is the atoning death of Jesus. The need for such a statement may indicate that there was some dispute among the opponents (and perhaps the community itself) as to the efficacious nature of, or need for, Jesus' death. The significance attached to Jesus' blood for John should not go unnoticed for it is taken up again later in 1 John (5.6, 8) as well as in Revelation (1.5; 5.9; 7.14; 12.11; 19.13).

The concept of sin is also introduced in v. 7. Sin is an extremely important issue in 1 John, as the frequency of the appearance of sin vocabulary indicates. The noun 'sin' (ἁμαρτία) occurs 17 times in 1 John, while the verb 'to sin' (ἁμαρτάνω) occurs 10 times. Such an emphasis suggests that a variety of questions surrounded the presence and/or absence of sin in the community and its significance. Part of the community's understanding of sin is revealed in the Fourth Gospel. There the following ideas are found: (1) The world is guilty of sin which must be removed by (the sacrificial death of) Jesus (1.29). (2) Physical infirmity may sometimes be the direct result of sin, an implication of Jesus' words

---

19 Westcott, *The Epistles of St. John*, p. 21.

to the man healed at the pool of Bethesda (5.14), but such a causal relationship does not always exist, as Jesus' words about the man born blind indicate (9.2, 3). (3) Those who reject the testimony of Jesus will die in their sin (of unbelief?) (8.21, 24), but Jesus himself is without sin. In fact, those who reject Jesus' testimony believe that he is a sinner (9.16, 24, 31) – in contrast to those who believe him (9.25) – and come to conclusions at odds with his own words (9.34). (4) Part of the Paraclete's ministry is to convict the world (prove it wrong) concerning sin (16.9, 10). (5) Jesus' words in John 20.23 imply that believers play some role in the forgiveness of sins. (6) There are also several implicit statements about the forgiveness and/or the means of forgiveness of sins. For example, in Jn 13.1-20 footwashing is instituted as a sign of the continual cleansing available to the believer for post-conversion sins. Jesus also assigns cleansing and sanctifying power to his word (15.3) and the Father's word (17.17).

This initial mention of sin both prepares the readers for a theme which dominates the next few verses (1.8-2.2) and provides them with a general orientation for the discussions about sin that will follow both here and later in 1 John. Specifically, the readers are told that Jesus his (God's) Son is essential for sin's forgiveness and removal.

The primary emphasis of this passage, the relationship between 'walking in the light' and 'cleansing from sin', should not be missed. Just as the one who 'walks in the light' is characterized by fellowship with others in the community, so this one is characterized by cleansing from all sin by Jesus. By using the present tense form of the verb 'cleanse' (καθαρίζει) John implies that such cleansing through the blood of Jesus is an ongoing and continual part of 'walking in the light'. Thus, while this cleansing from all sin, no doubt, would be conceived of as including the believer's initial salvation experience, its primary emphasis here is upon the ongoing, post-conversion life of the believer.[20] Such an emphasis is similar to the meaning of footwashing in John 13, where as the first part of the disciples' preparation for Jesus' departure he gives them this sign of continual cleansing from sin.

In summary, John makes clear in v. 7 that one's walk in the light can be assessed by one's relationship to others in the community and one's relationship to sin.

---

20 Brown, *The Epistles of John*, p. 202, observes, 'Perhaps the best explanation...is to stress that the author of I John is not worried about *initial* justification but about the forgiveness of sins committed as a Christian. When people first believe and come to the light, their sins are forgiven. They may sin again; yet if they try to walk in the light, the blood of Jesus, which cleanses from all sin, cleanses from these sins as well.'

Verses 8-9
The initial pair of 'if' clauses in vv. 6-7 is followed by another pair in the next two verses.

Verse 8. The phrase 'If we claim' alerts the reader to the fact that another of the opponents' (false) claims is being considered. Again the author adopts first person plural language ('we') as a means of (hypothetically) identifying with the claim. Rather than being unrelated to the first false claim, the latter seems to issue out of the former. The statement about cleansing from sin at the end of v. 7 suggests that if one is to walk in the light, such cleansing is necessary. However, the opponents seem to reject the need for this cleansing by denying that they have sin. While it is difficult to ascertain the precise meaning of the claim 'We have no sin', certain aspects of the phrase's meaning are discernible. In the Fourth Gospel (9.41; 15.22, 24; 19.11) 'to have sin' is characteristic of those who have encountered the illuminating light of God in the person of Jesus and yet choose to remain in darkness by rejecting his testimony. Their encounter with Jesus and their failure to believe result in their 'having sin'. In 1 Jn 1.8, however, those who make the claim 'to have no sin' do not appear to have rejected the testimony of Jesus outright, but to believe that on the basis of their initial response to the Gospel they have no need for the cleansing which results from the blood of Jesus. It is possible that such an attitude was based upon certain portions of Jesus' teaching in the Fourth Gospel. In a discussion with the Jews in John 8, Jesus makes the point that 'the one who commits sin is a slave to sin' (8.34). In contrast, 'whoever the Son makes free is free indeed' (8.36). Perhaps the opponents in 1 John had taken these words of Jesus to mean that when the Son set one free from sin, one was free from sin permanently, despite any (sinful) actions.[21] If so, this would explain the adamant rejection of the need for such continual cleansing.

To those who would claim 'to have no sin' and, consequently, have no need of such cleansing, the writer offers a stern denunciation. 'If we claim to have no sin we deceive ourselves...' Earlier John charged that those who walk in darkness while claiming fellowship with God were lying. He now increases the intensity of the guilt by noting that here it is self-inflicted. The emphasis in the (Greek) phrase is upon the word 'ourselves' which stands first. The point is not that others have caused this to happen, nor that they have fallen into error against their will, but

---

21   Brown, *The Epistles of John*, p. 206, notes, 'their claim may have reflected the thesis that actions committed by the believer were not important enough to be sins that could challenge the intimacy with God acquired through belief.'

rather that those who make such claims have entered into such deception actively. While in the Fourth Gospel the term here translated 'deceive' (πλανάω) occurs twice in reference to (false) accusations made against Jesus (Jn 7.12, 47), the noun form has already appeared in 2 John 7 with reference to the false message of the deceivers which was expected to be taken throughout the community. In its other occurrences in 1 John the term is used by the writer to alert his readers about various aspects of the false teaching that confronts the community. In Revelation the term appears in numerous contexts to describe the work of those who oppose God and his people (2.20; 12.9; 13.14; 19.20; 20.3, 8, 10). John's use of 'deceive' at this point both increases the intensity of the false claimants' guilt and introduces a term which will become synonymous with false teaching. By deceiving themselves they become deceivers.

Just as in v. 6, the improper action of the claimants is accompanied by an assessment of their relationship to the Truth. While those who claim to have no sin may base such a belief on their relationship to the Truth (Jesus/God), in point of fact, their claim reveals that the truth is not in them. In this charge the author seems to accomplish three things. First, these words suggest an intended progression of intensity with regard to the guilt of those who make these claims: those who lie do not do the truth, those who deceive themselves reveal that the Truth is not in them. Second, by this statement those who claim 'to have no sin' – in whom the Truth is not – are clearly distinguished from the Elder and his readers in whom the Truth remains forever (2 Jn 2). Third, in a subtle way this charge reveals the similarity between those who claim to have no sin and the Devil (their father?) of whom Jesus said, 'the Truth is not in him' (Jn 8.44). Verse 8, then, declares that claims to intimacy with the Truth are to be regarded as deception unless they are made on the basis of the cleansing brought by the blood of Jesus.

Verse 9. Again the writer balances the false claim of the opponents with a declaration about appropriate conduct and belief (cf. vv. 6-7). For a second time he introduces the corrective declaration with an 'if' (ἐάν) clause. Rather than deny having sin, John's readers are instructed to confess their sin. In the Johannine literature confession vocabulary occurs primarily in christological contexts (Jn 1.20; 9.22; 12.42; 1 Jn 2.23; 4.2, 3, 15; 2 Jn 7),[22] having reference to sin on this occasion alone. In contrast to a (deceptive) claim which denies sin, the readers are instructed to acknowledge their sins honestly before a God who is faithful

---

22 In Rev. 3.5 the risen Jesus promises those who are victorious in the church at Sardis, 'I will confess (ὁμολογήσω) your name before my Father and before his angels.'

and righteous. The occurrence of the verb 'confess' (ὁμολογῶμεν) in the present rather than past tense suggests that the confession that John advocates is to be a continuing, regular part of the community's life.[23] Given the other Johannine uses of the term it may be safe to conclude that this confession must be genuine, unhindered by the opinions of others, and public (at least in the sense that one is open to the community about confession).

Significantly, the term 'sins' appears here in the plural form (unlike vv. 7-8 where the singular occurs), indicating that John has specific and concrete acts of sin in mind. While the Fourth Gospel defines sin primarily as that of unbelief resulting in estrangement and alienation from God (cf. esp. Jn 16.9), the Fourth Gospel also suggests that other concrete manifestations of sin do exist (cf. Jn 5.14; 8.21-46). The idea here conveyed is that the confession called for is to be full and complete.

Earlier John exhorts his readers to walk in the light because he (God) is both the Light and in the light. Now the reader is encouraged to confess his or her sins owing to the fact that God is faithful and righteous. In describing God as faithful John may have in mind the words of Deut. 7.9 where God is said to be faithful in mercifully keeping his covenant promises. Such a meaning is not far removed from its significance here. If the writer is addressing believers, as was argued above, then the obvious point is that even when one has sinned, God can be trusted for forgiveness. In its other Johannine occurrences the word 'faithful' (πιστός) is primarily used to describe the faithful action of a believer (3 Jn 5), the faithful witness of believers (Rev. 2.10, 13; 17.14), Jesus as faithful witness (Rev. 1.5; 3.14; 19.11) and the faithful character of the words of Jesus (Rev. 21.5; 22.6). It is also used to encourage Thomas to continue to be a believer; one who has faith rather than doubt in Jesus. The believer who has sinned can confess sins with the assurance that God is faithful to forgive them.

Confession of sins can be made not only because God is faithful but also because he is righteous (δίκαιος). In the Fourth Gospel this same term is used to describe the just nature of Jesus' eschatological judgment. It is clear on that occasion that Jesus' righteous judgment is based upon the righteous judgment of his Father, whom he hears and seeks to please

---

23 Cf. esp. the comments of C.H. Talbert, *Reading John: A Literary and Theological Commentary on the Fourth Gospel and the Johannine Epistles* (New York: Crossroad, 1992), p. 20, ' "If we regularly confess [present tense] our sins [Prov 28.13], he is faithful and just [Deut 32.4; 1 Clement 27.1; 60.1], and will go on forgiving [present tense] our sins and cleansing us from all unrighteousness" (v. 9). Regular confession yields regular forgiveness of guilt and cleansing from the stain of sin.'

(Jn 5.30). While elsewhere in this Epistle John will use the term in reference to moral purity (cf. 2.1, 29; 3.7, 12; cf. also Jn 17.25), in 1 Jn 1.9 the emphasis is clearly upon God as one capable of rendering righteous judgment with regard to sin.

Confession of sin before this faithful and righteous God will produce a twofold result. The faithful God of the covenant will meet such confession on behalf of believers with remission of sins. The term 'forgive' (ἀφίημι) literally means 'to let go' or 'to release'. It is used on one occasion in the Fourth Gospel (20.23) for the forgiveness of sin in which believers appear to play some role. Just as one who walks in the light finds oneself in fellowship with others (v. 7), so the one who confesses finds himself or herself forgiven of sins.

In addition to forgiveness, John states that 'we are cleansed from all unrighteousness'. By including this phrase the author accomplishes several things. First, it appears that John uses the term translated 'unrighteousness' or 'wrongdoing' (ἀδικίας) as an intentional play on the Greek word for righteous (δίκαιος). It is the righteous one (δίκαιος) who is able to cleanse from unrighteousness (ἀδικίας). Second, it is clear that the phrase 'and cleanse us from all unrighteousness' is intended to parallel the latter part of v. 7, 'cleanses us from all sin'. Third, it is significant that while in v. 7 cleansing is attributed to the blood of Jesus, in this verse it is attributed to God.[24] This move is in keeping with John's habit of using terms for God which in other places were reserved for Jesus (cf. the discussion of light in v. 5). Fourth, it may be that by the specific mention of both forgiveness *and* cleansing John intends to make a distinction between forgiveness and purification. While it is true that the terms 'sins' (ἀμαρτίας) and 'unrighteousness' (ἀδικίας) appear as virtual synonyms later in 1 John (5.17), here it is hard to avoid the conclusion that the writer intends to make some distinction between these aspects of God's response to confession. On this reading, the believer's confession results both in the removal of sins' guilt, which produced estrangement from God, and in the destruction 'of the power of sin in the human heart',[25] which defiles one before God and impedes the believer's life as one born of God. Fifth, it is perhaps not without significance that the verbs in this verse are all in the present tense, suggesting that confession, forgiveness and cleansing are to be ongoing activities. 'Regular confession yields regular forgiveness of guilt and cleansing from the stain of sin.'[26] Finally, there is an emphasis on the completeness

---

24   Schnackenburg, *The Johannine Epistles*, p. 82.
25   Cf. Marshall, *The Epistles of John*, p. 114, esp. n. 14.
26   Talbert, *Reading John*, p. 20.

of the cleansing. As in v. 7 the cleansing is for all (πάσης) unrighteousness.

In contrast to those who deny the need for the cleansing which comes from the blood of Jesus, John's readers are encouraged to acknowledge their sin in order that their fellowship with God might be preserved. If walking in the light entails fellowship with one another, the results of the confession of sin at least imply the preservation of fellowship with God and the continuation of their walking in the light.

1 John 1.10–2.2

The third and final pair of three 'if' clauses appears in 1.10–2.2. Once again, the reader is alerted to the fact that another of the opponents' false claims is being considered. As was the case with the first two claims, there is a connection between this claim ('we have not sinned') and the previous one ('we have no sin'). In point of fact, the second and third claims are so similar that it is possible to treat the phrases as virtually synonymous. Evidence for this possibility includes the fact that each of the claims reveal that the claimant is not in fellowship with God, but is alienated from him and is involved in deception of the worst kind. Additionally, in the corrective statement that follows each false claim (1 Jn 1.7, 9; 2.2), the author makes reference to the cleansing of sin(s).

However, given the distinctive statements of each phrase and the progressive intensity of guilt involved in each claim, it may be best to assign a different emphasis in each case, while affirming the basic continuity of the claims. One way to detect the different emphasis in v. 10 is to note that the verb in the phrase 'we have not sinned' (οὐχ ἡμαρτήκαμεν) occurs in the (perfect) past tense, which appears to indicate that the claimants believed themselves to be free from personal sin. Although to say that v. 8 refers to the principle of sin while v. 10 denotes sinful acts may go beyond the Johannine language, it may not be going too far to say that in v. 8 there is a denial of the personal guilt produced by sin, while in v. 10 there is a denial of having committed sin.[27] Despite the apparent incongruity of the claim that one had never sinned (as a result of becoming a believer), it may be that even this claim is in some way attributable to the teaching of the Fourth Gospel. Specifically, it could be that the false teachers understood belief in Jesus to entail a sinless state similar to that reflected in Jesus' words to his opponents (whom he regards as children of the Devil) in Jn 8.46 where he challenges them, 'Can any of you prove me guilty of sin?' On this view, anyone who becomes a child of God is like Jesus, without sin.

Whether this third claim is synonymous with the second, or the author

---

27   Brown, *The Epistles of John*, p. 211.

wished to convey a different emphasis, it is followed by the strongest of the denunciations to accompany any of the claims. Earlier, John charged that those who walk in darkness while claiming fellowship with God are lying, while those who claim to have no sin are deceiving themselves. Now he charges that those who claim 'we have not sinned' make him (God) a liar. Several observations should be made about this charge.

First, throughout this passage it is not always clear whether the author has God or Jesus in mind when he uses the pronouns 'he' or 'him'. Some of the ambiguity may be intentional for, as has been seen, 1 John is fond of using terms to describe God that in the Fourth Gospel are used to describe Jesus. In the phrase 'make him a liar', it seems certain that the author has God in mind. On this view, the one who is in the Light (v. 7), who is faithful and righteous to forgive and cleanse (v. 9) is the one who is here made a liar by the claims to sinlessness. Second, the verb in the phrase 'we make' (ποιοῦμεν) is often used in the Fourth Gospel in charges that Jesus makes himself something other than what he is. These charges include that he makes himself to be: God (5.18; 10.33) or the Son of God (19.7); greater than Abraham (8.53); or a king (19.12). The irony of such accusations is that in the Fourth Gospel Jesus did not simply make himself (through his claims) to be God, greater than Abraham, and a king; he really is! Just as the opponents of Jesus in the Fourth Gospel misunderstood Jesus' identity, in 1 John those who claim to be sinless indicate that they misunderstand God's identity. Third, the motif of lying and deception, which began in v. 6, culminates in v. 10 with the charge that God is made a liar. Clearly, this is the most heinous of the charges, for it makes a liar of the one who is faithful and righteous, who is the Light and walks in the light. Such claims equate the Father of salvation with the father of lies (the Devil; Jn 8.44); they treat with contempt the salvific work of God, implying that it is invalid and unnecessary. The present tense verb 'makes' suggests that the act of 'making God a liar' is an ongoing act. To lie or even deceive oneself is bad enough, to make God a liar is the height of culpability.

In addition to making God a liar, this claim reveals that God's word is not in such ones. It would seem clear that at the very least the phrase 'his word' (ὁ λόγος αὐτοῦ) has reference to the revelation Jesus proclaimed in the Fourth Gospel and which is now being proclaimed by John and his community. But such an understanding of the phrase may not exhaust its meaning. While it is true that in the Fourth Gospel the Logos is never spoken of as being (dwelling) in the (heart of the) believer,[28] to argue that Logos here does not have a christological meaning ignores evidence

---

28   Schnackenburg, *The Johannine Epistles*, p. 82.

in the text to the contrary. Already in v. 1 the phrase 'word of life' has been used in a way that combines reference to Jesus and the proclamation about him. Given this earlier hint, together with the author's love of ambiguity, it would appear safe to see in 'his word' a reference both to Jesus and the proclamation about him.[29]

This interpretation fits well with the growing emphasis on the absence of truth in those who make the kinds of false claims as recorded in these verses. The charge that 'we do not do the truth' in v. 6 and that 'the truth is not in us' in v. 8 culminates in the charge that 'his word is not in us' in v. 10. Such growing intensity parallels a similar development in the deception and lies motif noted earlier in these same verses. Those who make these false claims reveal that they are not intimate (have no fellowship) with the Truth. It should perhaps be noted that as in the previous sections the author has used first person plural pronouns (we/us) in order to identify (hypothetically) with these claims.

1 John 2.1. A couple of general observations about the nature of this verse should be offered before the verse is examined in detail. First, it should be noted that although a chapter division separates 1.10 from 2.1, such a division is artificial as the first two verses of this chapter continue the thought begun in 1.5. Second, in contrast to the first two pairs of 'if' clauses, where the second 'if' clause immediately follows the first, here the two parts are divided by a phrase in which the author addresses his readers directly. By using a combination of 'my little children' and the first person singular 'I', instead of the customary plural 'we', the author goes to great lengths to insure that his previous statement in v. 10 is not misunderstood.

For the first time in 1 John the author makes use of familial language in addressing his readers. Both 3 and 2 John reveal that the Elder is comfortable in referring to those under his spiritual oversight as (his) children. On those occasions he uses a specific Greek word for children (τέκνα). Two times in the Fourth Gospel (1.12; 11.52) and four times in 1 John (3.1, 2, 10; 5.2) this same term is used to refer to children of God. Once in 1 John (3.10) this word has reference to children of the devil, while once in the Fourth Gospel (8.39) it refers to the children of Abraham. From this evidence it appears that the writer normally uses the term (τέκνα) when speaking of the spiritual children of a specific individual. It is somewhat surprising, then, that the author employs a different word for children in 2.1. On this and six other occasions in 1 John (2.12, 28; 3.7, 18; 4.4; 5.21) a diminutive term (τεκνία), meaning

---

29 Cf. Smalley, *1, 2, 3 John*, p. 34.

'little children', appears. One of the significant things about this word's usage in 1 John is that it always occurs in a form of direct address. Not only does this form of address have an affectionate and endearing quality about it, but it also appears to have a deeper significance in the Johannine community owing to the fact that Jesus himself employs this very term once near the beginning of the farewell discourse in the Fourth Gospel (13.33). Such a usage has, no doubt, influenced the writer's own habit at this point.[30]

This familial language is followed by a personal appeal to the readers. To draw the readers' attention to the importance of his appeal, the author uses a formula ('these things I write to you') similar to that which appears in 1.4 ('these things we write to you'). Earlier this formula was used to draw attention to the purpose of the entire work. Here, the phrase focuses upon this section, with 'these things' having particular reference to the preceding verses dealing with sin. The desire to impress upon the readers a very important point is also revealed in the shift from the 'we' language which has dominated ch. 1, to 'I' language. Specifically, the writer clarifies his earlier statement about sin in order that it not be misunderstood. Rather than being an advocate for sin, as the earlier statement may have been interpreted, through the use of a (ἵνα) purpose clause John makes clear his desire that his readers do not commit sin. Coming as it does on the heels of 1.10, such a statement appears to be in some tension with what precedes and will follow it (2.2). However, this much is clear: whatever John may mean in v. 10, it is evident that the statement there is not to be taken as an acknowledgment that sin is considered to be an appropriate course of action for the believer. In point of fact, as revealed in 2.1, John desires that his readers live without sin. It appears that he fully believes living without sin is possible for his readers. Given the broader context of 1 John, such a sinless walk is consistent with walking in the light, having fellowship with God, and making confession and cleansing a regular part of one's life. It is likely that this expectation of living without sin is deemed to be possible owing to the way in which God (1.7) and Jesus (3.3) function as standards of purity for the believer in 1 John. Perhaps Jesus' sinless walk, as described in Jn 8.46, also contributes in some fashion to this expectation on John's part.

It is only after this statement of clarification that the second 'if' clause in this third and final pair appears. In order to underscore his desire for

---

30 Another Greek word for children (παιδία) also appears in direct address in 1 John (2.14, 18). This term of endearment appears to have been influenced by Jesus' example in the Fourth Gospel (21.5) as well.

his readers to live without sin, John continues to depart from his practice of using first person plural language ('we'), as in vv. 7 and 9, where the action described is advocated for the reader. Instead he employs the phrase, 'And if any should sin...' By this subtle shift the reader understands that sin should be the exception rather than the rule for the believer. Only after this statement does the first person plural 'we' reappear.

In those situations where a believer does sin, she or he is not without hope or provision for the removal of sin. Reverting back to first person plural language, the author writes 'we have a Paraclete with the Father, Jesus Christ the Righteous One'. Earlier the reader has learned that it is the blood of Jesus that cleanses the believer from all sin (1.7) and that confession (before God) results in forgiveness and cleansing (1.9). Thus, for Jesus to be mentioned at this point as a remedy for sinful activity on the believer's part is not surprising. Here, Jesus is described as a Paraclete. What might such a designation mean? Several observations can be offered in response to this question.

First, the reader of the Fourth Gospel knows already that Jesus is considered to function as Paraclete, for in his words of comfort to the disciples in the Farewell Discourse he says, 'Even I will ask the Father and he will give you another Paraclete, the Spirit of Truth, in order that he might be with you forever' (Jn 14.16-17). Thus, the reader is not completely unprepared for this description of Jesus. Second, given the fact that Jesus is implicitly called a Paraclete in the Fourth Gospel, it is somewhat surprising that the term appears to have a different emphasis if not a different meaning in 1 Jn 2.1 than it does in the Fourth Gospel.[31] The context of 1 John indicates that here the term 'Paraclete' is best translated as 'advocate', 'intercessor', or 'legal counsel', for in this verse Jesus functions as an intercessor with the Father. This basic meaning is found in most every occurrence of the word 'Paraclete' outside the Fourth Gospel.[32] The only place in the Fourth Gospel where the term has a legal meaning is 16.8-11. There it is revealed that the Paraclete will function as prosecuting attorney to convict the world of sin, righteousness and judgment. In addition, the Paraclete will be with the disciples (14.16), teach them all things (14.26), remind them of everything that Jesus said (14.26), lead them into all truth (16.13), and speak only what he hears (16.13) in a way that glorifies the Son (16.14). Third, although the meaning of Paraclete is somewhat different in 1 John than in the Fourth

---

31 An observation which goes back at least to the time of Origen (*On First Principles* 2.7.4).

32 This includes the use of παράκλητος (or the loan word פרקיט) in rabbinic, Philonic, and the Patristic literature.

Gospel, there are ways in which Jesus' description as Paraclete in 1 Jn 2.1 is consistent with his actions on the disciples' behalf in the Fourth Gospel. Specifically, in John 17 Jesus reveals that he has protected the disciples whom the Father had given him (v. 12) and he intercedes with the Father for the disciples' continued preservation (v. 15).[33] Fourth, not only does the description of Jesus as Paraclete emphasize his action when a believer commits sin, but it also reveals Jesus' essential role in facilitating fellowship between the Father and believers as well as bringing additional meaning to Jesus' work of cleansing, mentioned earlier (1.7). As the Father is the one who has been described as the Light, the one who is in the light, as being faithful and righteous to forgive sin, reconciliation with him through the Son is clearly necessary.

Since the Father has earlier been described as righteous (δίκαιος) in the forgiveness of sin and cleansing from all unrighteousness (1.9), it comes as no surprise that Jesus, who functions as Paraclete on the believers' behalf, is also described here as righteous (δίκαιον). This observation is consistent with the Fourth Gospel's description of Jesus as righteous with regard to the nature of his eschatological judgment which is based upon the Father's own righteous judgment (Jn 5.30). Thus again, the reader is helped to appreciate the essential unity between the Father and the Son. Since Jesus, like the Father, is righteous, his work as Paraclete will be successful. It is perhaps not without significance that in both verses where Jesus is named to this point in 1 John, the name Jesus Christ has appeared, as in 2 John 3, 7 (however, cf. 2 Jn 9 where 'Christ' occurs).

In v. 2 the reader learns that not only is Jesus a Paraclete on the believer's behalf, but he is also an atoning sacrifice. A great theological debate has raged around the Greek word (ἱλασμός) found at this point in the text. Does the term reveal that Jesus is understood to be the sacrifice by which forgiveness and cleansing are obtained, or does it convey the idea that God must be appeased by the blood sacrifice of his Son? While it is impossible to rule out the idea that Jesus serves as a propitiating sacrifice that appeases the wrath of an angry God, several clues in the Johannine literature suggest that this is not the best interpretation of the term (ἱλασμός) in its Johannine context.

First, the focus of attention to this point in 1 John has been upon the blood of Jesus as cleansing agent with regard to sin. Specifically, the blood of Jesus becomes the basis for the forgiveness from God experienced by the believer. Thus, the term translated 'atoning sacrifice' (ἱλασμός) is defined in part by its connection to the blood of Jesus which

---

33   Schnackenburg, *The Johannine Epistles*, p. 86.

cleanses from sin. Second, there is no indication in the Johannine literature that God is an angry deity who must be appeased. Rather than an angry God who must be appeased by the blood of a sacrifice, God is portrayed as a loving Father who initiates the plan of salvation by sending his Son into the world to lay down his life on its behalf (cf. esp. Jn 3.16-17). While the thought of propitiation (appeasement) might be present in certain Old Testament texts and passages in the Apostolic Fathers,[34] such an idea appears to be absent from the Johannine literature, and, consequently, such an interpretation at this point in 1 John seems to be intrusive rather than natural. The primary emphasis of the term (ἱλασμός) in this verse is to make clear the idea that Jesus' atoning death is not only the basis of cleansing and forgiveness of sin but is also the grounds of his intercession with the Father. It is not without significance that the present tense verb 'is' appears in connection with the description of Jesus as atoning sacrifice. By this means the reader learns that Jesus' atoning death has a continuing significance, it continues even now to atone for the sins of those who believe in him.

John quickly goes on to indicate that Jesus' atoning death, which makes possible the forgiveness of sin, did not take place for believers only ('our sin'), but in order to make forgiveness available to the whole world by atoning for all its sin as well. Such a statement clearly reveals that, from the writer's vantage point, the scope and extent of the atoning sacrifice is universal in nature. The difference between those who experience forgiveness of sin and those who do not revolves around the appropriation of forgiveness through confession of sin and belief in the Son. The extraordinary character of this assertion is revealed in the fact that while God's love and provision of salvation for the world is affirmed at various points in the Fourth Gospel (3.16-17; 4.42; 6.33, 51; 12.46-47), the vast majority of Gospel passages indicate that the world is viewed as being in (sometimes) hostile opposition to Jesus (1.10; 7.7; 8.23; 9.39; 12.31; 15.18-19; 16.33; 17.9, 14, 16, 25; 18.36). That the offer of Jesus' atoning death includes such enemies not only reveals the full extent of God's love for the world, but also indicates something of the community's soteriological expectations with regard to salvation of those beyond their boundaries. Such a conception of the scope of Jesus' atoning death is no doubt also connected to the community's missionary and evangelistic efforts. If, as is sometimes suggested, the secessionists are laying claim to a privileged position with regard to salvation, John's statement about the extent of Jesus' atoning death for the sin of the whole world would be a powerful critique of their elitist position.

---

34   Cf. the helpful discussion of this material in Brown, *The Epistles of John*, pp. 217-22.

Reflection and Response — Part Three

Reflection

Perhaps the most prominent theme in 1 Jn 1.5–2.2 is the discussion of sin and the believer. Sin is a reality so serious that one ignores it and its consequences at one's peril. Those who walk in the light find themselves in fellowship with other believers and their sins forgiven. It is the blood of Jesus that cleanses believers from all sin and becomes the basis of forgiveness. In order to experience such forgiveness believers must confess, not deny their sin to God who is faithful and righteous to forgive all sin and cleanse from all unrighteousness. However, despite the availability of forgiveness, sin is not an activity to be tolerated in the community. In point of fact, believers are to avoid sin at all costs. It is not to be part of the Christian life, but rather an exception that must be dealt with appropriately. In the event that a believer does commit sin, that person is to confess that sin, for Jesus the righteous one is our advocate with the Father. Jesus' advocacy is based upon his own atoning sacrifice concerning our sins. This sacrifice, which is universal in scope, is efficacious and results in the forgiveness of confessed sin. In order to facilitate reflection on this most important issue, a series of questions are here raised.

Generally speaking, what is the attitude of fellow Christians toward sin and its presence among believers? How are these attitudes similar to and dissimilar from that found in 1 Jn 1.5–2.2? How seriously does the Church take 1 John's teaching to live in ways that seek to avoid sin at all costs? Are there churches that come to mind that might be considered examples of communities which seek to be faithful to this teaching? What are the characteristics that prompt this identification? What concrete community actions might be offered as evidence of communities that take sin seriously? Conversely, are there churches that do not appear to be concerned with the presence of sinful activity among members? What prompts the identification of these communities? In what ways do churches make provision for confession and cleansing from sin? Are these opportunities sufficient for the life of the community?

As helpful as these questions are to generate reflection about sin and the Church, such reflection is inadequate for the task without reflection on our own lives and the presence or absence of sin. Therefore, a few additional questions are now asked in order to generate reflection of a more personal nature. What is my own attitude to sin? Am I more aware of and concerned about the sin of others or the sin that may be present in my own life? How often do I reflect on my life in ways that result in facing the sin that remains in me? How am I distracted from taking the issue of sin in my life seriously? In what ways have I sought to confront sinful behavior in my life and that of my brothers and sisters? What kind of testimony does my life give with regard to my attitude toward sin and its seriousness? What is my attitude toward the atoning death of Jesus and his work as advocate? Is it one that presumes upon his sacrifice by treating sinful attitudes and actions as insignificant, or does it take seriously sin and its consequences? When is the last time I have felt the Holy Spirit's power bring conviction to my heart with regard to sinful activity? How have I responded to such ministry? In what ways have I made use of the provisions for forgiveness made available by Jesus and his Church?

Response

What kind of response may be made to such a serious issue as sin in my life and that of the Church?

First, using the reflection questions as a guide, examine your life seeking to discern sinful attitudes or behavior that are not pleasing to God. It might facilitate your response to make a list of the specific things that have been revealed.

Second, consult with a trusted brother or sister as a means of testing whether there are areas that need attention of which you might not be aware.

Third, having prayerfully identified those areas for which forgiveness is needed, confess these sins to God, receiving the intercession of Jesus and cleansing through his blood.

Fourth, as a sign of your confession, forgiveness and cleansing, participate in a footwashing service where washing may be received from and rendered to others as a sign of the continual cleansing available from Jesus.

1 John 2.3-17

In turning to the next portion of 1 John, four things become apparent. First, there is a great deal of thematic continuity between this text and the preceding one. In addition to containing responses to false claims, the sections are connected by the following terms: 'liar', 'his word', 'walking', 'from the beginning', 'the word which you have heard', 'I write', 'darkness', 'light', 'eyes', 'children', 'forgiveness of sin' and 'the world'. Second, although 2.3-17 continues a number of emphases from the previous passage it also introduces several Johannine themes that figure prominently in the remainder of the book. These include: knowing God, keeping his commands, the love of God and brother, the prohibition against loving the world, overcoming the evil one, and remaining. Third, while this section does not stand together as tightly as the previous one, there are signs that it too forms a major section in 1 John. The primary evidence that these verses should be treated together is related to the way in which love functions prominently as the evidence that one knows God. Standing near the beginning (v. 5), middle (v. 10) and end (v. 15) of the section are such discussions of love. By this means not only are the boundaries of the passage revealed, but the reader is also introduced to a theme which figures prominently in two other major sections of 1 John (3.11-18; 4.7–5.5). Fourth, it is equally clear that this passage can be divided into three subsections as each subsection (vv. 3-11, vv. 12-14, vv. 15-17) appears to have its own individual structural characteristics.

1 John 2.3-11

This first subsection is introduced by v. 3 and is loosely structured around three claims found in vv. 4, 6 and 9. Each claim is introduced by the phrase 'the one who says' (ὁ λέγων) and each appears to be based upon a preceding statement.[35] This subsection may itself be further divided into three smaller units: vv. 3-5, vv. 6-8 and vv. 9-11.

Verse 3. The section begins (v. 3) with the phrase 'in this we know', a phrase which will recur from time to time in 1 John (cf. 2.5; 3.16, 24; 4.6). The phrase appears to be a means by which the author reassures his readers about a specific issue or point. In v. 3 it not only serves this purpose, but (with the addition of 'and') also functions as a transitional textual marker indicating a shift and a new beginning in the book. Similar textual markers are found elsewhere in 1 John (2.28; 3.19). While the discussion in the following verses is clearly connected to what precedes (1.5–2.2), this phrase ('and in this we know') goes with what follows ('that we have known him').

In ways not dissimilar to the function of 1.5, in v. 3 the author introduces 2.3-17 with a topical statement. In the face of patently false claims to fellowship with God and false claims of sinlessness on the part of the opponents, the readers are given assurances with regard to how they can be certain about their knowledge of (and relationship to) God. Quite obviously, knowing God is at issue here. For John, this knowing is not to be understood as the accumulation of certain facts or information; nor is it to be understood as the acquiring of secret revelatory information as in

---

35 On the structure of 2.3-11, cf. the very helpful discussion in D. Rensberger, *1 John, 2 John, 3 John* (Nashville: Abingdon Press, 1997), pp. 58-59.

certain of the mystery religions; nor is it abstract or philosophical in nature. Rather, in the Johannine tradition, as in the Hebrew Scriptures, knowing must be understood relationally. This knowing is based upon experience and conveys the idea of intimacy with, not knowledge about, God. Thus, 'to know' is frequently used in the Old Testament with reference to sexual intercourse. Therefore, to know God in 1 John is to experience and understand him.[36]

It is significant that the verb 'to know' twice appears in this verse. In its first occurrence, the verb appears in the present tense, which points to a current habitual state of knowing. By this means, the readers are assured of their ability to be certain, on an ongoing basis, of their knowledge of God. The second use of the verb 'to know' occurs in the (perfect) past tense. Here the knowing has reference to something known in the past, which is still known in the present. At the very least, this would appear to point to the readers' initial belief in Jesus and may call to mind Jesus' words in Jn 17.3 where eternal life is equated with knowing God.[37] Thus, the use of this somewhat redundant formula ('we know that we have known') prepares the readers for the means by which they may be assured, a means withheld until the next part of the verse.

How can the readers know that they have known him? 'If we keep his[38] commands.' In the Fourth Gospel the command of the Father is the basis of Jesus' voluntarily laying down his life (10.18) and the basis of all that Jesus says or does (12.49). The command of the Father is also explicitly identified with eternal life (12.50). Not only does Jesus receive commands from the Father, but the disciples also are given commands in turn by Jesus. Two things should be noted about these commands. First, the command that the disciples receive is consistently tied to love. (a) Jesus instructs the disciples to love one another (13.34-35), a command to

---

36   Didymus the Blind, *Commentary on 1 John*, ACCS, XI, p. 178, observes: 'Often in the Scriptures the word *know* means not just being aware of something but having personal experience of it. Jesus did not know sin, not because he was unaware of what it is but because he never committed it himself. For although he is like us in every other way, he never sinned. Given this meaning of the word *know*, it is clear that anyone who says that he knows God must also keep his commandments, for the two things go together.'

37   Cf. Smalley, *1, 2, 3 John*, p. 47.

38   Although the name Jesus Christ is the nearest antecedent for the pronoun αὐτοῦ, it appears from 2.5 that God is here meant. However, given John's love of ambiguity, the very close relationship between the Father and Jesus in the Johannine literature, and the way John intentionally assigns characteristics to God or Jesus which the Fourth Gospel has assigned to the other, it might be best not to define the αὐτοῦ in too restrictive a fashion.

which appeal is made in 2 John 5. (b) Keeping the commands that Jesus gives reveals that the disciples love him (Jn 14.15, 21), are loved by him (14.21; 15.10), and are loved by the Father (14.21). (c) Jesus' command for the disciples to love is based on his own example of loving them (15.12) and remaining in the love of the Father (15.10). Second, there is an extremely tight interplay between keeping the commands and loving Jesus. In point of fact, the issue seems to be very clear. One's claim to love Jesus is invalid unless it is accompanied by the keeping of the commands, specifically, loving one another. While there has been no mention of love to this point in 1 John, in the light of the Fourth Gospel the reader would be prepared for the direction the author will now take. Therefore, based upon the Fourth Gospel and what has preceded in 1 John, the reader may already be deducing that just as one cannot claim fellowship with God without walking in the light, one cannot claim to know God without keeping his commands.

Just as knowing God is more than understanding certain facts, so keeping the commands is more than simple conformity. It is, of course, possible to understand 'keeping the commands' as either a condition for knowing God or a characteristic of knowing him.[39] However, such interpretive options would appear to be too one-dimensional in nature. Rather, this statement looks more like an example of the integrated way in which John views theology and ethics. For John, it is a matter of praxis, whereby the keeping of God's commands not only reveals that one knows God but is also itself a part of knowing God.[40]

Before leaving v. 3 it should perhaps be noted that the author resumes usage of the first person plural 'we' in this verse.

Verses 4-5. The first of three claims found in 2.3-11, each introduced by the phrase 'the one who says' (ὁ λέγων), occurs in v. 4. Immediately recognizable is the shift from first person plural language ('we') to third person singular language ('the one who'). What explains this shift? Perhaps it is best understood as an indication that the author is quoting the claims of the opponents at this point nearly verbatim.[41] Just as in 1.6, where the claim to fellowship with God while walking in darkness places the claimant in direct opposition to the God who is himself light,

---

39 For this distinction cf. the oft-cited quote from R. Bultmann, *The Johannine Epistles* (trans. R.P. O'Hara, L.C. McGaughy and R.W. Funk; ed. R.W. Funk; Philadelphia: Fortress Press, 1973), p. 25.
40 An idea which Brown, *The Epistles of John*, pp. 278-79 esp. n. 5, comes close to suggesting.
41 So Brown, *The Epistles of John*, p. 253.

so here in 2.4 the one who claims to have known God while not keeping his commands demonstrates his or her ignorance of God rather than knowledge of him.

Two things are revealed about the one who claims to have known him while not keeping his commands. First, such a one is identified as a liar. Given the earlier associations with lying in 1.6-10, it becomes apparent that the one who lies not only deceives, but is also ultimately identified with the Father of lies, the Devil (Jn 8.44), rather than with God. Second, the one who makes such claims also reveals that 'the truth is not in this one'. Clearly what is at stake in such a statement is more than abstract truth but identification with Jesus, who is 'full of truth' (Jn 1.4) and *is* the Truth (Jn 14.6). Perhaps this statement is to be read either in light of 1.10, indicating that far from such a person having an intimate knowledge of God, the Truth himself is not in them, or at the least that the Spirit of Truth, who is closely associated with Jesus and is said to be in the believer (Jn 14.17), is not in such a one.[42] Earlier it was noted that there is a very tight interplay between walking in the light, walking in truth, doing the truth and keeping the commands. This same interplay is found here in 2.4.

Verse 5 returns to the positive theme of keeping the commands begun in v. 3, which has been expressed negatively in v. 4. Several aspects of this verse merit comment. Here John departs from his practice of identifying with his readers by use of the first person plural 'we' and from his use of the third person 'the one who says' in favor of a clause ('whoever keeps his word') which is both broader and more inclusive than those previously used. The shift (to an indefinite relative clause) indicates that the net is cast as widely as possible with regard to who is included in this statement: *whoever* keeps his word.

There is also in this verse an unexpected shift from keeping his 'commands' to keeping his 'word'. On one level this shift might be explained merely as stylistic variation, for it is clear from the Fourth Gospel (14.21-24) that 'keeping my (Jesus') commands' and 'keeping my (Jesus') word' can be used interchangeably. But there are also hints in the Fourth Gospel that there is more to this shift in vocabulary than stylistic variation. Through this specific phrase the reader is reminded of the following things: (1) the solemn statement of Jesus in John (8.51) that anyone who keeps his word will never ever see death; (2) Jesus himself keeps his (God's) word (8.55); (3) the connection between 'keeping Jesus' word' and persecution (15.20; 17.14); (4) Jesus' challenge that 'If you remain in my word, truly you are my disciples' (8.31); (5) the fact that the disciples

---

42 For this suggestion cf. Schnackenburg, *The Johannine Epistles*, p. 97.

before them (the readers) had indeed 'kept your (the Father's) word' (17.6); and (6) that a very close connection exists between keeping his words and love (14.21-24). Thus, keeping the word of Jesus and/or the Father points beyond itself to a deep reciprocal relationship between the believer, Jesus and God. It might not be going too far to say that with the shift from 'commands' to 'word', the reader is being prepared for the focus on the Johannine command par excellence: the love command.

But whose word is to be kept? As in 2.3, there is some degree of ambiguity as to whether the pronoun 'his' has reference to God or Jesus. Knowledge of the Fourth Gospel alone does not bring complete clarity to the issue as the Gospel contains reference both to God's word and Jesus' word. If, as was suggested in 2.3, 'his' has reference to God, it is likely to have that reference here in v. 5 as well. However, given the way 1 John seems to delight in assigning to God characteristics attributed to Jesus in the Fourth Gospel, it is unwise to exclude *any* reference to Jesus in this pronoun. Specifically, the close proximity of 'the word' in 2.5 to 'the Word of Life' in 1.1 and 'the word' in 1.10 may suggest a very close relationship between the word to be kept and the 'Word of Life'.[43] The present tense use of the verb 'keeps' (τηρῇ) indicates that this activity is to be ongoing and might appropriately be translated 'whoever continues to keep his word'.

In v. 4, the one who claims to know God but does not keep his commands is called a liar and the truth is not in this one. Given the relationship between keeping the commands and truth, one might expect in v. 5 an explicit statement mentioning the relationship of truth to the one who keeps his word. But again a shift in terminology and emphasis occurs. Instead of being told that the one who keeps his word has the truth in him or her, a rather astounding statement is made: 'truly in this one the love of God has been perfected'. This middle phrase in v. 5 begins with the Greek word (ἀληθῶς) which, often translated 'truly', conveys much more than that particular English word. In the Fourth Gospel it occurs in a variety of texts where the emphasis is upon the indisputable nature of that which is under consideration. For example, Jesus calls Nathaniel a 'true' Israelite (1.47); the Samaritans say of Jesus, 'this is truly the savior of the world' (4.42); after the feeding of the 5,000 some say, 'This is truly the prophet coming into the world' (6.14); Jesus says, 'If you remain in

---

43   G. Strecker, *The Johannine Letters* (trans. L.M. Maloney; ed. H. Attridge; Minneapolis, MN: Fortress Press, 1996), p. 41, goes so far as to say that keeping the word 'requires faith in the sending of the Son (cf. 5.4-5) and rests on the "word of life" (1.1b). In anyone who fulfills this claim, that is, by trusting in the "word of life," the ἀγάπη τοῦ θεοῦ has "truly" reached its goal.'

my word, you are truly my disciples' (8.31); and the disciples who received Jesus' word 'truly' believe that he came from the Father (17.8). Thus, here in v. 5, the emphasis of the term is upon the indisputable nature of the evidence. Specifically, the perfection of the love of God is evidence that one keeps his word and, consequently, knows God. There would appear to be an intentional contrast between the one in whom the 'truth' does not dwell (v. 4) and the one in whom 'truly' the love of God has been perfected (v. 5).

At this point v. 5 introduces a term of great significance for 1 John, love (ἀγάπη). In fact, 20 per cent of the New Testament occurrences of 'love' (ἀγάπη) and 'to love' (ἀγαπάω) are found in the Johannine Epistles, which comprise only 2 per cent of the New Testament.[44] Such a heavy concentration of love vocabulary alone is enough to indicate something of the term's significance, but as shall be seen, its significance goes far beyond mere numbers. On this occasion the term appears in the phrase 'the love of God'. A fair amount of uncertainty exists with regard to the precise meaning of the phrase, as it is open to several interpretations. Does it mean God's love, human love for God, or a divine kind of love? Interpreters of the passage are completely divided on this issue. This same phrase occurs once in the Fourth Gospel (5.42), where the emphasis appears to be on God's love. It also occurs on three other occasions in 1 John (3.17; 4.9; 5.3), where, with the possible exception of 5.3, the meaning is also God's love. To this evidence might be added references to the love of the Father (Jn 15.10; 1 Jn 2.15; 4.12), all of which rather clearly mean God's love. Perhaps special note should be taken of 1 Jn 4.12 which not only speaks of God's love, but also of this love being perfected in the believer. Of course in the Johannine literature it is impossible to separate God's love in the believer from the believer's love for God, Jesus and other believers. Thus, while in 2.5 the dominant idea is God's love, given the other dimensions of love in the Johannine literature and John's fondness of double meaning, it might be wise to view the other aspects of love as at least potentially present in the phrase 'the love of God'. The reader must await 1 Jn 4.10-12 for an explicit statement about the integral connection between God's love, the believer's love for God and the believer's love for others.[45]

If this is the best understanding of 'the love of God' then rather clearly the emphasis in v. 5 is upon God's gracious love being perfected in those who keep his word. In the Fourth Gospel, God's love is manifest above all by the giving of his unique Son (τὸν υἱὸν τὸν μονογενῆ) in order that

---

44 Brown, *The Epistles of John*, p. 254.
45 Brown, *The Epistles of John*, p. 255.

all who believe might not be destroyed but have eternal life (Jn 3.16). His love of the Son extends back before the creation of the world (17.24), is evidenced by the Father placing all things in the Son's hands (3.35), is closely connected to the Son's laying down of his life for others (10.17), and is the basis of the Son's love for the disciples (15.9). The Father's love for the disciples (17.23) is closely tied to their love for the Son (14.21) and the keeping of his word (14.23). Thus, when reference is made to God's love in 1 Jn 2.5, it connotes an eternal, self-giving, reciprocal love which is perfected in the believer who keeps his word.

In the one who keeps his word, truly the love of God has been perfected. The Greek term here translated 'perfected' (τετελείωται) appears five times in the Fourth Gospel. There, it is used to describe the 'completion' of the work given to Jesus by God (4.34; 5.36; 17.4), the 'complete' unity of the believers in order that the world might believe (17.23), and the 'completion' of the Scripture (19.28). In 1 John all four occurrences of the term are in reference to the perfection of love (1 Jn 2.5; 4.12, 17, 18). Obviously, the term means to bring to completion, maturity or wholeness. In this context it has reference to a dynamic completion of God's love in the life of the believer. Part of John's purpose is to prepare his readers for his emphasis on *the* command to love one another (2.7). Thus, the concrete expression of keeping his word is to be manifested in the love of God toward brothers and sisters.

The perfect tense form of the verb 'perfected' suggests that the process of maturation of the love of God in the life of the believer began at some point in the readers' past. More than likely this point of beginning coincides with the time at which knowledge of God began. As noted earlier, the perfect tense of the verb in the phrase 'we have known' (ἐγνώκαμεν) occurs in v. 3. The passive voice of the verb 'has been perfected' indicates that God's love is a gift to the believer who knows him and keeps his word. Rather than seeing God's love as a reward for keeping his word, or simply as evidence of their knowledge of God, it is more in keeping with the Johannine view to see all these elements as integrally related to one another; one does not exist without the other. Knowing God, complete obedience and perfection of love go together.

The last part of v. 5 both rounds off the discussion in vv. 3-5 and prepares the reader for what follows in vv. 6-8. In v. 3 the formula 'and in this we know' functioned to indicate the beginning of a new section and stood with that which follows. In v. 5 the phrase appears to go with that which precedes it, serving to signify the end of this small unit (vv. 3-5) and again reassuring the readers that it is possible to be certain of what they know. However, instead of the expected reassurance ('that we have known him'), the focus of what is known changes from 'that we have known him' to 'that we are in him'. This manner of expression is an important one in the Fourth Gospel, being used to express the idea of intimacy, unity and solidarity. It is employed to express the relationship of the Son and the Father (14.20; 17.21, 23), the Son and the disciples (14.20; 17.21, 23), and the unity that should exist among the disciples (17.21, 23). Here the idea offers additional confirmation to the readers that their relationship to God is secure. Not only can they know that they have known him (an expression which itself implies intimacy), but they can also know that they are in him, thus sharing intimate fellowship with him, something the writer claims for himself (and those with him) as early as 1.3. In addition to reassuring the readers of their relationship to God, this phrase also prepares the readers for the next short section (vv. 6-8) within the larger unit which, among other things, deals with 'abiding in him' and 'being in him'.

Verses 6-8. The second of three claims found in 2.3-11 occurs in v. 6. As noted earlier, the phrase 'the one who says' (ὁ λέγων) may be an indication that in what follows the writer is coming close to a verbatim quotation of the opponents' claims. In contrast to the first (v. 4) and last (v. 9) claims to appear in this section, where each claim is accompanied by an example of action that serves to invalidate the claim, on this occasion the claim is accompanied by the action such a claim necessitates. The content of the claim is 'to remain (or abide) in him'. Several aspects of this claim should be noted. First, the reader is encouraged to see the connection between v. 5 and v. 6, in part by the fact that a very similar phrase stands on either side of 'the one who says'. Standing before it, at the end of v. 5, is the phrase 'in him we are' (ἐν αὐτῷ ἐσμεν), while standing after it in v. 6 is the phrase 'in him to abide' (ἐν αὐτῷ μένειν).

Second, the theme of remaining or abiding is a major motif in the Fourth Gospel and thus its appearance here would be picked up on immediately by the reader. Several ideas are present in the Gospel. Generally speaking, remaining conveys the idea of permanence in contrast to that which is temporary (Jn 8.35) and is associated with eternal life (6.27). More specifically, to remain/abide frequently appears in contexts that have reference to the believer's relationship with Jesus (6.56; 8.31; 15.4, 5, 7, 9, 10). Thus, those who make such assertions are claiming for themselves an ongoing intimacy with God/Jesus.

As noted earlier, on this occasion the claim is not accompanied by an action that serves to invalidate it (as in 1 Jn 2.4), but rather is accompanied by an action that the claim necessitates in order for it to be valid. The very next word in the Greek text underscores the fact that those who make such claims to intimacy with God are *obligated* to act in a fashion consistent with the claim. While this Greek word (ὀφείλει) is often translated as 'ought' or 'should', such translations are too weak as they fail to convey the word's full meaning. Rather than conveying the idea that the author is suggesting a commendable course of action which the reader may or may not choose to follow, the term carries with it the idea of necessity or obligation, usually a moral or ethical obligation.[46] Its use elsewhere in the Johannine literature (Jn 13.14, 19.7; 3 Jn 8; 1 Jn 3.16; 4.11) confirms this understanding of the term. In order to underscore the obligatory nature of this action the emphatic third person personal pronoun (αὐτὸς) is utilized, resulting in a translation something like, 'The one who claims to abide in him, must *himself* walk as that one walked'. Therefore, if one makes a claim to an intimate relationship with God, that person is obligated to a particular kind of walk or life.

Specifically, the one who makes this claim '*must* himself walk as that one walked'. Again, the familiar metaphor of walking occurs in the Epistles. Here the emphasis is upon one's identification with the character and activity of Jesus. Just as the one who claims fellowship with God must walk in the light as he is in the light (1.6, 7), so the one who claims to remain in him must walk as that one walked. And just as keeping his commands is both evidence of one's knowledge of God and a way of knowing him (2.3), so walking as that one walked is both evidence of one's remaining in him and is a way of remaining in him. In 1 Jn 1.7 the standard of conduct for the believer is God. Based on this one might expect God to be the standard in 2.6 as well. However, two things indicate that on this occasion Jesus is now the standard. First, as the reader will learn, in 1 John the pronoun 'that one' (ἐκεῖνος) always has reference to Jesus (cf. 3.3, 5, 7, 16; 4.17). In addition, the (aorist) past tense use of the verb 'walked' (περιεπάτησεν) indicates that the writer has a particular course of action in mind. More than likely the life of Jesus as described in the Fourth Gospel is here in mind. In order that the reader does not miss the point the writer uses 'just as' (καθὼς) to make clear that the believer is obligated to walk 'exactly as' Jesus walked.[47]

While it is possible to take v. 7 as a new beginning within the argument of 1 John, based in part upon the appearance of 'Beloved' which stands at the beginning of the verse, such an interpretive decision does not pay sufficient attention to the role vv. 7-8 play in continuing the thought of v. 6. As has already been noted, vv. 3-11 are structured around three claims, the second of which is found in v. 6. Thus, the broader structure suggests that there should be some connection

---

46 M. Wolter, 'ὀφείλω', *EDNT*, II, pp. 550-52 (551).
47 Brown, *The Epistles of John*, p. 262.

between v. 6 and vv. 7-8. Although 'Beloved' can designate the beginning of a new section in the Johannine Epistles, it does not always do so. Rather than indicating a new beginning here in 1 John, the appearance of 'Beloved' accomplishes several things. First, from 3 John the reader learns that this form of address is a favorite of the Elder, indicating the genuine affection that he has for those under his care. Thus, its appearance here comes as no surprise. Second, given the significant role of the Beloved Disciple in and for the Johannine community, the reader understands that the use of the term 'Beloved' is no mere polite form of address but has theological connotations closely associated with the model figure of the community.[48] Third, use of the term ('Αγαπητοί) continues the development of the theme of love, which is introduced in v. 5. Those in whom the love of God has been perfected are now addressed as 'Beloved'. Fourth, it is significant that at the very point where the writer seeks to inform the readers about love, he himself uses an expression that conveys his own love for his readers.[49] Fifth, perhaps most importantly, 'Beloved' functions to inform the reader as to the nature of Jesus' walk (mentioned in v. 6) and, by implication, how the reader is to walk.

What is the nature of the walk required of those who remain in him? Not surprisingly, instruction about the character of this walk takes the form of command. Earlier in this section (vv. 3-4), knowledge of God is closely connected to keeping his commands. It should be noted that the plural commands of vv. 3-4 become the singular command in vv. 7-8. This shift in number is not altogether unexpected in that already in 2 John (4-6) the plural and singular forms of command stand side by side and will continue to do so throughout 1 John (3.22-24; 4.20–5.3). Not unrelated to this is the fact that for the Johannine community all the commands focus upon and revolve around *the* one command. Although this command is not identified at this point, for a variety of reasons there would be no question in the reader's mind as to which command the author writes.

That which exemplifies how Jesus walked and how the reader is to walk is not a new command but an old one. In contrast to the actions of the opponents, who are not content to remain in the teaching of Christ (2 Jn 9) but go beyond it in various ways (perhaps even claiming that such 'new' commands originate with the Paraclete who will 'lead the disciples into all truth'; Jn 16.13), the author seeks to make clear that the origin of this command is quite ancient. In order to accomplish this task,

---

48 Brown, *The Epistles of John*, p. 264.
49 Westcott, *The Epistles of St. John*, p. 52.

he is not content simply to contrast the ancient basis of his words with the recent origins of his opponents' words. Rather, by making mention of an 'old' command he appeals to the commonly held view of the day which equates the credibility of a belief or idea with its antiquity. In other words, the older an idea or belief, the more likely it is to be true. In this case, the command is very old indeed for it goes back to the beginning, which often in the Johannine literature has reference to Jesus' ministry. One of the obvious parallels is found in 2 Jn 5 and 6, a passage devoted to a discussion of this very command. Therefore, this command is even older than the community itself. Not only is the age of the command underscored, but it is also identified as 'the word which you heard'. This designation suggests at least two things for the reader. First, it underscores the legitimacy of the old command for there are those who have heard it from the beginning themselves. Second, as noted earlier in 1 John (1.1, 10), there may be an intentional ambiguity in the use of the term 'word' (λόγος), which can have reference both to the message about and person of Jesus. Thus, it is made clear that the character of the believers' lives (walk) is not determined by recent theological innovations, but by a command identified with the community's life from the beginning.

On a previous occasion (2 Jn 5 and 6) the Elder wished to underscore that the command of which he speaks is not a new command but one as old as or older than the community itself. For the most part the same point is made in 1 Jn 2.7. If in 2 John the immediacy of the situation caused the Elder to focus solely on the importance of the antiquity of the command over against the novelty of the opponents' teaching, by the time of 1 Jn 2 it is clear that further reflection about the nature of the command has taken place. For here, the reader learns that despite the earlier disclaimer with regard to the command's novelty, the command is indeed a new one. This shift in thought is indicated in part by the use of the word here translated 'yet' (πάλιν), which stands at the beginning of v. 8 and results in a meaning something like 'yet despite the fact that the command is old, still it is new'. Thus the reader is alerted to the fact that the argument is taking a distinctive turn.

How is it that the command can be both old and new? Two things seem to be in mind with regard to the newness of the command. On the one hand, it is new because it is still fresh, it has not become obsolete. On the other hand, it appears that the writer is reluctant to give up on language that has its origins in Jesus' own words in the Fourth Gospel (13.34). This language is retained despite the fact that identification of the command as new creates some tension with what has earlier been stated (v. 7) and might play into the hands of the opponents. Thus, this new command is the old command, 'the word which you have heard'.

In 2.6 the reader is instructed to walk as that one (Jesus) walked. The next phrase ('which [ὅ] is true in him and in you') draws out the implications of this earlier statement by indicating how Jesus walked; he himself walked according to the love command. Primarily, this walk is exemplified by Jesus' voluntary death on behalf of his friends (Jn 15.12-17), which demonstrates a love that has no rival. His love is complete both qualitatively and quantitatively, 'he loved them until the end/completely' (εἰς τέλος; Jn 13.1). It is Jesus' love for the disciples that becomes the basis for his command for them to love one another (15.12). According to 1 Jn 2.7, not only is this true in Jesus' walk, but it is also true in those who remain in him, as the final words of the phrase ('and in you') indicate.

Just as the last phrase in 2.3 introduces 2.4-5 and 2.5 provides a transition from 2.3-5 to 2.6-8, so the final phrase in 2.8 provides a transition from 2.6-8 to 2.9-11. Here the reader learns that living according to the love command is integrally connected to the shining of the true Light and the passing away of the darkness. Such a statement clearly draws on the language of the Fourth Gospel's prologue (1.4-5) where the pre-incarnate Light shines in the darkness and the darkness cannot overtake it. The reader learns at least three things through this statement. First, it affirms the basic continuity of the Light's pre-incarnate and incarnate breaking into darkness. Second, it also affirms the way in which those who remain in him stand in continuity with the Light. Third, the statement reintroduces the idea of contrast between those who identify with darkness over against those who identify with the Light.

Verses 9-11. The third of the three (ὁ λέγων) claims found in vv. 3-11 occurs in v. 9 and builds on the last part of v. 8. This verse may be regarded as a thesis statement which is followed by positive (v. 10) and negative statements (v. 11) illustrating the main point.[50] In some ways the claim in v. 9 is a parallel to the claims in vv. 4 and 6. In each of them there is a claim of intimacy with God. It may be that the claim to be in the light is a special one in that earlier God has been identified as the Light (1.5) and as in the light (1.7). As with the claim in v. 4, this one is accompanied by an example of an action that serves to invalidate the claim. Here the claim is to be in the Light while hating one's brother or sister.[51] There are more references to hating in the Fourth Gospel than

---

50   Talbert, *Reading John*, p. 24.
51   The term translated 'brother' (ἀδελφός) here is best understood as including both men and women.

any other book in the New Testament and as many in 1 John as in any other book aside from the Gospel. Nearly all the references in the Fourth Gospel are to the world's hatred which Jesus experiences and/or his disciples will experience (3.20; 7.7; 15.18-19, 23-25; 17.14). Therefore, when learning of those who claim to be in the light while hating a brother or sister, the reader of 1 John immediately makes a connection between such ones and those who oppose Jesus. These people have more in common with the world than those who believe in Jesus. Those who make such claims, while hating their brother or sister, reveal that they are in the realm of darkness up to the present moment (ἕως ἄρτι). As revealed earlier, this realm is one that is diametrically opposed both to the realm of God (1 Jn 1.5) and to walking with Jesus (Jn 8.12). The contrast with v. 8 is significant. The ones who claim to be in the light while hating their brother or sister remain in darkness at the very moment that darkness is passing away and the Light is already shining.

Verse 10 offers a contrast between those who claim to be in the light and those who actually abide in the light. Whereas the earlier claim to be in the light is invalidated by the act of hating one's brother or sister, here the activity of loving one's brother or sister reveals one to be in the light. The mention of love at this point in the text accomplishes several things. First, it at last reveals the contents of the command that was introduced earlier in 1 Jn 2.3. Second, it makes more explicit the character of the walk that is true in Jesus' walk and the walk of those who believe in him (esp. 2.6, 8). Third, it provides an example of the way in which 'the love of God has been perfected' in those who keep his word (cf. 2.5). Therefore, those who love their brother or sister demonstrate their intimacy with God, who is identified in 1 John as both Light (1.5) and Love (4.16). Those who love in this way demonstrate the realm of their existence; they remain in the Light, a realm that is characterized by illumination, among other things.

The metaphor of walking, so familiar in the Johannine Epistles, is extended in the last part of v. 10, where the text reads, 'And there is no scandal in him'. Several observations should be offered about this phrase. It is not altogether clear whether the pronoun 'in him' has reference to the one who remains in the light or to the Light itself, as the Greek pronoun found here (αὐτῷ) can be taken as either masculine (referring to the one who remains) or neuter (referring to Light). It should be noted that in this verse, Light is the nearest antecedent to the pronoun. On this view, the reader understands the phrase 'and there is no scandal in him' to mean that there is no cause for stumbling in the light for it rather naturally illumines one's path, an idea also found in the Fourth Gospel (1.4-5, 9). Such an understanding is not far removed from that found in

1 Jn 1.5 where it is stated 'God is Light and in him is no darkness at all'. What is striking about this interpretation is the way in which the phrase 'in him is no darkness at all' (καὶ σκοτία ἐν αὐτῷ οὐκ ἔστιν οὐδεμία) so parallels grammatically and theologically the phrase 'in him there is no scandal' (καὶ σκάνδαλον ἐν αὐτῷ οὐκ ἔστιν) in the Greek text. Despite the fact that 1 John says 'his word is not in us' of the ones who say 'we have not sinned' (1.10) and 'in this one the truth is not' of the one who claims a knowledge of God but does not keep his commands (2.4), on balance it appears best to take 'in him' as having reference to the Light.[52]

The Greek noun translated 'scandal' or 'stumbling block' (σκάνδαλον) appears only here and in Rev. 2.14 in the Johannine literature. From the use of the verb form in the Fourth Gospel, the reader would understand that the term is used in a metaphorical or figurative sense. In Jn 6.61 Jesus asks those who had believed in him whether they were scandalized (σκανδαλίζει) by his words about eating his flesh and drinking his blood. The reader shortly learns that many of his disciples departed and did not walk with him after that point (6.66). In the farewell materials (16.1) Jesus explains to the disciples that he is warning them about the coming hatred and persecution so that when it comes to pass they will not be scandalized. These texts suggest that the reader would understand this term (σκάνδαλον) to mean a spiritual stumbling block. Specifically in 1 Jn 2.10 this term (σκάνδαλον) would be taken as having reference to departing from the faith, the temptation to sin and/or enticement to apostasy. The reader learns that there is no cause in the light for such falling, for the Light illumines one's path.

On this view, there is no cause for offense in the light. However, it might not be going too far to suggest that there is no cause for offense in the one who remains in the light. For those in whom 'the love of God has been perfected' would love their brother and sister and not cause them to stumble. If the believer is in view even in a secondary sense here, then it is probable that the phrase 'and there is no scandalon in him' includes the idea that there is in such a one no cause for stumbling: either their own stumbling or others.[53]

If v. 10 offers the positive side of the thesis stated in v. 9, then v. 11 offers the negative side. In contrast to the one who loves brother and sister, the one who hates does not remain in the light but rather has an intimate relationship with darkness. This verse is no mere duplication of the statement made in 2.9, but rather is an emphatic development of that thesis statement. The idea of v. 9 is developed in several ways. First,

---

52 Cf. the discussion in Smalley, *1, 2, 3 John*, p. 61.
53 As suggested by Westcott, *The Epistles of St. John*, p. 56.

there is the use of intentional repetition. Darkness is not simply mentioned once but three times in v. 11. Second, there is a steady increase in the use of predicates in this section (one in v. 9 – '*is* in darkness'; two in v. 10 – '*remains* in the light...scandalon *is* not in him'; three in v. 11 – '*is* in darkness...*walks* in darkness...the darkness *has blinded*'). Third, there appears to be a progression in terms of the severity of the involvement with darkness.

The verse begins with the idea expressed in 2.9, 'the one who hates his brother or sister is in darkness'. As seen in v. 9 the one who hates his brother or sister reveals that he or she is not in the light, but sides with the world in its hatred of Jesus and those who believe in him. They dwell in a realm that is diametrically opposed to God. Not only is the one who hates described as dwelling in this realm, but such a one is also described as walking in darkness. Since it is known from the Fourth Gospel that the one who follows Jesus does not walk in darkness (8.12), the reader understands that those who are described as walking in darkness in 1 Jn 2.11 are far from following Jesus. The reader also learns that one who walks in darkness 'does not know where he or she is going' (οὐκ οἶδεν ποῦ ὑπάγει). Rather than being in the light they do not even know where they are going. This statement is a clear reference to the words of Jesus in the Fourth Gospel (12.35) where he instructs the crowd to walk in the light lest darkness overtake them because 'the one who walks in darkness does not know where he is going' (οὐκ οἶδεν ποῦ ὑπάγει). Such a warning cannot help but to alert the reader about the perilous position of those who walk in darkness. Unlike Jesus who in the Fourth Gospel says, 'I know where I came from and where I am going' (8.14), these individuals do not know where they are going. The idea may also be a warning that any who follow such people are in a most perilous situation indeed, for they can lead others astray, a warning not unlike that expressed in 2 Jn 8-11.

The final part of v. 11 reveals that darkness is not simply a realm or neutral place of abode. Aside from the aimlessness of walking and not knowing where one is going, darkness is identified as a sinister force that is active in its malevolence.[54] For at this point the reader learns that the darkness has blinded the eyes of those who hate brother or sister. The tense (aorist) and voice (active) of the Greek verb translated 'has blinded' (ἐτύφλωσεν) emphasize both the malicious activity of darkness as well as the decisive moment, over a long period of time, at which the eyes were blinded. Such devastating results of walking in darkness may be compared to the results of lying in 1.6-10 which begins with

---

54 Cf. esp. the helpful remarks by Brown, *The Epistles of John*, p. 275.

lying (v. 6), leads to self-deception (v. 8) and eventuates in calling God a liar (v. 10). In both passages one's choices result in the most extreme consequences. Perhaps it should be observed at this point that in the Johannine literature darkness is associated with sin (cf. Jn 9.39-41). In this way too 1.5–2.2 and this passage are connected.

No doubt the reader is also struck by the contrast between the blind eyes of the one who hates his brother or sister and the eyes of the Elder (and those with him) which saw 'that which was from the beginning' (1.1), the foundation of the community's existence and belief. There may also be a hint here that just as 'the Light shines in the darkness and the darkness cannot seize or overtake it (κατέλαβεν)' so the darkness cannot seize or overtake (καταλάβῃ) those who walk in the truth (Jn 12.35). Such knowledge would be reassuring to the readers at a time when those who walk in the darkness have been overtaken by it.

Verses 12-14. The next subsection of 1 Jn 2.3-17 are verses 12-14. It is clear that these verses belong together from their structure, design and content. One of the distinguishing marks of these verses is their poetic nature, revealed by the fact that they have a remarkable symmetry or balance. As a result, most modern translations set them out in a way that draws attention to this dimension. These verses fall into two sections of three statements each, beginning with a form of the word 'write', followed by 'to you', a specific title ('children', 'fathers' or 'young men'), a designation that a new Greek clause begins (indicated by the Greek term ὅτι), and an assertion about the particular group just mentioned. Although somtimes thought to stand in isolation from that which surrounds it, these verses show a remarkable degree of contiunity with that which precedes and follows them in the text of 1 John. On the one hand, these verses make use of a number of themes and topics that have appeared earlier in 1 John (i.e. 'forgiveness of sins', knowledge of the one 'from the beginning', and 'the word of God remains' in you). On the other hand, they prepare the reader for the warning that follows (vv. 15-17) and the section concludes on the new commandment (2.3-17). Unlike the previous verses (1.5–2.11) no attention is given to false claims or inappropriate actions that invalidate claims to knowledge of God. Instead, in vv. 12-14 the focus is wholly on the positive attributes of the readers. These verses appear to be a summary statement about the status of those who have fellowship with the writer and his community and serve to reassure them of their forgiveness of sins, knowledge of God and relationship with the Word, and to encourage them to stand in or build upon these strengths—despite the negative emphases and stern warnings found in the book to this point. While these verses present several additional interpretive challenges for the reader, each of these difficulties is examined as it occurs in the text.

The initial statement of the first section occurs in v. 12 and begins with 'I write to you, children'. This phrase continues the use of 'I write' which has been characteristic of 1 John to this point (cf. 2.1, 7, 8; cf. also 'we write' in 1.4) and thus emphasizes the continuity of what follows with what has come before. It also makes use of a term of endearment, 'children' (τεκνία), which has also previously appeared in 1 John (2.1). As noted earlier this term not only has a familial connotation but takes on special significance for readers familiar with the Fourth Gospel in that Jesus used this very term in making reference to his disciples in the Farewell Materials (13.33). Its appearance at this point serves to underscore the transition from the subject of 1 Jn 2.11, those who walk in darkness, to the positive descriptions of the Johannine believers in vv. 12-14. Given the other uses of 'children' in the Johannine literature, it would be unwise to take this term in any other way than as a reference to the entire community.

This initial phrase is followed, as is the case in each of the six 'I write to you' clauses in vv. 12-14, by a Greek word (ὅτι) which can be translated as 'that' or 'because'. How should the reader take this term? Does it mean that the author is writing in order to tell the reader what he has to say, or is the writer explaining to the reader why he writes? While it is possible to insist that on this occasion the term must mean either 'that' or 'because' exclusively, it appears more likely that the meaning may indeed be a combination of the two. This suggestion is made because (1) it is questionable if the typical Greek reader would generally make such hard and fast distinctions with regard to this term,[55] and (2) it appears that the reader is both reminded of what has just been said and instructed as to the reason for these words.[56]

The content of the initial statement of affirmation made to all Johannine believers is 'your sins have been forgiven on account of his name'. Such a statement conveys a number of things to the reader. The emphasis on the forgiveness of sins reminds the readers that unlike those who deny their sin and, therefore, their need for forgiveness, the readers have experienced forgiveness. This statement implies that they have confessed their sin and experienced cleansing and purification (1.7, 9). It also suggests that they walk in the light and have fellowship with one

---

55   As Marshall, *The Epistles of John*, pp. 136-37, notes, 'Greek readers did not make the sharp distinction between the two uses of the conjunction which springs to the mind of the grammarian!'
56   Smalley, *1, 2, 3 John*, p. 71.

another (1.7). Thus, this declaration indicates that the readers have responded appropriately when faced with the issue of sin. But unlike the emphasis of the previous verses (1.7-2.2) on the need for continual forgiveness, the thought in 2.12 reveals that here the focus of attention is upon their initial experience of forgiveness, that is, the time of their conversion. This emphasis is made clear by the appearance of the (perfect) tense of the verb 'forgiven' (ἀφέωνται), which points to a past experience the results of which continue to be felt in the present. This mention of forgiveness also anticipates additional discussions of sin in 1 John (3.4-10; 5.16-18, cf. also 4.10).

The fact that such forgiveness is possible 'on account of his name' comes as no surprise to the reader, for while a number of things are done in the name of Jesus in the Johannine literature, the phrase 'in his name' is closely associated with belief in Jesus both in the Fourth Gospel (1.12; 2.23; 3.18; 20.31) and in 1 John (3.23; 5.13). This idea also dovetails nicely with the fact that in antiquity a person's name stood for the whole person, one's character, strengths and qualities.[57] To say that forgiveness of sins is 'on account of his name' indicates that while God is the one who grants forgiveness of sins, as stated in 1 Jn 1.9, Jesus is the one through whom forgiveness is mediated; for it is his blood that cleanses from all sin (1.8), it is Jesus who serves as an advocate (παράκλητον) with the Father who grants forgiveness (2.1), and it is Jesus who is the atoning sacrifice (ἱλασμός) not only for 'our' sins but those of the whole world (2.2). Therefore, in this opening statement of affirmation the readers are reminded of the importance of their initial belief in Jesus and are reassured that his atoning blood is efficacious for them.

The other two lines of this first stanza are found in v. 13. Here the same formula occurs as in the previous statement, 'I write to you...' However, on this occasion the words 'fathers' and 'young men' replace 'children' in the second and third lines respectively. If, as was seen in v. 12, 'children' has reference to the entire community, here it appears that a distinction is being made between two specific groups within the community, 'fathers' and 'young men'. While it is possible to take these terms as having reference to groups of leaders within the community (based in part on the use of 'fathers' in 1 Tim. 5.1 in relation to elders and the use of 'young men' in Acts 5.6 and 10), such an understanding fails to convince owing to the fact that the only evidence of a leadership title in the Johannine literature is that ascribed to 'the Elder'. In addition, there is no corroborating evidence that either 'fathers' or 'young men' functioned as a title within the community, unless it is here. The reader

---

57   L. Hartman, 'ὄνομα', *EDNT*, II, pp. 519-22 (519).

is more likely to see in these terms a reference to two groups of individuals within the larger group of 'children' comprised of older and younger believers.

Such an understanding of 'fathers' fits this context very well indeed. For not only is 'fathers' a polite form of address for one's elders (cf. Acts 7.2 and 22.1), but it is also a sign of reverence for those older or more mature in the faith (1 Tim. 5.1). In 1 Jn 2.13, the reader is likely to see a reference to those whose belief in Jesus is long-standing. These fathers are declared to 'know the one from the beginning'.[58] Thus, the reader understands them to stand in solidarity with the writer of 1 John (and those with him) whose intimate acquaintance with 'that which was from the beginning' is made the basis of his authority for writing (1.1-4). At the same time, this assertion about the fathers places them in diametric opposition to those who have falsely claimed a knowledge of God/Jesus but whose claims are betrayed by their actions (cf. 1.6-2.6). It also makes very clear that the fathers are those who keep his command and love one another. Thus, they know that they have known him (2.3-11). Such a statement is, no doubt, reassuring in the light of the stern language used with regard to the claims made in 2.4-11.

Like the first two lines of the first stanza, the third line also begins with the phrase 'I write to you...' On this occasion the group addressed is 'young men'. Such a division into 'fathers' and 'young men' is not an unnatural one, for in antiquity there appears to be no known middle age category such as is the case in contemporary society. 'Young men', of course, calls to mind the strength and vigor of youth. It has the meaning of one who is young in years in its other New Testament occurrences (Mt. 19.20, 22; Mk 14.51; 16.5; Lk. 7.14; Acts 2.17; 5.10; 23.18, 22). If 'fathers' has reference to those more mature in the faith, then it follows that 'young men' has reference to those who are younger in the faith. Of these it is said, 'You have been victorious over the evil one'.

This phrase conveys several things to the reader. First, there is a play on words in the Greek text between 'young men' (νεανίσκοι) and 'have been victorious' (νενικήκατε) which is not evident in the standard English translations. This word play highlights the fact that it is the young strong ones who are victorious. Second, the idea of being victorious over, which is primarily a Johannine emphasis in the New Testament, is familiar to the reader from the Fourth Gospel (16.33) where Jesus himself states, 'I have been victorious over (νενίκηκα) the world'. This victory includes both the world that hates him (15.18-16.4) and its ruler who is

---

58 'The one from the beginning' should in all likelihood be taken as having reference to Jesus, as 1 Jn 2.14 will make clear.

already being judged (16.11). Later in 1 John, the readers learn that those who are 'born of God have been victorious over the world' (5.4). Thus the reader is encouraged that the 'young men' have, like Jesus, been victorious in facing adversaries. Third, the appearance of 'being victorious' terminology in 2.13 introduces a theme that will reappear with some degree of regularity in 1 John. Fourth, it is significant that although the (perfect) tense of the verb places emphasis upon a victory that has taken place in the past the results of which are still felt in the future, the impression remains that there is still some fighting to do. Finally, mention of 'the evil one' makes clear that the believer's battle is ultimately with a dominant source of evil. Earlier subtle references in 1 John to such a sinister figure have come in the form of allusions to the father of lies (1.6, 10) and the malevolent force of darkness which is capable of blinding the eyes of certain individuals who claim to be in the light (2.9-11). In the Fourth Gospel evil works are identified as part of the realm of darkness (3.19) and characterize the world (7.7). Jesus' prayer in Jn 17.15 comes very close to identifying 'the evil one' as a personal force who is otherwise known as the Devil (8.44; 13.2), the ruler of this world (12.31; 14.30; 16.11) and Satan (13.27). By the time of 1 John it appears that 'the evil one' is one of the preferred titles for this figure (2.14; 3.12; 5.18, 19?), along with the Devil (3.8, 10). Thus, the readers of 1 John are being encouraged that instead of fearing the one who is able to blind their eyes, they have been victorious over this evil one, something of which they will be reminded near the book's end (5.18).

Verse 14 contains the entire second half of this poetic section, which resembles the first half to a remarkable degree. There is a fair amount of word-for-word repetition, with some significant modifications – both of which present challenges for the reader. One of the more significant interpretive challenges involves a shift in the formula 'I write to you…' from the present tense (γράφω) to the aorist past tense (ἔγραψα). One way of explaining this shift is to take the present tense as having reference to 1 John and the aorist tense as having reference to some other work written by the author, such as the Fourth Gospel or 3 or 2 John. As noted in the Introduction, it appears that 1 John follows chronologically 3 and 2 John as well as some form of the Fourth Gospel, so this interpretive option is at least theoretically possible. Additional support for this interpretation might also come from the fact that in 3 John 9 this identical aorist tense form of the verb (ἔγραψα) clearly has reference to a letter the Elder previously sent. There are, however, a couple of problems which make this view unlikely. While appeal to previously written documents may explain the shift from the present tense to the past tense, it does not explain the repetition which is found in v. 14. Neither is there much internal evidence to suggest that the content of 2.14 could have been derived from 3 or 2 John.[59] Even the appeals to the Fourth Gospel do not prove altogether convincing.

Another approach is to understand the shift in tense as a stylistic variation in order to avoid the monotony of six identical uses of the present tense verb 'I write'. But as with the previous view, this explanation does not adequately explain the repetition found in these two verses.

Still another way to explain this variation in verbal tense is to take the aorist tense verb (ἔγραψα) as an epistolary aorist, a means by which the writer puts himself or herself in the situation of the reader upon receiving and reading the letter. While such a use of the aorist tense was common in antiquity and cannot be ruled out, the problem of repetition and the reason for the shift in tense are still left unexplained.

It may not be insignificant that to this point in 1 John all seven occurrences of the verb 'I write' are in the present tense. From 2.14 onwards, the final six occurrences are in the aorist tense. Thus, it may be safe to assume that the reader would see in the shift from the present tense to the aorist tense some sort of transition.[60] But exactly what sort of transition is here implied? First and foremost the shift to the aorist tense alerts the reader to the fact that despite the repetitious nature of v. 14, what follows is not *mere* repetition for there are significant changes occurring in the second part of this poetic section. Thus, the shift in tense is a means by which the reader is prepared for the important departures that v. 14 contains. If the aorist tense 'I have written' serves to alert the reader to the changes introduced in v. 14, it follows that each additional occurrence of the aorist tense form (ἔγραψα) later in 1 John would convey to the reader a sense of continuity with regard to the book's developing argument; a development which culminates in the work's final section (5.13) where the term appears for a final time. Significantly, this text re-emphasizes the reason for the composition of 1 John.

Therefore, as v. 14 begins the reader is cautioned to give special attention to the changes that are encountered in v. 14. One such modification occurs in the first statement in this second stanza, where the text reads, 'I have written to you, children'. Despite the fact that a different Greek word for children occurs here in v. 14 (παιδία) than appeared in v. 12

---

59 Despite the many fine points in favor of this made by Strecker, *The Johannine Letters*, pp. 55-56.
60 Smalley, *1, 2, 3 John*, pp. 76-78, suggests that the shift to the aorist tense indicates a transition within vv. 12-14 to a further discussion of the statements made in vv. 12-13. The present tense looks back to the previous sections of 1 John while the aorist anticipates vv. 15-17.

(τεκνία), it is clear that this word, like its synonym in v. 12, has reference to the entire community. This word for children occurs three times in the Fourth Gospel. Twice it is used to convey something about the nature of the relationship between a parent and child (4.49; 16.21). To this basic meaning is added the fact that in one of his resurrection appearances (21.5), Jesus uses this term with reference to his disciples, a point which would not be lost on the readers of 1 John. Neither is it without significance that this address of children is immediately followed by a statement that makes reference to the Father, suggesting that the focus here is upon the intimacy of the father–child relationship.

Earlier in 2.14, the children have been reminded that their 'sins have been forgiven on account of his name'. Now the children are told that they 'have known the Father'. As in the first half of the section so here the perfect tense is used, this time to convey the idea that their knowledge (ἐγνώκατε) of the Father had a definite point of beginning, the effects of which are still felt in the present. In 1 John, knowledge of the Father implies that one has eternal life, which resides with the Father (1.2); fellowship with the Father and Son, as does the writer of 1 John (1.3); and has experienced forgiveness of sin by the Father through Jesus the Paraclete (2.1). Mention of knowledge also reminds the reader of the emphasis with which this section began, where assurances are given as to how they can know that they have known him (2.3). In that section, knowledge of God is very closely connected to keeping his commands, and keeping the commands closely connected to loving one's brothers and sisters. Thus, in being assured that they have known the Father, the readers are assured that they are keeping his commands and love their brothers and sisters. Such knowledge stands in stark contrast to the false claims to know God described earlier in this section.

Aside from the shift to the aorist 'I have written', the second line in this stanza of the poetic section matches the second line in the first stanza exactly: 'I have written to you, fathers, because you know the one from the beginning.' Whereas the other lines of this stanza are significant in part because of the variations they contain, the significance of this line is found in the fact that it is, for all practical purposes, identical to its counterpart in the first stanza. Such repetition suggests that the importance of this particular statement of assurance. As before, this line emphasizes the fathers' long-standing in the community, their solidarity with the writer, their opposition to those who make false claims to knowledge of God, and their obedience in keeping his commands and loving the brothers and sisters. Thus, they 'know that they have known him'. As such, this repetition reminds the readers of the stability and certainty of their faith as represented by their spiritual fathers in the community.

The third line of the second stanza mirrors the opening address in the third line of the first stanza with the exception of the shift in tense: 'I have written to you, young men'. As noted in the discussion on v. 13, it appears that those younger in the faith specifically are being addressed at this point. But unlike the third line of the first stanza, the opening address is not immediately followed by 'you have been victorious over the evil one'. Rather, the line is expanded at this point to read, 'because you are strong and the word of God remains in you'. It would not surprise the reader to find that the 'young men' are described as strong for the image of youth carries with it the idea of strength and earlier they are said to have been victorious over the evil one. Thus in this context it would appear that their strength is a spiritual one which comes from God and in any case reassures the readers of their strength as over against their opponents. In addition, the 'young men' are assured that 'the word of God remains' in them. Such a statement stands in marked contrast to that of 1.10, where the word of God does not remain in those who claim not to have sinned and as a result make God a liar. The implication is that these 'young men' have confessed their sin and are empowered and strengthened by the presence of the word of God in their very being.[61] If the contrast with 1.10 is intentional, then not only does the word of God have reference to Jesus' proclamation but also to his person as seems to be the case in 1.2, 10 where 'the Word' appears to contain at least a secondary christological reference.[62] At this point, the same statement made in the third line of the first stanza reappears in v. 14: 'and you have been victorious over the evil one'. Again the 'young men' are reminded that just as Jesus has been victorious over his adversaries, so they have been victorious over the evil one—the one who blinds the eyes of some of the 'brothers' and 'sisters' and, no doubt, stands behind the self-deception, lies and making of God a liar described in 1.6-10. It is interesting that whereas 'you have been victorious' (νενικήκατε) is in the perfect past tense, the verbs in the statements 'you

---

61   Given the fact that reference is made to 'the Father' and 'the one from the beginning' in the first two lines of the second stanza, some interpreters see in 'the word of God' a reference to the Holy Spirit, thus discerning an early trinitarian statement in 2.14. This reading appears to be a bit artificial as 'the word of God' is not found elsewhere in the Johannine literature as a reference to the Spirit.

62   The idea of the word of God remaining in the young men is not far removed from Jesus' words in the Fourth Gospel (15.7) where he says: 'If you remain in me and my words (τὰ ῥήματά μου) remain in you, ask whatever you desire, and it will be done for you.'

are strong' and 'the word of God *remains* in you' are in the present tense implying that the victory has been won in the past with the effects still felt in the present while the strength and the remaining of the Word are present realities. Such statements once again serve to reassure the readers of their (ongoing) relationship with God.

Verses 15-17. These three verses advance the argument of 1 John in several ways. Most immediately, they follow rather naturally vv. 12-14 which contain a number of assurances made to the readers with regard to their standing in the faith. Verses 15-17 build upon these previous verses by warning the readers that despite their standing it is imperative that they be vigilant so as not to be enticed to love the world or its desires. On a larger scale, these verses form a fitting conclusion to the second major section within 1 John (2.3-17) which has focused primarily on the issue of love. As such it makes clear that love of God is diametrically opposed to love of the world.

Verse 15 begins with the general prohibition of vv. 15-17: 'Do not love the world, nor the things of the world.' To this point in 1 John love terminology has been used exclusively in a positive manner. Mention has been made of 'the love of God' (2.5) and 'loving one's brother and sister' (2.10). Here the reader learns that it is possible to love the wrong thing(s). Such an idea, while introduced at this point in 1 John, is not new to readers of the Fourth Gospel, where it is revealed that 'men loved darkness more than light' (3.19) and that some 'loved the glory of men more than the glory of God' (12.43). While it is possible to take the prohibition of 1 Jn 2.15 in the weaker sense of 'Do not take a fancy to the world',[63] such a rendering does not do justice to the fact that the same Greek root word for love (ἡ ἀγάπη) is used here as in its other occurrences in 1 John, nor does it take sufficient account of the contrast between love for the world and love of the Father, which is prominent in this verse.

The first mention of 'the world' in 1 John reveals that Jesus' death is an atoning sacrifice for the sins of the whole world (2.2). However, in 1 Jn 2.15 it becomes apparent that the world is not simply a place or realm to be embraced in an undiscerning manner, for there is an inherent danger in loving the world. This idea is consistent with the picture of the world found in the Fourth Gospel. There, despite the fact that God loves the world and sends his Son as its Savior (1.29; 3.16-17; 4.42; 10.36; 11.27; 12.47; 16.28; 17.18, 21, 23; 18.37), the world does not know Jesus (1.10; 14.17; 17.25) as it is under the power of its ruler (12.31; 14.30), is closely

---

63   As Bultmann, *The Johannine Epistles*, p. 33 n. 19, suggests.

aligned with darkness and in need of illumination (1.5, 9; 3.19; 8.12; 9.5; 12.46), and is ultimately judged (9.39; 12.31; 16.8, 11). Thus, it is primarily a place of opposition to Jesus and his mission (8.23; 15.18-19; 16.20, 33; 17.14). This means that his disciples are not of the world and need to be kept (from the evil one) while in it (17.6, 11, 14-16). Given the context of 1 Jn 2.15 and the backdrop of the Fourth Gospel, it appears safe to assume that the connection between the world, darkness (2.8, 11) and the evil one (2.13-14) would not be lost on the reader at this point. The world, despite God's love for it and Jesus' atoning sacrifice on its behalf, is in the realm of darkness and under the influence of the evil one. Therefore, neither it nor the things belonging to the world are to be loved.

The second part of v. 15 contains the first of three antitheses that serve to clarify this prohibition against loving the world. Reminiscent of the constructions in 1.6–2.2, the first antithesis begins with an 'if' clause: 'If anyone loves the world, the love of the Father is not in him.' This contrast makes clear the diametric opposition between these two loves. The phrase 'the love of the Father' occurs only here in the New Testament, but rather clearly reminds the reader of the description of the one who keeps his word: 'in this one the love of God has been perfected'. The one who keeps his command has within this love of God, which manifests itself in love for one's brother and sister. Just as it is impossible to be in the light while hating one's brother (or sister), so it is impossible to love the world and the Father simultaneously. As with 'the love of God' in 2.5, it is possible to take 'the love of the Father' as having reference either to the believer's love for the Father or to the Father's love in the believer. Since aspects of both meanings are present in 2.15, it is best to take the phrase as having reference to both the Father's love in the believer and the believer's love for the Father. The appearance of 'the love of the Father' then serves to underscore the unity of 2.3-17 by drawing on terms and themes from its different subsections. In particular, the phrase 'love of the Father' not only points back to 'the love of God' found in 2.5, which is manifested in love for one's brother and sister, but also points back to mention of the children who have known the Father in 2.14. In this way, the first antithesis in this subsection helps to connect the prohibition against loving the world to the assurances of salvation upon which the previous subsection focuses.

The second antithesis of vv. 15-17 is found in v. 16. Like the statements of assurance in vv. 12-14, v. 16 begins with the word 'because' (ὅτι): 'Because everything in the world…is not of the Father but of the world.' While the first antithesis (v. 15b) was devoted to the first part of the general prohibition ('Love not the world'), the second antithesis focuses on the second part of the general prohibition ('nor the things of the world'). This conclusion is borne out in part by the similarity between the phrases 'the things in the world' (τὰ ἐν τῷ κόσμῳ) and 'everything in the world' (πᾶν τὸ ἐν τῷ κόσμῳ). Reference to the rather open-ended 'the things in the world' in v. 15a gives way to the more specific 'everything in the world' in v. 16. By this means the reader understands that the words that follow offer an expansion of the previous thought.

The reader may very well expect this second antithesis, like the first, to proceed to its conclusion in an uninterrupted fashion. However, on this occasion, the antithesis is interrupted by examples that illustrate the kinds of things that are in the world. Three examples are offered as representative of the things that belong to the world. The fact that there are three examples should not be taken to suggest that there are three and no more, but may have more to do with the author's preference for listing things in threes (i.e. the three claims in 1.6-10, the three claims in 2.4-9, and the two stanzas comprised of three parts each in 2.12-14). The three examples may also be related to the tendency in antiquity to list sources of evil in threes.[64]

The first example of 'everything in the world' is 'the desire/lust of the flesh'. The Greek word that appears here (ἐπιθυμία) is actually a neutral term which may be translated as either 'desire' or 'lust' depending upon its context.[65] There are several indicators that its occurrences in 2.16-17 are not neutral but convey a negative message. It is clear that in this context the 'desire of the flesh' is identified as an example of the things in the world. As such, this 'desire' stands in opposition to the love of God and reveals a love of the world. This love of the world demonstrates that this desire is aligned with darkness, a realm which is under the influence of the evil one. Finally, from its only appearance in the Fourth Gospel the reader knows that this term (ἐπιθυμία) has sinister associations. There, Jesus says to those who are unable to hear him, 'You are of your father the Devil and you wish (θέλετε) to do his desires/ lusts (ἐπιθυμίας)' (8.44). Therefore, when first encountering this term in 1 John, the reader is not predisposed to take it in a neutral sense but as associated with the Devil.

In its other two occurrences in the Johannine Epistles the term 'flesh' is used to describe Jesus having come in the flesh, his incarnation (2 Jn 7; 1 Jn 4.2). In the Fourth Gospel 'flesh' is used in a similar fashion on one occasion (1.14), has reference to Jesus' flesh – the bread from heaven – which must be eaten (6.51-56), and can stand for that which is earthly over against that which is heavenly or of the Spirit (1.13; 3.6; 6.63; 8.15;

---

64 Brown, *The Epistles of John*, p. 307.
65 H. Hübner, 'ἐπιθυμία', *EDNT*, II, pp. 27-28 (27).

and possibly 17.2). Given this Johannine background, it would appear that the 'lust of the flesh' in 1 Jn 2.16 has reference to all those things which are part of a life controlled by and focused upon that which has its origins in the world rather than in God. This phrase would rather clearly include the idea of inappropriate sexual desires and passions (as it does in Gal. 5.16; Eph. 2.3; 1 Pet. 2.11; 2 Pet. 2.10, 18), but not be focused exclusively upon them here.[66]

The second example of 'everything in the world' is identified as 'the lust of the eyes'. For a second time the word 'lust' (ἐπιθυμία) appears and surely conveys to the reader the same negative qualities as does its first appearance, only this time the lusts pertain to the eyes rather than the flesh. The eye is a common metaphor in antiquity. As the primary sensory organ of the body, the eye is that which receives a variety of stimuli. Owing to this fact, the eye, despite its value, can cause offense and must be disciplined, even severely (Mt. 5.29; 18.9; cf. also 7.2-5). Because of its strategic role, the eye can be used as having reference to the conscience. If the eye is healthy, the whole body has light, if the eye is bad the whole body has darkness (Mt. 6.22-24). The eyes have been mentioned twice in 1 John to this point. The author appeals to 'that which we have seen with our eyes' as a means of underscoring the validity of the community's testimony (1.1). Thus, the eyes play a significant role in establishing the tradition upon which the belief of the community is based. The reader also knows that it is possible for the darkness to blind one's eyes (2.11). Now the reader learns that losing one's sight is not the only danger with regard to the eyes. There are lusts that appeal to and are received by the eyes which compete with God for one's love. The precise nature of the 'lusts of the eye' is not altogether clear in 1 Jn 2.16. Given the eyes' primary association in the Fourth Gospel with being spiritually blind, there may be an implicit warning here that the lust of the eyes results in being made spiritually blind, an idea which would reinforce the point made in 2.11. It is, of course, possible that the reader knows from the Old Testament that the eyes can be used in association with sinful sexual desire (Gen. 39.7; Job 31.1), pride (Isa. 5.15) and greed (Jer. 22.17). While certainty on this point is beyond reach, it is safe to conclude that none of these Old Testament ideas would be completely foreign to the meaning of 'lust of the eyes' in 1 Jn 2.16.

The third example of 'everything in the world' departs from 'the lust of...' pattern. Instead it speaks of 'the pride of life' (ἡ ἀλαζονεία τοῦ βίου). The phrase very literally means something like 'the arrogant boasting of

---

66 As is often argued by various interpreters. Cf. esp. Schnackenburg, *The Johannine Epistles*, p. 122.

material possessions', as the word translated 'pride' has the connotation of 'ostentatious, empty pride' or 'arrogant boasting'. This word stands with a term which can be translated as 'life' (βίος). However, unlike the Greek word used in the Johannine literature to speak of the (eternal) 'life' (ζωή) which comes from God, this word has reference to the possessions, wealth or inheritance of material existence, as its occurrence in 1 Jn 3.17 makes clear.[67] Perhaps there is even a subtle play on Jesus' words in Jn 10.10, 'I came in order that you might have life (ζωήν) and have it fully.' In 1 Jn 2.16 the reader is warned about the danger of having a life (βίον) full of the things of the world.[68] At any rate, through this example the readers are warned about the seduction of wealth, a seduction which can result in a false confidence in one's possessions or abilities. This arrogant boastful lifestyle not only reveals a love of the world, but leads to a lack of love and care for one's brothers and sisters—a sign that the love of God does not remain in such a one (cf. 1 Jn 3.17).

At this point the author returns to the main thought of the third antithesis, 'Because everything in the world...is not of the Father but is of the world.' Just as 'love of the world' and 'love of the Father' are antithetical (2.15), so everything that has its origins in the world does not have its origin in the Father. Thus, everything that belongs to the world is opposed to the Father. By this contrast, the fundamental division between the Father and the world are underscored for the reader. The appearance of the word 'Father' not only continues the theme of the children in 1 John, but it also undercores the importance of fellowship with (1.3), forgiveness by (2.1) and knowledge of (2.14) the Father.

The third and final antithesis of this section is found in v. 17. Here the primary contrast is between the transitory nature of this world and its lusts on the one hand, and the permanence of the one who does the will of God on the other hand. The reader learns in this last clarification of the general prohibition 'love not the world...' that like the darkness (2.8) so too the world and its lusts are in the process of passing away. The same verb (παράγεται) occurs in both 2.8 and 2.17 to describe this 'passing away'. Its appearance in the present tense signifies a continuing process that is not yet complete, but its completion is inevitable. The world and its lusts are in the process of passing away as inevitably as darkness is in the process of giving way to light. Not only does mention of the world and its lusts passing away cause the reader to look back to a similar statement about darkness in 2.8, but it also anticipates the

---

67 H.-J. Ritz, 'βίος', *EDNT*, I, p. 219.
68 Brown, *The Epistles of John*, p. 312.

discussion of the 'last days' in the next section (2.18-27) and the subsequent discussion of the appearing of Jesus (2.28–3.4). Thus, this mention of the world and its lusts passing away introduces, in a subtle fashion, the idea of the return of Jesus into the argument of 1 John. The reader would not take 'the world' in a neutral sense but very much like its use in 2.15 as in the realm of darkness and under the influence of the evil one. Mention of the world's lusts is, rather obviously, a reference to the examples found in v. 16: the lust of the flesh, the lust of the eyes and the arrogant boasting of material possessions. Not only do these things have their origin in the world rather than the Father, but they also are transitory and, therefore, will not endure.

In contrast to the transitory nature of the world and its lusts, the reader learns that 'the one who does the will of God will remain forever'. Given the emphasis on love of God in vv. 15-16, it is somewhat surprising that reference is made at this point in 1 John to 'the one who does the will of God' rather than 'the one who loves God'. This unexpected shift serves to remind the reader that the person who keeps his (God's) commands (2.3) is the one who loves brother and sister (2.10). Such a move continues to underscore the fact that in the Johannine literature there is no division between theology and ethics. The reader is also mindful, from the Fourth Gospel, of the emphasis that Jesus places upon doing 'the will of the one who sent me' (4.34; 5.30; 6.38, 39; cf. also 7.16-17). For Jesus, doing 'the will of the one who sent me' means placing God's will and purposes above his own (5.30), equating the doing of his will with physical nourishment (4.34), and acknowledging his absolute dependence upon the Father (5.30). Those who desire to do the will of God know that Jesus' teaching is not his own but that of 'the one who sent me' (7.16-17). Jesus identifies the purpose of God's will as eternal life for those who see and believe the Son, which results in being raised on the last day (6.38-40). Thus, in contrast to those who love the world and its lusts, those who do God's will remain forever, for they are participants in eternal life[69] – a mode of existence characteristic of life with God.

Reflection and Response – Part Four

Reflection

Love is the dominant theme of 1 John and is introduced in 1 Jn 2.3-17. Here the readers learn that 'keeping the commands' and 'knowing God'

---

69 Schnackenburg, *The Johannine Epistles*, p. 124, observes, 'In GJohn the phrase "to abide forever" is identical in meaning with "to have eternal (divine) life".'

go hand in hand. It is impossible to know God without keeping his command to love one's brother or sister. Keeping the command to love one another reveals that the love of God has been completed or perfected in the believer. This command, which is no recent invention, comes from Jesus himself. Despite its antiquity, it is ever-new owing to the fact that it continues to be a present reality for the one who knows God. Keeping the command is manifested in love for fellow believers and reveals that one walks in the light. Conversely, those who hate a brother or sister reveal that they are walking in darkness and do not know where they are going for the darkness has blinded their eyes.

Not only is love defined in contrast to hate but it is also contrasted with love of the world and the desires of the world. These desires are defined as the desire of the flesh, the desire of the eyes and the pride of life. Believers are not to love the world and its desires, for everything associated with the world is passing away, as is darkness itself. But the one who does the will of God by keeping his commands remains forever. It is the contrast between love of God and love of the world that is the focus of this reflection and response section. In order to facilitate this reflection a series of questions are raised.

How are love of God and love of the world distinguishable today? In what individuals or groups are you able to see the love of God manifested? What characteristics of these individuals and groups led you to make this identification? What concrete examples of love have you seen in the lives of others and how prevalent are those acts in the Church today? Conversely, what groups or individuals do you know who exhibit love of the world and its desires? Why do you make this association between them? Why are the desires of the world so attractive and such a danger to believers? What are contemporary examples of the desire of the flesh, the desire of the eyes and the pride of life? How pervasive are these desires in the world today and in the Church? Are there any visible signs that this world and its desires are passing away? What are they?

On a more personal level, what or whom do I love? In what ways is the love of God present in my life? How would I describe my love and concern for fellow believers? In what ways am I affirmed or critiqued by the community with regard to the presence or absence of love in my life? In what ways have I experienced the love of God through other brothers and sisters? What has been the significance of such experiences? How seriously do I take the diametric opposition between love of God and love of the world? How am I tempted to choose between the two? With what concrete manifestations of the desire of the flesh, the desire of the eyes and the pride of life do I contend? In what ways do this world and its desires appear to be permanent rather than passing away and how does this affect my attitude toward it?

Response

How may I respond to the question of my love and allegiance to God or the world?

First, prayerfully consider your life identifying the people, things and desires that you love.

Second, evaluate your affections in light of 1 John's teaching about love of God and love of the world, focusing specifically upon those areas where your life does not reflect the teaching of this passage.

Third, discern with a trusted brother or sister, the ways in which you are 'keeping the commands' and the ways in which you struggle with the desires of the world.

Fourth, through the reading of Scripture, times of prayer and corporate worship, allow the reality of the return of Jesus to transform your attitudes toward and affections for the world and its desires, in order that the love of God might be made complete in you.

1 John 2.18-27

At this point the argument of 1 John develops in two specific ways. First, this section continues the theme of the passing away of the darkness, the world and its lusts, by introducing the idea of 'the last hour', which in turn is followed by a discussion of the return of Jesus (1 Jn 2.28–3.3). Thus, there is an emerging eschatological dimension to the book. Second, while indirect reference has been made to the opponents by mention of the false claims in the previous two sections, the opponents receive direct attention in 2.18-27, making even more explicit the nature of the false teaching and deception faced by the community. The section itself appears to be roughly structured around the address to 'children' in 2.18 and the three emphatic uses of 'you' in vv. 20, 24 and 27, resulting in the following subsections: vv. 18-19, vv. 20-23, vv. 24-26 and v. 27.

Verses 18-19. The section begins with the same term of endearment previously used in addressing the readers in 2.14. Several things are conveyed by means of this address. First, it is evident that the entire community is included in the term 'children' (παιδία). Second, this particular word reminds the readers of their intimate relationship with the Father, a relationship characterized by knowledge of the Father. Third, given the way in which 'children' follows so closely on the reference to 'the one who does the will of God', the readers are reassured of their secure position as children of the Father despite the passing away of the world and its lusts, on the one hand, and the appearance of antichrists and deceivers, on the other hand.

It is not altogether surprising that after the previous references to the transitory nature of darkness, this world and its lusts, that the readers should learn of 'the last hour'. Mention of this phrase, which occurs only in this verse in the whole of the New Testament, introduces more explicitly than before the idea of the culmination or end of history. This unique phrase is likely a combination of ideas from the Fourth Gospel and the Johannine community. From the Fourth Gospel the reader is familiar with the concept of 'the last day' which is closely associated with the resurrection of the dead (6.39, 40, 44, 54; 11.24) and final judgment (12.48). The reader is also familiar with 'the coming hour' which is closely associated with true worship (4.21, 23), the resurrection of the dead (5.25, 28), Jesus' hour of glorification (2.4; 7.30; 8.20; 12.23, 27; 13.1; 17.1) and departure (16.25), persecution (16.2, 4) and the scattering of the disciples (16.32). In addition, the book of Revelation can speak of the hour of Jesus' coming (3.3), the hour of persecution (3.10) and the hour of judgment (9.15; 11.13; 14.7, 15; cf. also 18.10, 17, 19).

There is a sense in which the ideas of 'last hour' and 'last day' merge in the Johannine literature. Clearly, the appearance of 'last hour' in 1 Jn 2.18 would alert the readers to the fact that the end of time is approaching with its accompanying characteristics (resurrection of the dead, judgment, etc.). At the same time, the appearance of 'last hour' instead of 'last day' would serve to highlight the continuity between this 'last hour' and Jesus' hour as well as underscore the idea of the immanence of the end – it is not only the 'last day' but the 'last hour'.

The declaration 'it is the last hour' is closely followed by a statement about the arrival of antichrist, an event which should not take the readers by surprise for it is something which they 'have heard'. The phrase 'just as you have heard' suggests that knowledge of the coming of antichrist is common in the community, but unlike a number of other pieces of Johannine teaching this teaching is not said to have been heard 'from the beginning' (2 Jn 6; 1 Jn 1.1; 2.24; 3.11). This omission suggests that the origin of the teaching about antichrist is a somewhat recent development within the community. While it is possible to take the phrase 'just as you have heard' as a sign that John is either making reference to or drawing upon current apocalyptic speculation with regard to a rather well-defined view of the antichrist, such an understanding appears to outdistance the evidence in a few ways. First, such an explanation does not give sufficient attention to the fact that there are no references to antichrist in any extant literature before 2 and 1 John. The fact that the term appears in this literature for the first time suggests that perhaps it has its origins in the Johannine community rather than outside it. Second, if it is probable that the term 'antichrist' has its origin in the Johannine community, then it would appear likely that the phrase 'just as you have heard' has reference to the Elder's own previous teaching (and warning) about the coming of antichrist (2 Jn 7), not to some emerging view of antichrist in the first century. Third, it is significant that nowhere in the Johannine literature is the term 'antichrist' used as having reference to *the* antichrist, a figure that finds a place in many eschatological discussions. What is perhaps most telling is the fact that the term 'antichrist' is not used in the Apocalypse for the arch enemy of Jesus, the Beast. Rather, quite in keeping with its previous occurrence in 2 John, antichrist in 1 John is associated with false teaching with regard to Jesus as Christ and Son of God.[70]

The prediction that the reader has heard, that 'antichrist is coming', has turned out to be a reality. The prediction, though, is contrasted with the reality in several ways. First, while the prediction may have led the reader to expect the appearance of *an* antichrist, in point of fact, '*many* antichrists have come'. However, such a statement is not as unexpected as it might at first appear for in 2 John 7, where the deceiver and the antichrist are equated, the reader learns that 'many deceivers have gone out into the world'. The presence of many antichrists is also in keeping with the meaning of the term in the Johannine literature, where antichrist is associated with false teaching and/or deception. Second, use of the temporal marker 'even now' underscores the reality of the prediction that antichrist is coming by emphasizing that the current situation is clear for all to see. Third, the prediction that antichrist 'is coming' is contrasted with the reality through use of the (perfect) past tense verb 'have come' (γεγόνασιν) indicating that the arrival of the antichrists is a past action—the effects of which are still felt in the present.

---

70   The first mention of the word antichrist outside the New Testament is Polycarp's letter to the Philippians (7), where he quotes 1 Jn 2.18 word for word with reference to false teachers. This Johannine definition of antichrist continues in the writings of Origen (*Against Celsus* 79), Tertullian (*Against Heretics* 33; *On the Flesh of Christ* 24; *Against Marcion* 1.22; 3.28; *Against Praxeas* 31), *Clementine Homilies* (2, 17), Cyprian (*Epistles* 69.3; 73.4), and Augustine (*On Baptism* 3.19.26; 4.16.21; 6.31.59-60; 7.15.29; 7.28.54). The term is used for the eschatological arch enemy of Jesus as early as Origen (*Against Celsus* 46), Tertullian (*Concerning Flight in Persecution* 12), Victorinus (*Commentary on the Apocalypse* 12.3), Lactantius (*Divine Institutes* 19), *Revelation of John*, Hippolytus (*Treatise on Christ and Antichrist*), and Augustine (*City of God* 18.52-53; 20.18-19; *On the Psalms* 106.33; *Sermon* 7.9.7; *John* 29.8).

The coming of many antichrists is sufficient evidence (ὅθεν) for the readers to know that 'it is the last hour'. This verse, which begins with mention of the last hour, returns to that theme at the end, thus structurally locating the discussion of antichrist within the discussion of the last hour. As noted earlier, mention of the last hour rather clearly has reference to the passing way of this world and anticipates a discussion of the appearing of Jesus which follows in 2.28–3.3. While it is possible to take reference to the last hour simply as a mistaken calculation about the end of time, such an understanding does not appear to do full justice to the richness of the meaning of this idea for 1 John. This is true for several reasons. First, the primary issue in this verse is an emphasis upon the immanence of the end not upon date-setting. Second, it is significant that in the biblical tradition the concept of time is somewhat ambiguous. Not only is one day with the Lord as a thousand years (2 Pet. 3.8), but also the prophetic tradition is characterized by a telescoping of future events where, within the prophetic vision, events appear to be closer than they actually are. Added to this is the idea that with the death and resurrection of Jesus and the sending of the Spirit, the last days have arrived (Acts 2.17). Third, the concept of history within the Apocalypse indicates that the apocalyptic vision of the end relativizes human history. This suggests something of the ambiguity of the understanding of history. The emphasis upon immanence and the somewhat ambiguous or open-ended understanding of history fits remarkably well within modern explanations of time and history, where many thinkers following the lead of Albert Einstein are convinced that time itself is relative.[71] Perhaps a helpful way to think about the early Christian understanding of the immanence of the end is to see a fundamental change in the way history was viewed as a result of the coming of Jesus. Until the life of Jesus, history might be described as moving step by step straight toward the end. However, with the coming of Jesus history has been brought very near the end but now rather than running straight toward it, history runs alongside the end, meaning that the end is never very far away, despite the passage of time.[72]

The identity of the antichrists is addressed in v. 19, where several things are revealed. One of the first things to strike the reader in this verse is the emphasis placed upon a Greek phrase (ἐξ ἡμῶν) which can be translated as 'of us' or 'out of us'. It is clear that this phrase is intended to

---

[71] Cf. A. Einstein, *Relativity: The Special and the General Theory* (trans. R.W. Lawson; New York: Wings Books, 15th edn, 1961).

[72] For this suggestion cf. J.H. Newman, 'Waiting for Christ', *Parochial and Plain Sermons*, VI (London: Longmans, Green & Co., 1896), p. 241.

draw the reader's attention for not only does v. 19 begin and end with the phrase, but also the phrase occurs five times in this verse alone! By this means the reader learns that the antichrists are defined by their position over against the community.

Specifically, it is revealed that at one time these antichrists were part of the Johannine community for they 'went out from us'. The specific moment of this 'going out' is likely in the reader's mind as the (aorist) past tense is here used, a tense which identifies a specific past action. While it is difficult to be certain of such a point, the Elder's warning about the arrival of deceivers and antichrists in 2 John 7 may be evidence of the moment when the antichrists first went out. The language of 'going out' not only reminds the reader of the deceivers' actions found in 2 John 7, but also suggests that the antichrists are in the company of Judas, who himself 'went out' into the night (of deception; Jn 13.30). Thus the words 'they went out from us' indicate that at one time these individuals were part of the community and apparently indistinguishable from other community members.

However, lest the readers come to a premature conclusion, they quickly learn that while these antichrists may have 'gone out from us', they were not 'of us'. In the Greek text there is a word play on the phrase translated 'out of us/of us'. The gist of the statement appears to be, while these antichrists gave every appearance that they were in fellowship with the community, in fact they were not. The next phrase explains how this lack of fellowship was discerned — by the actions of the antichrists. Their leaving the community is evidence that they did not continue in intimate fellowship with the community. These words remind the reader of the earlier emphasis on the need for absolute consistency between one's claims and one's walk (1.6–2.11). Just as those who claim to know God but walk in darkness reveal that they do not do the truth (1.6), so those who do not remain in the community's fellowship reveal that they are not 'of us'. At the same time, these words underscore the importance of 'remaining', which conveys the idea of very close intimacy, as seen in 2.6.

Does such severe language mean that those identified as antichrists were never really 'of us'? In seeking an answer to this question three things should be remembered. First, it is clear that the writer is concerned that those who are currently part of the community's fellowship might be susceptible to the deception of the antichrists. In 2 John 8 the Elder can speak of this as losing the full reward for which one has worked. Such language suggests that it would be incorrect to conclude that all those who might follow the lead of the antichrists were at no time 'of us'. Second, it is not uncommon for the writer of 1 John to state things in the starkest (almost hyperbolic) fashion possible to make clear his point. For example, after affirming that a Paraclete is available for believers who sin (2.2), the author asserts those who are born of God do not sin (3.9), before taking up the issue of sin and the believer again near the book's end (5.16-18). This mode of discourse at least allows for the fact that at one time those now identified as antichrists may indeed have been believers in Jesus.[73] Third, such an understanding would come as no surprise to readers of the Fourth Gospel who are familiar with a variety of individuals at different locations on the journey of belief. There are disciples who truly believe (Jn 2.11), 'believers' whom Jesus does not believe (2.23-24), disciples who do not believe (6.64-66), secret disciples owing to the fear of the Jews (19.38), and believing Jews whom Jesus calls children of the Devil (8.31, 44). It is only after a steady parade of a variety of individuals that Jesus reveals the criterion for true discipleship, 'If you remain in my word you are truly my disciples' (8.31). Such an emphasis would hardly be lost on the readers of 1 Jn 2.19, 'For if they were of us, they would have remained with us'. Such language also hearkens back to the necessity of maintaining proper fellowship with the writer and his community, who has fellowship with both 'the Father and his Son Jesus Christ' (1.3).

Rather than being overly discouraged by the depletion of their numbers owing to the departure of the antichrists, the readers are encouraged that even these troubling events did not happen by chance but were in accord with the divine will. This is conveyed in the Greek text by a construction (an ellipsis) where part of the sentence must be supplied by the reader. Very literally the verse reads, 'but in order that it might be manifested that none of them were of us…' The reader must supply the words 'they went out from us'. The end result is twofold. On the one hand, there is the drawing of a clear line of demarcation between the Johannine believers and the antichrists; none of the antichrists were 'of us'. On the other hand, these words reassure the readers that by this revelation of the antichrists the will of God was accomplished.

Verses 20-23. Having begun this major section (2.18-27) with a discussion of the antichrists and their relationship with the community (vv. 18-19), the focus now shifts to readers and their knowledge of the truth. This subsection (vv. 20-23) is the first of three that begin with the emphatic second person plural 'you'. On this occasion, its appearance signals a change in focus from the antichrists to those faithful in the community

---

73   Smalley, *1, 2, 3 John*, p. 103.

and prepares the readers for the other uses of the emphatic 'you' in vv. 24 and 27.

If the antichrists may be defined by the fact that they are no longer part of the community (and never were 'of us'), the readers are defined by the fact that they have an anointing from the Holy One. While it is never stated that the antichrists do not have an anointing, the contrast which the appearance of the emphatic second person plural 'you' causes may imply as much. At the least, such emphasis would suggest that the readers' anointing is not inferior to any anointing that may have been claimed by the antichrists.

The Greek term translated 'anointing' (χρῖσμα) occurs only three times in the New Testament with all of its appearances in this section of 1 John. The readers may very well see a play on words in the use of this term for its stem lies behind the word 'Christ' (Χριστός) as well as antichrist (ἀντίχριστος). It is this connection that perhaps may explain its usage here. Given the fact that the word Christ means 'anointed one' and that reference is made to the Spirit's descent upon Jesus in Jn 1.32-33, it would seem likely that reference to the believer's 'anointing' in 1 Jn 2.20 is closely associated with the activity of the Holy Spirit. A comparison of the function of the 'anointing' in 1 John and the function of the Paraclete in the Fourth Gospel bears out this understanding of 'anointing'. Both are spoken of as being received by (Jn 14.17; 1 Jn 2.27), abiding in (Jn 14.17; 1 Jn 2.27) and teaching all things to (Jn 14.26, 1 Jn 2.20, 27) the believers.[74] As followers of 'the anointed one' the believers are reminded that they themselves have an 'anointing'.

This anointing is from 'the Holy One'. Again, it is not altogether clear how the reader would understand this phrase as in the Johannine world it could have reference either to God the Father or to Jesus. From the use of 'he' in v. 25, it appears that the primary reference to the Holy One in v. 20 is to Jesus. Such an understanding would certainly be in keeping with the fact that in the Fourth Gospel Jesus is called 'the Holy One of God' by Peter (Jn 6.69). If the readers understand this anointing as coming from Jesus, it would also be in keeping with the fact that in the Fourth Gospel Jesus promises to send the Paraclete to his disciples (15.26; 16.7). However, given John's love of ambiguity, the fact that in the Gospel the Father is also involved in the sending of the Paraclete (14.16-17, 26), and that in the Septuagint, God can be referred to as 'the Holy One' (Hab. 3.3), one should not be too quick to exclude perhaps a (secondary) reference to the Father.

The purpose of this anointing is related to knowledge on the believers'

---

74   Cf. esp. Brown, *The Epistles of John*, pp. 345-46.

part. But at this point, the text of 1 John becomes uncertain, with ancient manuscripts offering two different readings. Some manuscripts read, 'And you have an anointing, and *you know all things* (πάντα)', while others offer, 'And you have an anointing, and *you all know* (πάντες)'.⁷⁵ On the one hand, if the later reading is followed, the words may be a response to claims the antichrists may have been making about possessing a superior knowledge, claims which would imply that only those in their circle had access to such knowledge. On this view, the readers are told that they 'all' (each and every one) 'know' as a result of their anointing. Thus, the alleged claims of the antichrists would be proven to be unfounded. If this reading is adopted, the use of 'all' (πάντες) in v. 20 serves as a sharp contrast with its previous appearance in v. 19 where the term is translated 'none'. On the other hand, if the former reading is followed, the emphasis is upon the readers' 'complete' knowledge as a result of the anointing which they have from the Holy One, a knowledge which would make any additional teaching (from the antichrists) unnecessary. On this view, the anointing functions just as Jesus says the Paraclete will function, 'That One will teach you all things (πάντα)' (Jn 14.26). Thus, the readers are reminded that they are in the exact situation Jesus foretold and, as such, should not be susceptible to the deception of the antichrists. Evidence that the reading 'you know all things' is to be preferred may also be found in v. 27, where the same general sense is affirmed, 'the anointing teaches you concerning all things', which is followed by the theme of the Truth and the lie, just as is the case in vv. 20 and 21.

Verse 21 seeks to make clear to the readers that they, as a result of their anointing, are knowledgeable of the truth. This is accomplished in part by the reappearance of the (aorist) past tense 'I have written', which was introduced in 2.14. The readers' thoughts would likely go back to the first appearance of this phrase in 2.14 where there is a close connection with their knowledge, as children and fathers, of the Father and that which was from beginning respectively. It is not surprising, then, that the issue of the readers' knowledge closely follows the phrase, 'I have written to you' in 2.21 as well. Clearly, here the readers are addressed as those who know the Truth, not as those who lack knowledge of it. At least two things are accomplished by this approach. First, the readers are confirmed in their belief and knowledge, perhaps against the claims of the antichrists that they alone possess a superior wisdom. Second, the groundwork is laid for admonitions with regard to the readers' future course of action given later in the passage. Earlier, the readers' knowl-

---

75 Manuscript support for πάντα is broad and rather early, while that for πάντες is quite early but somewhat narrow.

edge of God was closely tied to keeping his commands (2.3-4), which is manifested in the perfection of love (2.5). At various points throughout this earlier section, the actions of the opponents reveal that their claims are false and that they are devoid of the truth ('we do not do the Truth' — 1.6, 'the Truth is not in us' — 1.8, 'his Word is not in us' — 1.10). The appearance of similar language in 2.21 ('I have not written to you because/that you do not know the Truth') makes clear to the readers that the writer does not regard them as he does the opponents as being devoid of the Truth. Rather, he emphatically affirms their knowledge of (and relationship to) the Truth. Reappearance of the language of deception and lies, which is prominent earlier in the book (1.6, 8, 10; 2.4), underscores the contrast between the readers' knowledge and the teaching of the antichrists. No lie has its origin in the Truth. Lies and the Truth are as irreconcilable as Light and darkness (1.5-6), as love and hate (2.9-11). The primary point of this verse is that the knowledge of all things which the anointing has brought to the readers is sufficient to enable them to discern between the lies of the antichrists and the Truth. As before, it should be observed that the term 'Truth' is likely to be closely associated in the readers' minds with Jesus, thus preparing for the transition to the christological discussion that follows.

Verse 22 begins rather abruptly with a rhetorical question which might startle the reader somewhat given the fact that in the Greek text there are no connecting particles standing between the various clauses. The question itself reveals something of the content of the anitchrists' deceptive teaching. 'Who is the liar', who stands in such sharp contrast to the Truth (v. 21), 'except the one who denies that Jesus is the Christ'? The appearance of the words, 'the liar', reminds the reader of what has come before in v. 21 and at the same time conveys something about the magnitude of the lies involved. While it is possible to take 'the liar' as having reference to the liar *par excellence*, it likely appears in this form for the purposes of emphasis and contextualization. Such an understanding is in keeping with the grammatical emphasis of the following phrase which may be translated literally as 'except the one who denies that Jesus is not the Christ'. The appearance of this double negative in the Greek text, which cannot be adequately reproduced in a grammatically correct English translation, conveys to the readers the sense of the absoluteness and completeness of the antichrists' denial. In fact, the words 'Jesus is not the Christ' may even be very close to a verbatim quotation of the antichrists' words. Thus, by means of this question the reader learns that there is a christological dimension to the antichrists' deception which is no doubt connected to the earlier statements about the contradictions between their claims and their walk.

But what exactly is meant by the words 'Jesus is not the Christ'? Unfortunately, the Epistles themselves do not provide a complete answer to this question. However, despite the ambiguity that surrounds the content and meaning of the antichrists' claims, a few aspects of their view may be discerned. While it is clear that they are denying Jesus is the Christ, it would be improper to take this statement to mean that they rejected Jesus altogether. Rather, it should be remembered that the antichrists were at one time indistinguishable from other members of the community and so would have had some degree of appreciation of and commitment to the person of Jesus. Thus, their belief that Jesus is not the Messiah would not necessitate a complete rejection of Jesus, as is true of 'the Jews' in the Fourth Gospel. Nonetheless, Jesus is not believed to be the Messiah. What is the basis of this assessment? In all likelihood, this understanding is related to the fact that the antichrists are not confessing 'Jesus coming in the flesh' (2 Jn 7). As noted earlier, although the precise meaning of 2 John 7 is not clear, it does seem to be sufficiently evident that the antichrists' view is related in one way or another to the Incarnation. If their position be interpreted to mean that Jesus never came in the flesh (an understanding 1 Jn 4.2 seems to support) then the implication might be that since Jesus was not, properly speaking, a human, then he could not be the (Jewish) Messiah. There is some evidence, in close temporal proximity to the Johannine Epistles, for the existence of false teachers who denied that Jesus was clothed in the flesh. This is found in Ignatius' letter to the *Smyrnaeans* (5) which was written around 110-115 CE. However, it is not clear whether these individuals reject Jesus as the Messiah on that basis.[76] While it is possible to go further afield in search of historical analogies,[77] perhaps it is enough at this point simply to look in the directions to which the Epistles themselves point.

The one who utters the lie, 'Jesus is not the Christ', is the antichrist. While this reference to the antichrist might be taken as pointing to the eschatological opponent of Jesus, nothing in the Johannine Epistles warrants such an interpretive move. Rather, *the* antichrist is the one who

---

76   It is interesting that Ignatius goes on (*Smyrnaens* 6.2) to describe these individuals as not believing in the blood of Christ and not being concerned with love, attitudes which the false teachers of 1 John apparently share.

77   It is not uncommon for commentators to identify the Johannine antichrists with the teaching of Cerinthus, which Irenaeus describes in his *Against Heresies* 1.26.1. Cerinthus is said to have taught that Jesus was the human son of Mary and Joseph, a man more righteous, prudent and wise than other people. At his baptism the Christ descended upon him in the form of a dove, which led to the proclamation of the unknown father and the performing of miracles. Before Jesus suffered and died, the Christ departed from Jesus. One of the problems with this identification is that it does not seem to agree with the description of the false teaching as contained in 1 John.

denies that Jesus is the Christ. As 2.18 indicates, many antichrists have come, all of whom no doubt share in this lie. What is more, the one who denies that Jesus is the Christ, that is, the antichrist, is the one who denies both the Father and the Son. Although a bit more on the rationale for this statement is given in the following verses, here it is important to note that denial of Jesus as the Christ carries with it a denial of the Father and the Son. Such an observation should not come as a complete surprise to the reader given the emphasis placed upon the essential unity of God the Father and his Son Jesus Christ in other places in the Epistles (cf. 2 Jn 3, 9; 1 Jn 1.3). This statement makes even more apparent that the position of the antichrists stands in diametric opposition to the community's teaching, which can be summarized in part by the purpose statement found near the conclusion of the Fourth Gospel (20.31), 'But these things have been written in order that you might believe that *Jesus is the Christ, the Son of God...*' In this light, the teaching of the antichrists is clearly identified as in the realm of the lie and not the Truth.

Verse 23, the last verse in this subsection (2.20-23), offers an explanation of why denial of Jesus as the Christ entails a denial of both the Father and the Son. Structurally, this is accomplished by means of a perfect antithetical parallelism, in this case a construction where the main point is stated both negatively and positively. The negative statement comes first, 'Each one who denies the Son neither has the Father'. One of the first things to attract the readers' attention is the fact that in this sentence the normal order, 'Father and Son', is inverted with Son standing before Father. The effect of this move is to focus the readers' attention on the importance of Jesus and to underscore the fact that denial of the Son entails denial of the Father. While the antichrists might well disagree with this assessment, the readers know that the Son and the Father are one (Jn 10.30); that the Son who is in the bosom of the Father makes him known (1.18); that without the Son one cannot know or see the Father (14.7); that if one comes to the Father it must be through the Son (14.6); that the one who does not honor the Son does not honor the Father (5.23); and that the one who hates the Son hates the Father (15.23). Therefore, a denial of the Son means that one is cut off from the Father and, despite arguments to the contrary, cannot make valid claims to 'have' him.

In the Johannine literature the term 'deny' (ἀρνέομαι) functions in contexts where one's public acknowledgment of Jesus is at issue, often against the background of possible suffering and/or persecution. Those who do not deny include John the Baptist (Jn 1.20) and members of the churches in Pergamum (Rev. 2.13) and Philadelphia (Rev. 3.8), while Peter serves as the example of one who denies Jesus (Jn 13.38; 18.25, 27).

In 1 John to deny Jesus means to reject identification with him, regarding his role in salvific significance as inconsequential. The one who denies the Son 'does not have the Father'. The readers are not completely unprepared for the expression 'does not have' as they have seen one very close to it in 2 John 9. Here as there, the expression seems to echo covenantal language conveying the idea of a personal and intimate relationship with God. The ideas of 'knowing' and 'remaining', seen earlier, may not be too far removed from that of 'having'.[78] Thus, the one who denies Jesus does not have a personal and intimate relationship with God.

This negative statement is balanced structurally by a positive one. In contrast to those who deny the Son, and consequently do not have a relationship with the Father, those who confess the Son also have the Father. If to deny the Son is to reject identification with him and treat his role in terms of salvific significance as inconsequential, to confess him is to acknowledge identification with him, embracing the salvation which his blood makes possible. Therefore, the readers are told yet again that a relationship with the Son is absolutely essential in order to have a relationship with the Father.[79]

Verses 24-26. The next subsection of 1 Jn 2.18-27 follows, consisting of vv. 24-26. This subsection, as the one that precedes (vv. 20-23) and the one that follows (v. 27), begins with an emphatic use of the second person plural pronoun 'you' (ὑμεῖς). By this means an intentional contrast is being drawn between the antichrists who deny the Son and the readers who confess him.

Structurally, v. 24 is a stanza or strophe with three lines which may be divided in the following fashion:

> Let that which you have heard from the beginning remain in you;
> If that which you have heard from the beginning remains in you,
> you also remain in the Son and the Father.[80]

---

78   The idea of 'having' Jesus or God is found in various early Christian documents which appear to originate in close temporal proximity to the Johannine Epistles. Cf. the writings of Ignatius (*Magnesians* 12.1; *Romans* 6.3), Hermas (*Mandate* 12.4.3), and 2 *Clement* (2.3). Cf. Brown, *The Epistles of John*, p. 354.
79   In the Fourth Gospel the confession of Jesus is hampered owing to the fear of the Jews who had decided that any who confessed Jesus would be expelled from the synagogue (Jn 9.22; 12.42). In the Gospel according to Matthew (10.32-33) Jesus says, 'Therefore, whoever confesses me before men, even I will confess him before my Father who is in heaven; but whoever denies me before men, even I will deny him before my Father who is in heaven.' Cf. also Rev. 3.5 where Jesus says, 'The one who is victorious will be dressed in white clothing and I will not erase his name from the book of life and I will confess his name before my Father and before his angels.'
80   The strategic significance of remaining is made clear in v. 24 as the term (μένω)

As can be seen, in the first line of this verse the readers are instructed to allow that which they have heard from the beginning to remain in them. Given the immediate context of this verse and its broader Johannine context, it would seem certain that the phrase 'that which you heard from the beginning' has reference to the teaching of and about Jesus. This understanding is likely owing to the things which the readers of 1 John would associate with 'the beginning'. Specifically, the reader knows that the bedrock of the community's faith rests upon 'that which was from the beginning' (1.1), that the 'fathers' of the community have known 'the one from the beginning' (2.13, 14), and that the love command was heard from the beginning (2 Jn 6). Given the emphasis placed in the immediate context (1 Jn 2.22-23) upon the confession that 'Jesus is the Christ', it would appear virtually certain that the readers would understand the instruction to 'let that which you have heard from the beginning remain in you' as having reference to the community's belief that Jesus is the Christ (cf. esp. Jn 20.30-31). In these words the readers would no doubt see a contrast between the certainty of the teaching they possess (which goes back to the beginning) and the suspect teaching of the antichrists which appears to be of somewhat recent origin. The idea that this belief or teaching should remain in the readers is reminiscent of 1 Jn 4.14 where the readers are told 'the word of God remains in you', and of Jesus' words in Jn 15.7, 'if my words remain (μείνῃ) in you'. Thus, the readers are likely to equate the teaching they received from the beginning with the Word of God and/or Jesus.

The idea expressed in the first line continues to be of interest as it reappears in the second line of the stanza in a somewhat modified form. What was expressed as a command in the first line becomes part of a conditional clause in the second and third lines – which grammatically stand together. The appearance of this conditional clause (ἐὰν with the subjunctive) conveys to the reader both the challenge of fulfilling the condition and the anticipation of its fulfillment.[81] Thus, the second line of this stanza is not mere repetition but prepares the reader for the third line.

The third line of the stanza reveals that if the condition is fulfilled ('If that which remains in you from the beginning'), the result is that 'you remain in the Son and the Father'. Several observations should be offered about this line. First, it is clear that the language of 'remaining' conveys the idea of intimacy. Thus, those who allow 'that which they heard from the beginning to *remain*' in them have a personal, intimate

occurs three times in this one verse, once in each of the three lines.
81   So Bultmann, *The Johannine Epistles*, p. 40, and Smalley, *1, 2, 3 John*, p. 119.

relationship with the Son and the Father. Secondly, it appears that the ideas of 'remaining', 'having' and 'being in' are functional equivalents in 1 John. By this means, the lines of demarcation earlier drawn between those who 'have the Son and the Father' and those who do not are underscored. Third, this third line emphasizes for the readers that contrary to the teaching of the antichrists, the readers are in a very assured position—they remain in both the Son and the Father. Not only do they have an 'anointing' which insures that they know all things, but they also have the word they have heard from the beginning which insures their relationship with the Son and the Father.

Verse 25 gives the appearance of both continuing the thought of the previous verses and at the same time pointing to that which follows. On the one hand, the connections between the content of the verse with that of v. 24 is clear, while on the other hand, the author does on occasion use 'And this is…' as a means of introducing a new idea, as in 1.5 and 3.23. However, in 2.25 the choice appears to be a false one for this verse both continues the thought of the previous verse and points to that which follows.[82] Consequently, the content of 'this' in v. 25 is not unrelated to the ideas of 'remaining', 'having' and 'believing in' which appear to have converged in vv. 23-24. Thus, as v. 25 begins, the reader anticipates discovering even more about the nature of this 'remaining' and 'having'.

In what follows, the reader is not disappointed, for here a significant term is introduced which appears nowhere else in the Johannine literature. The significance of the new term is clear from the fact that in this verse, both the subject and the verb are from the same root word, 'And this is the promise (ἐπαγγελία) that he promised (ἐπηγγείλατο) to us'. The appearance of this unique term invites the reader to ponder its meaning by drawing on the Fourth Gospel in new and fresh ways. By this point the reader is not troubled by the ambiguity of the identity of 'he' who promised. In point of fact, this very ambiguity encourages the broadest possible understanding of the promise here discussed, as it calls upon the readers to draw upon the Fourth Gospel in creatively new ways. It comes as no surprise that eternal life is connected to this promise at the end of v. 25, for throughout the Fourth Gospel Jesus often speaks of the availability of eternal life and the role he and the Father have in it (cf. Jn 3.15-16, 18, 36; 5.24, 6.40, 47, 51, 54, 58). When read in the light of 1 Jn 1.2, the reader is struck by the fact that eternal life in 2.25 is promised by Eternal Life himself (1.2). Thus, there is little chance that the reader would see Jesus or his teaching as being very far removed from eternal

---

82   The phrase, 'And this is…' functions in the same transitional way in 5.11 and 5.14.

life. Eternal life, then, is perhaps one way of describing what it means to remain in the Son and the Father and to allow that which they heard from the beginning to remain in them.

This subsection (vv. 24-26) comes to a close in v. 26. By the phrase, 'These things I have written', the reader is alerted to at least two things. First, this phrase reminds the reader of the earlier appearances of 'I have written' where there is an emphasis upon the reader's knowledge of the Father (2.14) and the Truth (Jesus). Thus, there is an expectation that the phrase will function in a similar fashion on this occasion as well. But in 2.26, the emphasis is upon those who actively oppose the Truth, 'those who are deceiving you'. Second, the earlier appearances of 'I have written' both indicate a development of thought within the book and at the same time are a means by which continuity with that which comes before is maintained. In this verse the development of thought is that the 'antichrists' and 'liars' are now called 'deceivers'. The continuity with what comes before is maintained by the fact that as early as 1 Jn 1.8 the idea of deception among those who make false claims is known to the reader. It is perhaps not without significance that just as deception and lies are associated in this passage, in 1.6-10 the idea of deception (1.8) is surrounded by that of lies (1.6, 10). While the reader has known of the existence of deceivers since 2 John 7, where their coming is foretold, a sense of the gravity of the current situation is conveyed by their description in this verse. The phrase 'those who are deceiving' is a present tense participle which conveys the idea that these individuals are habitually attempting to deceive John's readers. Given their success in deceiving former members of the community, the threat they pose is all too real. However serious the situation, the author does not convey a sense of desperation but rather his words convey a sense of confidence in the midst of adversity.

Verse 27. The third and final subsection in this portion of 1 John consists of a single verse. Like vv. 20 and 24 it too begins with the second person plural pronoun 'you' standing in an emphatic position at the beginning of the sentence. As in the two previous subsections so here such emphasis contrasts in a very dramatic fashion the readers with the opponents, who are called deceivers in this verse. This verse is not only tied to vv. 20 and 24 by means of similar beginnings, but by making reference to the key terms 'anointing' (v. 20) and 'remaining' (v. 24), it ties the entire section together.

In response to the danger posed by 'those who are deceiving you', the readers are reminded yet again of the 'anointing' they have received. While much of what was said in v. 20 is assumed here, v. 27 is not simply a restatement of the previous discussion. In point of fact, several new moves are made in this final subsection. First, the readers have been told previously that they 'have an anointing from the Holy One'. In this verse they are told that they have 'received' (ἐλάβετε) the anointing. Such language not only suggests that a specific reception is in mind, but also reminds the reader of the command Jesus gave to his disciples in Jn 20.22 to 'receive the Holy Spirit', the fulfillment of which appears to have taken place outside the narrative of the Fourth Gospel.[83] Thus, it is likely that the readers are being reminded of their own Spirit baptism by the appearance of the term 'received'. Second, while v. 20 states that the readers 'have' an anointing, in v. 27 the readers are told that the anointing 'remains' in them. In this one statement, two of the dominant themes found in vv. 20 and 24 are combined underscoring the close connection that exists between the 'anointing' and 'that which you have heard from the beginning'. Thus, 'the anointing' and 'that heard from the beginning' are not to be played off against one another but are understood in a complementary fashion. As in its earlier occurrences, reference to remaining carries with it the idea of intimacy. Third, the more general statement of v. 20, 'You have an anointing and know all things', gives way to a more detailed discussion of the teaching role of the anointing in v. 27. Not only do the readers know all things, as a result of the anointing, but they do not have need that anyone should teach them. By means of this bold statement a couple of things are accomplished. On the one hand, the polemic against the antichrists and deceivers continues by making clear that there is absolutely nothing which the false teachers have to teach that the readers need to learn. On the other hand, this statement continues to underscore the fact that the role of the Paraclete as teacher within the Johannine community is unrivalled. This statement is consistent with the Johannine attitude toward teaching generally, a title and function which is reserved positively for Jesus (Jn 1.38, 49; 3.2; 4.31; 6.25, 59; 7.14, 28, 35; 8.20; 9.2; 11.8, 28; 13.13-14; 18.20; 20.16; 2 Jn 9), the Father (8.28), and the Paraclete (14.26), and negatively for Nicodemus (3.10), Balaam (Rev. 2.14), the Nicolatians (2.15) and Jezebel (2.20; 24).[84] In fact the point of 1 Jn 2.27 is not too far removed from Jesus'

---

83   On this interpretation cf. J.C. Thomas, 'The Spirit in the Fourth Gospel: Narrative Explorations', in T.L. Cross and E. Powery (eds.), *Spirit and Mind: Essays on Informed Pentecostalism* (Festschrift D.N. Bowdle; Lanham, MD: University Press of America, 2000), pp. 87-104.

84   The only exceptions to this trend are John the Baptist, who is once called Rabbi (Jn 3.26), and the man born blind (9.34), who is asked with derision by the Jews if he being born wholly in sin would teach them.

quotation of Scripture in Jn 6.45, 'And they are all taught by God'.[85]

Does this stark statement mean that there is to be no place in the community for the role of teacher? In one sense, this is precisely what the phrase means, for to think otherwise would be to ignore the unrivalled position of the Paraclete, the negative assessment of nearly all (human) teachers and the egalitarian nature of the community. However, as with many aspects of the Johannine Epistles, things are not always as straightforward as they seem. For one thing, despite the protestations to the contrary, the Elder does a fair amount of teaching in 1 John. While it is true that he avoids teaching terminology except with reference to the anointing, much of what he says would technically qualify as instruction. Two things should be remembered in trying to understand this paradox. First, this is not the only place in 1 John where tensions exist that on the surface would strike one as contradictory ideas. For example, after acknowledging the possibility that Christians might sin (1.6–2.2), in 3.4-10 it will be stated flatly that one who is born of God does not sin. The book will then close with an admonition for believers to pray for those who sin in order that they might be forgiven. Such a tension indicates that it is possible for the author to teach while denying the need for a teacher.[86] Second, it is altogether likely that the kind of instruction which the author shares with his readers is understood in the community, not so much to be teaching, as witnessing.[87] Such terminology is much more at home in the Johannine literature and might offer more of an insider's way of thinking about the distinctions here being made with regard to teaching.

The rest of the sentence presents several interpretive challenges to the reader, in part, owing to a difficult if not clumsy grammatical construction. The main question is whether the sentence should be divided into parts or be approached as one extended and complicated sentence. On the whole it seems best to take the second half of v. 27 as constituting one extended sentence, the main part of which is found in the first and last clauses, 'But as his anointing teaches you concerning all things… remain in him/it'. The middle clause 'and is true and is not a lie' would be viewed as a parenthetical statement with the clause 'and just as he taught you' picking up on the previous 'as'.

In the face of opposition by those who seek to deceive the readers, they are encouraged to remain in the teaching that comes from the anointing. The strong conjunction 'but' (ἀλλ') serves to contrast the

---

85 For the suggestion cf. Rensberger, *1 John, 2 John, 3 John*, p. 83.
86 As Marshall, *The Epistles of John*, p. 163, points out.
87 For this suggestion cf. Brown, *The Epistles of John*, p. 375.

teacher(s) of which the readers have no need with the teacher they do need. The one who teaches them is 'his anointing', a rather clear reference to 'the Holy One's anointing' from v. 20. In the Fourth Gospel Jesus taught that the Paraclete would 'lead the disciples into all truth' (16.13) and 'teach them all things' (14.26); now his anointing does just that. The present tense verb 'teaches' no doubt conveys the idea that the anointing continues to be active in teaching the community. But before the reader has a chance to digest these powerful words, a parenthetical statement breaks into the sentence emphasizing the fact that the teaching that comes via the anointing 'is true and is not a lie'. By this means, the trustworthiness of the anointing's teaching is affirmed, as is the continuity between the content of the anointing's teaching and the person of Jesus, who is the Truth. At the same time, the deceitful nature of the false teaching, hinted as early as 1.6-10, is exposed as is its relationship to the Devil, who is the father of lies according to Jesus (Jn 8.44). Although the readers may be in danger of getting lost in the parenthetical statement, their attention is quickly brought back to the primary clause in this part of v. 27 by the words 'and just as he taught you'. Two things are of particular interest about this phrase. First, the Greek word translated 'just as' (καθὼς) makes clear that the teaching mentioned in this clause is very much the same as that mentioned in the first part of this long sentence. Second, the (aorist) past tense verb 'taught' replaces the present tense verb 'teaches' found earlier. The change in tense may be a way of tying the present teaching activity of the anointing with its past activity and given the fact that the Paraclete's teaching is in conformity to that of Jesus it may even point back to 'that which was heard in the beginning'. Regardless of when they are taught, the teaching of the anointing is trustworthy. Therefore, the readers are instructed to remain in the teaching of the one who remains in them. This final clause is where the emphasis of the sentence lies[88] and is yet another example of 1 John's integrated understanding of theology and ethics.

Reflection and Response—Part Five

Reflection

Despite the presence of deceivers and antichrists in the community, the believers are encouraged by the fact, not that they have human teachers to counter the effects of the false teachers, but that they have received an anointing that enables them to be certain about a variety of things. This

---

88 Strecker, *The Johannine Letters*, p. 76.

anointing with the Holy Spirit comes from the Anointed One, who in this passage is called the Holy One. Fulfilling the promises made about the Paraclete by Jesus in the Fourth Gospel, this anointing insures that the believers know all things. The believers are encouraged to remain in this anointing for by it they know all things and have no need for anyone to teach them. This anointing, which is true, is not a lie. It stands in contrast to the deceivers and the deception of their false teaching. In contrast to those outside the community, the believers have been taught by the Spirit. It is in this teaching that they are to remain. They can be secure, knowing that they are in the truth.

What is the significance of the anointing for us? Several questions are offered to facilitate reflection on this topic.

What role does the Spirit play in the Church today? In what ways is the Spirit active as teacher in the Church? What specific teaching functions may be attributed to the Spirit? Are there attempts to domesticate the Spirit? How do individuals try to control the anointing? Why are such concerns about the Spirit's teaching activity present? What are the dangers involved in assigning a significant teaching role to the Spirit? How may one discern the difference between authentic and inauthentic teaching of the Spirit?

In what ways have I personally experienced the teaching ministry of the Holy Spirit? Exactly how has the Spirit been active? Are there any criteria by which I am able to distinguish between true and false teaching attributed to the Spirit in worship or other settings? Through what means has the Spirit functioned as teacher in my life? How sensitive am I to this teaching activity? What obstacles prevent me from being open to his teaching? When am I the most comfortable with his direction?

Response

First, identify those times of which you are absolutely certain the Holy Spirit acted as a teacher in your life.

Second, assess the content of the teaching in light of that which is known to be authentic teaching from the biblical text.

Third, with other members of the community respond in concrete ways to the things which the Spirit makes clear.

Fourth, in consultation with leaders in your local church, seek ways to create a community atmosphere open to the teaching ministry of the Holy Spirit.

1 John 2.28–3.10

As the reader comes to the next major section of 1 John several things become apparent. First, several textual indicators reveal that 2.28–3.10 stands together as a literary unit. The passage is bounded near its beginning (2.29) and end (3.9) with reference to 'those who are born of God'. There is frequent reference to the term 'children' (τέκνα) in these verses. Emphasis is given to the contrast between 'those who are born of God' and 'those who are children of the Devil'. In addition, there are seven occurrences of the construction 'each one who' (πᾶς ὁ) followed by a participle (2.29; 3.3, 4, 6a,b, 9, 10).[89] Taken together, these indicators suggest that these verses rather clearly hold together in a special way. Second, this section continues some of the emphases and ideas of previous sections by use of 'remaining', 'love', 'children of God', 'manifestation' of Jesus, 'sin and righteousness', 'deceive' and 'the Devil'. Third, at the same time, this section develops previous themes, like eschatology, in new and creative ways, while introducing new ideas and themes such as 'confidence before God' and 'the return' of Jesus. Finally, the reader also observes that this section falls into the following subsections each beginning with a term of endearment: 2.28–3.1 ('little children'), 3.2-6 ('beloved') and 3.7-10 ('little children').

1 John 2.28–3.1

The words 'and now' (καὶ νῦν) in v. 28 accomplish several things. As in 2.18 the phrase marks a new beginning in the movement of the book. In addition, the words have a transitional function indicating movement from the previous section to the new one. Finally, the reader sees some temporal significance in the phrase, for 'and now' acquires additional significance in light of 'the last hour' discussed in the previous section (2.18). Once again, the readers are called 'little children' (τεκνία) as they had been earlier in 1 John (2.2, 12). This term of endearment, which always appears in a form of direct address in this book, is especially significant owing to the fact that Jesus used it to refer to the disciples in the Farewell Discourse in the Fourth Gospel (13.33). No doubt, such language reassures the readers, coming as it does on the heels of a section devoted to a discussion of antichrists and deceivers.

Not only do the words 'and now' hearken back to the previous section, but the following phrase 'remain in him' is identical to the phrase with which v. 27 concludes. Therefore, the reader cannot help but

---

89 While nine participles are preceded by articles in this section, two of these constructions are not preceded by the word πᾶς.

think of that which follows as connected to the previous discussion. Nor can the reader ignore the emphasis represented by such repetition; these are very important words. While there is some question as to whether the phrase 'remain in him/it' in v. 27 is best understood as a statement or a command, either of which is grammatically possible in Greek, in v. 28 it is very clear that the phrase is a command: the readers are being instructed to 'remain in him'. Growing out of the admonitions about the threat of false teaching and the presence of the anointing which teaches the readers all things, this command puts the readers on notice that the antidote to false teaching and deception is remaining in him. The close and intimate relationship conveyed by the word 'remain' would surely remind the reader of Jesus' words in the Fourth Gospel (15.4), 'Remain in me, even as I remain in you', which precede his teaching about the vine and the branches. Remaining is an absolute necessity.

The reason for this command to 'remain in him' is spelled out by means of a purpose (ἵνα) clause, which is particularly rich in meaning: 'in order that when he is manifested we may have confidence and not be ashamed before him at his coming'. The phrase 'when he appears' in the Greek text is very literally 'if he appears'. But the English translation 'if' does not convey the meaning of the Greek word (ἐάν) in this sentence. In the Greek text there is no question about whether he *will* be manifested. The question is *when* this will take place. This understanding is much like the word's use in the phrase 'when (ἐάν) I die', found in Tob. 4.3. The manifestation of Jesus is familiar to the reader of 1 John for the word appears twice in 1.2. From this previous occurrence, which draws heavily upon the term's use in the Fourth Gospel, the reader understands it to be especially connected to the unfolding revelatory purposes of God, culminating in the resurrection appearances of Jesus to the disciples (21.1, 14). In 1 John the term is also closely associated with the author's (and those who stand with him) testimony about Jesus. Here the reader is called upon not only to contemplate the richness of the past revelatory events, but also to anticipate additional revelatory experiences which still lie in the future. The clear implication being that Jesus, who had been manifest before, will be manifest again to those who believe in him. Such an idea is obviously in accord with the teaching of Jesus in the Fourth Gospel where promises of resurrection 'at the last day' combined with the promise to return for his disciples (14.3) carry with them the (implied) promise of additional manifestation(s), even though the word 'manifest' is not used in precisely this way in the Fourth Gospel. The idea that the readers would be making this interpretive move is supported by the general eschatological character of the context as they have already learned that 'this is the last hour' (1 Jn 2.18).

It is important to remain in him so that when he is manifested 'we might have confidence'. The reader is familiar with the term here translated 'confidence' (παρρησίαν) from its numerous occurrences in the Fourth Gospel, where it is used primarily in the sense of 'openly' or 'plainly'. The first of its occurrences in 1 John reveals the shift in meaning the term undergoes from the Fourth Gospel to 1 John. Here the readers encounter it as a source of assurance in the face of the manifestation of Jesus. Their 'remaining in him' enables them, rather than being uncertain of their position, to greet his return as hopeful and joyful – as children would greet their father. Thus, understandings of confidence which focus on the ability to speak with candor and boldness especially in the presence of a superior are not far off the mark,[90] except that here the assurance involves the return of one who has been called God. But such is the assurance of one who remains in him.

The other main part of the purpose clause is more difficult for the reader to understand for it is a bit more complicated. The phrase in question is open to two somewhat different interpretations. The phrase can be translated 'and that we might not be ashamed at his coming'. This translation suggests a psychological understanding of the word 'ashamed'. On this reading, the shame is generated by the individual in the light of the appearance of Jesus. In support of this interpretation is a preposition (ἀπ') which normally means 'from' or 'away from', and the fact that the verb can be taken as a middle voice in which the subject acts on oneself. At the same time, there is reason to translate the phrase as 'and that we might not be put to shame by him at his coming'. This translation suggests a judicial context for the meaning of the phrase. Support for this understanding includes the fact that the verb might better be understood as a passive, indicating that the shame is something inflicted upon an individual. In addition, talk of 'confession' and 'denial' (2.22-23) in the preceding section with regard to the antichrists, perhaps implies that Jesus will himself confess some and deny others, a reality expressed in Rev. 3.5. Given the fact that the reader is given hints in both directions, perhaps it is not going too far to suggest that both ideas are here present. One should remain in him in order to avoid being ashamed of oneself before him and being put to shame by him. Such an under-

---

90   Perhaps it is here that the meanings of the term in the Fourth Gospel and in 1 John overlap slightly. The assurance of the one who remains in him might be related to the confidence which Jesus demonstrates in speaking 'openly' in the face of opposition in the Fourth Gospel. It was said of the early Christian martyrs that they had the confidence to speak on earth against their opponents and the confidence to speak in heaven to their God. Cf. Brown, *The Epistles of John*, p. 381.

standing fits nicely with the emerging view of the Christian life in 1 John where it is very difficult to separate divine and human roles.

The context for these ominous words is 'his coming'. Here for the first and only time in the whole of the Johannine literature the word 'parousia' appears. In antiquity the term was often used to describe the visit of a king or ruler. While its appearance here may be an indication that the readers are aware of this term, as it becomes a standard part of early Christian vocabulary to describe the return of Jesus, it is clear from its context in 1 John that the return of Jesus is in view whether or not the readers are familiar with the term. Its occurrence at this point, along with the previous mention of Jesus' manifestation and the broader context of the last hour, makes clear to the reader the significance of the admonition to remain in him. This is a time when the return of Jesus is in sight. One must remain in him or be in danger of being ashamed before him and put to shame by him.[91] It should perhaps be observed that a play on words exists in the Greek text, as the words for confidence (παρρησίαν) and appearing (παρουσίᾳ) sound very much alike.

Verse 29 both develops the thought of v. 28 and points to a major issue in those verses which follow. With the opening phrase, 'If you know that he is righteous' the readers are alerted to a couple of things. First, this phrase extends the thought of the previous verse by describing the nature of the one who is coming; this one is righteous. Earlier the reader has been told that God is 'faithful and righteous to forgive our sins and cleanse us from all unrighteousness' (1.9). Two verses later the reader learns 'we have an advocate with the Father, Jesus Christ the Righteous One' (2.1). Thus, the reader is not taken by surprise in 2.29 to find the description 'he is righteous'. This statement, as the earlier one in 2.1, is consistent with the Fourth Gospel's description of Jesus as righteous with regard to the nature of his eschatological judgment which is based upon the Father's own righteous judgment (Jn 5.30). Such a description is especially at home in 1 Jn 2.29 given the implied context of eschatological judgment in 2.28. While reference to the Father cannot be ruled out, at least in a secondary sense, it appears that primary reference is being made to Jesus in the phrase 'he is righteous'. Second, this phrase should not be taken to suggest a lack of knowledge on the reader's part

---

91   Smith, *First, Second, and Third John*, p. 75, offers these summary statements: 'As John returns to the matter of the opponents, the antichrists and deceivers, so now he again strikes the eschatological note with which he began this section. Here it no longer has an ominous ring and yet there remains more than a hint of warning (v. 28). Plainly, those who abide in Christ...will have confidence and no cause for shame at his coming. The nuance of warning overlaps a foundation of assurance.'

with regard to the statement 'he is righteous'. Rather, it is an invitation to the reader to engage in self-reflection and contemplation with regard to whether or not the reader really believes that he is righteous.[92]

If the reader knows that 'he is righteous', then the reader should also know[93] that 'each one who does righteousness has been born of him'. By this means, the readers are being reassured, in no uncertain terms, of their intimate relationship and close standing with the Father and the Son. What is true of the Father and Son in terms of character is also found to be true in the activities of the believer. Their righteous character is being revealed by their righteous actions. What is more, their righteous conduct reveals that they have been born of him (who is righteous).

As in other places in 1 John, there is some ambiguity with regard to the meaning of 'him' in this verse. It is possible to take the word with reference to Jesus since he is the subject in the verse immediately preceding this one. However, the reader is now accustomed to the fact that the author moves rather easily between his references to the Father and the Son. This stylistic tendency together with the fact that in the Johannine literature believers are spoken of as children of God all but assures the reader that a shift in attention from the Son to the Father has occurred. Reference to being born of him introduces into 1 John an idea that becomes prominent as the book moves forward. The reader no doubt understands such imagery in the light of the Fourth Gospel where it is revealed that those who believe in him are given authority to become children of God, a birth that takes place through God's own activity (Jn 1.12). It is later revealed that such a birth (from above) takes place by means of the Spirit (3.3-5). Thus, all those who do righteousness reveal that they are children of God, born of the Spirit. This accounts for the similarity in character between God and his children.

Before leaving 2.29, it should perhaps be noted that this verse contains the first of seven occurrences of the construction 'each one who...' (πᾶς ὁ) in this section, revealing something of the significance of the phrase, 'each one who does righteousness'.

1 John 3.1. In the previous verse the reader is encouraged to engage in self-reflection and contemplation with regard to whether or not the reader really believes that he (the Father) is righteous and, subsequently,

---

92 Brown, *The Epistles of John*, p. 382.
93 Despite the fact that two different Greek words appear in this clause both of which are translated 'know' (εἰδῆτε and γινώσκετε), there does not appear to be any difference in meaning. Rather, this appears to be an example of Johannine style with regard to variation in vocabulary.

upon the fact that each one who does righteousness is born of him. The implications of this reality result in a virtual explosion of emotions in 3.1. The reader is alerted to the extraordinary significance of being 'born of him' by the appearance of two specific words at the beginning of the Greek sentence, each of which conveys special meaning. Standing at the very beginning of the sentence is the word translated 'see' or 'look' (ἴδετε), a term which conveys several things to the reader. First, the word reminds the reader of a formula of revelation found in the Fourth Gospel, for example, 'Behold the Lamb of God'. In places where this formula occurs something of the identity of an individual is revealed by one who is speaking prophetically (cf. Jn 1.29, 36, 47; 19.14, 26-27). Second, the term also reminds the reader of the invitation issued by Jesus and his followers on occasion in the Fourth Gospel to potential believers in Jesus to 'come and see' (1.39, 46; 4.29). Third, the appearance of the word here in 1 Jn 3.1 is unusual in two ways. It occurs in the second person plural rather than the second person singular as is normal and ordinarily the term has reference to things actually seen rather than to a concept.[94] The latter point may indicate that the readers are actually expected to visualize this reality in this verse.[95] Thus, the appearance of the term itself indicates something of the extraordinary nature of 'being born of him'.

The second word in the Greek text (ποταπὴν) is no less significant for it conveys the idea of astonishment. This unusual word, for how great something is, introduces a note of wonder into the passage. This one word expresses both the quality and quantity of the Father's love. At one and the same time it emphasizes both how much love there is and how amazing this love is. Perhaps a translation like, 'what extraordinary love' is not far from the mark. This extraordinary love has been given by the Father. The appearance of the word 'Father' with reference to God at this point underscores for the reader the theme of 'being begotten' and makes clear that believers are children of the Father. The fact that the verb 'has been given' (δέδωκεν) occurs in the perfect past tense may serve to emphasize that this gift was bestowed at some point in the past but is still felt at the present. It is likely that the readers would here be reminded of the moment of their initial belief. The extraordinary quality and quantity of the Father's love is conveyed by means of a purpose (ἵνα) clause: 'in order that we might be called children of God'. This magnificent love is made known in believers being called children of God.

It is significant that though the readers have been addressed as children before in 1 John, here they are specifically called the children of God. In

---

94   Westcott, *The Epistles of St. John*, p. 95.
95   Brown, *The Epistles of John*, p. 387.

order to underscore this distinct emphasis, there is a shift in vocabulary in this verse. For the first time a different word for children occurs in the Greek text of 1 John (τέκνα). Part of the reason for this shift may be related to the use of this term in the Fourth Gospel, where it appears three times, twice in the phrase 'children of God' (1.12; 11.52), once in the phrase 'children of Abraham' (8.39). The occurrence of these words at this point in 1 John clearly draws upon the rich theological meaning of the phrase in the Fourth Gospel where very near the beginning of the Gospel it is stated that 'whoever received him were given authority to become children of God, to those who believed in his name' (Jn 1.12). The nature of this birth is clarified both in the very next verse in the Fourth Gospel (1.13), where it is described as being born of God, as well as in the Nicodemus dialogue (Jn 3.1-15), where it is identified as a birth from above and connected to the work of the Spirit. In Jn 11.52 the phrase 'children of God' means all who believe. The fact that 'children of God' here builds on this understanding is borne out by the fact that in 1 John each occurrence of the phrase 'children of God' follows a passage that speaks of believers being born of God.[96] Nor is it without significance that in the Johannine literature, believers are never called 'sons of God' but always 'children of God', as the term son (υἱός) is reserved exclusively for Jesus.[97]

The reality of the believers' status as 'children of God' is confirmed in three ways. First, the Greek verb, which lies behind the phrase 'we might be called', appears in the passive voice with the subject unnamed. This use of the verb is an indirect way of indicating that God is the one who calls believers children of God. The act of calling believers children of God not only identifies them as such but constitutes them to be children of God. Thus, this naming is a creative divine act. Secondly, the status of believers as children of God is not something confined to the future, but is a present reality, as the emphatic expression 'And we are'[98] reveals.[99] Thus, the extraordinary nature of God's love is, like eternal life, a present reality for the believer.

A third more negative confirmation of the believers' status as children of God follows fast on the heels of the first two. Here the reader learns that receipt of God's extraordinary love in the form of becoming his

---

96   C. Haas, M. de Jonge and J.L. Swellengrebel, *A Translator's Handbook on the Letters of John* (London: United Bible Societies, 1972), p. 77.
97   With the exception of the eschatological promise found in Rev. 21.7.
98   Despite the fact that some manuscripts omit the phrase καὶ ἐσμέν, evidence for its inclusion is quite strong and convincing.
99   Westcott, *The Epistles of St. John*, p. 96.

children entails a separation from and enmity with the world. Earlier in 1 John (2.15-17) the world is revealed to be a sphere opposed to God and a threat to believers. Specifically, the readers learn that the love of the Father and the love of the world are diametrically opposed. In 1 Jn 3.1 the world continues to be understood as such a place of opposition. The sentence, 'The world does not know us because it did not know him', makes connections with the readers in powerful ways. It makes clear that those who are God's children are not known by the world owing to their relationship with Jesus, an idea clearly expressed in Jn 15.19. In the first part of the sentence the word 'know' appears in the present tense indicating that for the believers, such lack of knowing by the world is an ongoing reality. They do not know the believers just as those who do not keep his commands do not know God (1 Jn 2.4). The reason for this situation is made prominent in the second part of the sentence where the world's lack of knowledge of the believers is tied to a lack of knowledge of him by the world. The fact that the second appearance of the verb 'know' in this sentence appears in the (aorist) past tense reveals that this lack of knowing occurred at a specific point in the past. Though the immediate context suggests that the identity of 'him' in 3.1 is God, there are reasons to believe that reference is now being made to Jesus. Not only is the reader familiar with the ways in which reference is made to God and Jesus almost interchangeably at many points in 1 John, but there is also evidence from the Fourth Gospel that points in this direction. Specifically, the reader is informed by the fact that the same words that appear in 1 Jn 3.1 are used to describe the world's response to Jesus (the Logos) in the prologue of the Fourth Gospel (1.10): 'He was in the world, and the world was made through him, and the world did not know him (καὶ ὁ κόσμος αὐτὸν οὐκ ἔγνω).'[100] By being introduced to this idea at this point, the readers are being encouraged to interpret their uneasy and painful relationship with the world as an additional sign of their being children of God. At the same time, there is an anticipation of later instruction with regard to the believers' relationship to the world (1 Jn 4.8-10).

Verses 3.2-6
The next subsection of 2.28-3.10, which begins with another term of endearment ('Beloved'), continues the thought of the previous subsection (2.28-3.1) in several ways while introducing and developing other ideas and themes. These include the 'children of God', the 'manifestation of

---

100   Though a different word order is found in 1 Jn 3.1, the words themselves are identical: ὁ κόσμος...οὐκ ἔγνω αὐτὸν.

Jesus', the 'return of Jesus' and 'sin', a topic which appeared in 1.5–2.2 and will be developed later in the final subsection (3.7-10) of this passage (2.28–3.10).

Verse 2. The beginning of this subsection is marked by another term of endearment with the appearance of 'Beloved', a word that has occurred previously in 2.7. Being addressed as 'Beloved' at this point reminds the readers of the magnificent nature of the love bestowed upon believers described in 3.1. The rest of v. 2 is devoted to exploring present and future dimensions of this identity as 'children of God'. Through a combination of 'children of God' language introduced in 3.1 and the 'now' of 2.28, emphasis is placed upon the present reality of the believers' identity as children of God. There should be no doubt in the minds of the readers with regard to this identity with all that it means. This is a reality that already exists in their lives, a reality based in the phenomenal love which God has for his 'Beloved'.

But just as the language 'children' conveys something of the readers' nature, so it implies the idea of their development. Not only have the readers experienced new life as children of God in the present, but they also learn that there is a dimension of their lives as God's children which is future. This future dimension of their lives involves both certainty and uncertainty. There are aspects of the believers' future existence with God that are as yet unclear. This is because 'it has not yet been manifested (or revealed) what we shall be'. Appearance of the word 'manifested' (ἐφανερώθη), which is used to describe Jesus' return in 2.28 and also occurs with this meaning in the next part of 3.2, suggests to the readers that details of their future existence will not be revealed until the manifestation of Jesus at his return. As to the precise nature of their future existence, 'what we shall be', the believers must await Jesus' manifestation. Just as the disciples in the Fourth Gospel were unable to see Jesus more perfectly until after his resurrection, so the readers are unable to envision their future lives as children of God until Jesus' future manifestation.

However, the fact that there is some uncertainty with regard to the nature of the believers' future existence as children of God should not lead the readers to despair, for there are aspects about the future of which they are certain. This certainty is indicated by the appearance of 'we know' (οἴδαμεν), language that has earlier occurred to underscore the knowledge the readers have as a result of the anointing they received (2.20), their knowledge of the truth (2.21) and their knowledge that God is righteous (2.29). Here, their knowledge focuses upon three specific points. First, the readers know that he will be manifested. Uncertainty about the precise nature of their future existence does not mean that there is any uncertainty for the believers about the manifestation of Jesus. As in 2.28 the phrase 'when he is manifested' in the Greek text is literally 'if he is manifested'. But as in its earlier occurrence there is no question here about whether he *will* be manifested, but *when* he will be manifested. Though it is possible to translate the phrase 'when *it* is manifested' instead of 'when *he* is manifested', it is virtually certain that reference is being made to Jesus and the manifestation of his return. Second, Jesus' manifestation in his return will bring along with it a transformation of the believers, resulting in the believers being like him. This transformation could possibly mean that as a result of Jesus' manifestation the believers will have a body that is no longer confined by earthly limitations – like Jesus who, after the resurrection in John 20 appears to be able to enter rooms despite doors being locked. At the least, there is the suggestion that the believers' future existence will be of a different order and on a different level than that currently known. Thus, the readers are encouraged that despite the fact that 'it has not yet been manifested what we shall be…we shall be like him'. Such an assurance would, no doubt, be of great comfort to the readers of 1 John and leave them with a sense of hopeful expectation.[101]

Third, this transformation into his likeness is evoked in and by the radical transforming moment when 'we shall see him just as he is'. Although there is, no doubt, at least a secondary reference to God in the pronoun 'him', the primary reference seems to be to Jesus, who will be manifested at his return and whom the believer will be like. Hints as to the meaning of 'see him as he is' may be discerned in part by the development of the theme of seeing God and/or Jesus in the Johannine literature. In the Fourth Gospel the theologically rich idea of seeing God is very much tied to Jesus. Though the prologue can state that 'no one has seen God at any time' it quickly goes on to qualify this with the words, 'the only begotten God, the one in the bosom of the Father, that one has made him known' (Jn 1.18). Such language suggests that Jesus, the Logos and only begotten of the Father, has a special knowledge of and communion with the Father. The suspicions that the Son has 'seen' the Father are confirmed later in the Fourth Gospel when Jesus reveals that those who have seen the Son have seen the Father as well (14.9). But despite such statements as these Jesus' prayer reveals that seeing the (full) glory of the Son awaits the disciples in heaven, where he was before (17.24). Something of the nature of such seeing may be hinted at in the vision(s) of Jesus given to John in the Apocalypse, where the

---

101 Smith, *First, Second, and Third John*, p. 77.

prophet is drawn further and further into the very presence of Jesus. This seeing involves experiencing Jesus, for as the visions continue, different dimensions of Jesus' person are manifested, all of which have a definite effect upon the prophet. The phrase to 'see him just as (καθώς) he is' conveys the idea of direct and immediate access. In the Johannine literature the culmination of the desire for direct and immediate access to Jesus comes in Rev. 21.22, where the reader learns that there is no temple in the New Jerusalem, for the Lord God Almighty and the Lamb is (ἐστιν) its temple, and in Rev. 22.4 where the saints in the presence of God and the Lamb will see the face of God and have his name written upon their foreheads. While all these ideas may not be present in 1 Jn 3.2, the idea of 'seeing him as he is' at least points in this direction. In sum, the transforming experience of 'seeing him as he is' results in the believers' transformation into his likeness. Special mention should perhaps be made of the fact that first person plural language ('we') appears consistently throughout this verse underscoring the communal aspect of even this experience.

Verse 3. In the light of the glorious future that awaits the children of God, the readers are admonished to take appropriate action to prepare for this future. Specifically, 'Each one who has this hope in him purifies himself just as that one is pure'. At this point the language switches from the corporate first person plural ('we') of the preceding verse to 'each one who' (πᾶς ὁ) as a way of emphasizing that the following moral demand is placed upon each and every reader.[102] This is the second occurrence of the 'each one who' construction in this section (cf. 2.29) and may indicate that this issue was one of dispute with the opponents,[103] though this is far from certain. While a common term in other parts of the New Testament, for the first and only time in the Johannine literature the term 'hope' occurs. From the immediate context it appears that the term has reference to the manifestation of Jesus at his return, which includes the transforming experience for the believer of becoming like him when 'we see him just as he is'. The expression 'to have hope on/in him' suggests that the hope of the believer for the future is securely grounded,[104] for it is based in one who is not of this world.[105]

Since the reader has this extraordinary hope of seeing him just as he is, it follows that he or she must be prepared to see him as he is. According

---

102 Smalley, *1, 2, 3 John*, p. 148.
103 Smalley, *1, 2, 3 John*, p. 148.
104 Smalley, *1, 2, 3 John*, p. 148.
105 Strecker, *The Johannine Letters*, p. 91.

to this verse, the one who prepares for such a vision purifies (ἁγνίζει) himself or herself just as he is pure (ἁγνός). Several aspects of this statement merit comment. First, it should perhaps be noted that the term translated 'purifies' occurs only here and in Jn 11.55 in the whole of the Johannine literature. Normally, in the Greek Old Testament it is a word that is used to describe ceremonial or ritual purification as its appearance in Jn 11.55 does. However, here in v. 3 the term appears to be used in a moral sense. The idea conveyed is that just as one must remove ritual impurity to enter into the presence of God in his tabernacle, temple or city, so one must take steps to ensure one's moral purity in anticipation of seeing him as he is. Second, it is not without significance that the verb 'purifies' appears in the present tense, indicating that the reader is called to be continually vigilant with regard to purifying oneself. Third, this is the only place in the New Testament where Jesus is described as 'pure' (ἁγνός). While such a statement at first glance might seem an inappropriate way to describe Jesus, given the context of the Johannine literature, its appearance here makes sense to the reader. Specifically, Jesus has earlier in 1 John been called 'righteous' (2.1). It is his blood that cleanses from all sin (1.7). In addition, the Fourth Gospel suggests that Jesus is sinless (8.46) and describes him as sanctifying himself (Jn 17.19). Thus, even before the clarification of the following verses regarding purity, the reader understands that this word, ordinarily used to describe ritual purity, is being transformed into a term that focuses on moral purity. Fourth, the following verses will leave no doubt that the purity here described is concerned primarily with the issue of sin and the fact that Jesus is himself sinless (3.5). Fifth, one of the primary emphases of this verse is the fact that Jesus becomes the standard of purity for the believer. If the child of God is to see him as he is, then the believer must take the appropriate steps to ensure that he or she is in a state of purity modeled on Jesus' purity. Sixth, the present tense verb in the phrase 'just as that one is (ἐστιν) pure' reveals that Jesus' purity is a continuing reality which exists into the present.

The admonition for the believer to purify self in order to experience the transformative moment of 'seeing him as he is' coincides with Johannine thought, for there has been and will continue to be a consistent emphasis upon the necessary divine–human cooperation in the experience of eternal life. Jesus will be manifested to the child of God, but he or she must prepare for his manifestation.

Verse 4. In this verse and those that follow, the nature of the purity to be pursued by the child of God is clarified, as for a third time the reader's attention is directed to the issue of sin. To this point the reader has learned that sin is a reality which must be addressed directly by the believing community. Apparently, the deceivers were claiming to be without sin and, therefore, without need for the cleansing brought by the blood of Jesus (1.7–2.2). The readers are there told that they should not sin, but *if* anyone does sin there is an advocate with the Father, Jesus Christ the Righteous One. In the poetic section of 2.12-13 the reality of the forgiveness of sin experienced 'on account of his name' by those within the community is underscored.

The thought of 1 Jn 3.4 is introduced by the third appearance of the 'each one who' formula in this section. While in 2.29, the formula is used to describe 'each one who does righteousness' (πᾶς ὁ ποιῶν τὴν δικαιοσύνην), in 3.4 it is used to describe 'each one who does sin' (πᾶς ὁ ποιῶν τὴν ἁμαρτίαν). The similarity of these phrases suggests that the readers would see some intentional contrast between the 'doing of righteousness' and the 'doing of sin', rather than taking the latter construction as emphasizing the actual realization of sin as is sometimes suggested.[106]

Part of the interpretive challenge of v. 4 is to determine how the readers would understand the relationship between sin and lawlessness found in this verse. It is possible to take v. 4 as a definition of sin and lawlessness with these terms being seen as synonyms, as the phrase 'and sin is lawlessness' at the end of the verse might imply. But there are reasons to believe that the readers would see a certain escalation in the development of thought in the phrase 'each one who does sin also does lawlessness'. On this view, there is a relationship between sin and lawlessness, but it is not a synonymous one. Rather, it would appear that those who commit sin are those who *even* commit lawlessness. That is to say, perhaps the readers would see in this phrase an increasing severity of culpability rather than taking sin and lawlessness simply as synonyms. Namely, one who does sin is *even* guilty of lawlessness.

One of the clues that would alert the reader to the fact that these terms are not mere synonyms is the fact that in the Greek text the term lawlessness (ἀνομία) appears with the definite article, suggesting that this is a specific and well-known lawlessness, not lawlessness generally. Further, this is the only place in the Johannine Epistles where this word appears, while the term 'law' (νόμος) does not appear in them at all. The virtual absence of this language suggests that the meaning of lawlessness in 3.4 does not have primarily to do with observance of the Torah as such for the connection between sin and law-breaking is not a strong

---

106   A proposal made by Westcott, *The Epistles of St. John*, p. 101, among others.

one here.[107] While there has earlier been an emphasis upon the connection between keeping his commands and knowing God (2.3-4), there the reader learned that keeping the commands is focused upon the love command as the following verses make clear (2.5-17). The escalation of language, the use of the definite article and the unique appearance of 'lawlessness' language all suggest that the reader would not understand such terminology in a generic fashion but rather take it as having a specific connotation.

Several pieces of evidence suggest that the word translated 'lawlessness' (ἡ ἀνομία) should better be translated as '*the* Iniquity'. First, such a suggestion is based, in part, upon the fact that, as noted earlier, the term appears in the Greek text with the definite article. Second, the section which immediately precedes this one in 1 John (2.18-27) contains reference to the appearance of false teachers and antichrists which indicate that it is the last hour. Further, the immediate context of this term's appearance is the manifestation of Jesus at his return. Third, in addition to the Johannine thematic hints that point toward this interpretation, within a variety of strains of early Christian thought there is evidence for precisely this meaning of 'lawlessness'. As early as the Thessalonian correspondence, this language is used to describe 'the man of lawlessness' whose appearance will precede the return of Jesus (2 Thess. 2.3-4). This theme is developed in the *Didache* (16.3-4), the *Epistle of Barnabas* (4.1-4; 18.1), and in one version of the longer ending of Mark (16.14), the so-called Freer manuscript, where the phrase 'this age of lawlessness' appears. In each of these texts, the idea of eschatological evil is in view.[108] It seems likely, then, that the readers would see in these words technical terminology for '*the* Iniquity', a definite and well-known expectation of eschatological opposition to God. Thus, the primary emphasis of v. 4 is to indicate that 'each one who does sin' is not only involved in sinful acts but is at the same time taking part in the eschatological opposition to God – for sin is iniquity. That the verb in v. 4b occurs in the present tense underscores the fact that one's sinful activity is even now eschatological iniquity. The broader implication of this verse is clear: one cannot confidently prepare for the manifestation of Jesus at his return and at the same time take part in active rebellion against him.[109]

Verse 5. The thought of the next verse is closely connected to that of the previous one. This close relationship is conveyed in part by the fact that

---

107 Smalley, *1, 2, 3 John*, p. 154.
108 Schnackenburg, *The Johannine Epistles*, p. 171.
109 Marshall, *The Epistles of John*, p. 177.

the sentences are connected by the word 'and' (καί). Appeal is once again made to the readers' knowledge as a means of exhortation. Earlier this term (οἴδατε) had been used to emphasize the readers' authentic 'knowing' in contrast to the false teachers' lack of 'knowing' (2.20-21). On this occasion the certainty of their 'knowing' is focused upon Jesus and his relationship to sin. Thus, they are being reminded of one of those basic truths foundational for the community. Specifically, the readers are told 'that one was manifested in order that he might take away sins'. The appearance of the pronoun translated 'that one' (ἐκεῖνος) is an obvious reference to Jesus, as this term is used exclusively in 1 John with reference to him. Once again the word 'manifested' appears in 1 John and has earlier been used in reference to the Incarnation of Jesus as a whole (1.2, cf. also 3.8),[110] as well as to the manifestation of Jesus at his return (previously in this section; 2.28; 3.2). Here in v. 5, the term appears to have reference to the Incarnation as a whole. The purpose of his manifestation is underscored for the reader by the appearance of a purpose (ἵνα) clause translated 'in order that'. The language used to describe the purpose of his manifestation is very similar to that found in the Fourth Gospel (1.29) where John identifies Jesus as 'the Lamb of God who takes away the sin of the world'. It is difficult to believe that such similarity would be lost on the readers of 1 John. It is virtually certain that they would understand the verb translated 'take away' (ἄρῃ) in a very similar fashion to the way it is understood in Jn 1.29. While it is not made explicit for the reader exactly how Jesus takes sin away, enough hints have already been given in 1 John to suggest how the readers would understand it. The reader has already learned that 'the blood of Jesus cleanses us from all sin' (1 Jn 1.7), that Jesus is an advocate with the Father on behalf of the believer who might sin (2.1), and that Jesus is the atoning sacrifice for our sins and those of the whole world (2.2). Such knowledge would no doubt inform the readers' understanding of the way Jesus takes away sins. In Jn 1.29, the Lamb of God is said to take away the *sin* of the world, but in 1 Jn 3.5, that one takes away *sins*. The shift from the singular 'sin' to the plural 'sins' may very well convey to the reader the idea that not only is sin in its totality taken away, but also the sinful acts of each individual believer, which are themselves a manifestation of evil and opposition to Jesus.[111] Such an emphasis would be in keeping with the phrase 'each one who' in v. 4.

Not only do the readers learn that Jesus was manifested to take away

---

110   A thought not unlike that found in the Fourth Gospel where the Baptist uses the same term to describe his manifestation to Israel (Jn 1.31).
111   Brown, *The Epistles of John*, p. 402.

sin, but in the final part of v. 5 they also learn of the complete antinomy that exists between Jesus and sin. In the phrase translated 'and sin is not in him at all' emphasis is clearly upon the term 'sin', as it stands first in the Greek sentence. The statement that Jesus is without sin does not come as a complete surprise to the reader for the implication of the Fourth Gospel is that Jesus has no sin (8.46). The statement 'and sin is not in him at all' (καὶ ἁμαρτία ἐν αὐτῷ οὐκ ἔστιν) is very close to that of Jn 7.18 where Jesus says of himself 'and unrighteousness is not in him at all' (καὶ ἀδικία ἐν αὐτῷ οὐκ ἔστιν). Such a statement is consistent with the earlier descriptions of Jesus in John as righteous (2.1) and pure (3.3). The appearance of the present tense verb 'is' serves to underscore for the reader that Jesus' sinless life continues into the present. The implication of v. 5 for the broader argument of 1 John is that if, as v. 3 states, the children of God are to purify themselves as that one is pure, this purification will involve a complete renunciation of sin by the believer for 'sin is not in him at all'. Again Jesus serves as the perfect pattern for the believer.

Verse 6. This verse falls rather naturally into two related parts, each of which begins with the phrase 'each one who', the fourth and fifth time this particular construction appears in this section. By this means, the readers learn that there are two mutually exclusive categories of individuals: those who remain in Jesus and those who sin. It is in this way that the very challenging discussion of sinlessness found in vv. 7-10 is introduced into the argument of 1 John.[112] The continuity of thought that v. 6 shares with the previous verse(s) is easy to see for here the implications of Jesus' diametric opposition to sin are brought to their natural conclusion. If his purpose in coming was to take away sin, and if there is absolutely no sin in him at all (v. 5), then it follows that those who are intimately related to Jesus would be rather far removed from sin themselves. The first part of the verse contains the bold statement, 'Each one who remains in him does not sin'. Despite the fact that these words follow somewhat naturally on the thought of v. 5, they cannot help but strike the readers as quite staggering for several reasons. First, the optimism with regard to the readers' ability not to sin is remarkable given the fact that their experience, as might be deduced from 1 John, appears to include a not always successful battle with sin. In point of fact, the tone of a number of passages in this work reveal that the readers are being warned on more than one occasion about sin and its consequences for the believer. Second, the idea that one could live without sin appears to have been condemned earlier in the Epistles at least in the

---

112   Rensberger, *1 John, 2 John, 3 John*, p. 90.

form proposed by the false teachers (1 Jn 1.8-10). For this same point now to be made about the readers would be confusing at the least. Third, the declaration made in 3.6 appears to stand in contradiction to other statements found in 1 John, where the possibility, even reality, of believers' sinning is acknowledged (cf. esp. 1.6–2.2). Thus, the reader is presented with a formidable challenge when seeking to understand the thought of 1 John at this point, a challenge that only becomes more difficult as the section (vv. 7-10) continues.

Challenging though this verse may be, the text itself contains hints that assist the reader in understanding the verse. One of the most important clues is the emphasis here placed upon 'remaining' or 'abiding' in him. To this point in 1 John the term here translated 'remain' or 'abide' (μένω) has appeared in contexts that underscore the intimate relationship which exists between the believer and God or Jesus. On the one hand, in its first occurrence, the reader finds the language of 'remaining' tied to specific kinds of ethical activity: 'whoever claims to remain in him ought to walk just as that one walked' (2.6). On the other hand, the next occurrence of the term in 1 John (2.10) shows that one's actions, in this case loving one's brother, reveal that one remains in the light. Additionally, the reader learns that the one who does the will of God 'remains' forever (2.17). Conversely, if one goes out from the community, it is a sign that such an individual was never really part of the community, otherwise they would have 'remained' with us (2.19). Admonitions to let that which was from the beginning 'remain' in you are tied to whether or not one remains in the Son and the Father (2.24). It is also remembered that the chrisma received from him remains in the readers (2.27). The nearest occurrence of the term to 3.6 is in the first verse of this section (2.28), where remaining in him is tied to not being ashamed at his appearing. Thus, the idea conveyed by the phrase, 'each one who remains', is one of intimate fellowship and very close relationship. The idea of divine indwelling is not far from view here.[113]

Consequently, whatever the precise nature of the believer not sinning, it is clear that such ability is enabled by 'remaining in him'. This idea fits nicely with that of the Fourth Gospel (15.4) where the mutual indwelling (remaining) of the believer and Jesus is likened to branches dwelling in a vine. Just as the branches are unable to do anything on their own, so here the child of God is unable to avoid sin except for remaining in him. Thus, the main idea seems to be that the one who has such an intimate relationship with Jesus is kept from sinning by the relationship itself. Earlier in 1 John (2.18-27), 'remaining in him' is the antidote to false

---

113 Brown, *The Epistles of John*, p. 403.

teaching and deception. Here, 'remaining in him' is the antidote to sin. As such, the one who remains in Jesus not only avoids sin, but also avoids the impurity of involvement in *the* eschatological iniquity that opposes Jesus. In the light of the earlier statements about the believer and sin in 1 John, it would seem that this sinlessness would be connected to the admonitions and provisions for the purifying of oneself. That is to say, the one who remains in him would not deny the need for cleansing through Jesus' blood and would make use of this Paraclete's ministry of intercession on behalf of the believer. While there is an inherent tension in this interpretation, it seeks to make sense of the readers' knowledge to this point in the argument and at the same time convey something of the tension felt by the reader given this most startling statement.

By this time the reader has grown accustomed to the antithetical parallelism found throughout 1 John. Therefore, the reappearance of this literary feature does not surprise the reader at this point. Specifically, in the first part of v. 6 the primary point is made in a positive fashion, while in the second part of the verse a similar point is made in a negative fashion. The appearance of the 'each one who' formula underscores for the reader that a comparison is being made with the previous statement as well as preserving the antithetical parallelism. It may not be going too far to suggest that the construction carries with it an instructive intention which constitutes a warning for the community.[114] In the first part of the verse it was observed that each one who knows the intimacy of remaining in him does not sin. In the second part of the verse it is now stated that 'the one who sins has neither seen him nor known him'. Just as the one who claims to have fellowship with God but walks in darkness reveals by one's actions that one is far from the truth (1.6-10), so the one who sins invalidates by their actions any claims to knowledge of or intimacy with Jesus. The reader would appreciate the contrasts between the phrases 'the one who remains' and 'the one who sins', for in both cases the same formula is used and in both cases a present tense participle occurs to emphasize the fact that remaining or sinning characterizes the individual in view. It is striking that for the one who sins, there is a complete denial of any knowledge of Jesus. While it may be possible that the use of 'seeing' and 'knowing' language points to claims made by the deceivers, it is not without significance that one of these is the very term that the reader finds at the beginning of 1 John (1.1) to describe the unique qualifications and authority of the writer(s). If the writer is, in part, qualified to write to the community by having seen Jesus with his own eyes, then such a one is in the unique position of assessing whether

---

114 Strecker, *The Johannine Letters*, p. 96.

or not others have seen him. Such a denial of the deceivers' claims would be especially pointed and stark. Similarly, denial of the deceivers' knowledge of him is reminiscent of the earlier discussion of how one can know that they know him (2.3-17),[115] where the litmus test is the keeping of his commands—namely, love for one's brother or sister. There is, then, a convergence of thought in v. 6b, as mention of knowledge of him (or the lack thereof) reminds the reader of how one knows that one knows him and it hints in a subtle fashion that not keeping the commands may indeed be related to the sinning here described. At the same time, such a convergence points the reader toward the next major section of 1 John (3.11-18) where 'love one another' forms the center of the work's thought.

Verses 3.7-10
The final subsection of this larger passage is signaled by the appearance of another term of endearment. It also contains a warning not to be deceived, which forms the basis of the discussion in the following verses. Specifically, 'those who do righteousness' are contrasted with 'those who do sin', while those who are 'of the Devil' are contrasted with those 'born of God'. A final indication that these verses stand together is the fact that very near the beginning and end of these verses are references to those who either do (or do not do) righteousness.

Verses 7-8. For a third time in this passage 2.28–3.10, a term of endearment begins a subsection. This term is the same one, 'little children' (τεκνία), that appeared at the beginning of the passage in 2.28. Among other things, appearance of this term reminds the readers of their special status as children inasmuch as this is the same word used by Jesus with reference to the disciples on one occasion in the Farewell Materials of the Fourth Gospel (13.33). It also contributes to the continuity of the broader passage and prepares the reader for the coming reference to 'the one born of God' later in this section (v. 9).

Following this direct address is the primary point of this subsection. The readers are warned in no uncertain terms 'let no one deceive you'. Apparently, this warning is focused upon the threat posed by those seeking to influence the readers with regard to their view of sin and its consequences. The stark nature of the warning suggests that there may even be individuals who otherwise would be deemed to be trusted members of the community that may be advocating a less than vigilant

---

115   In ways similar to Jesus' words about the Jews in the Fourth Gospel (16.3), the deceivers are denied any claim to authentic knowledge of him.

attitude toward sin and the believer. This is the only place in the Johannine literature where the word 'no one' (μηδείς) occurs and may appear here to add to the emphasis of the warning. The fact that this warning follows fast on the heels of the statement about sin in v. 6 suggests that not only is this position being advocated by some within the community who were not without influence, but it also indicates that such a careless attitude toward sin is a real threat to the spiritual life of the community. It would not be going too far to say that the rest of the content of vv. 7-10 is devoted to spelling out the reasons why this admonition is so important.

The warning is followed in the next two verses (vv. 7-8) by a contrast between 'the one who does righteousness' and 'the one who sins'. While there may be those who confuse the issue, it is really very simple.[116] 'The one who does righteousness is righteous, just as that one is righteous. The one who does sin is of the Devil, because the Devil sins from the beginning.' The structure of the formula used in these verses would appear to lead the reader rather naturally to make a comparison between the two. The reason is that each formula begins with the words 'the one who does' and concludes with words about the origin of one involved in the action just described. Whatever claims there may have been about the nature of righteousness, or whatever definitions were being offered, the truth is quite clear; the actual doing of righteousness is determinative in whether or not one is righteous. As in many places in the Johannine literature, there is here no line of demarcation between theology and ethics. One cannot claim to be righteous without doing righteousness. While it may be going too far to say that the doing of righteousness makes one righteous, it is not going too far to say that part of one's identity as righteous is very much connected to the doing of righteousness. Such a cooperative relationship between God and the believer is quite similar to the thought expressed earlier in 1 John (2.3) on the relationship between the assurance of one's knowledge of God and the keeping of his commands. The idea here expressed coheres well with an earlier statement, very similar in structure to this one, where the reader learned that 'the one who does righteousness has been born of him' (2.29). Just as the doing of righteousness is consistent with the actions of one born of him, so the doing of righteousness is consistent with the actions of one who is righteous.

Given the earlier parallelism, the readers might expect at this point a statement something like 'the one who does not do righteousness is not righteous'. However, instead of this the readers are pointed to the origin

---

116 Smith, *First, Second, and Third John*, p. 83.

of their righteous activity. For a third time in 1 John and a second time in this passage, Jesus is called righteous. He is the Righteous One who serves as an advocate with the Father for the believer who has sinned (2.1), and the readers' knowledge of his being righteous is the basis of their knowledge that 'the one who does righteousness has been born of him' (2.29). Having learned earlier that they must purify themselves 'just as' (καθὼς) that one is pure (3.3), now they learn that there is an intimate connection between their own doing of righteousness and his being righteous. Specifically, their lives of righteousness are to conform to his being righteous, thus the language 'just as (καθὼς) that one is righteous'. It appears that his being righteous is both a model for their own lives and, at the same time, an empowerment for such living. In this context, it is clear that Jesus' righteousness includes his purity and being without sin. Therefore, the one who remains in him does not sin, but rather does righteousness because he himself is without sin and is righteous.

The second part of the parallelism occurs in the first part of v. 8. The opposite of doing righteousness in this verse is identified as 'doing sin'. To this point in 1 John, the following things regarding sin have been made clear to the reader: sin is not an inconsequential issue for the child of God; it is connected to the eschatological Iniquity; Jesus came to take away sin; there is no sin in him; each one who remains in him does not sin; and the one who does sin has neither seen nor known him. Consequently, the reader is not wholly unprepared for the explicit and powerful words of v. 8: 'the one who does sin is of the Devil because from the beginning the Devil sins'. Given all the reader knows about sin to this point, it is not surprising to learn that those who are involved in such practices have an innate connection to the Devil. The Fourth Gospel reveals that the Devil is a murderer from the beginning (8.44), that he is the father of lies (8.44) and that he put betrayal of Jesus into Judas' heart (13.2). In fact, on one occasion Judas can even be spoken of as a Devil (6.70).

Though this is the first occurrence of the name 'the Devil' in 1 John, mention has already been made of this enemy of Jesus in earlier references to the evil one (2.13-14). Interesting enough, all four occurrences of the words 'the Devil' occur in this section of 1 John; three occurrences here in v. 8 and one in v. 10.[117] The idea that one who sins is of the Devil is especially challenging to the reader given the fact that those who are part of the community are said to be victorious over the evil one (2.13-14). Now to discover that sinful activity reveals one's allegiance to this enemy of Jesus rather than victory over him is quite a sobering reve-

---

117 Brown, *The Epistles of John*, p. 404.

lation. By this means the readers are reminded that sin finds its origins in the Devil, because 'from the beginning the Devil sins'. It is significant that the words 'from the beginning' stand first in the Greek sentence indicating that emphasis is being placed here. While the precise meaning of the phrase 'from the beginning' is not altogether clear in this verse, it would appear that at least a partial reference is being made to the story of beginnings as found in the book of Genesis. Not only must it be assumed that the writer and readers would have access to and knowledge of such a story, but there are also hints within the Johannine literature that indicate this story was of more than passing interest to the community. As the readers know, the Fourth Gospel makes reference to this story in 8.44 where the Devil is described as 'a murderer from the beginning' and 'the father of lies'. Added to this is the fact that in the next major section of 1 John, another allusion to this story is found where reference is made to Cain ('of the evil one'), who murdered his brother. Therefore, whatever else might be conveyed by the phrase 'from the beginning' it is clear that part of the readers' understanding would include the idea that the Devil has been involved with sin as long as it has existed. Not only has the Devil been sinning from the beginning, but also as the present tense verb 'sin' suggests, he continues to sin right up to the present. Thus, the parallelism found in vv. 7-8a is sufficient to drive home the point to the readers that one's actions reveal something about one's character owing to the allegiance such actions reveal. Specifically, just as it is true that the one who does righteousness is revealed to be closely connected to the one who is righteous, so it is equally true that the one who sins is like the one who has always sinned and continues to sin.

A rather heavy Greek grammatical construction marks the transition from a description of the activity of the Devil to that of the Son of God in v. 8b. Such emphasis ensures that the reader's attention is focused squarely upon Jesus and his work. [118] The sentence literally reads, 'for this reason was manifested the Son of God, in order that he might destroy the works of the Devil'. The reader's attention is also focused in this verse upon the fact that here one encounters the first of seven occurrences of the full title 'the Son of God'. While reference to Jesus as God's Son has consistently marked the work from near its beginning (1.3, 7; 2.22, 23, 24), here the full title occurs. Perhaps its introduction at this point in the argument of 1 John is related to the broader context of this section where attention has been given to the 'children of God' and will

---

118   Haas, de Jonge and Swellengrebel, *A Translator's Handbook on the Letters of John*, p. 84.

be given to the children of the Devil. In addition, this more emphatic reference to the Son stands in greater contrast to the Devil. It is made very clear in this part of v. 8, by means of a purpose (ἵνα) clause, that *the reason for the manifestation of Jesus in his incarnation is the destruction of the works of the Devil*. That the incarnation as a whole is here in view is supported by the fact that the Greek word translated as 'manifested' (ἐφανερώθη) appears in the aorist past tense indicating a specific manifestation at a certain point in time. The reader is told that the Son of God has come with the express purpose of putting an end to the Devil's sinful activity. The word translated 'destroy' (λύσῃ) is the same one used by Jesus in the Fourth Gospel (2.19) to describe the destruction of 'this temple' (his body). It conveys the idea of demolishing, tearing apart or deconstructing the structure (works) constructed by the Devil. What are the 'works of the Devil' in 1 Jn 3.8? Rather clearly they are identified with his sinful activity in which he and others are involved. In this regard, v. 8b stands parallel to the thought of 3.5 where the purpose of Jesus' manifestation is that 'he might take away sin'. Thus, destroying the works of the Devil and taking away sin are the same things.

Verse 9. The first part of the last antithetical parallelism of this section is contained in v. 9. For a sixth time in this passage the formula 'each one who' appears. It is paired with a seventh and final one in v. 10b. The formula builds upon the theme that since Jesus is sinless, children of God should be without sin. Specifically, this verse picks up on several ideas that have been expressed earlier in the passage. It combines the idea of having 'been born of him' expressed near the beginning of this section in 2.29 and the broad theme of 'children of God' which occurs at various places in this passage, with the emphasis upon avoidance of sin on the part of the believer. Here, it is made explicit that the believers have been born of God, an idea stated less explicitly in 2.29. Drawing on the rich Johannine theme of birth from above, this image now comes to be equated with the doing of righteousness, avoidance of sin, and being a child of God. The perfect tense word translated 'has been born' conveys at least two things to the reader. First, it focuses attention upon the fact that this birth took place at a specific point in the past. Second, it underscores the fact that the effects of this birth are still in place: the one born of God in the past is still born of God in the present.

Again the idea of the sinless life of the believer is hammered home to the reader in the words 'each one born of God does not do sin'. The phrase is very similar in form to that found in v. 6, 'each one who remains in him does not sin'. In v. 9, an explanation is offered in support of this statement regarding the believer being without sin. In fact, this statement is strategically located as the heart of v. 9 standing in the middle of the verse that has a chiastic structure.

> Each one who is born of God
> > Does not sin
> > > Because his seed remains in him
> > And he is not able to sin
> Because he is born of God

Specifically, the verse begins and ends with references to being born of God. Then standing on either side of the statement ('because his seed remains in him') are those words that affirm that the believer is without sin. The believer is sinless because 'his seed (σπέρμα) remains in him'. That is to say, because God's seed remains in the believer, the believer does not sin. Such an idea at the very least implies that because God's seed remains/abides in each one born of him, the believer is able to live a life in which sin is not present. This much is clear. But how would the reader understand the words 'the seed of God'? How would it be understood to enable the one born of God to avoid sin in his or her life? And how would the reader deal with the tension such a statement creates given the earlier statements in 1 John focused upon encouraging believers not to sin?

There are a number of ways in which the reader might understand the phrase 'the seed of God'.[119] Two options present themselves as meriting attention. It is possible to take 'the seed of God' as having reference to the 'Word' or 'Truth' of God. Evidence that points in this direction comes from both the Fourth Gospel and 1 John. In the Fourth Gospel Jesus speaks of the fact that the Word does not remain in certain individuals (Jn 5.38) and says that there is no place for his word in his opponents (8.37). The Fourth Gospel also records Jesus' instruction to those who would truly be his disciples to remain in 'my word' (Jn 8.31). In addition, the idea of 'the Word' remaining in believers is one that has appeared on several occasions to this point in 1 John (1.10; 2.14, 24). Thus, identification of 'the seed of God' with 'the word' makes good sense within the Johannine literature.

Another interpretive option is to see 'the seed of God' as having reference to the Spirit. Support for this interpretation comes from various directions. First, it is difficult not to see in the phrase 'the seed of God' some reference to the Johannine view of birth from above as described in the Fourth Gospel. As noted earlier, this idea is introduced as early as the prologue (1.13) and receives extensive attention in the Nicodemus

---

119   Brown, *The Epistles of John*, pp. 413-15, offers a helpful survey and evaluation of the various interpretive options.

passage (3.5-8) where the Spirit is clearly identified as making birth from above possible. Second, it is also very clear from the Fourth Gospel that the Spirit of Truth will and does remain in the believer (14.16-17).[120] Third, as seen above there is very good reason for understanding the 'chrisma that remains in you' (2.20, 27) as having primary reference to the Spirit. Fourth, later in 1 Jn 3.24 the relationship between remaining and being given of the Spirit is mentioned (3.24; 4.13). Consequently, while there is good reason to see a reference in 'the seed of God' to 'the word', there may be even better reasons to see here a reference to 'the Spirit'. This is not to suggest that the readers would see any sort of tension between the word and the Spirit, but rather to suggest that the Spirit would be the primary referent when the readers see 'the seed of God'. The import for the readers at this point is that the Spirit, which remains in the believer, is that which enables him or her to live in such a way that sin is avoided entirely.

Before leaving this part of v. 9, it should perhaps be observed that the statements of both v. 6 and v. 9 underscore the importance of 'remaining'. Just as remaining in him in v. 6 enables one not to sin, so here the remaining of the seed in the believer enables one not to sin. One of the implications of such statements is that in order for one to remain sinless or to live without sin, the believer must remain in him and his seed remain in the believer. The adverse of this would also appear to be true. If the believer does not remain in him or his seed remain in him or her, a life that avoids sin is not a possibility.

If the previous statements about the believer and sin and these about the believer being sinless are difficult to reconcile, the tension only gets worse in the last part of v. 9. For here the claim that the believer is sinless is even more emphatic in the last part of v. 9 than anything which has preceded it. Specifically, owing to the seed that remains in the believer, such a one 'is not able to sin, because he has been born of God'. If the previous statements suggest that a life without sin is a *possibility* for the child of God, this one implies that it is an *impossibility* for the child of God to sin. But what would such an extreme statement mean to the readers? In seeking to make sense of such a rigid statement, it must from the outset be admitted candidly that on the surface these words underscore yet again the fact that those who identify with Jesus as God's children are to live without sin in their lives owing to their relationship with God, his Son and his Spirit. To dismiss this statement without feeling its full force is to do an injustice to the text by failing to give it a fair hearing.

---

120 Thomas, 'The Spirit in the Fourth Gospel: Narrative Explorations', pp. 97-99.

Still, these strong words in v. 9, that a believer is not able to sin, are difficult to reconcile with previous (and later) statements about the possibility of a believer sinning. One attractive solution to this problem, which has some grammatical support, is to emphasize the point that in this passage the Greek verb for sin (ἁμαρτάνω) always appears in the present tense. On this interpretation the reader is being told that the one who is born of God does not sin habitually, as a course of habit, but rather occasionally sins. In other words, while there is the possibility of a 'Christian sinning' there is no possibility of a 'sinning Christian'. This interpretation is appealing, owing in part to the fact that it seems to fit so well with the experience of believers. Yet, at the same time, such an interpretation does not quite seem to do justice to the vigor and intensity of John's words. For in some ways it pulls the teeth from John's language and at least suggests that sin in the life of the believer is not *that* unusual.

Perhaps the key to understanding this passage, as suggested above, is the word 'remain/abide' (μένω), which occurs twice in this text: in v. 6, 'Each one who remains in him does not sin'; and in v. 9, 'Each one born of God does not do sin because his seed (σπέρμα) remains in him'. The comments of John Wesley are particularly helpful at this point. He believed that while it was possible for those born again to commit outward sin, outward sin was the result of a process which comes dangerously close to ending in the loss of one's faith. Wesley explains by way of case study:

> He fell, step by step, first, into negative, inward sin, not 'stirring up the gift of God which was in him,' not 'watching unto prayer,' not 'pressing on to the mark of the prize of his high calling': then into positive inward sin, inclining to wickedness with his heart, giving way to some evil desire or temper: next he lost his faith, his sight of a pardoning God, and consequently his love of God; and, being then weak and like another man, he was capable of committing even outward sin.[121]

While Wesley may overstate the case, in the light of 1 Jn 1-2, which is testimony to the fact that a believer might sin (not testimony of a backslidden believer), his interpretation does preserve the force and power of 1 John's words. Specifically, one who sins is siding with the Devil and chooses not to 'remain' in Jesus. Sin, then, is not inconsequential but disrupts one's relationship with God, which can lead to complete estrangement. At what point the seed of God ceases to remain in the believer is difficult to determine and 1 John does not reflect upon this possibility directly. However, the point of this passage should not be lost sight of. It is to remind the readers that sin (ultimately) leads to the

---

121 J. Wesley, *The Works of Wesley: Sermons*, I (ed. E.H. Sugden; Grand Rapids: Francis Asbury Press), pp. 307-308.

Devil and must be avoided at all costs. Such an interpretation does not relieve the tension between the differing statements with regard to sin and the believer. However, perhaps the tension between chs. 1–2 and ch. 3 ensures that the readers do not become complacent about sin, but take a no-nonsense approach to this altogether pivotal issue. If so, the tension should be retained in order to accomplish this purpose.

Verse 10. Before being able to move directly to the second part of the antithetical parallelism, the reader encounters a most significant statement. Part of its significance is revealed by the fact that it interrupts the parallelism in a way reminiscent of the statement in 2.1 which interrupted a pair of 'if' (ἐάν) clauses. But the content of the statement itself reveals that in some ways the entire discussion has been moving toward it: 'in this is manifest the children of God and the children of the Devil'. The words 'in this' or 'by this' appear to point both to what has preceded and what follows. That is, the presence or absence of sin in one's life reveals whether one is a child of God or the Devil. One's family identity becomes manifest by one's actions. The adjective translated 'manifest' (φανερά) appears only here in the Johannine literature, but is from the same word family (φανερόω) that has occurred earlier in 1 John (1.2; 2.19) and frequently in this section (2.28; 3.2, 5, 8). It is used to convey the idea of Jesus' manifestation in the Incarnation (1.2), the manifestation of the deceivers (2.10), the manifestation of Jesus' return (2.28; 3.2), the manifestation of the believer's existence at Jesus' return (3.2) and the manifestation of Jesus to take away (3.5) and destroy sin (3.8). Thus, for the reader to learn that the believer's family identity is to be made manifest through his or her actions conveys an ominous sense of awe. Their actions are very important, even in ways that transcend the present.

Balancing the reference to the now familiar 'children of God' is the phrase 'children of the Devil'. Although this is the only place in the whole of the New Testament where the precise phrase 'children of the Devil' occurs, its appearance here is neither out of place nor surprising. On the one hand, the Johannine reader knows that it is informed by the Fourth Gospel (8.44) where Jesus charges that his (Jewish) opponents are children of their father the Devil, a passage which appears to form the background of a previous discussion in 1 John (1.6-10). On the other hand, the previous statements with regard to the origins of sinful activity culminates rather naturally in this phrase. While it is true that individuals are never spoken of as 'being born of the Devil' in the Johannine literature, the phrase 'children of the Devil' cannot be far removed from such an idea.[122]

---

122   A conclusion reached as early as Origen, *Homily on Ezekiel* 9.1.

The second part of v. 10 contains the last half of the antithetical parallelism. This is the last occurrence of the 'each one who' formula that characterizes this section. In v. 9 the formula was used to underscore the fact that 'each one born of God does not sin', while here the statement is put more negatively: 'each one who does not do righteousness is not of God'. This phrase emphasizes the idea that one's righteousness or being without sin is not merely passive. One must actively pursue righteousness and be sinless. Perhaps such a statement would remind the reader that 'remaining in him' requires active participation on the believer's part. The words 'not of God' parallel 'of the Devil' in v. 8.

Surprisingly enough, the sentence does not end here as the reader has every right to expect. Rather, appended to this statement by use of 'and' (καὶ) is another which both clarifies what has come before and provides a transition to that which follows. Righteousness is not to be understood as some vague, abstract concept. On the contrary, it is to be understood very concretely as the presence or absence of love. On this occasion, it appears that the term normally translated 'and' (καὶ) should better be translated 'namely' or 'that is' for despite the abrupt transition, it is clear that the last part of this sentence carries the first part forward in specific ways. Understood in this way the sentence reads, 'each one who does not do righteousness is not of God, namely, the one who does not love his brother'. Reference to the love command has already been made in 2.3-17 where keeping the commands, the perfected love of God, love of one's brother (and sister), walking in the light and love of the Father are intertwined. There, the one who hates his brother (or sister) is characterized as one who walks in darkness, does not know where he or she is going, but has been blinded by the darkness (2.10-11). Such ideas are in the readers' mind as they make the transition to the next major section of 1 John, where the love command takes pride of place and forms the heart of 1 John. Before leaving this section of 1 John a final observation should perhaps be offered. It is significant that the definition of righteousness as love for one's brother (or sister) reinforces the fact that for the Johannine community there is no line of demarcation between belief and practice, theology and ethics.

Reflection and Response – Part Six

Reflection

Among the many emphases of this passage is its focus upon the children of God. In fact, this is the theme to which all the other emphases of the passage are connected. It is clear that believers are children of God owing to the fact that God himself has called us/them such. The basis of this identity as children of God issues forth from the magnificence of God's love. Being children of God leads to confidence at the appearing of the Son and not being known by the world, just as Jesus was not known by the world. This hope in the return of Jesus and this relationship to God as his children also leads to purification of self, with Jesus as the standard of purity. Such activity is in conformity with and anticipation of the fact that at his appearing, 'we shall be like him for we shall see him just as he is'. Therefore, those who are children of God avoid sin at all costs. In point of fact, as long as God's children remain in him and his seed remains in them, they are not able to sin! Sinful activity is such an important issue that its presence reveals that those who sin are children of the Devil instead of children of God.

Who are the children of God in today's world? What are their distinguishing characteristics? How can individuals know if they have been called children of God by God himself? What attitude do they exhibit toward the return of Jesus? What is their relationship to issues of purity and holiness? In what ways do they continue to remain in him? What attitudes toward the world, sin and the Devil are manifest in their daily lives? Where do they draw the lines between themselves and the world, and what leads them to these specific boundaries?

On a more personal level, at what point did you know you had been called a child of God by God himself? What happened to you and what changes took place? When you think about the return of Jesus does it bring comfort to you or does it generate the fear of shame and rejection? What are the reasons for your reactions? How has your identity as a child of God and your relationship with Jesus pushed you toward purity of life? Of what specific things have you been convicted in this regard? What specific steps do you take to insure that you 'remain' in him and his seed remains in you? What are the boundaries between you and the world, sin and the Devil?

Response

In order to respond to the teaching of this text appropriately, consider the following things:

First, reflect on the story of your conversion, identifying the ways in which God spoke to you. It may help to write it out as well.

Second, look for opportunities to share your testimony with a believer and an unbeliever as the Spirit provides the chance.

Third, within the community of faith examine the boundaries between you and the world, sin and the Devil. With others, seek to determine the legitimacy of these and if they sufficiently reflect the distinction between the children of God and the children of the Devil.

Fourth, in times of personal and corporate prayer seek further direction from the Lord about your life as his child.

1 John 3.11-17

At this point the reader comes to the very center of 1 John, for not only does 3.11-17 stand logistically at the center of the book but, as suggested in the Introduction, it is also theologically the heart of the work. The passage appears to fall into three subsections. It begins with a somewhat formulaic statement in v. 11 where the call to love one another is given and is followed by two subsections which deal with hatred and murder on the one hand (vv. 12-15), and laying down one's life and love on the other hand (vv. 16-17).[123] In some ways v. 18 provides both the conclusion to this section and the introduction to that which follows in vv. 19-24. For the purposes of this commentary, it will be treated as part of the next section. It is clear that this section as a whole continues the thought of 1 John in a variety of ways. Language familiar from earlier in the work reappears here, such as 'love', 'hate', 'from the beginning', 'evil', 'know' and 'remaining'. At the same time it also introduces several new ideas, as the concept of love receives further definition and color.

Verse 11. This most strategic section begins with a sentence that both looks back to the previous verse(s) and forward to the following verses. The sentence begins with the word 'because' (ὅτι), which clearly points to the preceding discussion regarding sin and the believer. Its appearance here suggests that what follows is an explanation of the relationship between doing righteousness and loving one's brother. In form, the opening line of v. 11 resembles that found in 1.5. In the former passage the text reads, 'And this is the message which we have heard from him'. In 3.11 the text reads, 'Because this is the message which you heard from the beginning'. Adding to the similarity between these verses is the fact that these are the only two places in the whole of the New Testament where the word translated 'message' (ἀγγελία) occurs. It is sometimes suggested that these similar statements are so striking that 1.5 and 3.11 are intended to serve as the major structural markers in the book. However, such claims appear to outdistance the text by paying insufficient attention to the differences between the statements and the continuity that exists across these suggested major divisions within the book. None-

---

123 Rensberger, *1 John, 2 John, 3 John*, p. 96.

theless, the formula found in v. 11 both recalls the previous formula found in 1.5 and indicates that a new section has begun, albeit one that has striking connections with that which precedes and that which follows.

The message is identified as being 'from the beginning'. By this phrase the readers are reminded that the command to 'love one another' is no recent innovation, but has its origins in the very foundation of the community. In point of fact, on this occasion the phrase takes the readers back to the ministry of the earthly Jesus, who in the Fourth Gospel gives the command to love one another on more than one occasion (Jn 13.34; 15.12, 17). Of special note is the fact that just as in the previous section the sinless living of the believers is to be based upon Jesus' own sinless life, so in the Fourth Gospel the love command is based squarely upon the fact that the disciples are to love one another just as Jesus has loved them. The fact that the readers are told that they 'have heard' this from the beginning indicates that part of the instruction received when first incorporated into the community would have included this command. Part of the significance of this command is conveyed by means of a purpose (ἵνα) clause, translated 'in order that you might love one another'.

Although this is the first time the readers of 1 John have encountered the phrase 'love one another', several things may be assumed about it. First, as noted before, the place of this command within the Johannine tradition would be unrivaled owing to the fact that it originates with Jesus. Second, it is clear from 2 John 5 that the readers would have some knowledge that this command was itself under attack by the deceivers. Third, it is also apparent that the readers would see no difference between 'loving one's brother' and 'loving one another', aside from the fact that Jesus is so closely associated with the wording of the latter. Fourth, it may not be without significance that the phrase 'love one another' has not appeared earlier in 1 John. Its being withheld until just this point in the argument may be another of the ways by which the importance of this section is highlighted. Given its significance in the community, its occurrence here would certainly have an impact upon the readers. After its appearance at this point in 1 John, 'love one another' occurs on several other occasions in the work (3.23; 4.7, 11, 12), though clearly interchangeably with 'love of brothers' (3.14; 4.20-21). Fifth, it may not be without significance that the verb 'love' appears here in the present tense, implying that this is an ongoing characteristic of the believer. Sixth, the fact that the readers are admonished so strongly in this passage (and others) to love one another may be an indication that this aspect of the community's life is being challenged very seriously. In this statement, which serves as the heart of 1 John and indeed of Johannine theology, the gaps from the earlier discussion on love (2.3-17) are beginning to be filled in for the reader.

Verses 12-15
The strategic statement of v. 11 is followed by several verses devoted to the themes of murder, hate and the way these themes are intertwined. In fact, the subsection begins with a discussion of Cain's murderous act (v. 12), moves to a discussion of the love-hate relationship between the world and the community, and concludes by addressing the ways in which hatred and murder are connected.

Verse 12. The positive statement of v. 11 is followed somewhat awkwardly by v. 12. Throughout 1 John, the readers have become accustomed to the use of 'just as' (καθώς) when they are being exhorted about one matter or another (2.18, 27), but especially in connection to Jesus (2.6; 3.2, 3, 7). However, this pattern is disrupted in v. 12 which begins with 'not just as' (οὐ καθώς), signaling a change in emphasis. The reader who has been encouraged to 'love one another' is immediately confronted with a negative example; an example of one whose actions are not to be followed. For the first and only time in 1 John, explicit reference is made to an Old Testament story.[124] Here the focus of attention is upon Cain, who is described in a twofold fashion. First, Cain is said to be 'of the evil one'. Such a statement clearly identifies Cain with the Devil, even as a child of the Devil, and reveals that Cain's example is to be avoided at all costs by the believer. Second, Cain is described as one who 'butchered his brother'. The word translated 'butchered' (ἔσφαξεν) is a term which conveys the gruesome nature of the murder of Abel, who is never called by name in this passage, and the word is often found with reference to cutting the throat of sacrificial victims. Its only other New Testament occurrences are in the book of Revelation (5.6, 9, 12; 6.9; 13.3, 8; 18.24), often in texts where this dimension of the word's meaning is being emphasized. By the use of this term, something of the ghastly nature of Cain's actions is conveyed to the reader.

This twofold description of Cain is followed by the question, 'And for what reason did he butcher him?' By this means the dramatic emphasis of the discussion is underscored, even as a transition is made to Cain's motive for such a horrendous action. The reason is simply put: 'Because his works were evil and those of his brother were righteous.' It should come as no surprise to the reader that Cain's works are evil given the

---

124 It is interesting that the only other occurrence of οὐ καθώς in the New Testament (Jn 6.58) also occurs with reference to an Old Testament event.

earlier statement that he is 'of the evil one'. Thus, the short answer to this rhetorical question is that Cain's evil works, including the butchering of his brother, find their origin in the evil one. But the reader is also likely to see reference to the Fourth Gospel, where evil works are closely connected with hatred and unbelief (3.19-21; 7.7). Not only are Cain's works labeled as 'evil', but they are also contrasted with his brother's works that are described as 'righteous'. Such language is reminiscent of the description of Cain (as evil, πονηρός) and Abel (as righteous, δίκαιος) found in Josephus (*Ant.* 1.53). Clearly the contrast between the two brothers would not be lost on the readers. Nor would the fact that by means of this contrast the reader is being prepared for the transition to the next verse where the contrast between the world and the community is described. Before leaving this verse it should probably be observed that with the mention of the 'righteous works of his brother' the reader has seen the last reference in 1 John to the term 'righteous'. It appears to give way to 'love' from this point.

Verse 13. The contrast between the 'evil works' of Cain and the 'righteous works' of his brother prepares the reader for what follows in v. 13. If someone righteous, like the brother of Cain, could suffer owing to the evil of someone else, it should come as no surprise that such events can still transpire. The readers are instructed, 'Do not be astonished, brothers, if the world hates you'. Several observations should be offered on this verse. First, the negative form of admonition ('do not be astonished') occurs only in the Johannine literature and usually precedes a theological statement of some importance (Jn 3.7; 5.28).[125] Here it is a combination of encouraging the readers not to be taken by surprise by the fact that the world hates them, and reminding them in an implicit fashion of the theologically significant foundation these words have in the Johannine community. Second, it is significant that for the first and only time in 1 John, the readers are addressed as 'brothers and sisters'.[126] Such an address is particularly appropriate in this context for it appears between reference to the murder of a brother in v. 12 and the love for and of one's brothers, which figures prominently in the rest of this passage. Third, the phrase 'if the world hates you' is a very delicate construction that does not make clear on its own whether or not the readers were actually suffering hatred at that very moment. However, both the context and the present tense form of the verb 'hates' indicate the experience

---

125 Strecker, *The Johannine Letters*, p. 110.
126 The Greek term ἀδελφοί in this context is inclusive of both men and women, thus the translation 'brothers and sisters'.

nine theology, the gaps from the earlier discussion on love (2.3-17) are beginning to be filled in for the reader.

Verses 12-15
The strategic statement of v. 11 is followed by several verses devoted to the themes of murder, hate and the way these themes are intertwined. In fact, the subsection begins with a discussion of Cain's murderous act (v. 12), moves to a discussion of the love-hate relationship between the world and the community, and concludes by addressing the ways in which hatred and murder are connected.

Verse 12. The positive statement of v. 11 is followed somewhat awkwardly by v. 12. Throughout 1 John, the readers have become accustomed to the use of 'just as' (καθώς) when they are being exhorted about one matter or another (2.18, 27), but especially in connection to Jesus (2.6; 3.2, 3, 7). However, this pattern is disrupted in v. 12 which begins with 'not just as' (οὐ καθώς), signaling a change in emphasis. The reader who has been encouraged to 'love one another' is immediately confronted with a negative example; an example of one whose actions are not to be followed. For the first and only time in 1 John, explicit reference is made to an Old Testament story.[124] Here the focus of attention is upon Cain, who is described in a twofold fashion. First, Cain is said to be 'of the evil one'. Such a statement clearly identifies Cain with the Devil, even as a child of the Devil, and reveals that Cain's example is to be avoided at all costs by the believer. Second, Cain is described as one who 'butchered his brother'. The word translated 'butchered' (ἔσφαξεν) is a term which conveys the gruesome nature of the murder of Abel, who is never called by name in this passage, and the word is often found with reference to cutting the throat of sacrificial victims. Its only other New Testament occurrences are in the book of Revelation (5.6, 9, 12; 6.9; 13.3, 8; 18.24), often in texts where this dimension of the word's meaning is being emphasized. By the use of this term, something of the ghastly nature of Cain's actions is conveyed to the reader.

This twofold description of Cain is followed by the question, 'And for what reason did he butcher him?' By this means the dramatic emphasis of the discussion is underscored, even as a transition is made to Cain's motive for such a horrendous action. The reason is simply put: 'Because his works were evil and those of his brother were righteous.' It should come as no surprise to the reader that Cain's works are evil given the

---

124   It is interesting that the only other occurrence of οὐ καθώς in the New Testament (Jn 6.58) also occurs with reference to an Old Testament event.

earlier statement that he is 'of the evil one'. Thus, the short answer to this rhetorical question is that Cain's evil works, including the butchering of his brother, find their origin in the evil one. But the reader is also likely to see reference to the Fourth Gospel, where evil works are closely connected with hatred and unbelief (3.19-21; 7.7). Not only are Cain's works labeled as 'evil', but they are also contrasted with his brother's works that are described as 'righteous'. Such language is reminiscent of the description of Cain (as evil, πονηρός) and Abel (as righteous, δίκαιος) found in Josephus (*Ant.* 1.53). Clearly the contrast between the two brothers would not be lost on the readers. Nor would the fact that by means of this contrast the reader is being prepared for the transition to the next verse where the contrast between the world and the community is described. Before leaving this verse it should probably be observed that with the mention of the 'righteous works of his brother' the reader has seen the last reference in 1 John to the term 'righteous'. It appears to give way to 'love' from this point.

Verse 13. The contrast between the 'evil works' of Cain and the 'righteous works' of his brother prepares the reader for what follows in v. 13. If someone righteous, like the brother of Cain, could suffer owing to the evil of someone else, it should come as no surprise that such events can still transpire. The readers are instructed, 'Do not be astonished, brothers, if the world hates you'. Several observations should be offered on this verse. First, the negative form of admonition ('do not be astonished') occurs only in the Johannine literature and usually precedes a theological statement of some importance (Jn 3.7; 5.28).[125] Here it is a combination of encouraging the readers not to be taken by surprise by the fact that the world hates them, and reminding them in an implicit fashion of the theologically significant foundation these words have in the Johannine community. Second, it is significant that for the first and only time in 1 John, the readers are addressed as 'brothers and sisters'.[126] Such an address is particularly appropriate in this context for it appears between reference to the murder of a brother in v. 12 and the love for and of one's brothers, which figures prominently in the rest of this passage. Third, the phrase 'if the world hates you' is a very delicate construction that does not make clear on its own whether or not the readers were actually suffering hatred at that very moment. However, both the context and the present tense form of the verb 'hates' indicate the experience

---

125 Strecker, *The Johannine Letters*, p. 110.
126 The Greek term ἀδελφοί in this context is inclusive of both men and women, thus the translation 'brothers and sisters'.

of hatred by the world is already a reality for the community. The appearance of such a delicate construction is one means by which the readers are admonished to take courage in the face of hatred for it points to their righteous standing, in the same line as that of Cain's brother. Fourth, talk of the world's hatred cannot help but evoke thoughts of the Fourth Gospel for the readers. They remember Jesus' warning that such hatred was certain to follow and that it was a sign of his followers' solidarity with him—for the world hated Jesus before they hated his followers (15.18-25; 16.1-4; 17.14). Fifth, in this verse the world is clearly an alien place for the child of God, just as it was for Jesus, despite his role in its creation. In this, its appearance here continues the thought of 1 Jn 2.15-17 and 3.1.

Verse 14. Resuming the thought of v. 11 and responding to the description of Cain and the world in vv. 12-13, v. 14 begins with a great deal of emphasis on the word 'we'. In contrast to Cain and the world 'we know that we have passed out of death into life, because we love the brothers'. The shift from the second person plural of the previous verses to the first person plural 'we' adds to the emphatic nature of this opening. Clearly, the knowledge of the readers is being underscored in ways that build upon earlier uses of this word for 'know' (οἶδα). They know all things through the chrisma they have received (2.20) and receive certain instruction because they know the truth (2.21). In the previous section this word is used to describe the fact that the readers know 'he is righteous' (2.29) and that they know of the manifestation of his return (3.2, 5). Thus, the appearance of the emphatic 'we know' would be quite reassuring to the readers who have just been admonished to love one another, but know the reality of being hated.

The sentence falls into two parts, structured around two occurrences of the same word (ὅτι) which may be translated 'that' in its first occurrence and 'because' in its second, both of which focus on the content of the readers' knowledge. The first aspect of the readers' knowledge to be emphasized is that 'we have passed out of death into life'. This phrase is a particularly graphic way to describe the transformation the readers have experienced. One aspect of this phrase that merits comment is the fact that this very phrase is found in the Fourth Gospel in the mouth of Jesus. In a solemn saying Jesus remarks, 'Truly, truly I say to you, the one who hears my word and believes in the one who sent me has eternal life, and does not come to judgment but has passed out of death into life' (Jn 5.24). It is difficult to believe that the readers would not see in the words of 1 Jn 3.14 a fulfillment of those spoken by Jesus in the Fourth Gospel. On this view, they carry the implicit message that the readers have heard his word and believed in the one who sent him. Therefore, they have already passed out of death into life. That is to say, they have eternal life. The verb (μεταβαίνω) itself conveys the idea of movement from one (spiritual) abode to another as its appearance in Jn 13.1 demonstrates, where Jesus knew that he would pass out of this world to the Father. Not only this, but the perfect tense of the verb indicates that this transformation took place at a particular point in the past, but its effects are still felt. In other words, the readers passed over from death at a specific point in the past (probably the time of their initial belief) and they continue to abide in life in the present. Even the prepositions 'out of' (ἐκ) and 'into' (εἰς) found here offer explicit support to the idea of movement from the sphere of death to that of life. Highlighting the fact that these are two spheres of existence, it is significant that both death and life appear here in the Greek text with the article. Although the word 'death' (θάνατος) often has reference to physical death in the Fourth Gospel (11.4, 13; 12.33; 18.32; 21.19), it also is clearly used to describe spiritual death. This is particularly true of its occurrence in Jn 5.24, where the one who passes from death unto life will hear his voice and be raised from the dead (5.25-29). Spiritual death is also in view in Jn 8.51. The idea that the reader has passed out of death into life also suggests that everyone abides in the sphere of spiritual death until they pass over from it into that of life. In the Johannine community this passage is accomplished by birth from above through the Spirit. Clearly the realm of life is that brought by Jesus to those who believe in him. The life now experienced sets the believer free from the realm of death. It is eternal life, which is experienced now and is a guarantee of resurrection life.

Not only do the readers know that 'we have passed out of death into life', the readers know this 'because we love the brothers'. The second part of this sentence is signaled by the second appearance of the Greek term here translated 'because' (ὅτι). The reason the readers can have such confidence and assurance that they have passed out of death into life is because of the knowledge that comes from their experience. The criterion, the test of their transformation, is love of the brothers and sisters. This fact alone reveals that they are unlike Cain and the world who are dominated by murder and hatred. Rather than domination by murder and hatred, their experience is one of love for the brothers and sisters. Such love is grounded in Jesus' desire for his followers (Jn 13.34) and is the identifiable characteristic that reveals an individual is one of his disciples (13.35). Thus, the presence of such love among the readers is proof of their transformation. While love does function in an evidential fashion in this text, the broader Johannine understanding of love would suggest that love also plays some role in the actual transformation of the believer out of death into life. It may be significant that 'brothers (and sisters)' appears here in the plural. As such, this may be a means by which the readers are reminded that such love must be focused on specific individuals.

Just as the presence of love for the brothers and sisters reveals that one has passed out of death into life, so the absence of love for the brothers and sisters reveals that one remains in death.[127] There is no middle ground when it comes to love. It is absolutely essential to one's identity and nature as one who remains in life. It is significant that the verb 'remains' is in the present tense on this occasion, revealing that one continues in the sphere of death even now, owing to a lack of love for the brothers and sisters. Such statements as those found in v. 14 would not only assure the readers of their place in life but also encourage self-examination with regard to the presence or absence of love in their lives and relationships.

Verse 15. This verse both builds off the thought of v. 14 and returns to the themes introduced in vv. 12-13 as it rounds out this subsection (3.12-15). The entire community is addressed by means of the phrase 'each one who', as v. 15 develops the thought of v. 14 by intensifying its thought significantly. Specifically, 'the one who does not love' of v. 14 becomes 'each one who hates', revealing that there is no middle ground when it comes to the presence or absence of love. Not only does the shift from not loving to hating take place, but the rhetoric escalates as the sentence spirals up to the point that 'each one who hates his brother is a murderer'! Such a startling statement builds the argument of 1 John in several ways. First, it combines the ideas of murder by Cain (v. 12) and hatred by the world (v. 13) in an explicit fashion at this point. Such a combination indicates that these two ideas are so very closely related that one is no less culpable for hatred than for murder, so serious is the matter of hatred. Second, the appearance of the term 'murderer' no doubt here brings images of Cain to the reader's mind, for he stands as the great example of one whose hatred of brother results in his butchering of him. Third, occurrence of the term 'murderer', literally 'man-killer' (ἀνθρωποκτόνος), could not fail but to result in the readers' identification of 'one who hates' with the Devil, who is himself referred to by means of this same term in Jn 8.44. Adding to its significance is the fact that these are the only two places in the whole of the New Testament where this particular term occurs. In the Fourth Gospel, it is found in the

---

127 This is only one of two places where the verb 'remain' appears in a negative sense in the Johannine literature (cf. also Jn 12.46).

context where Jesus accuses his adversaries: 'You are of your father the Devil and you desire to do his lusts. That one was a murderer from the beginning, and he does not stand in the truth, because the truth is not in him.' Thus, the one who hates brother or sister is being identified in an explicit way with the Devil. Hatred on the part of individuals reveals that those who hate share the nature of their father the Devil. This statement also makes explicit the intent of 1 Jn 3.10 where the children of the Devil are identifiable by the fact that they do not do righteousness, that is, they do not love the brother or sister.

Again appeal is made to the common tradition of the community by means of the words 'and you know that'. On this occasion, the readers are reminded that 'the murderer does not have eternal life remaining in him'. The closest one comes to this idea within the Johannine literature is Rev. 21.8 where murderers (φονεῦσιν) are included in a list of those who will 'have their part in the lake of fire, which is the second death'. The point is clear enough, those who hate to the point of taking life give adequate proof that they are not among those who live in the realm of life, for their actions reveal that their abode is that of death. Consistent with much of Johannine thought, it is interesting that here the text speaks of eternal life remaining in the individual. This is not altogether unexpected as several things can be spoken of in the Johannine literature as remaining in the believer. These include: the Word (1 Jn 2.14; Jn 5.38), the anointing (χρῖσμα) (1 Jn 2.27), the Seed of God (3.9), the love of God (3.17), and the Truth (2 Jn 2). In addition, the Father (1 Jn 3.24; 4.12, 13, 15-16), Jesus (Jn 6.56; 15.5) and the Paraclete (Jn 14.17) may also be spoken of in this way.[128] Such stern language is no doubt directed to the deceivers but is also probably addressed to individuals within the community as well. Thus, it would not seem to be going too far to see here an implicit warning to those in the community that if one does not remain in him, evidenced by the practice of love for the brothers and sisters, one could forfeit the gift of eternal life.[129] Such a warning is quite consistent with the emphasis in the previous section upon remaining in him in order to live without sin. On this view, hatred is indeed a mortal danger.[130]

Verse 16-17
In contrast to the previous subsection (vv. 12-15) which was devoted to the negative example of Cain and the world, the final subsection (vv. 16-

---

[128] Westcott, *The Epistles of St. John*, p. 113.
[129] Bultmann, *The Johannine Epistles*, p. 55.
[130] Strecker, *The Johannine Letters*, p. 114.

17) of this passage (3.11-17) focuses upon the positive example of Jesus and the implications of his life of love for the believers' lives.

Verse 16. The words 'in this' in the phrase 'in this we have known love' point ahead for the definition of love to the 'that' clause which constitutes the second part of v. 16a. Yet again appeal is made to the common tradition of the community. The perfect past tense 'have known' indicates that a particular event from the past, with results that abide in the present, is here in mind. As the sentence unfolds, it becomes clear that here the common tradition has to do with Jesus' death on the cross. The more immediate referent of what is known is 'love', which appears in this verse with the definite article indicating love in its absolute sense. Appearance of the word 'love' clearly picks up on its mention at the beginning of this section (v. 11), where the message heard from the beginning is identified as 'love one another'. 'Love of the brothers (and sisters)' appears in the middle of this section as the evidence that the readers have passed out of death into life (v. 14), while lack of love reveals that one remains within the sphere of death. Thus, the definition of love offered in v. 16 is of more than passing interest to the readers for it has come to be identified as the essential characteristic of the believer in 1 John.

The definition of love here offered is given in narrative form. That is to say, love is defined by means of an example; 'that one (ἐκεῖνος) laid aside his life on our behalf'. Rather clearly, 'that one' has reference to Jesus, who, says 1 Jn 2.2, is an atoning sacrifice (ἱλασμός) for our sins and those of the entire world. The reader also knows that it is the blood of Jesus that cleanses the believer from sin (1.7). When these ideas are combined with the passion of Jesus as described in the Fourth Gospel, the sacrificial nature of this verse becomes clear. The imagery of 'laying aside one's life' occurs only here and in the Fourth Gospel in the New Testament. Specifically, this is the way Jesus speaks of himself in the Good Shepherd Discourse (Jn 10.11-18). The fact that such similarity of language appears in the Fourth Gospel strongly suggests that the common tradition of the community is, at this point, to be equated with that found in the Fourth Gospel. The imagery is that of laying aside one's life as if a garment, an image reflected in Jn 13.4, where Jesus lays aside his garments before washing the feet of the disciples. The (aorist) past tense of the verb 'laid aside' reveals that a particular laying aside is in view. Clearly it is that of Jesus' voluntarily laying aside his life on the cross, a life no one takes from him. It should also be observed that standing in the place of emphasis in the Greek text is the phrase 'on our behalf', underscoring how such a sacrifice is directly connected to the readers.

Such an example of love is not something simply to be pondered, but carries with it an ethical obligation of the most binding character. Following fast on the heels of the statement about Jesus' death are these words: 'we are also obligated to lay aside our lives on behalf of the brothers'. These words immediately remind the reader of Jesus' own words in the Fourth Gospel (15.13): 'Greater love than this no one has, that he lay aside his life for his friend.' Therefore, the command of 1 Jn 3.16 is not simply a deduction drawn from Jesus' actions but is based directly upon his words in the Fourth Gospel. In this regard, Peter's offer to lay aside his life for Jesus earlier in the Fourth Gospel (13.37) is ironically in accord with these later words. In 1 Jn 3.16b 'we' stands in an emphatic position. 'We', as opposed to Cain and those who hate the brothers, have an obligation to love as Jesus loved. If the evidence of remaining in life is 'loving the brothers (and sisters)', then it appears that the evidence of loving the brothers (and sisters) is 'laying down our lives on their behalf'. The absolutely mandatory nature of these words is conveyed by the phrase 'we are obligated'. The verb that stands behind this phrase (ὀφείλομεν) occurs at several places in the Johannine literature (1 Jn 2.6; 4.11; 3 Jn 8; Jn 13.14; 19.7) and usually describes an ethical obligation for the believer that is based upon the example of Jesus.[131] Here such an obligation to lay aside one's life is clearly based upon the example of Jesus laying aside his life. The fact that the verb translated 'are obligated' is in the present tense and the verb 'to lay aside' is in the (aorist) past tense indicates that this obligation, which can take place but once, is an ongoing part of the very definition of the believer. One must be ready at any moment to make that once and for all sacrifice. The plural 'lives' reveals that such love is to be exhibited by the community in a variety of contexts. Although there is no indication in 1 John that the community faced the kind of persecution which could result in the martyrdom of its members, there is some evidence to suggest that such an eventuality might be an expectation of the readers. First, Jesus' words of warning in the Fourth Gospel about possible future excommunication and martyrdom (16.2-3) would no doubt be part of the readers' thoughts on this subject. Second, the fact that the readers were living in the 'last hour', which the arrival of antichrists indicates (1 Jn 2.18), might also bring with it the expectation of martyrdom in the last days. Finally, it is clear that at least some in the broader Johannine community did at some point suffer in precisely this way, Antipas serving as the chief example (Rev. 2.13). Thus, in contrast to those who hate and take life, the believers are to love and give life. This is their abode; this, their domain.

---

131   Brown, *The Epistles of John*, p. 449.

Verse 17. If the laying aside of one's life is rarely a possibility for the believer, other sacrifices are called for more regularly. Verse 17 may be set out in the following fashion.

> If anyone has the life (possessions) of this world
> and sees his brother having need
> and shuts up his compassion from him,
> how can the love of God remain in him?

The construction of this sentence in the Greek text itself informs the reader in a couple of ways. First, it is significant that the first three lines of this sentence are not complete in themselves but look forward to the end of the sentence where the kind of person being described is revealed.[132] In this way the sense of drama for the reader builds until the end of the sentence. Second, the phrase with which v. 17 begins 'if anyone has' (ὅς δ' ἂν ἔχῃ) suggests a situation that is expected to occur on a regular basis. Thus, as opposed to the once and for all laying aside of one's life, the readers now learn of a laying aside that is expected to occur with a great deal more regularity.

The first statement in v. 17, 'if anyone has the life (βίον) of this world' describes members of the community who have 'goods, possessions, or livelihood'. While it might be safe to assume that in themselves these things are neither good nor bad, the addition of the phrase 'of the world' alerts the reader that such may not be the case on this occasion. For the reader knows that one of the dangers facing the believer is 'love of the world and the things of the world' (2.15). One such thing of the world, singled out for specific mention in that warning, is 'the pride of life (βίου)' (2.16), an arrogant ostentatious pride in one's material possessions. Therefore, one of the connotations that the phrase 'the life of the world' would have for the reader is one filled with warning about the seduction of riches. At the same time, mention of 'the life of the world' would also remind the reader that the things they will be called upon to lay aside are transitory in nature, because the world itself (and its lusts) is passing away (2.17).

The second statement in v. 17 builds upon the first one in several ways. One of which is that it is the person who 'has the life (possessions) of this world' who 'sees his brother (or sister) having need'. The word translated 'see' carries with it the idea of gazing upon another, implying that the one who has the possessions of this world has become aware of the situation of the one who has need. Another way the second part of the sentence builds upon the first is by means of the contrast created

---

132 Brown, *The Epistles of John*, p. 449.

between the one who 'has possessions', on the one hand, and the one who 'has need' on the other hand. Although it is not altogether clear what kinds of needs are here in mind, it would appear safe to assume that they would include things like food, clothing, shelter and work. Perhaps the kinds of things Gaius was prepared to offer to the Johannine missionaries in 3 John are not far from the need envisioned in this verse.

The third statement, in turn, builds upon the previous two. The one who has possessions, and who sees the brother's (or sister's) need is now described as locking up his or her compassion. The word translated 'compassion' (σπλάγχνα) literally means 'intestines' and conveys the ancient idea that this part of the body was the seat of its emotions. In this, its only occurrence in the Johannine literature, the term draws on the idea that love is an act which utilizes the emotions. The implication is that 'having the life of this world' and 'seeing the need a brother has' should result in an appropriate engagement of the emotions to enable a loving response on the part of the believer. But instead of such a response, what is described in this part of v. 17 involves the 'shutting up' or 'locking away' (κλείσῃ) from the brother or sister in need the very center of one's emotions. Such a response effectively seals one off from the opportunity to respond to such need in love.[133]

This verse closes with a rhetorical question so stark in nature that the reader must supply the rather obvious answer. If a person 'has' and 'sees' and 'locks up', 'how can the love of God remain in him (or her)?' This section, therefore, concludes as it began with an explicit statement about love of one's brother (or sister). The love of God mentioned here is no doubt the same love of God as mentioned earlier in 1 John (2.5) which can be spoken of as having been perfected or completed in the life of the one who keeps his word. Clearly such love is a gift from God himself and enables the believer to love the brothers (or sisters). And at the same time, it is evidence to the believer that he or she has passed out of death into life. Just as it is possible to say that eternal life does not remain in the murderer (v. 15), so it is possible to say that the love of God does not remain in the one who locks away his or her compassion from community members in need.

It seems likely that these words are aimed in the direction of the deceivers and false teachers whose understanding of the faith may have excluded, or at least minimized, the need for the kind of love here

---

133   On this point the insightful remarks of Rensberger, *1 John, 2 John, 3 John*, p. 101, should be cited: 'People must shut off their inner selves, the emotions of care and concern and the bodily sensations that accompany them, in order to maintain an indifference to others in need. Only when they have walled themselves off emotionally can they wall themselves off theologically and materially as well.'

described. Such a position might be like that found in Ignatius' description of his opponents in *Smyrnaeans* (6.2): 'For love they have no care, none for the widow, none for the orphan, none for the distressed, none for the afflicted, none for the prisoner, or for him released from prison, none for the hungry or thirsty.'[134] There is also an implicit warning to the readers that the gift of being a child of God can be forfeited if the love of God does not remain in the believer. In such a case, one 'can experience a renewed subjection of one's self to the rule of the world and of death'.[135]

Reflection and Response—Part Seven

Reflection

The theme that dominates the passage that stands at the center of 1 John is devoted to a further exposition of love. Specifically, love is identified as the message which was heard from the beginning, is contrasted with hate, and is identified as the sign that one has passed from death unto life. In contrast to hatred, which leads to the slaughter of one's brother or sister, love exhibits itself in laying down one's life for one's brother or sister, following the example of Jesus. Concrete expressions of such love include opening one's heart of compassion to a brother or sister in need and giving of one's possessions.

The following questions are designed to assist in reflecting upon this theme. If love and hatred are exhibited in concrete acts, what do the actions of the Church reveal about its character? In what ways does the Church demonstrate a loving attitude to brothers and sisters in need? Has the Church, or some within the Church, been involved in the 'slaughter' of its own? What specific examples come to mind? How has the church been most successful in living in accordance with the teaching of this passage? What are its greatest failures?

When reflecting on this theme more personally, do you detect the presence of hatred and love in your own life? What temptations do you have to hurt another brother or sister? If hatred grows from a seed of hard feelings to the murder of another, what is the furthest point you have made on that journey? When did you experience this and how have you responded to it? What acts of love and compassion are currently part of your life? What are the regular acts of love and compassion in your life? Can you identify a recent event when you acted in a spontaneous way toward a brother or sister in need? Based upon the presence

---

134   Cited according to the translation of K. Lake, *Apostolic Fathers*, I (London: Heinemann, 1912), p. 259.
135   Strecker, *The Johannine Letters*, p. 116.

or absence of love and hatred in your life, would you be considered a child of God or a child of the Devil?

Response

How can we respond to such challenging questions?

First, it is important to begin with an honest evaluation of your life with regard to the presence or absence of love and hatred. Therefore, assess your life by means of the reflection questions.

Second, pray specifically about the things that are troubling about your life with regard to hatred. Make this a regular matter of prayer until you hear from God.

Third, commit yourself to the Lord and a trusted member of the community to turn from evil acts to loving ones. This involves two steps. Identify the individual(s) with whom you are at odds and make preparation to render an act of compassion and love to him or her when the next opportunity presents itself. In addition, identify those within your community who are in need and, along with others, act in ways to alleviate their need.

Fourth, in order to maintain an open heart of compassion, be intentional about reflecting upon and responding to the needs around you in both long-term and spontaneous ways.

1 John 3.18-24

With this section, the structure of 1 John begins to take a new turn by revealing a concentric contour. This is to say that after building to the last passage (3.11-17), which stands at the heart of this work as well as the heart of Johannine theology, each of the subsequent sections begins to mirror a preceding section. This passage (3.18-24) shows a number of points of continuity with the one that stands on the other side of the central one regarding love for one another. In that passage (2.28–3.10), as with this one, the section begins with a term of endearment, explains how one can have confidence before God, and encourages purity of life. 1 Jn 3.18-24 may be divided into the following subsections: the introductory statement of v. 18 is followed by the focus upon the heart that condemns (vv. 19-20). The confidence which results from a heart that does not condemn (vv. 21-22) gives way to a discussion of both the identity of the believer and keeping of his commands (vv. 23-24).

Verse 18. In many ways v. 18 could be treated as the conclusion to the preceding section for it continues in a concrete fashion the emphasis and theme of that passage by extending the thought of vv. 16-17 in particular. However, there are also reasons for seeing this verse as an introduction to the next section, for it begins with a term of endearment, as have a number of sections in 1 John, and it introduces the next section by means of a specific word, 'truth'. Thus, v. 18 may be thought of as something of a bridge or transition from one section of the book to the next. Its discussion here rather than in the previous section is more a sign of the inadequacies of proposed outlines for the book than a sign that the verse has less continuity with the preceding than with the following section.

This verse begins with a return to the term of endearment 'little children', which picks up on the children of God emphasis of 2.28–3.10. It also shows that this is the preferred term of endearment for the readers of 1 John at this point. A serious admonition follows 'little children' which contains both negative and positive elements. The prohibition, 'let us not love in word nor tongue' is followed by the admonition, 'but in work and truth'. This particular construction may suggest that the temptation to love in theory but not in practice was all too real for those in the community, for this construction is normally used to indicate that a certain activity should be stopped or avoided.[136] It is clear that what is being prohibited is a love confined to empty words or a theoretical commitment to love, but one which lacks the concrete acts identified in v. 17. The relationship between the terms 'word and tongue' and 'work and truth' may be explained in any number of ways. It is possible that the words in each phrase are to be understood simply as synonyms or seen to show some kind of progression in thought from one word to the next. However, there is reason to believe that the reader would take the second word in each pair as expressing the reason for the first.[137] On this interpretation, it is the 'tongue' that expresses the 'word' of love, while the 'work' of love finds its origin in the 'Truth'. Viewed in its context, there is a condemnation of verbal expressions of love for those in need, that are not accompanied by acts of love which involve giving of oneself and one's material means. In contrast to 'the works of the Devil' (3.8) and the 'evil works' of Cain (3.12), the work here identified has its origin in Truth. Appearance of the word 'Truth' (ἀληθείᾳ) at this point in 1 John would not only point to the origin of the 'work' of love here prescribed, but would also point beyond itself to the deeper christological associations Truth has in the Johannine literature. Simply put, Jesus, whose love is the model for believers, is the one who enables the love that must remain in the believer. This particular combination of words (ἐν ἔργῳ καὶ

---

136   Plummer, *The Epistles of S. John*, p. 86.
137   Brown, *The Epistles of John*, p. 452.

ἀλνθείᾳ) reminds the reader of 3 John 8, where those who receive and support the Johannine missionaries are called 'coworkers in the Truth' (συνεργοὶ...τῇ ἀληθείᾳ). Gaius' work of hospitality (3 Jn 5) is a striking example of the concrete acts of love called for in 1 Jn 3.18.

Verses 19-20. These two verses form one rather complicated and obscure sentence in the Greek text,[138] which presents a number of interpretive challenges. The sentence begins with the phrase 'and in this' which can refer to that which follows, but here rather clearly has reference to that which precedes. As such, it is on the basis of the concrete acts of love in work and Truth (v. 18) that 'we shall know that we are of the Truth'. The verb translated 'we shall know' is in the future tense and implies a possible future crisis that the readers may face. What generates this crisis is not stated, but it seems likely that the issue concerns how one can know whether or not he or she is 'of the Truth'. To know that one is 'of the Truth' means knowing that one's life, especially as it relates to love of the brothers, finds its origin and enablement in Jesus who is *the* Truth in the Johannine literature. Such knowledge should be a source of confidence for the believer.

The next phrase is not so easily understood, for after reading these words of comfort, the readers are now emphatically brought into the very presence of God by means of the words 'before him' which stand first in the Greek phrase at this point. It is difficult to know precisely how the readers would understand this phrase, owing to the differing images that are called forth in it. On the one hand, it could be a means to underscore God's role as judge so that the reader sees himself or herself as standing before the judge of all judges. On the other hand, the sentence begins with words of comfort to the believer, words that might not sit as well with the imagery of judgment. How might these images and ideas be reconciled? In the parallel passage to this one (2.28-3.10), the idea of having confidence before God is connected to the appearing of Jesus at his return. While such imagery involves the idea of judgment, its primary emphasis is that of self-examination and purification of self. In 3.19, there may be an intentional ambiguity about the precise meaning of being 'before him' so as to include any number of occasions when the believer might find themselves before him, to include times of prayer, a topic that is taken up later in this section.

---

138   Brown's comments, *The Epistles of John*, p. 453, are particularly hard hitting. He states: 'We have already seen that the epistolary author is singularly inept in constructing clear sentences, but in these he is at his worst... At the least, it offers the Prologue competition for the prize in grammatical obscurity.'

It is while before him that 'we convince/assure our heart'. The problem at this point is how to understand the Greek verb (πείσομεν) normally translated as 'convince' or 'convict'. Unfortunately, no help is gained from its use in other Johannine contexts for this is its only occurrence in the whole of the Johannine literature. If the verb is translated in its normal fashion, it is very difficult to see on what point the believer is trying to convince himself or herself. For that reason, it seems best to translate the verb as 'to calm' or 'to reassure', a meaning the word has in several ancient texts.[139] Thus it appears that 'we reassure our heart' as we are 'before him'. Although this is the only passage in which the word 'heart' occurs in the Johannine Epistles, the fact that the heart needs reassurance would surprise few readers. In the Fourth Gospel, the heart is clearly the center of a variety of activities and emotions such as discernment (12.40), purpose (13.2), distress (14.1, 27), sorrow (16.6) and joy (16.22).[140] The heart is viewed as the center of the human being and the seat of moral character. It is interesting that a term which comes to have this meaning in the Fourth Gospel occurs in such proximity to the term earlier translated 'compassion' (v. 17), which is also closely associated with the emotions. Perhaps the reader would see a parallel between that which is felt in the face of a brother in need and that felt in the face of God. One's response in one context is no doubt related to one's response in the other. It may be significant that 'heart' appears here in the singular, providing yet another link to v. 17 where singular nouns also appear.

As the sentence continues in v. 20, the heart's need for reassurance is made clear in the phrase, 'if our heart condemns us'. The term translated 'condemn' is a legal term that focuses on internal judgment rather than formal sentence. It conveys the idea of accusations which the heart, that center of the human being and seat of moral character, makes on the basis of its intimate knowledge of the individual. This Greek term literally means 'to know against' and may be used in this context to contrast the heart's knowing (καταγινώσκη) with that of God (γινώσκει). The context suggests that the heart's knowledge, as extensive as it is, is not complete or exhaustive. Not only can the readers know that they are 'of the Truth', owing to the acts of love manifest in their lives, but also because 'God is greater than our heart and knows all things'. In this most remarkable statement,[141] there is an intentional contrast between the

---

139   Cf., e.g. 2 Macc. 4.45 and Mt. 28.14.
140   Westcott, *The Epistles of St. John*, p. 136.
141   Schnackenburg, *The Johannine Epistles*, p. 186, says that this phrase is 'one of the major theological statements in 1 John'.

heart's ability to condemn (καταγινώσκῃ) and God's ability to know (γινώσκει). In this, God is greater than our heart. This is made clear for the reader in the last phrase in v. 20, where the reason for God's superiority over the heart is made explicit, because 'he knows all things', words which echo those of Peter in the Fourth Gospel (21.17). The heart's accusations may result from knowledge of sin or an exaggerated feeling of guilt.[142] Thus, its judgment may not always be trusted, owing to the imprecise nature of its knowledge. However, God's knowledge of the individual is complete. It is neither too strict nor too lenient. Just as the readers can rely upon the 'anointing' to teach them 'all things' (2.20), so here the reader may trust in the fact that 'God knows all things'. God's knowledge of the thoughts and intents of the heart, as well as its acts of love, should enable the readers to reassure their heart in moments of such accusations. It is not altogether clear why the readers need assurance on this point. It is possible that it is a response to the polemics of the deceivers who were challenging them about their standing before God. If so, just as the readers need no one to teach them owing to the 'anointing' they have received (2.27), so they have need of no one to condemn them owing to God's knowledge.

Verses 21-22. The next two verses also form one sentence in the Greek text and build off the previous two verses in a specific fashion. For a third time in 1 John the readers are addressed as 'Beloved'. On this occasion, its occurrence represents an emphatic turning toward the readers,[143] as it offers comfort to them after the troublesome discussion of the heart's accusatory condemnations and at the same time serves to connect this discussion in an explicit fashion with that of 3.11-17. By this means, the readers' attention continues to be directed toward love of brothers and sisters. With its appearance, the somewhat ominous tone of the previous verses (vv. 19-20) gives way to the more heartening ones which follow. The believers' reassuring their hearts by means of their own acts of love and God's complete knowledge of them results in hearts that do not condemn. This much is clearly meant by the phrase 'if our heart does not condemn us'. But included in this audience are also, no doubt, readers whose hearts are not offering condemning accusations. By means of yet another example of antithetical parallelism the argument of 1 John is developed as this statement ('if our heart does not condemn us') plays off the one in v. 20 ('if our heart condemns us'). Specifically, a heart that does not condemn means 'we have confidence with God'.

---

142 Schnackenburg, *The Johannine Epistles*, p. 186.
143 Strecker, *The Johannine Letters*, p. 123.

Several aspects of this phrase merit comment. First, the fact that the word 'confidence' stands first in the Greek phrase indicates that the readers would see the emphasis of the sentence being placed here. Second, the word translated 'confidence' has already appeared in another passage in 1 John where the readers were in need of assurance (2.28). There its meaning focuses upon the confidence one can have as a child of God at the appearing of Jesus. Rather than being uncertain of their place, they may have confidence and not be ashamed at his appearing. When the term reappears in 3.21, its earlier usage is no doubt still in the readers' ears. The same kind of confidence or boldness that one may have in the face of Jesus' appearing may be enjoyed already any time one is with God. Third, as in its earlier occurrence, confidence carries with it the idea of freedom of speech or the boldness a child has to speak to its parent. This aspect is particularly significant given the fact that one result of this confidence, identified in v. 22, is manifest in the believer's intercession with the Father. Fourth, supporting the idea that the believer can have confidence in the present is the present tense form of the verb 'have', indicating that confidence is a current possession. Fifth, the phrase translated 'with God' (πρὸς τὸν θεὸν) implies that the believer looks in the direction of God and has a friendly relationship with him. Thus, the anxiety found in v. 19 with regard to the accusatory heart when one is before God gives way to the confidence of a child freely speaking with its parent.

The results of such confidence are made all the clearer in v. 22 where the thought of this sentence continues. '*If* our heart does not condemn us' then owing to our confidence with God 'whatever we ask, we receive from him'. Such a statement is phenomenal and strikes the reader as being in the same category as those that speak about the believer being without sin and being perfected in love. That is to say, they seem like qualities confined to future existence.[144] But there can be no doubt that this is the actual current experience of the believers, for both the words 'ask' and 'receive' appear here in the present tense, indicating that such 'asking' and 'receiving' is an ongoing reality in their lives. It is also clear that *every* petition is granted. Though such language seems incredible, the readers would likely see in it a reference to and fulfillment of the words of Jesus found at various places in the Fourth Gospel (14.14; 15.7, 16; 16.23-24, 26-27). Despite the fact that this is the first explicit occurrence of petition language in 1 John, clear allusions have already been made with regard to 'confession of sin' among others (1.9). These references along with those which occur later in the work suggest that prayer

---

144 Marshall, *The Epistles of John*, p. 199.

is a regular part of the community's spirituality. No doubt such prayer is based on the model of Jesus in the Fourth Gospel (6.11; 11.41-42; 17.1-26).

The confidence that results in such asking and receiving is grounded in this reality: 'because we keep his commands and do the things that are pleasing before him'. While it is possible to reduce this statement to a contractual arrangement between God and the believer, where each party has certain obligations to one another, such an understanding does not do justice to the integrative nature of Johannine theology and ethics. Rather, this statement reveals something of the reciprocal nature of the relationship that exists between God and his children. The relationship between receiving that which is requested and obedience to God is grounded in Jesus' words in the Fourth Gospel (14.15; 15.14, 17) and so is at the basis of the community's self-understanding. But the reciprocal nature of this relationship goes even further. The implication is that the more one keeps the commands and does those things that please him, the more one is in a position to ask and receive. Such an implication prepares the way for future words about the relationship between receiving and obedience found in 1 Jn 5.14, where such asking is to be in accordance with his will.

By mention of 'keeping his commands'[145] the reader is taken all the way back to 2.3-17, where the idea is first taken up in 1 John. In that context there is a clear understanding that keeping the commands may be understood as keeping *the* command of 'loving one another'. Such an understanding is confirmed in 3.11-18 where this command is given pride of place in the book. Now, keeping the commands also includes for the reader, the loving act of laying aside one's life on behalf of one's brother or sister and the loving act of laying aside one's possessions on behalf of a brother or sister in need. Therefore, at this point in the argument of 1 John 'keeping the commands' is informed by all that precedes it and carries with it the idea that love requires the expression of practical acts of love. Thus, the asking and receiving described in v. 22 are bounded on either side by references to the love command. The believer has confidence owing in part to a knowledge of the loving acts in v. 19 and the ground of one's asking and receiving is keeping his commands which focuses on the love command. This asking and receiving is also grounded in 'doing the things pleasing before him'. Again

---

145 Brown, *The Epistles of John*, pp. 461-62, notes: 'In Johannine literature keeping the commands or divine word leads to many good things (beside having one's requests granted), e.g. never seeing death (John 8.51); being given the Paraclete (14.15-16); being loved by the Father (14.21); having the Father and the Son indwell (14.23); remaining in Jesus' love (15.10).'

explicit reference is made to the tradition of the Fourth Gospel. On this occasion, Jesus' words in 8.29 forms the basis of these words. There, Jesus says, 'I always do things pleasing to him'. While the readers would probably see little difference between 'keeping his commands' and 'doing the things that are pleasing before him', this latter phrase offers them yet another example of Jesus as the model for their own behavior. Just as the believer is to be pure as he is pure, and to love as he has loved, so the believer is to please God as he has pleased him. It should probably be noted that both the verbs, 'keeping' and 'doing', are in the present tense, implying that both activities are ongoing and regular in the believers' lives.

Verse 23. This verse begins with a formula, 'and this is the command', which is connected to what precedes and points forward to what follows. It is clear that here the formula focuses the readers' attention upon a further definition of 'the command', a concept that has received no little attention to this point. This definition of 'the command' of God follows closely the discussion of the 'commands' of God. Such a move from the plural 'commands' to the singular 'command' has occurred earlier in 1 John (2.3-8) and, as a result, would not come as a surprise to the readers on this occasion. However, what follows is surprising to the readers on two counts. First, instead of the command being defined in a singular fashion, as one expects given the move from 'commands' to 'command', it is given a twofold definition in v. 23. Second, it is also a bit of a surprise that the love command does not follow this formula immediately, for the love command has been very closely and consistently tied to 'the command' at various points in 1 John. 'The command' is defined in 3.23 in the following way, 'that we might believe in the name of his Son Jesus Christ and that we love one another just as he gave a command to us'. Such a powerful statement would be pregnant with meaning for the readers.

It should be noted from the outset that this sentence's construction reveals 'believing' and 'loving' are integrally connected activities and are not to be seen as alternatives or in competition with one another as to which is more important. They are clearly two aspects of one command. This is borne out by the fact that they stand together as the definition of the command and are both part of the same purpose (ἵνα) clause in the Greek text. It is also significant that for the first time in this work the language of 'believing' appears. It is somewhat surprising that the first occurrence of this language in 1 John comes well after the book's midway point, given the fact that this term (πιστεύω) is an extraordinarily important one in the Fourth Gospel. Its appearance here introduces the reader to language that will become frequent from this point onwards in 1 John, occurring five times in the remainder of the book (4.1, 16; 5.1, 5, 10, 13). However, it should be observed that though 'believing' terminology is only introduced at this point, the idea of 'believing' has at least been alluded to earlier in 2.22-23, a passage which deals with 'confessing' Jesus. This earlier theme prepares the readers in some ways for the emphasis on believing that develops in the latter part of 1 John.

The first part of the command, 'that we might believe in the name of his Son Jesus Christ' is part of the fabric of the community's tradition as revealed in the Fourth Gospel. The idea of believing in his name is strategically positioned in the Fourth Gospel. Its first appearance comes in the prologue and with it the promise that those who believe in his name are given 'the authority to become children of God' (Jn 1.12). Its last occurrence is found very near the conclusion of the Fourth Gospel in the book's purpose statement where those who believe in his name have life as a result (20.31). As the idea of belief in Jesus is a central one in the Fourth Gospel, the concept would be a familiar one to the readers and fit naturally within their spirituality. In the ancient world the name stood for the authority and character of a person.[146] In some ways, the name was held to be synonymous with all that the person represents. In this verse, the particular title that appears leaves no doubt as to what is at stake in this name, for here 'his Son Jesus Christ' occurs. At various points the readers have observed that when a full version of the name occurs it signals that false teaching is soon to be addressed directly. Such hints occur in 2 John 3 and in the prologue of 1 John (1.3). In both cases, this earlier mention of the full version of the name gives way to admonitions about deceivers who apparently misrepresent and/or misunderstand Jesus and his work. This is true in 2 John 7 where an aspect of the Incarnation is apparently being denied. Neither are the expectations of the readers of 1 John disappointed in this regard as the significance of Jesus is stressed at a number of places (1.7; 2.1-2, 6, 12, 14, 28-29; 3.2-3, 5-7, 16) and it is revealed that there are those who do not confess him (2.22-24). Added to this is the fact that the very next major section of 1 John returns to the topic of the false prophets, antichrists and deception (4.1-6). To 'believe in the name of his Son Jesus Christ' is not only informed by the rich tradition of the Fourth Gospel, but also by that which the readers have previously learned in 1 John.

Specifically, to believe in his name here includes belief and confession of the following: that fellowship with the Father includes fellowship

---

146 Haas, de Jonge and Swellengrebel, *A Translator's Handbook on the Letters of John*, p. 97.

with the Son (1.3); that cleansing from sin is accomplished through Jesus' blood (1.7); that the righteous Jesus acts as an advocate for the believer (2.1) based on his atoning sacrifice (2.2); that he is a model for the believer's walk (2.6); that forgiveness of sin comes through his name (2.12); that he remains in the believer (2.14); that this Righteous One will be manifest at his appearing (2.28-29); that his mode of existence and purity are the model for the believer (3.2-3); that he came to take away sin and is himself without sin (3.5-6); that he came to destroy the works of the Devil (3.7); and that he laid aside his life on behalf of the believers. It should be evident that for the reader these are not simply doctrinal points to be affirmed, but are experiences which the believers undergo in various ways. This is what it means to believe in the name of his Son Jesus Christ. As for the fact that the admonition to believe comes in the form of command, it may be observed that this is consistent with Jesus' words in Jn 6.29 where he says, 'This is the work of God, that you might believe in that one who sent him'. As the readers already know, this same text appears to lie behind the warning given in 2 John 8.

The second part of the command is no less important than the first for several reasons. First, the words that appear here, 'love another', clearly have reference to those of Jesus spoken in the Fourth Gospel at various points (13.34; 15.12, 17). Such emphasis would not be lost on the readers. Second, this love command has been the subject of 1 John at various places to this point and will continue to be so in what follows. Third, neither should the significance of 'love one another' being paired with belief in his Son Jesus Christ be overlooked. Such a pairing reveals something of the reciprocal nature of these aspects of the command and indicate something of the way in which love and God are understood: an understanding that will become clearer at a later point in 1 John (4.7). This aspect of the command is further emphasized by identifying its origin as God (through Jesus) and indicating that the believer must love exactly as (καθὼς) Jesus commanded.

In some ways, then, it might be said that 1 Jn 3.23 combines those elements that are essential to Johannine Christianity.

Verse 24. Resuming the thought of v. 22, the readers' attention is again directed to 'keeping his commands', a phrase that has now been expanded to include both belief in his Son Jesus Christ and love for one another. But the readers soon discover that there is more at stake in keeping his commands than receiving those things requested. For 'the one who keeps his commands remains in him and he (remains) in him'. Thus, the reappearance of 'keeping his commands' is anything but mere repetition. The obedience demonstrated in keeping the commands reveals that this believer is in the closest relationship possible with God. This union between God and the believer goes beyond anything hinted at in the Fourth Gospel or the Johannine Epistles to this point, for here the idea is clearly one of mutual indwelling, remaining or abiding. It is altogether likely that such a statement with regard to mutual indwelling is directly related to the fact that the believers are described as children of God in 3.1 and that this theme receives a significant amount of attention in the verses that follow (3.2, 9-10). Although this is the first mention of God remaining or dwelling in the believer, the readers have been given hints in this direction from near the beginning of 1 John. For they have learned that it is possible to speak of 'Truth' (1.8), 'the Word of God' (1.10), 'the anointing' (2.27), 'his seed' (3.9) and 'eternal life' (3.15) as potentially remaining in an individual. To be told that God remains in the one who keeps his commands and this one is in him at the very least suggests something of the imparting of the divine nature to the believer. Even this idea is not altogether foreign to the reader for the eschatological possibility of being like Jesus appears as early as 3.2. However, this notion is intensified in 3.24 in at least two ways. First, the subject on this occasion appears to be God instead of Jesus (though absolute precision on this point is impossible to achieve). Second, in contrast to the promise of 3.2, this mutual indwelling is not an eschatological promise but a present reality for the believer. Stupendous as this statement is, it does follow well the discussions of the believer being without sin and the love of God being perfected in the believer. The theme of the mutual indwelling of God and the believer reappears later in 1 John (4.13, 15-16). It is significant that both the verbs 'keep' and 'remain' appear in the present tense indicating that both these are ongoing activities. The implicit message is that as long as one keeps his commands, God and the believer remain in one another. Obedience and mutual indwelling are inextricably bound together in 1 John.[147] Thus, the language of 'believing' and 'confessing' gives way to the more dominant language of 'remaining' to describe the relationship between God and the believer.

The phrase 'and in this we know' appears again in 1 John and, as in its earlier uses, it brings the readers assurance about a specific issue or experience. This time the verb 'know' appears in the present tense emphasizing the fact that the knowledge here described is currently experienced by the readers. The object of the assurance here offered by means of the phrase 'and in this we know' is 'that he remains in us'. If there should be any question as to whether or not the extraordinary idea of the mutual indwelling of God and the believer is true, the readers are

---

147   Smalley, *1, 2, 3 John*, p. 211.

now offered proof of such a statement. The proof of this relationship comes 'from the Spirit whom he gave to us'. The Spirit is mentioned here explicitly for the first time in 1 John and is identified as the means by which the believer can know that God remains in him or her. Though the readers are not told how the Spirit makes this reality known, sufficient hints have occurred in 1 John to give the readers some idea of how the Spirit works in this fashion in particular. The primary evidence of the Spirit's activity to this point in 1 John concerns the anointing the believers have received. This anointing knows all things (2.20) and teaches the believer all things, so much so that the believer has no need of human teachers (2.27). Such teaching would no doubt be made manifest in a variety of concrete ways. These ways might include the spoken testimony of various members of the community, the confirmation of one's status by means of one's walk witnessed by the brothers and sisters, Spirit-inspired confession, as well as prophetically spoken words. On this latter point it should be noted that many of the activities assigned to the Paraclete in the Fourth Gospel require a human spokesperson. It should also be noted that the broader Johannine community shows evidence of being a prophetic community with the presence of both true (Rev. 1.3; 22.6, 9) and false prophets (1 Jn 4.1; Rev. 2.20). Neither should it be ignored that the very next major section of 1 John returns to the idea of false teaching and even introduces the term 'false prophets' into the text at that point (1 Jn 4.1). Nor should it be ignored that apparently there is a close connection in 1 John between false prophets, spirits that must be tested, especially those who do not confess Jesus as being from God (4.1-3), and the spirit of deception (4.6). All of this is to say that the assurance the Spirit brings that God remains in the believer in all likelihood is understood by the readers to take many forms. If the anointing is an anointing by the Spirit, and the Spirit teaches all things, then one aspect of the Spirit's activity is assuring believers that he abides in them.

Reflection and Response – Part Eight

Reflection

The various themes found in this passage are held together by, connected to and carefully integrated with the idea of confidence before God. Knowledge of being in the Truth is accompanied by loving in work and truth. The presence of such acts sets our heart at peace, and even if our heart condemns us God is greater than our heart because he knows all things. A heart that does not condemn leads to confidence to speak openly with God, expecting to receive that for which we ask owing to the fact that we do his commands. His twofold command is to believe (by means of appropriating) all that Jesus Christ, God's Son, is and does, and to love one another. Such keeping of the commands is evidence of the mutual indwelling of God in the believer and the believer in God. Knowledge of this relational intimacy comes by means of the Spirit. Therefore, believers can be assured of their relationship with God by a number of means and have confidence before him to speak openly about their needs.

The following questions should help generate additional reflection on this topic. How is confidence before God understood in the churches with which you are familiar? What is the relationship between confidence before God and works of love in the Truth? In what ways is the expectancy of answered prayer connected to the doing of the command to love one another? How is the idea of receiving the things one requests understood, on the whole? What role does one's heart and its judgments or lack thereof play in the prayer life of the church? What is the meaning of believing in the name of his Son Jesus Christ to the churches with which you are acquainted? How does one experience mutual indwelling with God and what are the evidences of that experience? What role is the Spirit assigned in assuring believers of their knowledge of and relationship with God? Are there individuals you would identify as examples of this relationship with God? How would you describe them?

More personally, how would you describe your own relationship with God? What is the defining characteristic of your attitude toward God in times of prayer? Do you have the kind of confidence described in this passage? Have you ever experienced the temptation to allow your confidence to become arrogance in approaching God? In what ways are your own acts of love connected to your attitude to God in prayer? Has your heart ever condemned you when you have come before God in worship? Is your heart usually a good indicator of your spiritual state or are you prone to exaggerated feelings of guilt? When has God overridden your heart's judgments resulting in confidence before him? How would you describe that experience? What is the extent of your belief in the name of the Son Jesus Christ? What dimensions of his person and work (as described in 1 John) have you embraced and appropriated, and what dimensions have not been so embraced and appropriated? Have you ever been aware of the intimacy of mutual indwelling with God? When did this happen most recently and how did it come about? How has the Spirit's presence been manifested at such times?

Response

The following elements would appear to be among the appropriate responses to this aspect of 1 John.

First, prepare yourself for a time of prayer by examining your heart to discern if it offers any accusations or condemnations. If your heart condemns you in any way, ask the Lord for forgiveness and assurance of your mutual indwelling, embracing and appropriating all those dimensions of Jesus' person and work.

Second, make known your requests to the Lord openly and honestly, being conscious of the connection between receiving and doing his commands.

Third, as a sign of devotion to the Lord, commit to a specific course of action through which your keeping of the command to love one another is manifested.

Fourth, seek out and take advantage of times of worship in which other believers will actively pursue an outpouring of the Spirit on your behalf in order to insure your continual mutual indwelling with God.

1 John 4.1-6

The mirroring effect begun in 3.19-24 (which parallels 2.28–3.10) continues in this section as 1 Jn 4.1-6 reveals a number of points of continuity with 2.18-27. In ch. 2 the readers learn: it is the last hour; many antichrists have come; the believers have received an anointing which teaches them all things and makes the role of human teachers unnecessary; there are those who deny that Jesus is the Christ; it is impossible to have the Father without having the Son; and the necessity of remaining in that which they have received from the beginning. The number of points of continuity between the passages would not be lost on the readers. However, the latter passage (4.1-6) does not merely repeat the contents of the former (2.18-27), but continues to develop the argument of 1 John in a specific direction. It addition to the ways in which 2.18-27 informs one's reading of 4.1-6, the reader is also informed by the connections these verses share with 3.23. For in some ways it is possible to see in 4.1-6 and 4.7–5.5 a detailed exposition of the twofold command to 'believe in the name of his Son Jesus Christ and love one another', respectively. The structure of 4.1-6 falls rather naturally into two sections: vv. 1-3 focusing on the relationship between the Spirit and the proper confession of Jesus, and vv. 4-6 focusing on the line of demarcation between those who are of God and those who are of the world. The entire section is bounded on either side by references to spirits. In v. 1 the issue is the relationship of the spirits to God; in v. 6 the issue is how one distinguishes between the Spirit of Truth and the spirit of deception.

Verse 1. Once again the readers find that a section of 1 John begins with a term of endearment. The term used on this occasion ('Beloved') marks a new beginning both here and in the next section (4.7). Most recently 'beloved' has appeared in the context of encouragement for the readers that they have 'confidence before God' because their heart does not condemn them (3.21). Its appearance in 4.1 sustains the emphasis on love which precedes in 1 John and points to the next major section of the book which takes this issue up once again in detail (4.7-5.5). By this means the impending warning of vv. 1-6 is seen as based upon loving concern for the readers. The warning that follows ('Do not believe every spirit') comes in the form of a command and is noteworthy for several reasons. Except for the negative (μὴ), each word of this phrase begins with the same letter in the Greek text (παντὶ πνεύματι πιστεύετε), a construction that would no doubt attract the attention of the reader. In addition, the command 'do not believe' is in the present tense which could produce a meaning something like 'do not keep believing', which suggests a situation where believing every spirit was common. As in the previous section, the idea of believing likely includes more than mental assent but would perhaps encompass the experience of participation with a 'spirit'. But the most significant question about this phrase concerns the meaning of 'every spirit'. Exactly what do these words mean? While a precise answer must await an examination of the entire passage, at this point the readers would no doubt define the term 'spirit' in light of its first appearance in the preceding sentence in 3.24, where it clearly has reference to the Spirit of God. It is this appeal to the Spirit as the one who confirms that the believer may know of his or her mutual indwelling with God which makes the following discussion necessary. For here it becomes clear that appeals to (inspiration by) the Spirit are being made both by those in the community and those who have left it. Thus, while the Spirit is the means by which assurance of one's mutual indwelling with the Father is gained, it follows that believers must be able to distinguish between the work of the Spirit of God and the work of other 'spirits'.

The content of the Fourth Gospel as well as that of 1 John makes it abundantly clear that the readers would understand the Spirit to be at work in their lives. In fact, it might not be going too far to say that they have the Spirit dwelling within them (Jn 14.17; 1 Jn 2.27; 3.24). It appears likely that the deceivers also appeal to the Spirit as the basis of their own teaching and interpretive positions. Such a deduction is made in the light of a variety of hints found in the Johannine Epistles. In 2 John 8-11 it seems that those who do not 'remain in the teaching of Christ' but have 'gone beyond it' may have appealed to the work of the Paraclete as the basis of their interpretive innovations. There are also the hints found in 1 Jn 2.18-27 where it appears that the deceivers may have been making claims about their (unique?) anointing. Such hints find clarity in 4.1-6 as the relationship between the deceivers and the spirit that inspires them receives considerable attention. It is perhaps worth remembering that in the Fourth Gospel one of the functions of the Paraclete is to lead and guide the believer into all truth (16.13). Therefore, any claims to inspiration on the part of the deceivers could very well have been based upon Jesus' words in the Fourth Gospel.

Assuming that the Paraclete's ministry was being appealed to as the basis of the innovative teaching of the deceivers, the warning and instruction found in 4.1-6 is easy to understand. Owing to a variety of claims being made on the Spirit's behalf, the reader could no longer uncritically accept or become aligned with the content or actions of a 'spirit-inspired' individual. Rather, the reader must have a way of distinguishing between the various claims being made. As such, the readers of 1 John are instructed 'but test the spirits if they are of God'. The idea expressed by the word 'test' (δοκιμάζετε) is mainly a positive one with the meaning 'approve of' or 'accept as trustworthy'.[148] This is its only occurrence in the Johannine literature. Just as the believers are to stop believing 'every spirit' so they are to test the spirits. The verb translated 'test' occurs in the present tense and suggests that this activity is to be an ongoing part of the community's life. This verb's appearance in the second person plural ('you') indicates that each member of the community is entrusted with the responsibility of testing the spirits. It is a testimony to the egalitarian nature of the Johannine community that such a responsibility is not restricted to the leader(s) of the community, but is something expected of every believer.[149] The idea that believers must be prepared to make such determinations is already present in 2 John where they are called upon to distinguish between those who remain in the teaching of Christ and those who do not bear this teaching (vv. 9-11). In 1 Jn 4.1, the goal of such testing is to determine whether or not a given 'spirit' finds its origin in God or some other source.[150] What

---

148   G. Schunack, 'δοκιμάζω', *EDNT*, I, pp. 341-43.
149   In contrast to the emerging practice reflected in the epistles of Ignatius to place most responsibility for distinguishing between true and false teaching in the hands of the bishop. Passages relating to the importance of the bishop for Ignatius are scattered throughout his epistles.
150   This phrase (εἰ ἐκ τοῦ θεοῦ) is a typical Johannine expression. In point of fact, expressions like this one (εἶναι ἐκ) appear some 55 times in the Johannine literature,

would reference to these 'spirits' mean to the reader? The answer to this question begins to emerge in the next phrase.

The need for such testing is 'because many false prophets have gone out into the world'. With this statement it becomes clear that the testing of the spirits has reference to individuals who function in a prophetic capacity. Thus, the idea that there is some connection between the work of the Spirit and prophetic activity hinted in 3.24 is made clearer in 4.1. The testing of the spirits is the testing of the prophetic activity within the community.[151] The statement that 'many' false prophets have gone out into the world is fraught with meaning for the reader. It hearkens back to the language of 2 John 7 where 'many deceivers have gone out into the world' and is reminiscent of 1 Jn 2.18 where 'even now, many antichrists have come'. Although this is the only reference to false prophets in the Johannine Epistles, it is clear from its context that the false prophets are synonymous with the deceivers and antichrists mentioned earlier. In other words, these false prophets are identified with the false teachers who have left the community. Thus, testing the spirits is now understood to mean testing the S/spirit that inspires the words and actions of a given individual who claims Spirit inspiration as the basis of his or her activity. There is evidence in another Johannine writing that this very issue was a problem for at least a portion of the community. In the Apocalypse, the church at Thyatira is judged for its toleration of 'that woman Jezebel who calls herself a prophetess' but teaches and engages in 'sexual immorality and eating food sacrificed to idols' (Rev. 2.20-25). Similarly, a problem appears to exist in the church in Pergamum where false teaching is tolerated (2.14-15). On the other hand, the church in Ephesus successfully tests those who make false claims to be apostles (2.2), and both identifies and rejects false teaching (2.6).

Like the deceivers of 2 John 7, these false prophets have 'gone out into the world'. As the readers know, the language of 'going out' in the Johannine literature carries with it the idea of missionary activity. It conveys the idea that these false prophets are going out to reach as many people as possible with their false teaching. In 2 John, the readers are warned about the impending arrival of the deceivers, while in 1 Jn 4.1 the false prophets have already gone out from the community. The

---

compared to 28 times in the rest of the New Testament. Strecker, *The Johannine Letters*, p. 132 n. 7.

151   The need for discernment with regard to the Spirit's activity was a feature of early Christianity that was rather widespread. It is evidenced in the writings of Paul (1 Cor. 12.1-3; 14.29; 1 Thess. 5.20-21); *Didache* 11.1; 12.1; Hermas, *Mandate* 11.7; and *1 Clement* 42.4.

(perfect) past tense of the verb 'have gone out' places emphasis not only upon the time of their departure at a specific point in the past, but also upon the effects and duration of that departure. That the false prophets are here described as going out into the world conveys the idea that they have rejected the community for a world hostile to Jesus and those who believe in him (cf. Jn 3.19; 7.7; 16.33; 2 Jn 7; 1 Jn 2.18-19).[152] No doubt their going out reminds the readers that Judas also 'went out' – to betray Jesus (Jn 13.30).

Verses 2-3
The next two verses stand together as the thought of the book moves directly from the idea of testing to the test itself. The reader finds that the test is described in an antithetical fashion characteristic of the Johannine literature, with v. 2 conveying the message positively and v. 3 conveying it negatively.

Verse 2. The phrase 'in this you know' again appears in 1 John pointing the readers to what follows. On this occasion the Greek term translated 'you know' (γινώσκετε) could be taken as a command (imperative) or as a statement (indicative). Thus, the readers would either understand that they are being instructed to know (learn) something they do not yet know or that they are being reminded of something they already know. Here the latter appears to be the case. In part this interpretation is preferred because it is consistent with the fact that in 1 John a statement rather than a command always follows the phrase 'in this'. In 4.2 the readers are both being reminded that they know the Spirit of God and being provided with the means of being certain about such knowledge in the face of competing claims to knowledge of the Spirit of God. Mention of the Spirit of God clearly draws upon 3.24 where the readers are told that their ability to know of their mutual indwelling with God comes by means of the Spirit. It also appears likely that the words of Jesus in the Fourth Gospel with regard to the disciples' knowledge of the Paraclete (Jn 14.17) lie behind the idea of the readers' knowledge of the Spirit of God at this point in 1 John. If so, it is significant that Jn 14.17 also includes the idea that the world cannot receive the Paraclete because it does not know him.

The specific criterion of testing the spirits comes in the last part of v. 2. Very literally the text reads: 'Each spirit who confesses Jesus Christ in the flesh having come is of God.' The move from the 'Spirit of God' to 'each spirit' reveals the close connection between the Spirit of God and

---

152 Brown, *The Epistles of John*, p. 503.

the individual believer, here referred to as a spirit. Such a move indicates that the reader is to see one's confession of 'Jesus Christ having come in the flesh' as the result of the Spirit's activity, so much so that the believer may be referred to as 'each spirit' in this context. It is not necessary to take 'spirit' here as reference to one's 'human spirit', in contrast to the Spirit's activity in the believer, for there appears to be an intentional ambiguity in these words. The test of a spirit's origin takes the form of a confession. With notable exceptions (1 Jn 1.9), confession language occurs primarily in christological contexts in the Johannine literature (Jn 1.20; 9.22; 12.42; 2 Jn 7; 1 Jn 2.23; 4.2, 3, 15). Generally speaking, the idea of confession includes that of public proclamation, an idea that fits nicely in this passage. Thus, in making a public proclamation of Jesus by means of confession, the readers join their voices with that of John (the Baptist), in spite of any risks such confession might entail (Jn 9.22; 12.42).

The specific confession by which the origin of a spirit may be tested is 'Jesus Christ in the flesh having come'. What would the content of this confession mean to the readers? First, the appearance of the name Jesus Christ would alert the reader to the fact that false teaching is soon to be addressed, consistent with other places in the Johannine Epistles where the name Jesus Christ occurs. The most recent appearance of 'Jesus Christ' in 1 John has come in the occurrence of the formula 'believe in the name of his Son Jesus Christ' (3.23). As observed in the reading of that passage, there is in 3.23 a convergence of ideas that inform the meaning of belief in his name, ideas that come both from the Fourth Gospel and the first three chapters of 1 John. This convergence of ideas would scarcely be forgotten by the readers as they encounter the language of confession in 4.2. In point of fact, it is likely that this convergence would inform the content of the confession in direct ways. The location of the name Jesus Christ at the beginning of the phrase indicates that the emphasis of the confession here described is upon a person, not a fact or doctrine. As such, this confession involves the same experiential dimensions with and of Jesus as does belief in his name; a confession that is proclaimed verbally and confirmed through one's deeds.[153] Therefore, the confession described in 4.2 is not that of a proposition but of a living person.

Second, it would be clear to the readers from the sentence structure that a certain emphasis is being placed upon the fact that 'in the flesh' Jesus Christ has come. Such a statement calls to mind the extraordinarily important verse in the prologue of the Fourth Gospel, Jn 1.14, 'and the

---

[153] An interpretation found in the sixth-century work of Oecumenius, *Commentary on 1 John*, ACCS, XI, p. 210.

Word became flesh and dwelt among us'. Thus, 'in the flesh' conveys one of the community's foundational beliefs – that Jesus has come in the flesh. That there are some questions in the community about this belief is revealed for the first time in 2 John 7 where the readers learn that the deceivers are unable to confess 'Jesus Christ coming in the flesh'. Though flesh vocabulary does not appear in the prologue of 1 John, the emphasis there upon 'hearing', 'seeing' (with our eyes), and 'touching' (with and hands) the Word of Life indicates that this 'physical' dimension of Jesus' identity is and will be extremely important in the book. But as 1 John unfolds, it becomes evident that the issues surrounding the person of Jesus are not focused so much on the reality of the Incarnation, but rather upon its significance. At this point it should simply be observed that the many significant dimensions of Jesus' person that converge in the admonition to 'believe in the name of his Son Jesus Christ' found in 3.23 inform and are informed by the fact that his salvific significance is inextricably connected to his having come 'in the flesh'.

Third, the verb 'having come' would also be significant for the readers in determining the meaning of this confession. The form of this verb (perfect participle) stresses the fact that the past act of Jesus Christ coming in the flesh is still very much a living reality for the readers. In fact, this particular form of the verb underscores the point that here the person of Jesus Christ incarnate is being confessed, not some statement of faith about the fact of his Incarnation. It should also be noted that the language of his 'having come' points to the idea of the pre-existence of the Son who has come in the flesh. This confession, then, testifies to the fact that Jesus Christ, who has come in the flesh, is a present reality whose enduring significance is that he continues to be the incarnate Son who brings a variety of salvific benefits. Thus, the confession is a comprehensive one that includes much more than an affirmation of Jesus' Incarnation.

It is this Spirit-inspired confession that reveals the origin of one's Spirit-inspired utterances and actions. Here, the Spirit of God generates this confession as a result of and growing out of an experiential relationship to Jesus in the various dimensions of his person. In this case, the Spirit not only inspires speech and actions but the Spirit also validates them. In this verse one is not far from the thought of the Fourth Gospel where Jesus declares that the Spirit of Truth only speaks that which he hears (16.13). It should not surprise the readers then that the Spirit-inspired utterances that claim their origin in (the Spirit of) God must speak the truth about Jesus. The essential unity of Father and Son affirmed throughout the Fourth Gospel and the Johannine Epistles would demand no less.

Verse 3. The criterion of the test advocated in 4.1 is completed in v. 3 by means of the second part of the antithetical parallel. The positive statement of v. 2 that identifies the content of a confession revealing one is of God is followed by the negative statement in v. 3 which focuses upon the one who is unable to make such a confession. This sentence, joined to the previous one by means of 'and' or 'but' (καί), begins like its counterpart in v. 2 with the words 'each spirit that'. This repetition makes clear that attention is still being focused upon 'Spirit-inspired' individuals who speak and act in prophetic ways. However, as the sentence proceeds the parallel with v. 2 is disrupted by the appearance of an emphatic use of the negative 'not' (μή). Whereas the 'prophetic' figures in v. 2 'confess Jesus Christ coming in the flesh', in v. 3 the 'prophetic' figures 'do not confess' Jesus. Such an expression is quite similar to that of 2 John 7 where the deceivers are described as 'not confessing Jesus Christ coming in the flesh'. If confession of Jesus entails belief in all he is and all he accomplishes, lack of such confession is synonymous with unbelief and denial of him and the significance of his life (cf. esp. 1 Jn 2.22-23). This lack of confession might even be said to 'annul' or seek to 'destroy' his person and significance.[154] Another break in the parallelism between vv. 2-3 occurs where the reader expects to find the words 'Jesus Christ having come in the flesh'. In its place is simply the name 'Jesus'. This unexpected alteration conveys a couple of things to the reader. First, it is clear that the name Jesus is, in this verse, an abbreviated form of the fuller confession found in v. 2. It follows that just as the confession found in v. 2 builds upon and has reference to all those things that precede it in 1 John, so the name Jesus functions in a similar way in v. 3. Second, the appearance of the name Jesus reinforces the fact that belief in and confession of a person is very much the issue in these verses, not simply confession of a doctrine. If the Spirit-inspired confession of 'Jesus Christ having come in the flesh' reveals that this 'spirit' finds its origin in God, so any 'spirit'-inspired utterance which does not confess Jesus reveals that its origin is not from God. Just as the confession 'Jesus Christ coming in the flesh' is a kind of shorthand for a fuller understanding of his person and significance, so not confessing Jesus may be a kind of shorthand standing for utterances, beliefs and practices that advocate and embrace a false Christology. It would appear that the situation envisioned in 1 Jn 4.1-3 is one where 'spirit'-inspired individuals, speaking prophetically to the community, espoused teachings and practices at variance with the teachings and practices of

---

154   In point of fact, a number of ancient writers, though few Greek manuscripts, read 'annul' or 'destroy' (λύει) at this point instead of 'do not confess'.

the Johannine community as revealed in the Fourth Gospel. What might be known of their teaching? They appear to claim fellowship with the Father without the Son, have no place for Jesus' role in the forgiveness of sins, ignore his role as a model of behavior for their lives, and deny his messianic status. However, by not confessing Jesus, these individuals reveal that they do not speak on behalf of the Paraclete for his relationship to Jesus (the Truth) is so intimate that he is even called the Spirit of Truth (Jn 14.17; 15.26; 16.13).[155]

If such spirit-inspired teaching does not originate with the Spirit of God, what is the identity of the spirit that inspires it? The remainder of v. 3 provides an answer to this question. By means of the phrase 'and this is' the source of the spirit identified as 'not of God' in v. 3a receives further definition in the next phrase which literally reads 'that of the antichrist'. This phrase conveys a number of things to the readers. It makes clear that the spirit-inspired utterances and activities of those who do not confess Jesus have their origin in the antichrist, a term that has come to be associated with deception and false teaching in 2 John and 1 John. Occurrence of the word 'antichrist' in v. 3 also reveals that the false prophets described in 4.1 are to be identified with those individuals found in 2.18-27 who deny Jesus is the Christ and thereby deny both Father and Son.

It is also significant that the phrase 'that of the antichrist' is constructed in such a way as to necessitate that the readers supply some word or idea to complete the phrase. The word that makes most sense in this context is 'spirit'. If 'spirits' who confess Jesus Christ are identified with the 'Spirit of God', it makes sense that 'spirits' who do not confess Jesus would be identified with the 'spirit of the antichrist'. However, the fact that the word 'spirit' must here be supplied alerts the reader to the fact that the 'spirit of the antichrist' is not to be regarded as comparable to the 'Spirit of God'. It also indicates that the teaching and activities of 'spirit-inspired prophets' who do not confess Jesus belong to the realm or orbit of the antichrist. As in 2 John 7, antichrist appears here with the definite article 'the'. Yet, as noted earlier in 2 John 7 and in the reading of 2.18-27, nowhere is there the idea of the antichrist as *the* eschatological figure so often assumed in many discussions. Rather, it is clear that 'the antichrist' is identified with 'the deceiver' and 'the many deceivers' of 2 John 7, as well as the 'many antichrists' that have already come in 1 Jn 2.18. Antichrist, then, is a Johannine term used to describe deception and false teaching that rejects the Johannine view of Jesus and his significance

---

155 On the relationship between the Paraclete and Jesus cf. Thomas, 'The Spirit in the Fourth Gospel: Narrative Explorations', pp. 87-104.

in the salvation of the believer. It is this spirit of antichrist that the readers have heard is coming, as the Greek construction 'that which' (ὅ) instead of 'the one who' (ὅν) makes clear.

As in 2.18, the expectation of the readers based on 'that which we have heard' is fulfilled by the fact that even now, the spirit of the antichrist is already in the world. The appearance of the words 'even now' directs the readers' attention back yet again to 2.18 when they were told 'even now many antichrists have come'. This language also recalls the idea of 'the last hour' stated in 2.18. The appearance and position of the word 'already', at the end of the Greek sentence, places additional emphasis upon the fact that the spirit of the antichrist is already at work in the many spirits who do not confess Jesus. Such a statement points in the direction of the teaching of the Fourth Gospel about the present dimension of expected future realities (Jn 4.23; 5.25; 12.31; 13.31; 15.3; 19.28; 1 Jn 2.8). It would not surprise the readers to find that 'the world' is the place of operation for 'the spirit of the antichrist' in as much as the world has figured as a place hostile to Jesus and his followers in the Johannine literature and it is identified as belonging to 'the ruler of this world' in the Fourth Gospel (12.31). Therefore, the admonition to test the spirits is of utmost importance, for in the case of the Johannine community some of the spirits operative are, in reality, false prophets inspired not by the Spirit of God, as claimed, but by the spirit of the antichrist.

Verse 4. This verse marks the beginning of the second half of vv. 1-6. This subsection (vv. 4-6) begins with an introductory statement which reassures the readers that despite the presence of false prophets, they are of God (v. 4). At the center of this subsection stands an antithetical comparison between those of the world and those of God (vv. 5-6b). These verses conclude with a statement about the 'Spirit of Truth' and the 'spirit of deception' (v. 6c).

The subsection begins in v. 4 with the appearance of an emphatic use of the word 'you' which contrasts the readers with the false prophets, who are some of the 'spirits' just tested. Coming on the heels of v. 3 and its focus upon the presence of the antichrist in those who do not confess Jesus, such a contrast would serve to reassure the readers that they are not numbered with the false prophets. On the contrary, for a second time in this section (v. 2), the readers are told that they 'are of God'. On this occasion, the second person plural 'you' occurs making the point of divine origin all the more emphatic. The phrase translated 'you are of God' (ὑμεῖς ἐκ τοῦ θεοῦ ἐστε) carries with it the idea of origin with a literal meaning 'you are out of God'. Such a statement, which has been of primary importance in vv. 1-3, comes as no surprise here and dovetails nicely with the emphasis placed upon the readers' origin in God. They are God's children (3.1, 2, 10), having been born of him (3.9). Implicit in this statement is the equation drawn between the readers, who 'are of God', and those who 'confess Jesus Christ having come in the flesh', who are also 'of God' (v. 2).

The reappearance of the term 'children', which has occurred at a number of strategic points in 1 John (2.1, 12, 28; 3.7, 18), ensures that the readers do not miss the connection between finding one's origin in God and being his children. Not only are the readers reassured of their origin in God, in contrast to the false prophets, but they are also (re)assured that they 'have been victorious over them'. This is a very significant statement for the readers. The (perfect) tense of the verb (νενικήκατε) reveals that the victory they have experienced has occurred in the past but its effects are still felt by the readers. Strictly speaking, the verb's tense indicates that in some sense this battle is past. Such an idea is, of course, at one with that expressed earlier in 1 Jn 2.13-14, where in an address to the 'young men' the readers are told 'you have been victorious over the evil one'. Interestingly, the identical form of the word translated 'have been victorious' occurs in 2.13-14 as well as in 4.4. Therefore, the victory won over 'the evil one' is perhaps not far from the reader's mind at this point in 1 John. At the same time, it is clear that this statement with regard to the past victory of the readers over the false prophets is tempered by the fact that it comes in the context of instructions for the readers to test the spirits to determine their origin. The meaning of 'you have been victorious over them', then, is one which combines the idea of a present victory in the form of a successful withstanding of the false prophets' message with the assurance of success in facing the words and deeds of false prophets in the future. Because they are of God, the readers are assured, their victory is as good as won.

The reason offered for the victory experienced by the readers is found in the remainder of v. 4: 'because he who is in you is greater than he who is in the world'. The last time the word 'greater' appeared in 1 John it communicated the fact that 'God is greater than our hearts' and any condemnation they might bring against the readers (3.20). Its occurrence in v. 4 also involves a comparison. On this occasion, the comparison is between the one who is in the believers and the one who is in the world. Who is the greater one in the believers? Owing to the fact that this statement occurs in a context where a great deal of emphasis has been placed upon whether or not one's origin is of God (4.1-3) and that the readers are assured God remains or dwells in them and they in him (3.24), it is hard to avoid the conclusion that God would be identified as the greater one in the believers. However, the readers are aware of several statements in 1 John which imply that it is also possible to conceive of Jesus as being 'in' the believer (cf. 1.8, 10; 3.15). At the same time, it is clear that the idea of the Spirit being 'in' the believer is a major one in 1 John (cf. 2.27; 3.9, 24) and owing to the immediate context (3.24–4.6) would be especially appropriate here. The ambiguity of the phrase 'the one who is in you', the way in which God, Jesus and the Spirit can be understood to be in the believer, and the essential unity between Father and Son and by extension the Spirit, all combine to suggest that the readers would not be inclined to restrict the meaning of this phrase but would have a rather expansive understanding of the phrase, 'the one who is in you'.[156] However the words are understood, the one who is in the believer is greater than the one who is in the world and ensures that the readers have been victorious over the false prophets.

The readers would also likely see in the phrase 'the one who is in the world' a similar ambiguity. The nearest antecedent to 'the one who' is found in v. 3 where the phrase 'that of the antichrist' occurs. Thus, it is possible to see primary reference to the 'spirit' of the antichrist in the phrase 'the one who is in the world'. Such an interpretation is supported by the fact that the 'spirit' of the antichrist appears to stand behind the 'spirit' activity of the false prophets, those who do not confess Jesus. This interpretation is also supported by the fact that in the last verse of this section (v. 6) the spirit of deception is contrasted with the Spirit of Truth. From the meaning of antichrist in the Johannine literature, it is clear that 'the "spirit" of the antichrist' and 'the spirit of deception' function as synonyms. One of the problems faced by adoption of this interpretation is that the deceivers, and consequently the false prophets, are themselves described as antichrists who have come (2.18). Another complication with this interpretation is that in the Johannine literature, one figure above all others functions as God's adversary: the ruler of this world (12.31; 14.30; 16.11). The Johannine believers have already been victorious over this evil one (1 Jn 2.13-14), just as Jesus has been victorious over the world (Jn 16.33) having judged its ruler (16.11). The opposition of the Devil and his children to God is well documented in 1 Jn 3.8-10, as is the destruction Jesus brings to his works (3.8). Thus, it is difficult to avoid the idea that the Devil, the evil one, the ruler of this world is primarily in view in 4.4. However, it is unlikely that the readers would see a rigid division between the spirit of antichrist and the spirit of deception, on the one hand, and the Devil, on the other hand. A final observation on this verse should be offered before turning to v. 5. Clearly, the world stands here in the negative sense of being the place of hostility to God

---

156   Smalley, 1, 2, 3 John, p. 227.

and his purposes: a theme which has been emphasized at various points in 1 John.

Verse 5. The middle portion of this subsection (vv. 5-6b) begins in v. 5 where the first part of an antithetical comparison of those of the world with those of God occurs. Structurally, v. 5 is surrounded by the statements 'you are of God', which affirm the divine origin of the readers. The emphasis begun in v. 4 with the pronoun 'you' continues in v. 5 where the emphatic personal pronoun 'they' (αὐτοί) occurs for the only time in the Johannine Epistles. Such emphasis is clearly designed yet again to identify the false prophets in contrast to the readers. While the readers find their origin in God, the false prophets 'are of the world', with the term 'world' standing in a position of emphasis. At least two things are immediately communicated to the readers by such a statement. First, it reinforces the point that the false prophets, who 'have gone out into the world' (4.1), have their origin in the world, which is the place of activity of the 'spirit' of the antichrist. This point further underscores the idea that the 'spirit' that empowers their activity is not the Spirit of God, but 'that of the antichrist'. Second, following so closely on the heels of the statement 'greater is the one who is in you than the one who is in the world', there is the subtle message that these false prophets belong to the realm over which the victory has already been won.

'On account of this' origin in the world 'they speak of the world and the world hears (or listens) to them'. If not before, certainly by this point the readers are aware of the emphasis placed upon 'world', as this word occurs three times in v. 5 alone.[157] Such repetition serves to remove any doubt about the origin, source, and spirit at work in the false teachers. They are thoroughly integrated into the world. They speak its language and it listens. The idea of belonging to the world reflects Jesus' own language in the Fourth Gospel where he makes clear the division between his disciples and the world (15.19; 17.14, 16). Focus on the world in 1 Jn 4.5 reveals that a similar division is being envisioned here. On this occasion at least a couple of ideas are present in the term 'world'. It is identified as the portion of humanity hostile to Jesus and the place of activity for the 'spirit' of the antichrist and the false prophets. The verb translated 'speak' often appears in the Fourth Gospel to describe Jesus speaking. As such, its appearance in 1 Jn 4.5 might carry with it the idea of 'prophetic' speech. The fact that the verb appears in the present tense suggests that such speaking is an ongoing activity. Just as the writer and

---

157 In the Fourth Gospel the term (κόσμος) appears three times each in 1.10, 3.17, and 17.14, while appearing five times in 15.19.

those with him have heard 'that which was from the beginning' (1.1), so the world hears and gives receptive attention to its prophets. The world, which does not recognize Jesus, listens to its own. Perhaps these words also convey the idea that the false prophets' message is meeting with some degree of success.

Verse 6. The second part of the antithetical statement is found in v. 6. Again an emphatic personal pronoun ('we') occurs as a means by which the lines of demarcation between 'them' (the false prophets) and 'us' (the community) are made all the clearer. The emphatic statement found in v. 4, 'you are of God', gives way to 'we are of God' in v. 6. Before discussing a possible reason for this shift, it should be noted that in both cases the readers' origin in God is emphasized and that these statements stand on either side of the phrase 'they are of the world'. Such thematic repetition underscores the contrast between those of God and those of the world. It also serves to remind the readers yet again of their divine origin. While it is possible to see the word 'we' as having reference to the writer and those who stand with him, as in 1.1-4, it appears that here 'we' has reference to the writer, those who stand with him, and the readers. Such an interpretation accounts both for the 'authoritative' feel of these words and for the fact that the writer often identifies with the readers in first person language.

Just as the world listens to the false prophets, so 'the one who knows God hears (or listens) to us'. In 1 John, 'the one who knows God' keeps his commands (2.3) and love of God has been perfected in such a one (2.5). Such knowing includes knowledge of 'the one from the beginning' (2.13-14). As noted in the reading of those passages, this knowing is an intimate relational knowing, which is closely associated with the language of 'remaining' in him, being of him and being his children. In 4.6, the one who has this intimate knowledge of God 'hears us' (those in the community). The present tense verb 'knows' indicates that such knowing is envisioned as a continuous process. Just as the writer (and those who stand with him) 'has heard' the Word of Life (1.1-4), so those who know God give receptive attention to the community. Clearly, the idea being expressed hearkens back to the beginning of this section, which is devoted to warning the community not to believe every spirit but to 'test the spirits'. There, the criterion for the test focuses on the confession of 'Jesus Christ having come in the flesh'. The activity of the 'Spirit of God' is found in those who confess (and experience) Jesus in this fashion. Clearly, the Spirit is seen as active in this particular confession. In 4.6, the Spirit's activity not only enables one to hear the Johannine witnesses, but also (it is implied) inspires the Johannine witnesses to speak. Just as

Jesus' sheep know his voice and hear (listen to) it (Jn 10.27), so the one who knows God hears his (the Spirit's) voice through the Johannine witnesses.[158] Conversely, 'he who is not of God does not hear us'. Since those who are not of God are of the world, they listen to the false prophets who are themselves of the world. Just as the one who hates his brother or sister walks in darkness because the evil one has blinded his or her eyes (1 Jn 2.11), so the one who is not of God is unable to hear the Johannine witnesses for such a one hears the world instead. Such language is reminiscent of Jesus' words in the Fourth Gospel, 'you do not hear because you are not of God' (1 Jn 8.47). The readers would, no doubt, be comforted by the fact that their own experience parallels that of Jesus.

The phrase 'out of this' (ἐκ τούτου)[159] indicates that the words which follow grow out of the preceding discussion. Although it is possible to restrict the meaning of the phrase to the content of v. 6b alone (or primarily), such a restrictive understanding does not fully appreciate the way in which v. 6c functions as a conclusion to this entire section. Therefore, as a result of all that precedes, 'we know the Spirit of Truth and the spirit of deception'. Near the beginning of this section the readers are told 'in this you know the Spirit of God'. Now, at the end of the section, appeal is again made to the readers' knowledge and the basis of such knowledge. The present tense form of the verb 'know' underscores the fact that 'not believing every spirit' and 'testing the spirits' are to be ongoing activities. As a result, the readers' knowing is an ongoing reality as well.

It is possible to detect the activity of the 'Spirit of Truth' in various prophetic individuals by means of the confession they bear and their reception of Spirit-inspired words and activities. A number of things converge for the readers in the phrase 'Spirit of Truth', which appears only here in 1 John. It would be exceedingly difficult to ignore the fact that the title Spirit of Truth is a common one to describe the Holy Spirit in the Fourth Gospel (14.17; 15.26; 16.13). Owing to its associations in the Fourth Gospel, the Spirit of Truth would be pregnant with meaning in 1 Jn 4.6. Not least of these associations is the extremely tight connection that exists between Jesus and the Spirit of Truth, for Jesus is the Truth, an idea found in both the Fourth Gospel and 1 John. Thus, there is present in this phrase a connection between the 'Spirit of Truth' and the

---

158 Jesus also says in the Fourth Gospel, 'Each one who is of the Truth hears my voice' (18.37).
159 This is the only occurrence of ἐκ τούτου in 1 John. It occurs twice in the Fourth Gospel (6.66; 19.12).

christological confession described in v. 2. There would also be present in this title a subtle message about the relationship between the 'Spirit of Truth' and the Truth resident in the community, over against the 'spirit of deception' and the deception resident in the world. A final idea present for the readers in this title is the fact that in 1 John there is a close connection between the Spirit and God. Here in 4.6, the Spirit of Truth functions as a parallel to the Spirit of God in v. 2, thus continuing the tendency in 1 John of attributing qualities and characteristics to God that are attributed to Jesus in the Fourth Gospel. In the end, the Spirit of Truth is at work in those prophetic figures whose words and actions are in accord with the confession of 'Jesus Christ having come in the flesh'.

Standing in diametric opposition to 'the Spirit of Truth' is 'the spirit of deception', a title that occurs only in 1 Jn 4.6 in the New Testament. Although sometimes translated as 'the spirit of error' such an English translation obscures the fact that the Greek term in question (πλάνης) is from the same word family as the verb (πλανάω) translated 'deceive' (1 Jn 1.8; 2.26; 3.7) and the noun (πλάνοι) translated 'deceivers' (2 Jn 7). Just as 'the deceiver' is synonymous with 'the antichrist' in 2 John 7, so 'the 'spirit' of the antichrist' is synonymous with 'the spirit of deception' in 1 Jn 4.6. Thus, in this section's final statement it becomes very clear that 'the spirit of deception' is responsible for the many 'deceivers' who have gone out into the world to 'deceive' as many as possible, including members of the Johannine community. It is this spirit, 'that of the antichrist', that is manifest in the 'spirits' that do not confess Jesus. However, the community has nothing to fear for it knows the difference between 'the Spirit of Truth' (God) and 'the spirit of deception' (the evil one) and is capable of testing the 'spirits' present in their context for they have received the Spirit (3.24).

Reflection and Response – Part Nine

Reflection

Discernment is perhaps the most significant theme found in this passage. Believers are admonished no longer to believe every spirit but to test the spirits to see if they are of God. The presence of many false teachers makes such instruction necessary. It is significant that these comments are directed to the entire community, not simply a special group of leaders. This process of discernment involves two aspects. Prophetic activity attributed to the Spirit must be in conformity to the Spirit confession, 'Jesus Christ coming in the flesh'. Such confession focuses upon the significance of Jesus' Incarnation, his pre-existence, and the believers' experience of Jesus in a personal way. In addition to this confession, prophetic activity attributed to the Spirit must exhibit continuity with the community's experience of and belief in Jesus. Thus, there must be a dynamic interaction between these 'prophets' and the community to which they speak. The community, then, is the place where prophetic words and deeds must be tested to insure that they are the result of the Spirit of Truth rather than the spirit of deception.

A few questions should facilitate reflection on this topic. How widespread are the claims for prophetic activity in the Church today? Are there individuals whom you would regard as being true spokespersons for God? To whom are these individuals accountable? Does anyone test the words and/or deeds of these individuals? If so, how do these 'prophetic' figures respond to such testing? Are there individuals who claim prophetic inspiration whom you consider to be false prophets? What leads you to this conclusion? How are these individuals similar to and dissimilar from those whom you regard as true prophets? In your opinion, how involved is the Church in assessing contemporary prophetic activity?

What kinds of personal experiences have you had with those claiming to be prophetic figures? What are the attitudes and characteristics of such individuals? In what ways do their words and deeds measure up to the confession of Jesus Christ having come in the flesh? What is their relationship to the community? What individual known to you personally would you consider to be a genuine prophetic figure? How did you arrive at this conclusion and what criteria did you use in this process? Have you ever encountered an individual whom you considered to be inspired by a spirit other than the Spirit of Truth? What led you to this conclusion? In what ways are you actively involved in testing the spirits? What has proven to be the most reliable instrument(s) of discernment to you in this process? Have there been times when you failed to discern properly a situation involving prophetic claims? If so, what did you learn about this aspect of spiritual life?

Response

How can we respond to what the Spirit is saying to us in this matter?

First, evaluate your role in the testing of spirits. Determining the level of your own involvement, prepare yourself through worship, prayer and the reading of Scripture for future encounters with the 'prophetic'.

Second, assess your past responses to 'prophetic' activity using the criteria of the confession of Jesus Christ coming in the flesh and the interaction between the community and the spokesperson(s) as your primary instruments of discernment. Make a list of your successes and failures in this regard.

Third, observe and evaluate the messages and activities of those who claim to speak prophetically on behalf of the Spirit of Truth, paying careful attention to the criteria mentioned above.

Fourth, seek confirmation and/or correction from other members of the body. Celebrate the genuine words of the Spirit of Truth and under the guidance of your spiritual leaders carefully discern what your response should be to 'prophetic' activity that does not pass the test of discernment.

1 John 4.7–5.5

For the third time in 1 John the theme of love is discussed in some detail. Structurally, 4.7-5.5 finds its parallel in 2.3-17, where the subject was first raised. In addition to 2.3-17, 4.7-5.5 has also been preceded in 1 John by the discussion of love in 3.11-17, which functions as center of the book. Thus, by the time the reader comes to this passage, much has already been said about love. A review of those preceding passages reveals that a number of ideas which have appeared before in 1 John reappear in 4.7-5.5. However, despite the large number of common ideas, this section is anything but mere repetition. For in ways not unlike previous parallel sections in 1 John, 4.7-5.5 develops the thought about love in concrete and significant ways. This observation is illustrated by the fact that a good two-thirds of the love vocabulary appearing in 1 John is found in this passage alone. Specifically, 18 of 28 occurrences of the verb (ἀγαπάω) are found here, as well as 13 of the 18 occurrences of the noun (ἀγάπη).[160] Such a heavy concentration of love vocabulary suggests that the previous discussions of love function as a thematic prelude to this section, which then becomes the thematic climax on this topic in 1 John.[161]

This section may be further divided into three subsections: 4.7-10, 4.11-18 and 4.19-5.5. The first two of these subsections begin with the term of endearment, 'Beloved'. In addition, an admonition to the readers to love appears in the opening sentence of all three subsections. In each case, the admonitions to love are based upon God's love. Generally speaking, 4.7-10 grounds the admonition to love one another in the loving act of God who sent his unique Son into the world as an atoning sacrifice concerning our sins. The emphasis of 4.11-18 is upon the relationship between loving one another and 'remaining' — God in the readers and the readers

---

160 Brown, *The Epistles of John*, p. 545.
161 Strecker, *The Johannine Letters*, p. 142.

in God. The final subsection, 4.19-5.5, underscores the necessity of keeping the commands by loving one's brother or sister, the children of God. By this means the one born of God is victorious over the world.

In addition to the broad connections 4.7-5.5 shares with 2.3-17 and 3.11-18, this passage is also connected to 3.23 and 4.6 in specific ways. As observed earlier, it is possible to view 4.7-5.5 as an exposition of the second part of the command given in 3.23 'to love one another', following the exposition in 4.1-6 of the first part of the command to 'believe in the name of his Son Jesus Christ'. This section is also linked to 4.6 by the occurrence of the phrase 'of God' (ἐκ τοῦ θεοῦ) and reference to knowing God, which appear in both 4.6 and 4.7.

Verses 7-10

Verse 7. This section (and subsection) begins with the term of endearment, 'Beloved', which indicates that a new section has begun, as in 4.1, and is especially appropriate in this context for it introduces the third discussion of love in 1 John. Not only does the appearance of the term indicate a new beginning to the readers, but the words which follow also contribute to this sense. The first three words in the Greek sentence (translated 'Beloved, love one another') all begin with the same letter ('Αγαπητοί, ἀγαπῶμεν ἀλλήλους). This alliteration would not be lost on the readers. Found in these words is the third appearance of the words 'love one another' (cf. 3.11, 23). The fact that this identical phrase should occur yet again in 1 John hammers home to the readers the importance of this command. The phrase is informed both by the words of Jesus in the Fourth Gospel and all that precedes it in 1 John. Grammatically, the phrase expresses the idea of a command or exhortation (hortatory subjunctive) and leaves the impression that the entire section functions as an admonition. Such love clearly includes the concrete expressions of sacrificial love as found in 3.17.

The readers have learned that whoever loves their brother or sister walks in the light (2.8, 10), implicitly connecting love to God who is the Light (1.5). They have also discovered the tight connection between love for one another and eternal life (3.14-15). In 4.7 love is not only identified with God, but God is identified as the origin of love in the statement, 'Love is of God'. The Greek phrase translated 'of God' (ἐκ τοῦ θεοῦ) makes clear that the idea of origin is here in mind. Thus, the earlier allusions and hints give way to an explicit statement indicating that love issues forth from the very nature of God. Though further detail awaits them, the readers already know certain things about God's love. His love for the world is the reason he gave his unique Son 'in order that all who believe in him might not perish but have eternal life' (Jn 3.16). They know that the Father loves the one who loves the Son and keeps his commands (14.21-24). They also know that the Father's love for the Son is connected to the Son's love for the believers and their love for him (15.9-10; 16.27; 17.22-26). Therefore, when love is attributed to the nature of God, the readers have some idea of its meaning.

However, in this verse the focus of discussion is not primarily upon the nature of God's love. Rather, it is upon the implications of love's origin in God for the readers. As such, the admonition to 'love one another', with which the sentence begins, is based upon the fact that love originates with God. To drive home this point, the remainder of v. 7 indicates that because love is part of God's nature, the presence of love in one's life reveals one's relationship with God. Specifically, 'each one who loves has been born of God and knows God'. Earlier in 1 John a similar statement has been made about the one who does not sin (3.9). On that occasion it is observed that 'the one born of God does not sin'. The statement in 4.7 is made in a slightly different form, focusing more on the fact that the practice of love reveals one is born of God. The basic idea in both texts is that those born of God reflect his nature, they do not sin and they love. The reader might be a bit surprised that the phrase 'each one who loves' does not include the object of such love. While it might be possible to see in such an omission an attempt to focus on love more generally, such a reading would be odd given the fact that the general and immediate contexts of this verse are clearly concerned with love for one's brother or sister, love for one another. There is no attempt to explain the love found among those in the world. The readers know from the Fourth Gospel that the world loves its own (15.19), but the world's love is not here at issue. The present tense verb 'loves' indicates that such love is an ongoing part of this person's identity and life. It is the one whose life exhibits love habitually. Such activity reveals that such a one has been born of God. As in its other occurrences, the (perfect) tense indicates that this divine birth has taken place at some point in the past, but its effects are still felt in the present. The presence of love reveals that this divine birth has taken place and is, therefore, the result of such a birth. Just as love is 'of God', so the one who loves is 'of God'!

Not only is love evidence of one's divine birth, it is also testimony to the fact that one knows God. This verse makes explicit an idea that appears as early as 2.3-17. The one who knows God keeps his commands. The great command for the community is to love one another. Consequently, the one who loves reveals by keeping his command(s) that such a one knows God. The present tense verb 'knows' and the preceding discussion in 1 John reveal that this knowing describes an ongoing, intimate relationship between God and the believer. Simply put, one's practice of love testifies to one's origin in God and one's ongoing relationship with him.

Verse 8. In typically Johannine fashion the positive statement in v. 7 is followed by an antithesis in the negative, 'The one who does not love has not known God'. As can be seen, these antithetical statements are not exact, for there is no mention in v. 8 of being 'born of God', as in v. 7, and there is a change of tense in the verb from 'knows' (present) to 'has known' (aorist). The antithesis makes clear that despite any claims to knowledge of God, the absence of love reveals that such claims are invalid. The vigorous way in which this statement is made may remind the readers of earlier discussions about the deceivers who claim to have fellowship with God but do not walk in the light (1.6). It clearly picks up on this passage's parallel (2.3-17) where claims to know God are regarded as invalid if not accompanied by the keeping of his commands to love one's brother or sister. Thus, the presence of love is an absolutely essential aspect of the believer's life as a child of God.

The reason offered for such a statement is found in the last part of v. 8 where the relationship between God and love is clarified further still. In this part of the verse occurs one of the most famous statements in all of the New Testament, 'God is love'.[162] The earlier statements about the relationship between God and love find their full expression here. The connection between love and the light, and the fact that love originates with God, is explained by the fact that God is love. Naturally, then, the ones who love exhibit that they are of divine origin, children of God, born of God. One cannot know God without being loving, for God is love. One cannot be 'of God' without loving. One cannot claim parentage in God without loving—for God himself is love. An encounter with a loving God leads to a transformation of the person into a loving individual.[163] Such an idea is not far from John Wesley's doctrine of perfection in love.

The statement 'God is love' reveals something about who God is. It does not simply affirm that God loves. Rather, it indicates that love permeates all that God does. All his activity is loving.[164] Clearly, the

---

162   Brown, *The Epistles of John*, p. 549.
163   Marshall, *The Epistles of John*, p. 212.
164   C.H. Dodd, *The Johannine Epistles* (London: Hodder & Stoughton, 1946), p. 109, notes, 'But to say "God is love" implies that *all* His activity is loving activity. If He creates, He creates in love; if He rules, He rules in love; if He judges, He judges in love.'

thought of this phrase casts God in very personal terms. It should be noted that this phrase is not some abstract philosophical statement about God's nature. As with the statement 'God is light' (1.6) so this one is followed by its implications for the readers (4.11-12). But one does not have to wait until then to realize this is no abstract concept, for its meaning is defined in the following verse (9) where God's loving activity is described. Therefore, the reader would scarcely understand the statement 'God is love' apart from concrete expressions of that love. The construction of the phrase (ὁ θεὸς ἀγάπη ἐστίν), which makes clear subject and predicate, prohibits the readers from inverting it to mean 'love is God'. As evidence of the fact that these words do not attempt to explain the presence or absence of love in the world, but are focused here upon God's loving activity, the readers would know that not all love can be equated with God. In addition to the fact that the world loves its own (15.19), might be added what is said of some in the Fourth Gospel, 'they loved the glory of men more than the glory of God' (12.43). Structurally, the statement 'God is love' in v. 8 is a climax of earlier statements in 1 John and becomes the theme of much that follows in this section.

Verse 9. The antithetical statements of vv. 7-8 are followed by two verses that define by concrete example how the phrase 'God is love' is to be understood. Five times in this section (4.7–5.5) the words 'in this' begin a sentence (4.9, 10, 13, 17; 5.2). The first of these occurrences is found in v. 9 where these words connect vv. 7-8 to vv. 9-10 by pointing to that which follows. Immediately following the words 'in this' the readers come to a term that they have seen at various points. The verb translated 'has been manifested' (ἐφανερώθη) has earlier appeared in 1 John with reference to the ministry of Jesus (1.2; 3.5, 8) and to his parousia (2.28). In the Fourth Gospel it is used with reference to his resurrection appearances (21.1, 14). Although the subject of this verb is the phrase 'the love of God', the second half of the sentence makes clear that the Incarnation of Jesus is fully in view. The word order at the beginning of this sentence indicates that emphasis is being placed upon the verb 'has been manifested', drawing on its rich meaning in the Johannine literature.

The statement 'God is love' in v. 8 becomes 'the love of God' in v. 9, making clear that the previous statement is not to be understood in an abstract way. Rather the focus is upon the dynamic activity of God. The love of God, which may be perfected in the believer (2.5), has been manifested 'in us'. While it is possible to translate these words as 'to us', based upon the words' usage in Jn 1.14 and 9.3 it is likely that the better translation is 'in (or) among us'. How has the love of God been manifested in and among us? There is but one supreme answer. 'God sent his unique Son into the world, in order that we might live through him.' The readers would recognize in these words a clear reference to Johannine tradition as found in the Fourth Gospel, Jn 3.16. While there are certain variations between Jn 3.16 and 1 Jn 4.9, there are a number of ways in which the latter builds upon the idea expressed in the former. One of the first things to strike the reader is the word order of the sentence. Despite the fact that the love of God is being discussed, emphasis is clearly placed upon Jesus as the first words are literally, 'his Son, the unique one'. The fact that both nouns here are preceded in the Greek text by the definite article serves to underscore these aspects of Jesus' identity. From the Fourth Gospel and the Epistles the reader is well acquainted with the fact that Jesus is God's Son. Such an understanding is part of the very fabric of the community's tradition and has been the focus of attention in the battle with the false prophets. His significant role is made clear by the fact that one aspect of the command the readers have received is 'that we might believe in the name of his Son Jesus Christ'. In v. 9, this fundamental understanding is underscored by the appearance of the term often translated as 'only begotten'. However, this term (μονογενῆ) rather conveys the idea of 'only' or 'unique' child. Clearly its occurrence here serves to highlight the distinctive relationship that exists between God and his Son. This language also reinforces that in the Johannine literature while there are many 'children', there is but one Son. The term's appearance is also significant to the reader owing to the fact that this term occurs four times in the Fourth Gospel in extraordinarily important contexts. Its appearances there are focused on the Incarnation (1.14, 18; 3.16), God's love for the world (3.16) and belief in Jesus his Son (3.18).

It was this unique Son that God sent into the world. Although this is the first appearance of the verb 'send' in the Johannine Epistles, the Fourth Gospel is replete with references to the fact that Jesus is 'the one sent by the Father' (5.23-24, 36-38; 7.16-18, 28-29; 17.3, 18-25). The fact that the verb appears in the (perfect) past tense, 'sent', draws attention to the lasting effects of this action. Something of the magnitude of God's love is conveyed by the fact that this sending of the unique Son was into a world in open rebellion to God. He was sent to a place of hostility and hatred; a place that would not listen to him; a place now full of false prophets and the spirit of deception. Such an act, along with that of 2.2, suggests that God does not simply love those in the community, while forgetting the world, but loves the world to such an extent that, like Abraham, he was willing to sacrifice his only son. If his love is the model for the community, then their love must embrace more than just those inside the community, but must have implications for their relationship to the world as well. The purpose or result of this sending is 'that we might live through him'. This verb 'live' (ζάω) appears only here in 1 John though it is frequent in the Fourth Gospel (5.25; 6.51, 57-58; 11.25; 14.19). Given the parallel with Jn 3.16 and the fact that Jesus is himself the Life, even Eternal Life, the readers would likely see reference to living as synonymous with experiencing eternal life. It would not surprise the readers to find that such life comes 'though him', for he is the Life.

Verse 10. The thought of v. 9 is continued in v. 10, where a definition of love is offered. The last two words of the previous verse, 'through him', function as a bridge between vv. 9-10, as the latter now describes how 'we might live through him'. For a second time in this section, the readers are directed forward by the words 'in this'. The phrase is used in this verse to point to the definition of love. While the words 'in this is love' might be construed as having reference to love in an abstract or generic way, again the general and immediate contexts make clear that God's love is in view. The definition of love takes the form of a construction whereby human love is contrasted with divine love. In this antithetical construction, a negative statement precedes a positive one. The order itself conveys a couple of things to the readers. First, it moves from the fact that love is not defined as human ('our') love for God, but as God's love for 'us'. Second, beginning with this negative statement places additional emphasis upon the impotency of human love. The definition of love is 'not that we loved God, but that he loved us and sent his Son as an atoning sacrifice concerning our sins'. The emphatic use of the personal pronouns 'we', 'he' and 'us' would also alert the readers to the fact that the contrast here offered between human love and God's love is an extraordinarily important one. Such a combination of emphatic devices would not be lost on the readers.

In the first part of the antithesis, love is defined by what it is not. Love is not defined by 'our' love for God. It should perhaps be noted that the readers are not told that they do not love God, for it is clear that at least some of them do (2.5). Nor are they told that their love is temporary or episodic. In point of fact, the (perfect) past tense form of the verb 'loved' implies that their love has an enduring quality to it. Rather, the readers are informed that such love for God, however real and lasting, is not an adequate starting point for articulating a definition of God's love. The first part of the antithetical statement is contrasted with the second by means of the construction, 'not that...but that'. The only appropriate starting point for a definition of 'the love of God' is with God and the way he loves. It is 'not that we loved...but that he loved'. Significantly, the verb 'loved' here appears in the (aorist) past tense, which points to an act of love at a particular point in time. In this case, there is no question that the focus of this particular act of love is the Incarnation of Jesus, as v. 9 implies. However, v. 10 goes further to reveal that in this context the culmination of the Incarnation is Jesus' atoning death. 'God loved us and sent his Son as an atoning sacrifice for our sins.' For a second time in these two verses, there is reference to the fact that God 'sent' his Son. In this second occurrence, it is clear that this sending has as its goal the sacrificial death of Jesus to atone 'for our sins'. For a second time in 1 John Jesus is referred to as 'an atoning sacrifice', a term with which the readers are familiar. From its earlier appearance in 1 John (2.2), the readers know that in this term (ἱλασμός) several ideas converge. Jesus is the atoning sacrifice whose blood cleanses from all sin. His advocacy with the Father on behalf of believers is based upon his atoning sacrifice. His atoning death was not only for the sins of those who believe, but for those of the entire world. Thus, the readers now have spelled out for them the connection between God sending his unique Son into the world and Jesus' sacrificial atoning death. In 4.10, the focus is specifically upon the effects of Jesus' death for 'our sins'. The definition of love is both concrete and clear. God's love is such that he sent his unique Son into a hostile world to die as an atoning sacrifice to remove sins. God forgives those who have sinned against him and himself provides the means for the removal of sin at the greatest personal cost possible. Obviously, this definition of love informs what it means for believers to have the love of God perfected or completed in them.[165]

Verses 11-18
The next subsection begins by reaffirming the need to love one another, moves to a discussion of the connection between the perfected love of God and the indwelling of God in the believer, and concludes with the relationship of the perfected love of God and fear in the life of the believer.

Verse 11. The second subsection found in 4.7-5.5 begins with the sixth and final occurrence of the term of endearment 'Beloved'. Its appearance here is not only appropriate for the context, but hearkens back to v. 7 where the term begins this larger section and is followed by the exhortation to love one another, an exhortation that serves to define this entire

---

[165] Bede's comments, *Commentary on 1 John*, ACCS, XI, p. 213, are especially to the point: 'This is the greatest sign of God's love for us: when we were not yet able to seek him because of our many sins, he sent his Son to us, so that he might grant forgiveness to all who believe in him and call us back into the fellowship of his fatherly glory.'

passage. Following this term's final appearance in v. 11 is the phrase, 'if God so loved us'. The 'if' clause here does not express doubt about the nature of God's love, but rather assumes the reality of that love just described. In fact, one might even translate the Greek term (εἰ) as 'because' or 'since'. The readers would at once be struck by the emphasis placed upon the nature of God's love, a love manifested in the sending of his unique Son as an atoning sacrifice for 'our' sins. At the same time, the readers would hear the echo of Jn 3.16 in this phrase, given that three of the same words appearing in Jn 3.16 reappear in 1 Jn 4.11 in identical form ('God so loved'). Just as in Jn 3.16, so in 1 Jn 4.11 the Greek term translated 'so' (οὕτως) appears describing the incredible nature of God's love. Such echoes indicate that the words of Jn 3.16 continue to inform this section of 1 John.

Owing to the remarkable nature of God's love, the readers are again exhorted to love one another. This time the exhortation is conveyed by the language of obligation: 'we also are obligated to love one another'.[166] The emphatic personal pronoun 'we', along with the word 'also' (καί) serves to underscore the fact that 'our' loving actions are based upon God's loving actions. The verb translated 'we are obligated' (ὀφείλομεν) is by now a familiar one to the readers, having appeared in Jn 13.14, 19.17; 3 John 8; 1 Jn 2.6; 3.16. As the previous readings reveal, this term carries with it the idea of moral and/or ethical obligation. Its appearance in this verse indicates both that the reader is obligated to love and that this obligation to love is based squarely upon the fact that God has loved so much. Not only does this language remind the reader of earlier places where this verb occurs, but it also reminds the reader of other places where the believer's life must be consistent with the nature of God. This is true whether it involves walking in the light (1.6-7), avoidance of sin (3.4-10) or loving one another (4.1-10). The readers might expect that since 'God so loved us', 'we are obligated to love' God, especially since reference to the believer's love of God has just appeared in v. 8. However, the obligation of the believers, growing out of God's love, is to love one another. Such a shift is reminiscent of 1 Jn 1.7 where the one who walks in the light is said to have 'fellowship with one another', instead of to have fellowship with God as 1.6 may have implied. Again, one's relationship to God is made visible by one's relationship(s) to and in the community.

How would the readers understand the relationship between God's loving action and the obligation to love one another? Though never

---

166   The command to love one another appears in this form (ἀλλήλους ἀγαπᾶν) only here in the New Testament.

expressed as such, it would appear that the believers' love for one another would be viewed as an expression of the gratitude felt owing to the extraordinary love experienced in the atoning sacrifice of God's Son. It seems likely that for those who experience such unmerited love, this love would naturally overflow into the lives of brothers and sisters. At any rate, the message is clear: the love of God incarnate in Jesus, must become incarnate in the readers as well.[167]

Verse 12. The command 'to love one another' with which v. 11 concludes is followed by a direct reference to the community's tradition with the words, 'no one has seen God at any time', a statement which appears on several occasions in the Fourth Gospel (1.18; 5.37; 6.46). Its appearance here merits several observations. It is clear that the appearance of this statement would draw upon the readers' knowledge of the community's tradition. Therefore, its previous occurrences would in all likelihood inform its meaning on this occasion. In the Fourth Gospel, this statement conveys the idea that despite the fact that no one has seen God at any time, he is nonetheless accessible. He has been made known through his Son (1.18; 14.9). Thus, the appearance of this traditional statement creates the expectancy within the readers that they will be informed as to how access to God is gained. The sentence itself reveals that a great deal of emphasis is placed upon the fact that absolutely no one has seen God. Literally the sentence reads, 'God no one at any time has seen'. The appearance of these words in this order, makes clear such emphasis. In addition to word order, another aspect of this sentence would not be missed by the readers. Unlike Jn 1.18, 5.37, and 6.46, a different verb for seeing occurs in 4.12. Not only does this shift in terminology result in a word play in Greek between 'God' (θεὸν) and 'has seen' (τεθέαται), but it may also point to this term's appearance in 1 Jn 1.1-2 which draws upon the great incarnational passage in the Fourth Gospel (1.14) where the same term appears. Thus, in this one statement the readers are reminded of two important Johannine truths: no one has seen God at any time, but 'we' have seen the Word who became flesh, who reveals the Father. Therefore, the expectancy of access to God is very real for the readers at this point in the text. As for the idea of seeing God, the closest the readers come to this idea in 1 John is when it is said of Jesus that 'we shall see him as he is' when he is manifested at the parousia (3.2).

This traditional statement is followed by an 'if' clause where the command to love one another appears yet again. However, unlike the 'if' clause seen in v. 11, the clause in v. 12 does not imply certainty. Rather it

---

167 Brown, *The Epistles of John,* p. 545.

expresses an open-ended condition based upon the phrase, 'if we love one another'.[168] In v. 11, the obligation to love one another is tied to the fact that God loved 'us' so much. In this verse, the command follows the traditional statement about access to God and points to the last part of the sentence. If one loves in conformity to the love command, which issues out of God's own love, it is a sign of two things: 'God remains in us and his love has been perfected/completed in us.' On this occasion the mutual indwelling of God and the believers (3.24) gives way to a statement that focuses upon the fact that God dwells in the believers. This extraordinary statement goes some ways toward assuring the readers that although no one has seen God at any time, it is still not only possible to experience God, but also to have God indwell or remain in them. As before, the idea of 'remaining' points to an intimate and on-going relationship between God and the believers. The use of the plural 'us' may indicate that the readers would see in such language a corporate emphasis.

The connection between 'remaining' and 'love being perfected' would not surprise the readers for this very connection has been made earlier in 2.5. There it is said, 'Whoever keeps his word, truly in this one has the love of God been perfected'. The immediate context of 2.5 makes clear that the one who keeps God's word is synonymous with the one who keeps God's commands, which in turn is synonymous with those who love their brothers and sisters. At this point, the readers know full well that loving one another is *the* command. It is clear from the context that 'his love' in v. 12 has reference to God's love, which is said to have been perfected in 'us'. As noted in 2.5, the perfection of God's love means that it is brought to completion or is fully manifested. Since the love in question is God's love, the primary emphasis is upon the presence of God's love in the life of the believer, but it is hardly possible to separate God's love in the believer from the believer's love for God, Jesus and other believers. This is especially the case in 4.12, where love for one another clearly informs the meaning of 'his love' and is, no doubt, the goal or completion of God's love.

Despite the similarity between the ideas expressed in 2.5 and 4.12 with regard to the perfection of love, the statement in the latter should not be treated as mere repetition of the former. Two things distinguish the latter from the former. First, a compound form of the verb 'has been perfected' (τετελειωμένη ἐστίν) appears in 4.12 communicating a bit more emphasis than that in 2.5. Second, at this point the readers are much more fully

---

168 ἐάν plus the subjunctive (ἀγαπῶμεν) expresses some amount of uncertainty with regard to the outcome.

informed as to the nature of God's love and what it means for such love to be perfected in them. Since the concept appeared in 2.5 the readers have learned that such love requires sacrificial giving, even to the extent of the laying down of one's life (3.16-17). The fact that God sent his unique Son as an atoning sacrifice to remove the sins of a hostile world reveals that such perfected love takes the initiative in reconciliation, going so far as to provide the means for reconciliation. The extremes to which God's love goes indicates that his perfected love in the believer should know no limits. How would the readers understand the relationship between the two parts of v. 12? Is it because 'we love one another' that 'God remains in us and his love has been perfected in us', or do 'we love one another' as a result of his remaining and the perfecting of his love? Consistent with what has preceded in 1 John, it is probably best not to see the options as 'either...or'. Rather, these elements appear to exist in a very dynamic way. 'Loving one another' not only reveals that 'God remains in us and his love has been perfected in us', but 'loving one another' is also part of God's remaining in the believers and the perfecting of his love in them.

Verse 13. In the previous verse the readers are told that if they love one another, 'God remains in us'. This theme receives detailed attention in vv. 13-16, where a number of related themes and issues converge offering the readers the most comprehensive (and final) discussion of the mutual indwelling of God and the believer in 1 John. The transition from the statement in v. 12 to the fuller discussion in vv. 13-16 is provided by the third appearance in this section of the words 'in this' (cf. 4.9, 10). The phrase 'in this we know' at once draws on the fact of God remaining in the believers (v. 12) and points to the assurance of how one can be certain that God does indeed dwell in them (vv. 13-16). This is the sixth occurrence in 1 John of the phrase 'in this we know', a phrase by which the readers are assured of a variety of things. Specifically, 'in this we know' that 'we have known him' (2.3), 'love' (3.16), 'we are of the Truth' (3.19), 'he remains in us' (3.24b), and 'the Spirit of Truth and the spirit of deception' (4.6b).[169] In 4.13 'we know that we remain in him and he in us'. Clearly, this phrase extends the thought of v. 12, where God remaining in 'us' is the point. What the reader might not be prepared for is the way in which this phrase in v. 13 serves as an introduction to what follows in vv. 13-16. There is a sense, then, that all which follows in vv. 13-16 offers an explanation of this initial statement. It is not insignifi-

---

169 To this might be added 4.2 where the phrase 'in this you know the Spirit of God' occurs.

cant that the verb 'know' appears in the present, implying that such knowing is a continuous experience on the readers' part, reminiscent of 'believing' and 'knowing' in 4.1-2. The emphasis in v. 12 upon God dwelling in the believers, gives way in v. 13 to the idea of mutual indwelling. However, perhaps too much should not be made of this shift given that the expressions appear to be somewhat interchangeable in 1 John (cf. esp. 3.24). As with the verb 'know', so the verb 'remain' appears in the present tense, underscoring the idea that this mutual indwelling is an ongoing, continuous relationship.

The way in which the readers are initially assured of this mutual indwelling is that 'he has given to us out of his Spirit'. It is not surprising that assurance of mutual indwelling contains a reference to the Spirit, for a number of activities have already been attributed to the Spirit in 1 John. The readers have an anointing by which means they are taught all things and have no need of anyone to teach them (2.20, 27). In a verse very similar to 4.13, they have once before been reassured that they know God remains in them because he has given 'us' out of his Spirit (3.24). In addition, the Spirit of God who inspires prophetic work in the community is known to the readers by means of the confession of 'Jesus Christ having come in the flesh' (4.2). Owing to their status as children of God and the fact they know God, they also 'know the Spirit of Truth' (4.4-6). The point here is that the same God who dwells within the believers is the same God who has given of his Spirit. The presence and activity of his Spirit among them is evidence of the fact that he remains in the believers and they in him. They may be certain of their relationship with God for they see, hear and feel the presence of his Spirit. The near verbatim repetition of 3.24b in 4.13 may indicate that this statement about the Spirit and mutual indwelling forms part of the community's basic understanding of the function and role of the Spirit. Despite any problems caused by openness to the Spirit's work (cf. 4.1-6), there is no attempt in 1 John to domesticate the Spirit; rather the readers continue to be encouraged to expect the Spirit to work in distinct and concrete ways among them. Despite the apparent ambiguity associated with the activity of the Spirit, the overall sense of 1 John is that the Spirit has a vital role to play in the believers' lives. Here, they may know of their mutual indwelling with God by the fact that they have been given of his Spirit.

Verse 14. There are a couple of ways in which v. 14 is connected to v. 13. If, in v. 13, the readers are reassured about their mutual indwelling with God by means of the Spirit, in v. 14 they are reassured of that relationship on the basis of what 'we' have seen and 'our' witness. This sentence begins with a (καὶ...καὶ) construction, translated as 'both...and', which indicates that the two actions are closely related. On this occasion the statement reads, 'Both we have seen and we testify'. In addition to the 'both...and' construction, this sentence is marked by the use of the emphatic 'we'. By use of this construction and this language a very strong message is conveyed to the readers. Reappearance of the word translated 'see' (τεθεάμεθα) directs the readers' attention to its previous occurrences, not only in 4.12, but also in 1.1 and Jn 1.14. Its occurrence in v. 14 may reveal why this verb appears in v. 12 instead of the verb which occurs in the phrase 'no one has seen God at any time' at various places in the Fourth Gospel. The significance of its choice now becomes clear. The emphasis is upon 'seeing' or 'beholding' the Word which became flesh. In order to reassure the readers of their relationship with God, appeal is made to what one might call the very foundation of the community's faith: the Incarnation of Jesus. That which was 'seen' in this verse is the same as that which was seen in 1 Jn 1.1 and Jn 1.14. The reappearance of this verb also makes clear that while 'no one has seen God at any time', 'we' *have* seen his Son and, in turn, have 'seen the Father' (Jn 14.9). The occurrence of this verb in the (perfect) past tense places emphasis upon the continuing effects of such seeing.

In what sense is it possible to say that 'we have seen' God send his Son as Savior of the world? On one level, such a statement makes the claim that in the salvific life and ministry of Jesus 'we have seen' the effects of God sending his Son. But it should not be forgotten that in the Fourth Gospel a great premium is placed upon whether or not one believes 'in the one who sent me' (cf. Jn 6.29). Therefore, it is likely that in this verse visible sight (on the part of eyewitnesses) and belief in the God who sent the Son converge into an integrated 'vision' of God's loving act of salvation. This significant verb is followed by an equally important Johannine one: 'we testify/witness'. From both the Fourth Gospel and 1 Jn 1.2, the readers understand that the testimony of Jesus, the Beloved Disciple (cf. esp. 19.35), and others is foundational for the community. They also understand that testifying is an ongoing part of the community's life through the ministry of the Paraclete (Jn 15.26) and those in the community (15.27). Thus, it comes as no surprise that the word 'witness' or 'testify' occurs here in the present tense indicating that the ongoing witness of the community is part of that which reassures the readers about their relationship with God. This emphasis also offers another point of connection between vv. 13-14, in that one implication of v. 13 is that the Spirit enables this ongoing witness of the community.

At this point, the content of 'our' seeing and testifying is identified: 'that God sent his Son as Savior of the world'. This statement conveys several things to the readers. First, it reinforces the earlier emphasis placed upon the fact that God's love is expressed by sending his Son into the world as an atoning sacrifice for our sins (4.9-10). Second, in this verse the Son, who is earlier identified as the unique Son and an atoning sacrifice, is now described as 'the Savior of the world'. This title is peculiar given the fact that the verb 'save' is missing from the Johannine Epistles, though it occurs six times in the Fourth Gospel (cf. 3.17; 5.34; 10.9; 11.12; 12.27, 47). However, the identical title does occur on one occasion in the Fourth Gospel (4.42), where Jesus is called 'the Savior of the world' by the Samaritans who believe in him as a result of the Samaritan woman's testimony and Jesus' time among them. Third, the term 'Savior' in this context is informed by the fact that Jesus is earlier described as an atoning sacrifice for the sins of the world (2.2; 4.10) and that his blood is that which cleanses from all sins (1.7). No doubt, deliverance from death (3.14) and the giving of life (4.9) are also understood to be aspects of Jesus' identity as Savior.[170] Fourth, it would be obvious to the readers that mention of 'the world' lays stress upon the universal nature of the salvation he brings. Its location in the narrative of the Fourth Gospel indicates that the title is meant to convey a universal application, coming after Jesus has earlier been called 'the messiah' (1.41) and 'the king of Israel' (1.49) by his disciples. At the same time the title 'Savior of the world' continues to develop the idea that the atoning death of Jesus is limitless in its extent (1 Jn 2.2).

Verse 15. The thought of v. 14 is continued in this verse in specific ways. First of all, v. 14 indicates how one partakes of the salvation brought by the Savior of the world. In addition, this verse makes explicit that such testimony and confession results in mutual indwelling by specifically mentioning this theme once again. The verse begins with the words 'if anyone confesses', a construction which picks up on the idea that Jesus is the Savior of the world, by emphasizing the fact that anyone without exception can confess. Thus, the universal implications of Jesus' salvific work, seen in 2.2 and 4.14, continue to be developed in 4.15. This clause is a conditional one that includes a past tense (aorist subjunctive) verb, which focuses the confession upon a particular point in time. In all likelihood, the readers would see in this a reference to the time of their initial belief in and confession of Jesus. On this occasion, the verb appears as a third person singular, underscoring the fact that despite the corporate nature of this entire section, where first person plural is used in an almost exclusive fashion, confession must be made by individuals

---

170 Strecker, *The Johannine Letters*, p. 159.

as well as the entire community. The idea of confessing Jesus is by now a familiar one to the readers, for as early as 2.23 they are told, 'Each one who confesses the Son has the Father'. The theme of confession is a particularly important one in 4.2-3, where the idea of confession of Jesus is informed by the command to believe in his name (cf. 3.23). There is a sense in which it is appropriate to say that the confession described in 4.15 puts into words the testimony mentioned in v. 14.

The content of the confession 'Jesus is the Son of God' is also by now very familiar to the readers. As the reading of 3.23 reveals, this confession is no mere affirmation of a point of doctrine but reflects the fact that the one who confesses has become a participant in the many experiences made available by Jesus. The confession 'Jesus is the Son of God' appears to be a summary statement whereby the various dimensions of Jesus' work are reflected in this one declaration. In addition to the many things found in 1 John 1-3, this idea has come to focus on the fact that Jesus, the unique Son has come in the flesh, as an atoning sacrifice for our sins, being sent by the Father as Savior of the world. While this confession may suggest that the false prophets and deceivers were denying some aspect of Jesus' significance, it clearly indicates for the readers the singular importance of Jesus' person and work for the community.

The presence of this testimony (of that which was seen), the presence of this confession that Jesus is the Son of God, is evidence of God's mutual indwelling with the believer. Thus, not only does the presence of the Spirit reassure the readers about their relationship with God, but the presence of the confession that 'Jesus is the Son of God' also reassures them on this matter. The readers are aware that these two evidences are not unrelated to one another by the fact that it is the Spirit who enables and empowers such a confession, and it is this confession by which the activity of the Spirit is tested. Therefore, the integrative and holistic dimension of Johannine thought is once more very much in evidence.

The statement that underscores the relationship of this confession to mutual indwelling is itself an interesting one. Structurally, it begins and ends with the word 'God': 'God remains in him and he in God.' The form of the statement itself emphasizes the mutual indwelling of God and the believer, as the full form of the statement occurs. Both God and the believer are said to remain in one another. By this means, the readers are reminded of the intimate and personal relationship they have with God, as evidenced by the fact that they are able by means of the Spirit to 'confess' Jesus as God's Son in the fullest possible sense.

Verse 16. The final discussion of the theme of mutual indwelling in 1 John comes to a close with v. 16. This is not only indicated by the fact that v. 16 offers a fitting conclusion to the brief discussion of 'remaining' found in vv. 13-16, but also by the fact that the word 'remain' does not occur again in 1 John after its three appearances in v. 16. In these verses the readers are reassured of their relationship with God by the presence of the Spirit (v. 13) and the presence of the confession that 'Jesus is the Son of God' (vv. 14-15). In v. 16, a third means of reassurance appears: love. As in v. 14 a 'both...and' construction occurs, this time connecting the (perfect) past tense verbs 'we have known' and 'we have believed'. In another resemblance to v. 14, the 'both...and' construction is reinforced by appearance of the emphatic personal pronoun 'we'. In v. 16 the connection between the verbs 'we have known' and 'we have believed' is very close indeed. The appearance of these particular verbs together would, no doubt, remind the readers of a significant confession from the Fourth Gospel where these same two verbs appear—Peter's words to Jesus (Jn 6.69). There, Peter, who speaks on behalf of the other disciples, says, 'Both we have believed and we have known that you are the Holy One of God'. Such a parallel suggests that this combination is almost technical language for confession in the Johannine community. In 4.16 both verbs appear in the (perfect) past tense indicating that the readers' knowing and believing occurred at a specific point in the past but that the effects of their knowing and believing endure to the present. As in other places in 1 John, this point in the past may very well be the time of the readers' initial belief in Jesus.

In 1 Jn 4.16, the object of their knowing and believing is 'the love which God has in us'. This statement is important for several reasons. First, the present tense verb 'has' reveals that the love 'in us' is a present, ongoing experience and reality for the believers. This shift to the present tense from the past tense verbs in vv. 9-10 is in keeping with the way in which this verse seeks to reassure the readers about their current relationship with God. Second, love appears in an absolute sense in this verse, embracing God's love for the believers, the believers' love for God, and the believers' love for one another. If the readers might have difficulty separating these aspects of love from one another in other places in 1 John, such distinctions would seem impossible to make in 4.16. Third, 'the love which God has in (or among) us (ἐν ἡμῖν)' is clearly a reference to the sending of God's unique Son as an atoning sacrifice to be the Savior of the world. Such a meaning resonates with statements that define the community's understanding of the Incarnation of Jesus as found in Jn 1.14, 'And the Word became flesh and dwelt among us (ἐν ἡμῖν)'. As such, this statement is not far removed from the confession that 'Jesus is the Son of God'. On this view, God's love 'among us' is Jesus. At the same time, this expression appears to include reference to the way in which the readers have known the love of God 'in us' experientially. For the readers have come to know that the love of God is a transforming power in their lives, resulting in a change of character in keeping with that of their Father who is himself love. Thus, the basis of the reassurance given in v. 16 appears to include both these dimensions.

While it is possible to treat v. 16b as beginning a new thought in the argument of this section, a closer examination reveals that such a move does not pay sufficient attention to the text itself. This observation is primarily based upon the content of v. 16b where the refrain about mutual indwelling is heard yet again. Thus, it appears better to begin the new thought in v. 17 where the argument with regard to love goes in a slightly different direction. It is at the beginning of the sentence found in v. 16b that a very significant statement reappears: 'God is love.'[171] In v. 8, this statement developed the idea of the relationship between God and love. Not only does love originate with God (4.7), but also God himself is love. In v. 8, this statement forms the basis of the discussion in the following verses. The appearance of the statement 'God is love' in v. 16 is no less significant than its earlier occurrence, for here the implications of this statement for mutual indwelling are clearly delineated.

For a third and final time in vv. 13-16, the readers encounter a statement about mutual indwelling. The form of this statement in v. 16 is no mere repetition of the previous ones, for it is carefully crafted to underscore the essential relationship between love and mutual indwelling. Here 'the one who remains in love remains in God and God remains in him'. It should not be ignored that in this verse the verb 'remain' appears three times, as compared to its singular appearance in both vv. 13 and 15. Such emphatic use of 'remaining' language would not be lost on the readers. How does one remain in love? Based upon all that precedes in 1 John, it appears that one remains in love if the love of God has been perfected in the believer. Specifically, this love is manifested in love for one's brother or sister, a love which knows no limits in its sacrificial nature. In this sense, this (perfected) love is informed by the sacrificial atoning death of Jesus. That such perfect love is here in view is indicated not only by what precedes this verse but also

---

171   Bede, *Commentary on 1 John*, ACCS, XI, p. 216, offers these comments on the nature of God's love: 'And we believe in the love which God has for us, the same love he has for his only-begotten Son, because God did not want his Son to be an only child. He wanted him to have brothers and sisters, and so he adopted us in order that we might share his eternal life.'

by the fact that perfected love and love for one's brother or sister becomes the basis of the discussions that follow in 4.17-18 and 4.19–5.5 respectively. Just as the ones who have been given of the Spirit remain in God, and just as the ones who confess that 'Jesus is the Son of God' remain in God, so the ones who remain in love also remain in God. But what exactly does it mean to 'remain in love'? This question is answered in part by the readers' knowledge of Jesus' words in the Fourth Gospel (15.10), 'If you keep my commands you remain in my love'. Significantly, this very emphasis returns in 4.21–5.3. However, the very basic logic of this verse should not be missed. If God is love, then to dwell in him is to dwell in love.[172] The verse concludes with the phrase 'and God remains in him'. With this, the most emphatic statement about mutual indwelling in 1 John comes to an end. Therefore, at the end of v. 16, the reader now knows that assurance about 'our' mutual indwelling with God comes from the Spirit, the confession that 'Jesus is the Son of God' and the presence of love.

Verse 17. As noted earlier, it is possible to take v. 12 as an introduction to vv. 13-18, with the theme of mutual indwelling discussed at greater length in vv. 13-16 and the theme of perfected love discussed in vv. 17-18. If the role of vv. 13-16 is to reassure the readers about their relationship with God, it appears that the role of vv. 17-18 is to reassure the readers about the confidence they can have in the face of 'the day of judgment'. Thus, while these verses take the discussion in a slightly different direction, the continuity between vv. 13-16 and vv. 17-18 is easy to see. The transition, with its continuity and discontinuity, is indicated to the readers by the phrase 'in this', which may have reference either to that which precedes it (vv. 13-16) or to that which follows (vv. 17-18). Although it is possible to argue for one interpretation or the other in an exclusive fashion, it appears that the readers would likely take this phrase as a bridge between these sections. On the one hand, it points back to the discussion of the mutual indwelling experienced by God and the believer. On the other hand, it points forward to the discussion of the confidence the believers have in the face of 'the day of judgment'.[173] Such an interpretation of 'in this' leads the readers to the conclusion that it is in the mutual indwelling of the believer and God that 'love has been perfected among us'.

As in other places in 1 John, the love here described is the love of God completed in the believers, manifested in love toward one another. The

---

172   Marshall, *The Epistles of John*, p. 221.
173   Smalley, *1, 2, 3 John*, pp. 256-57.

(perfect) past tense 'has been perfected' conveys the idea of continuous activity grounded in the ongoing relationship of mutual indwelling between God and the believers. As such, the love which has been perfected is dynamic rather than static.[174] The love of God perfected through the intimacy of mutual indwelling has as its purpose and goal 'that we might have confidence in the day of judgment'. The idea of having confidence is not a new one to the readers, for it has appeared in 2.28 with reference to the believer's confidence at the appearing of Jesus and in 3.21 with reference to the believer's confidence before God when the heart does not condemn. In each case there is the idea of a freedom on the believer's part to speak openly before God or Jesus. Such an idea implies that one is unafraid of revealing one's true self. In this case, the confidence of the believers is found in the context of 'the day of judgment'. This phrase, which is literally 'the day of the judgment', occurs in this form (where the article 'the' accompanies both nouns) only here in the New Testament. The phrase conveys several things to the readers. First, it reminds the readers that Jesus has been given authority to judge (Jn 5.22, 27), so it might be possible to understand the phrase as 'the day of *his* judgment'. Second, this idea appears to be informed by 'the last day' imagery of the Fourth Gospel (6.39, 40, 44, 54; 11.24), 'the last hour' language of 1 John (2.18), and 'the hour of judgment' terminology of the Apocalypse (9.15; 11.13; 14.7, 15). Third, a very similar phrase (lit. 'the day of judgment') appears in several other New Testament documents, indicating that this idea was a somewhat widespread one in early Christianity (Mt. 10.15; 11.22, 24; 12.36; 2 Pet. 2.9; 3.7; Jude 6). Therefore, it seems certain that the readers would see in this language yet another appeal to their eschatological context where the return of the Lord is imminent. That one could have confidence in such a sober and crucial context would prove to be quite reassuring indeed.

In the last part of v. 17 the readers' confidence is very closely tied to their identity with Jesus: 'just as that one is, we also are in this world'. Throughout 1 John, Jesus has functioned as a model for the readers to imitate. They are obligated to walk as that one walked (2.6), be pure as that one is pure (3.3) and love as that one loved (3.16). In 4.17, appeal is made to Jesus' mode of being in the world. Given the context, it would appear that the readers would see in such a statement reference to the mutual indwelling of the Father and the Son, exemplified in the Son's perfect obedience in keeping the commands of the Father (Jn 15.9-10). Specifically, Jesus is the model of love. The fact that the verb 'is' occurs in the present tense indicates that there is no attempt to distinguish

---

174 Smalley, *1, 2, 3 John*, p. 257.

between the past, present and future works of Jesus, for in the Johannine literature he transcends space and time.[175] The readers can have courage in the face of the day of judgment owing to the fact that their character, obedience and relationship with the Father resemble those of Jesus. They are like Jesus for they too keep his (God's) commands (2.3-5) and are his (God's) children (3.9-10). The presence of the Spirit in their lives, the confession that Jesus is the Son of God and their perfection in love, all point to their mutual indwelling with God. Such a relationship in love transforms them into individuals who live in this world in the same way Jesus lives. Such an emphasis draws upon the fact that the disciples of Jesus are still in the world (Jn 17.11) and have a work to do in the world (17.18). Their faithfulness to and solidarity with Jesus gives them assurance to face his judgment for they conform to his model.

Verse 18. If the readers are encouraged in v. 17 by the fact that they have confidence on the day of judgment, owing to the love which has been perfected in them resulting from their mutual indwelling with God, in v. 18 they are encouraged by the fact that fear is not present in those who have perfect love. The readers are alerted to the fact that 'fear' is the primary focus of this verse in two ways. First, the word appears as a noun or verb four times in v. 18 alone! Second, the verse begins with the word 'fear' standing first and in a position of emphasis. Literally, the first phrase in v. 18 reads, 'Fear is not in love'. By this means the readers learn that the opposite of confidence is fear, with love producing one and eliminating the other. While it is possible to treat fear in an absolute sense, given the fact that its appearance follows v. 17 so closely, it is likely that for the readers the fear described in v. 18 is the 'fear' associated with 'the day of judgment'. On two occasions in the Fourth Gospel Jesus dispels fear. The fear of his disciples is dispelled by his words (6.19-20); the fear of Jerusalem by his fulfillment of Scripture (12.15). Otherwise in the Fourth Gospel, fear is associated with 'the fear of the Jews' (7.13; 9.22; 19.8, 38; 20.19) and Pilate's fear of Jesus (19.8). Clearly, fear has negative connotations in the Fourth Gospel. The immediate context of 1 Jn 4.18 makes clear that the love in question is the love of God which has been perfected. Just as Jesus is able to dispel fear, so fear is unable to coexist with God's love.

The next phrase in v. 18 is connected to the first by means of a term that normally functions to designate a contrast of some sort. However, on this occasion the term marks a climax instead.[176] 'But (ἀλλ') perfect

---

175   Strecker, *The Johannine Letters*, p. 165.
176   Haas, de Jonge and Swellengrebel, *A Translator's Handbook on the Letters of John*, p. 113.

love casts out fear.' For the first time in 1 John the readers encounter the term 'perfect love', which for them is identical to the phrase 'the love that has been perfected'. In both constructions there is reference to love in an absolute way; God's love for the believer, the believer's love for God, and the believer's love for one another. In this sentence the construction 'perfect love' is personified in that 'perfect love' is that which casts out fear. It is tempting to see in such personification a reference to God (who is love) and/or Jesus (who is the perfect example of love). In addition to 'day of judgment' language found in v. 17, the theme of casting out may also convey to the readers that the fear in v. 18 has to do with eternal punishment. However, while it may be assumed that evil will be cast out on 'the day of judgment', the readers have the assurance of Jesus' words that each one whom the Father has given him, 'I will never cast out' (6.37).

This statement is followed by one which underscores why love and fear cannot coexist: 'because fear has punishment'. Unfortunately, the phrase is somewhat ambiguous so that the precise nature of the relationship between fear and punishment is not made explicit. It could mean that fear is associated with punishment; that fear anticipates punishment; that fear carries punishment with it; or fear is itself punishment. Some light might be shed on this discussion by the term here translated 'punishment'. This Greek word (κόλασιν) is found in only one other place in the New Testament (Mt. 25.46), where it is identified as 'eternal punishment'. Given the other associations in this passage with 'the day of judgment', the readers would likely see in this phrase an allusion to eschatological punishment. The idea could very well be that fear of 'the day of judgment' anticipates the punishment which will come with it. For those who fear this day, instead of having confidence in it, already experience its punishment to a certain extent. Perhaps the idea here is not far from Jesus' words in the Fourth Gospel that 'the one who does not believe has already been judged'. While it is possible to speak of fear as its own punishment, the eschatological dimension of fear and punishment should not be overlooked in this verse.

This verse and subsection (vv. 11-18) concludes with the phrase, 'and the one who fears has not been perfected in love'. This verse, which begins with the somewhat abstract statement 'fear is not in love', concludes with a very personal one. The person who fears reveals that he or she is not perfected in love. For the one who has been perfected in love has confidence not fear in 'the day of judgment'. This statement also implies that there is a sense in which love is perfected in the believer and the believer is perfected in love.¹⁷⁷ As one presses further and further into the love of God, one finds oneself being perfected and transformed by the very love embraced. These words of assurance serve to encourage the readers not only about their mutual indwelling with God, but also about their place in 'the day of judgment'. Just as they can have confidence at his appearing (2.28), so they can have confidence at the judgment.¹⁷⁸

1 John 4.19–5.5

The final subsection of this section devoted to a detailed discussion of love is found in 4.19–5.5. Like those beginning in vv. 7 and 11, this subsection also begins with a form of the love command. While repeating some of the themes of the earlier passages, this subsection offers concrete examples of how love should function in the believers' lives. Intertwined with this emphasis on love is that of belief in Jesus, reminding the reader of the dual command given in 3.23. As found in other places in 1 John, this integrated discussion prepares the way for a more detailed examination of the person and role of Jesus (5.6-12).

Verse 19. This short verse is a significant one in the argument of 1 Jn 4.7-5.5. Primarily, it serves as an introduction to the discussion that follows in 4.20–5.5. By directing the readers' attention back to v. 10 and its emphasis upon the priority of God's love, v. 19 serves as a transition from that which precedes to the theme of love for brothers and sisters that follows. The verse begins with the third occurrence of the love command found in 4.7–5.5. The reappearance of this now familiar command alerts the readers to the fact that a new turn in the argument is being introduced. However, on this occasion there is some ambiguity as to how the phrase is to be understood. Grammatically, it is possible to take the underlying Greek phrase (ἡμεῖς ἀγαπῶμεν) either as making a statement (indicative) or giving a command (subjunctive). Given the fact that the verb is clearly a command in vv. 7 and 11, which stand at the beginning of each of the previous subsections in 4.7–5.5, and the fact that the entire section can be understood as an exhortation, perhaps it is best to think that the readers would be inclined to see in this verb an exhortation. It might not be going too far to say that by this point in 1 John, even the statement (indicative) describing 'our' love would carry overtones of

---

177 Cf. the words found in 1 *Clement* 49.5, 'By love all God's elect were made perfect' (ἐν τῇ ἀγάπῃ ἐτελειώθησαν).
178 Bede, *Commentary on 1 John*, ACCS, XI, p. 217, observes, 'The new convert is afraid that the strictness of the righteous Judge will condemn him, but love casts this kind of fear out and gives him assurance on the day of judgment.'

a command for the readers. In 4.19 the command to love one another is strengthened by the emphatic use of the pronoun 'we'. On the one hand, this emphatic pronoun serves to contrast the readers with those who fear 'the day of judgment' (vv. 17-18). On the other hand, this emphasis serves to contrast the readers with the 'he' (God) that comes in the second part of the verse. The plural 'we' also reminds the readers of the communal nature of love. As in vv. 16-18, love is used in an unqualified way. Specifically, no object of 'our' love is given. As before, the readers are likely to see in this a comprehensive understanding of love: God's love for us, our love for God, and our love for one another. Given the previous discussion in vv. 17-18, it is clear that this command would be understood as having 'perfect love' in mind.

The reason for this exhortation is given in the second part of the verse: 'because he first loved us'. 'We' are to love because 'he' loved first. Allusions to the priority of God's love for 'us' already appear in 4.10. However, in v. 19 this idea is made explicit by use of the term 'first', a word which compares 'our' love with 'his'. His love has priority chronologically as well as theologically. The (aorist) past tense of the verb 'loved' suggests a particular manifestation of God's love. Given the immediate context, there can be little question that this has reference to the sending of his unique Son as an atoning sacrifice to be the Savior of the world. This act of love precedes the love present in the believers' lives. Such a chronological priority carries with it the theological priority of God's love. His love makes 'our' love possible. The transformative experience of God's love not only obliges the readers to love but also empowers them to do so.[179] One implication of this reality is that just as God loved those undeserving of such love, so 'we' are enabled to love such people.

Verse 20. The connection between 'our' love and God's is developed in v. 20 where the readers encounter a formula reminiscent of those at the beginning of 1 John. Owing to its earlier use, the phrase 'if anyone says/ claims' would prepare the readers for a claim to intimacy with God, in this case love, that is invalidated by improper actions on the part of one making such a claim. It is likely that such language would remind the readers of the false teachers and, given the similarities to 3.17, may indicate that a particular situation is in mind. The specific claim in v. 20 is 'I love God'. Interestingly enough, though it is implied at various points, this is the first occurrence of the verb here translated 'love'

---

[179] As Bede asks (*Commentary on 1 John, ACCS*, XI, p. 217), 'From where would we get the power to love God if he had not loved us first of all?'

(ἀγαπῶ) in the Johannine literature which has God as the object. That this claim stands first in v. 20 suggests that God is included as one of the objects in the phrase 'let us love' in the previous verse. The claim to love God is clearly a claim to intimacy with him, not unlike previous claims in 1 John (1.6; 2.4, 6). However, the one who makes this claim and at the same time 'hates his brother or sister is a liar'.

Earlier in 1 John (2.9-11) the readers learned that 'not loving' is synonymous with 'hating'. In addition, it is known that the activity of 'hating' belongs to the realm of this world (3.13) and the one who hates one's brother or sister is a murderer, devoid of eternal life (3.15). It follows in 4.20 that the one who hates one's brother or sister while claiming to love God can be seen to be a liar. Not only is the claim 'I love God' shown to be a lie, but the life of the one who makes such a claim is also shown to be a lie. Such murderous activity of the world is diametrically opposed to the God who is love. The present tense verb 'hates' underscores the fact that the hatred of one's brothers or sisters here described is an ongoing activity. As the readers already know (1.10), to be a liar identifies one with the father of lies, the Devil (Jn 8.44). Thus, far from demonstrating love for God, these actions reveal that one's intimacy is with the Devil instead.

The verse concludes with a perfectly balanced statement which connects 'loving' with 'seeing'. It contrasts one's lack of love for a brother or sister who has been seen, with claims of love for God who has never been seen. The emphasis upon seeing and not seeing accomplishes two things at once. First, it conveys the idea that the brother or sister not loved has been seen in the past and is still in the vision of the unloving person. No doubt the reader's mind goes to the situation described in 3.17, where a 'believer' with the means of this life locks up his or her compassion and refuses to help a brother or sister in need. Such a graphic example reveals that the content of 4.20 is not hypothetical but drawn from the experience of the community. Love, then, is not sentimentality but concrete actions which embody this gracious experience. How can one who does not love a brother or sister, who is seen everyday in need, claim to love God? Second, the sentence draws upon the common Johannine belief that no one has seen God at any time (1 Jn 4.12; Jn 1.18). Just as the sight of the brother or sister in need is constant, so the lack of sight with regard to God is constant. In addition to the contrast between the brother who is 'seen' and the God who is 'unseen', the readers might also see in the reference to the God who is 'unseen' a critique of claims to mystical union with God which are not authenticated in concrete ways. There is also the possibility that reference to the God who is not seen would remind the readers that there are some among them who claim to love or know God who, in fact, have not seen him (3 Jn 11; 1 Jn 3.6). The final words in v. 20 make clear that it is impossible to love God and hate one's brother or sister. The thought here is not that one must love God in order to love one's brother or sister, or that one must love one's brother or sister in order to love God, but rather that love of God and love of brother or sister are impossible to separate. Therefore, the command to love in v. 19 is fulfilled in part by the emphasis upon the indivisibility of love for God and love for one another. Such an emphasis leads naturally to the next verse which recalls the content of 2.4 in specific ways.

Verse 21. This verse is connected to the previous one by use of the word 'and'. By this means the readers are led to draw a conclusion based upon that which precedes, particularly the content of vv. 19-20. In the Greek text emphasis is placed upon 'this command', indicating that the preceding discussion culminates in refocusing upon the command. Such an emphasis takes the reader back to 2.3-11, where reference is first made to 'his command' in 1 John. From this point onwards, the readers are left in no doubt that 'keeping his commands' has reference to the love command. This point is re-emphasized in 3.23, where it is expanded to include belief 'in the name of his Son Jesus Christ'. In 4.21 the command is said to come 'from him'. While it is possible to take 'him' as a reference to Jesus, the immediate context suggests that God is here in mind. Although it is true that Jesus gave the new command to love one another in the Fourth Gospel (13.34), the readers would not be surprised that the command could be regarded as coming from God. This is the case for at least two reasons. First, the idea that the command comes from God is familiar to the readers from 2 John 4, which unequivocally states, 'just as we have received a command from the Father'. Second, the readers are now quite familiar with the habit of 1 John to attribute things to the Father that the Fourth Gospel attributes to the Son.

While there is a certain repetition in 4.21 of previous statements in 1 John, there is also an advancement of the work's argument in this verse. Specifically, the content of the command takes a different form in this verse, 'in order that the one who loves God also loves his brother or sister'. Among other things, this is the first time in 1 John that love for both God and brothers and sisters has been spoken of positively.[180] But there is a complication at this point, for this form of the command does not match any command known to come from God or Jesus in the Johannine literature. Rather, there is a faint echo in this command of

---

180   Smalley, *1, 2, 3 John*, p. 264.

Jesus' words found in Mk 12.28-31. There, in response to a question from one of the scribes, he says, 'First, you shall love the Lord your God with your whole heart and your whole life and your whole mind and your whole strength. Second, you shall love your neighbor as yourself.' However, despite the similarity, in 1 Jn 4.21 there are not two commands but one: one command that involves love for both God and one's brother or sister. It appears that this command, which comes from God, is the climax of all that has come before it in 1 John to this point.[181] In this first explicit mention of the command since 3.23, the inseparability of these two loves is again underscored. Unlike the one who claims to love God but hates his brother or sister, the one who receives God's command loves both God and his or her brother or sister. Aspects of this verse will be developed in the next few verses.

1 John 5.1. Although a new idea is introduced at this point, it is clear from the way in which the theme of love recurs in this and the following verses that 5.1 continues the thought of the previous verses, particularly the thought of 4.21. The direction the argument 1 John takes in the next major section (5.6-12) is introduced as this section (4.7-5.5) draws to a close. In both 5.1 and 5.5, the idea of belief in Jesus occurs. In 5.1 the focus of belief is that 'Jesus is the Christ'. In 5.5 the focus of belief is that 'Jesus is the Son of God'. Such emphasis accomplishes at least two things for the readers. First, it reminds them of the idea expressed in Jn 20.31, the purpose statement of the Fourth Gospel, which says, 'These things have been written in order that you might believe that Jesus is the Christ the Son of God, and in order that you might have life in his name'. Thus, this foundational piece of Johannine tradition, which might appropriately be called the full Johannine confession,[182] may very well underlie these final verses of this section. Second, such emphasis prepares the readers for the next major section of 1 John (5.6-12) where discussion of the person of Jesus is very much the issue. This verse also prepares the way for the discussion of keeping his commands which follows in vv. 2-3.

The phrase 'each one who' is reminiscent of 2.29–3.10 and 4.7, where this construction occurs several times. Specifically, this formula focuses attention upon the fact that an individual response is required on the part of the readers, despite the communal orientation of the message of

---

181 Strecker's comments, *The Johannine Letters*, p. 173, are very much to the point: 'The dense interweaving of love of God and of the sisters and brothers, as presented in the ἵνα clause's connection of subject and predicate, constitutes the climax of the author's authoritative teaching to the Christian community.'

182 Brown, *The Epistles of John*, p. 535.

1 John. On this occasion, the formula reads, 'Each one who believes...' The present tense form of the word 'believes' indicates that the readers' belief is understood as an ongoing activity. As the readers know by this point, the idea of 'believing' in 1 John is closely identified with 'confessing'. Equally, the readers know that the idea of 'believing' in Jesus is no mere affirmation or passive acceptance of a point of doctrine, but carries with it an active participation in and experience of the person in whom belief exists; not simply belief in the fact but the person himself. Here the object of believing is 'Jesus is the Christ'. The significance of these words would be informed by 2.22, where the antichrists are described as not confessing that Jesus is the Christ. It is also informed by 3.23, where the various dimensions of Jesus' activity and person are drawn together in a comprehensive expression. In addition, the attention given to the fact that Jesus Christ has come in the flesh in 4.1-6 would not be lost on the readers. Thus, the understanding that Jesus is the Christ continues to take shape as 1 John unfolds. He is the unique Son, the atoning sacrifice, the Savior of the world. Belief that 'Jesus is the Christ' would include all these aspects of his identity and activity.

Each one who expresses this kind of comprehensive belief in Jesus 'has been born of God'. Several times the (perfect) past tense verb translated 'begotten' (γεννάω) is used in 1 John to describe the divine origin of the believer (cf. 2.29; 3.9; 4.7; 5.1, 4, 18). As in other contexts, here this form underscores the fact that the believer's birth has taken place at a point in the past and that the believer continues as one 'born of God'. As the readers know well by this point, the idea of birth from God is an extraordinarily important one in Johannine thought occurring in pivotal locations in the Fourth Gospel (1.12; 3.1-15) and 1 John. Earlier, those who do righteousness (2.29), those who do not sin (3.9) and those who love (4.7) are to said to have been born of God. Now, the connection between belief that 'Jesus is the Christ' and being born of God is placed alongside these other ideas. Clearly, such statements would not be understood by the readers in a contradictory way but rather as interconnected.

The second part of v. 1 combines the themes of divine birth and love in a new and creative way. In parallel with the phrase 'each one who believes', with which v. 1 begins, the phrase 'each one who loves' appears at the beginning of the second part of the verse. This structural parallel is a subtle encouragement to the reader to see the connections that are to emerge between 'belief' and 'love' in the verses that follow.[183] At this

---

183 Caesarius of Arles, *ACCS*, XI, p. 221, goes so far as to say that 'John immediately joined love to faith, because without love faith is useless. According to charity, faith belongs to Christians, but without love it belongs to the demons' (*Sermon* 186.1).

point the readers are likely prepared for the object of the phrase 'each one who loves' to be God or one's brother or sister, given these earlier emphases in 1 John. However, in what follows there is a departure from this somewhat established norm. Instead, the readers encounter a play on words which develops this theme in an unexpected way. The sentence reads, 'Each one who loves the one who has begotten loves the one who is begotten of him'. While it is possible to take this phrase as a maxim drawn from human experience, that the one who loves the father loves the child of the father, the immediate context makes clear that these words have specific reference to the believer's love for God and the believer's brother or sister. These words indicate that when one believes, he or she is born as a child of God into the family of God. This experience carries with it all the benefits of divine origin and the obligation of family life. In this case, the obligation includes love for both one's parent and one's siblings. The identity of the parent and siblings would be very clear to the readers. They are none other than the God who begets those who believe in his Son and the brothers and sisters who have been begotten by him. Once again, the readers are told that love for God entails love for one's brother or sister. In point of fact, this statement stresses the inextricable bond that exists between love for God and one another in ways that are hard to ignore. It follows that there is no love for one without love for the other. The believer's love described in this verse is comprehensive. This vigorous statement is a natural follow up to the idea expressed in 4.21.

Verse 2. For an eighth and final time the readers encounter the assuring phrase, 'in this we know'. As in its earlier occurrences the concept of knowing carries with it the idea of experiential knowledge. Although it could be seen to have reference to what precedes it in 5.1, it appears that this phrase points the readers forward to what follows in v. 2: 'In this we know that we love the children of God, when we love God and do his commands.' Though the theme is a familiar one to the readers, there are a couple of unexpected nuances found in v. 2. To this point in the argument of 1 John the readers have been assured that they love God if they love their brother or sister and keep his commands. However, in 5.2 this idea is inverted so that the readers are now assured of their love for the children of God by their love for God and the keeping of his commands. Because of this unexpected departure from previous thought, various translations invert the Greek phrase to conform to the earlier expression. However, such a move does not pay sufficient attention to the fact that this unexpected change conveys its own message about the believers' assurance as it relates to love of God and love of the children of God. Thus, it would seem wise to allow the text to have its say despite any problems it appears to create for the readers.

The assurance offered in v. 2 builds intentionally upon the statement found in the second part of v. 1. There the emphasis is upon the fact that the one who loves the Father must also love the child of the Father. In v. 2 the emphasis is reversed so that the one who loves the 'children of God' by this knows that he or she loves God and does his commands. The occurrence of the phrase 'children of God' not only builds upon the meaning of the phrase as it has developed throughout 1 John, but is also natural at this point for it makes clear that 'the one who has been begotten' in v. 1 has reference to the child of God.

The second part of v. 2 is introduced by a Greek word (ὅταν), which in this context conveys the idea of a constantly recurring action, and might best be translated 'whenever'. The readers can be assured of their love for the children of God whenever they love God and keep his commands. The inversion of how one can know about one's love makes explicit the integrated nature of love for the reader. It is impossible to separate love for the children of God from the love of God. The presence of one implies the presence of the other. Not only can the readers know that they love God when they love their brothers or sisters, they can know that they love their brothers and sisters when they love God. While such argumentation is open to the charge of circularity, it would not likely surprise the readers for it represents the kind of integrative and dynamic thought characteristic of 1 John.

The final part of this phrase 'and do his commands' is also somewhat unexpected for the readers are familiar with the phrase 'keeping his commands'. This unique expression, which occurs only here in the New Testament, would accomplish at least two things for the readers. First, it would reintroduce the idea of keeping the commands, which has been a major theme in 1 John. Second, it would perhaps combine the ideas of 'keeping the commands' with 'doing the will of God' (2.17), ideas implicitly connected with one another earlier in 1 John. Clearly, 'doing the commands' primarily involves loving one another in 1 John. It includes the idea of belief 'in the name of Jesus his Son' (3.23) and now is closely connected with love of God as well.[184]

Verse 3. The thought of v. 2 is developed further in v. 3 by the appearance of a formula familiar to the readers, 'This is the love of God'. The pronoun 'this' points to what follows as yet another definition of love is

---

184 In fact, Smalley, *1, 2, 3 John*, p. 268, can go so far as to say that this Greek construction is a hendiadys meaning, 'to love God is to keep his commands'.

offered and is facilitated by the appearance of the word 'for'. Earlier the readers learn that love is defined as enabling them to 'walk according to his commands' (2 Jn 6). Love is also defined by the fact that 'God loved us and sent his Son as an atoning Sacrifice concerning our sins' (1 Jn 4.10). In 5.3, the discussion of the love of God is clearly informed by the fact that the readers have assurance of their love for the children of God when they love God (v. 2). Consequently, the contents of v. 3 are read in light of the previous verse. In this light, 'the love of God', mentioned in this verse, appears to be primarily the love the believers have for God. The definition of love offered in this verse is conveyed by means of a purpose clause translated 'in order that we keep his commands'. The connection between loving God and 'doing his commands' is already implied in v. 2. In v. 3 the connection is made explicit. Loving God is 'keeping his commands'. Thus, the definition of the command continues to expand for the readers to include love for one another, believing in the name of his Son Jesus Christ, and loving God. The mention of 'keeping his commands' draws attention once again to the many parallels between this section (4.7–5.5) and an earlier one devoted to the theme of love (2.3-17). In the earlier passage it is made clear that 'keeping his commands' and 'keeping his words' describe the same activity. Here, these ideas are clearly synonymous with 'doing his commands' which is closely connected to 'doing the will of God'. Appearance of the phrase 'keeping his commands' also underscores just how integrated the idea of love is for the readers of 1 John.[185] The last phrase in v. 3, 'and his commands are not heavy' at once concludes the thought of v. 3 and at the same time leads to v. 4. The adjective translated 'hard' or 'burdensome' (βαρύς) is found only here in the Johannine literature. In this verse the word conveys the idea that the commands of God are not too difficult or heavy to carry out. The reason that his commands are not crushing is found in the next verse.

Verse 4. The thought of this verse is connected to the previous one by the word 'because' (ὅτι). By this means an explanation is offered to the readers why his commands are not burdensome or heavy. However, the readers might be a bit surprised by the following construction. Instead of the expected 'whosoever is born of God' the readers encounter 'whatsoever is born of God'. By this unexpected shift the readers are alerted to the fact that the emphasis here is more than could be conveyed by the expected construction. The construction is not unlike that found in the

---

185 There is also the echo of Exod. 20.6b which reads, 'those who love me keep my commandments'.

Fourth Gospel (3.6) where Jesus says, 'That which is born of flesh is flesh, that which is born of Spirit is Spirit'. Thus, this particular construction underscores the inclusive nature of the category of those who have experienced birth from God. Of course, by this point the readers are quite familiar with the concept of divine birth. As in other contexts, the verb occurs in the (perfect) past tense indicating that the birth took place at a specific point in the past with results which endure into the present.

The reason that his commands are not heavy is that 'whatsoever has been born of God is victorious over (overcomes) the world'. Appearance of overcoming language would remind the reader of the parallel passage to this one found in 2.3-17. Specifically, they have been told, 'I write to you young men because you have been victorious over the evil one' (2.13). A very similar statement follows in 2.14. In addition, the readers have been assured that 'greater is the one in you than the one in the world' (4.4). In contrast to its usage in 2.13-14, the present tense verb translated 'is victorious' indicates in 5.4 that the struggle in which the believer is engaged is an ongoing one. Consistent with its occurrence in other places in 1 John, 'the world' here has a negative if not sinister connotation. Its opposition to God and association with the evil one is very clear to the readers. In this sentence it appears that the world is seen as a threat to the believer. It is a place whose desires are clearly in diametric opposition to God, his will and his love. As such, it seeks to draw the readers away from God and into its own orbit, which is controlled by its desires and is the realm of 'that of the antichrist'. In this sense, it might be appropriate to say that the world threatens to make his commands burdensome. However, the believer is victorious over the world.

The readers are scarcely able to consider the identity of the source of the believers' victorious activity before they encounter a formula of definition which has earlier been used to offer further clarification of a point just made. On this occasion, the formula is used to define further the means by which such victorious activity takes place. 'And this is the victory which is victorious over the world, our faith.' Not only does the formula alert the readers to the importance of this statement but the sentence is also constructed in such a way that both the object 'the victory' (ἡ νίκη) and its adjective participle 'which has been victorious' (ἡ νικήσασα) are from the same root word. Such emphasis would not be lost on the readers. Neither is it insignificant that the verb tense of the latter is an (aorist) past tense, pointing to a decisive moment of victory at a specific point in the past. Perhaps one of the things the readers would associate with this past event is the fact that Jesus himself has claimed victory over the world in the Fourth Gospel (16.33). Specifically he says,

'I have been victorious (νενίκηκα) over the world'. Interestingly enough, these words are spoken in a context of encouragement to the disciples who (will) face tribulation at the hands of the world. Thus, at one level, this victory that has already been won would, no doubt, be associated with Jesus' own victory over the world. That there is a connection between Jesus' past victory and the believers' current victorious activity follows rather naturally. Such an impression is confirmed by the final words of v. 4, 'our faith'. The word 'faith', which appears only here in the Johannine Epistles and not at all in the Fourth Gospel, is closely associated with the verbs 'believe' and 'confess'. This association alone is enough to make clear the content of 'our faith', even if its content were not revealed in v. 5 which follows. For the readers of 1 John, the identity of 'our faith' is that Jesus is the Christ, the unique Son of God, who was sent as an atoning sacrifice to be the Savior of the world. This faith is an experiential one whereby the various aspects of Jesus' life and work are not just affirmed by the believers but also experienced by them. Thus, 'our faith' is the faith of the Johannine community that focuses upon Jesus Christ.

Verse 5. With this verse both this larger section (4.7-5.5) and this shorter subsection (4.19-5.5) come to a close. In several ways v. 5 functions as a bridge between this section (4.7-5.5) and the one which follows (5.6-12). It points forward to the content of 5.6-12 by the language, 'the one who believes that Jesus is the Son of God'. At the same time, this verse points back, not only to the preceding verse but also to the thought of 2.12-13. The entire verse takes the form of a rhetorical question, 'Who is the one who is victorious over the world except the one who believes that Jesus is the Son of God?' Having just learned of the significant role of 'our faith' in attaining victory over the world (v. 4), the readers now discover that this faith must be understood in very personal terms, for v. 5 makes clear that 'our faith' is to be equated with 'the one who believes'. In this sense then, faith as it appears in v. 4 is not something that stands on its own as a system of doctrine independent of believers, but is intimately connected with individual believers. Thus, v. 5 expands on the content of v. 4 in very personal ways. The phrase 'who is it that is victorious over the world' reveals that the victory that has been won (v. 4), is one that is an ongoing struggle and one that must be fought by individual believers. The Greek phrase translated 'the one who is victorious' is a present tense form which makes clear that the victory is not to be understood wholly as a past event, but must be fought for every day. Therefore, the victory of Jesus is the basis of the believer's victory but his victory does not eliminate the need for a continuous fight. Once again, the victory in question is over the world. For a third time, the term 'the world' appears in a two-verse span (vv. 4-5). Such emphasis would not be lost on the readers. In each occurrence the world is a place of hostility toward God and those who are born of him. Consequently, a victory over it says much about the victor's relationship both to God and the world.[186]

In form, this verse is very much like 2.22, where a similar rhetorical question is raised. There, as in 5.5, the words translated 'except' (εἰ μὴ) appear to indicate the specific identity of the individual in question. 'Who is the one who is victorious except the one who believes…?' Once again the present tense appears in the phrase 'the one who believes' indicating that believing is an ongoing activity. The phrase 'the one who believes' clearly expands upon the idea of 'our faith' in the preceding verse. This expansion can hardly be missed in the Greek text where 'the one who believes' (ὁ πιστεύων) and 'faith' (ἡ πίστις) are seen to be closely connected as they come from the same Greek root word. The content of this belief is 'that Jesus is the Son of God'. The close association that exists between the titles 'Christ' and 'Son of God' is clear to the readers from the Fourth Gospel (esp. 20.31) as well as all that precedes this verse in 1 John. As noted earlier, vv. 1-5 are surrounded by the belief that 'Jesus is the Christ' (v. 1) and that 'Jesus is the Son of God' (v. 5). By this means the readers are again reminded of the integral connection between love and what is believed about Jesus. While the titles 'Christ' and 'Son of God' are very similar in the Johannine literature, it is difficult to believe that the readers would not see in this occurrence of 'the Son of God' a reference to the fact that since God's love was revealed in the Incarnation of Jesus, faithfulness to his love requires faithfulness to a proper belief about Jesus.[187] Therefore, the twofold command of 3.23 is again underscored.

Reflection and Response—Part Ten

Reflection

Two of the major themes in 1 John are addressed for a final time in this passage; love and remaining. To be more exact, love in its various dimensions is tied to the mutual indwelling of the believer and God. Of the many aspects of love discussed in this section, one in particular is identified here for further reflection and response. As early as 1 Jn 2.5 the

---

186   At a number of places in the Apocalypse reference is made to the one who is victorious (Rev. 2.7, 11, 17, 26; 3.5, 12, 21). In each case a promise of reward is given. In 1 Jn 5.5 the focus is not on a reward but upon the content or basis of the victory.

187   Rensberger, *1 John, 2 John, 3 John*, p. 129.

readers have learned that it is possible for the love of God to be perfected or completed in the believer. This idea is mentioned four times in 4.7–5.5. In 4.12 it is stated that if we love one another God remains in us and his love is perfected (or completed) in us. In 4.17, the mutual indwelling of God and the believer results in his love being perfected in us with the result that we have confidence on the day of judgment. In the following verse it is revealed that perfect love casts out all fear of the judgment and that presence of such fear indicates the absence of perfected love. Thus, the perfection of his love in the lives of believers coincides with love for one another, mutual indwelling with God and the presence of confidence in the face of the final judgment.

Several questions are now offered as a means of facilitating further reflection on this issue. Who do you consider to be the greatest examples of love? What are the reasons for your assessment of these individuals or groups? Would you describe any of these individuals as persons of faith? What are the other characteristics of their lives? Are there individuals within the Church who function as models of perfect love? How would you describe their relationship with God? What role does the expectation of the return of Jesus play in their lives? Is this expectation a cause of joy or fear for them?

How has God's love been experienced in your life? How would you describe the impact of his love upon your own attitudes toward him and others? In assessing your life, what evidence is there that God's love is perfected in you? What obstacles stand in the way of such perfect love? What emotions are generated by the thought of the return of Jesus? If fear is present, how can it be removed and what can replace it? How often do you ask the Lord to perfect his love in you? How have you experienced the relationship between loving your brother or sister, remaining in God and the perfecting of love in your life?

Response

Among the appropriate responses to this dimension of this passage, perhaps the following merit consideration.

First, assess your life with regard to the presence or absence of perfect love in it, by means of your relationship to other believers and to God.

Second, describe the nature of your relationship with God to a fellow believer. Give specific attention to the way in which you experience mutual indwelling with him.

Third, based upon the biblical teaching about perfect love, seek to facilitate its development in your life by identifying and incorporating into your life the appropriate spiritual disciplines and exercises.

Fourth, periodically take stock of your life, judging it by means of your relationship to God, your spiritual brothers and sisters, and your attitude toward the return of Jesus.

1 John 5.6-12

As with the previous sections, the mirroring effect continues in 1 John, with 5.6-12 standing in parallel to 1.5–2.2. The points of similarity between the passages include: the phrase to 'make him (God) a liar' (1.10; 5.10); the emphasis upon the 'blood' of Jesus (1.7; 5.6, 8); and the way in which these sections begin—'And this is the message...' (1.5) and 'This is the one who came...' (5.6). In 1 Jn 5.6-12, the theme of witness is prominent, with witness vocabulary appearing ten times in these verses. The section may be divided into two subsections: vv. 6-8, which focus upon the witness of the Spirit and the water and the blood, and vv. 9-12, which focus upon the witness of God.

Verses 6-8

In the first subsection of 5.6-12, the emphasis is clearly upon the water, the blood and the Spirit. Each of these is seen as a witness, but there is some ambiguity as to the precise meaning of the terms, especially the water and the blood. Suffice it to say that this section is very thick with meaning. There is also a question about the original form of the text in vv. 7-8.

Verse 6. The first subsection begins with the demonstrative pronoun 'this' pointing back to Jesus the Son of God in v. 5. It is 'this' Jesus, the Son of God, who is believed by the one who is victorious over the world. This very Jesus is the one 'who came through water and blood'. Such emphasis is reinforced by the appearance of the name 'Jesus Christ' at the end of this phrase in v. 6. In addition, the phrase 'this is...' appears at several points in the Fourth Gospel as a confessional statement[188] and thus prepares the readers for what follows. For the readers there can be little question that the role of Jesus Christ in salvation is an unrivaled and essential one. The impression left is that Jesus alone is the one of whom this statement is true.[189] The phrase translated 'the one who came' is an idea familiar from the Fourth Gospel where Jesus is known as 'the one who is coming' (1.15, 27; 6.14; 11.27; 12.13). In 2 John 7 and 1 Jn 4.2,

---

188 Cf. esp. Jn 1.34 ('This is the Son of God'), 4.42 ('This is the Savior of the world'), 7.40 ('This is the true Prophet') and 7.41 ('This is the Christ').
189 Schnackenburg, *The Johannine Epistles*, p. 232.

this expression is used to describe Jesus coming or having come in the flesh. In 5.6 this expression occurs in the (aorist) past tense, which indicates that the activity of having come through water and blood has reference to a specific past event or past events.

While it is clear that Jesus Christ is 'the one who came through water and blood', it is not altogether clear what such a statement would mean to the readers. However, there are a variety of hints in the Fourth Gospel and the Johannine Epistles that assist in determining the likely meaning of these words. The first such hint occurs in the very next phrase of this verse, 'not in the water only but in the water and the blood'. At least two things are clear from this statement. It appears that all concerned (both readers and deceivers) agree that Jesus Christ came through the water. However, not all agree that Jesus Christ came through the blood. Thus, something new about the theological disagreement between the community and those who have left it is revealed to the readers in this verse.

With this helpful piece of information in hand, perhaps the best place to begin in the attempt to unravel this literary knot is with the term 'blood'. To this point, the term has appeared only one time previously in 1 John. Very near the beginning of the book, the readers are told that the blood of Jesus cleanses from all sin and unrighteousness (1.7-9). In all probability the occurrences of the term 'blood' in 5.6 would at the least carry this connotation for the readers. It is perhaps not insignificant that there seems to be some disagreement between the community and those who have left it over the value of and need for Jesus' blood. At the same time, the term would likely be informed by its somewhat limited but significant role in the Fourth Gospel. The first mention of blood in the Fourth Gospel is found in Jesus' words near the end of the Bread from Heaven discourse (Jn 6.53-56):

> Amen, amen, I say to you, unless you eat the flesh of the Son of Man and drink his blood, you do not have life in yourselves. The one who eats my flesh and drinks my blood has eternal life, and even I will raise him in the last day. For my flesh is true food and my blood is true drink. The one who eats my flesh and drinks my blood remains in me and even I in him.

The connection between Jesus' blood and eternal life reveals that his flesh and blood are essential components of bringing salvation. In this text, despite numerous arguments to the contrary, it is difficult to avoid concluding that the readers of the Fourth Gospel would see some allusion to the Eucharist by this emphasis upon Jesus' flesh and blood. The other mention of blood in the Fourth Gospel comes in the dramatic climax of Jesus' passion when a spear is thrust into his side and blood and water come forth (19.34). This story clearly grounds the significance of Jesus' blood as life-giving in his death on the cross and explains more fully John's words in 1.29 that Jesus is 'the Lamb of God who takes away the sin of the world'. Therefore, when the readers of 1 Jn 5.6 encounter reference to Jesus as 'the one who came through the blood', they would hardly be thinking in ways that exclude primary reference to his atoning death on the cross. It appears that it is this aspect of Jesus' identity and work which is being disputed by the false teachers confronted in 1 John.

Determining the meaning of 'water' for the readers in 5.6 is a bit more challenging, but in this case the Johannine hints are even more plentiful. Though the term 'water' does not occur in 1 John before this reference in 5.6, it occurs frequently in the Fourth Gospel. There water comes into play in connection with baptism (1.26, 31, 33; 3.23) and in the story of its transformation into wine (2.1-11). Water also appears with Spirit in the discussion of 'birth from above' (3.5), and the Spirit comes to be identified as the 'living water' which quenches thirst forever (4.7-15). Water is associated with miraculous healings (5.1-9; 9.1-34), and it is miraculously walked upon by Jesus (6.16-21). Later at his death (19.34), along with blood, water issues forth from Jesus' side.[190] Clearly, in the Fourth Gospel water plays a very important role, having remarkably rich associations. What would all this mean to the readers of 1 Jn 5.6? It is tempting to see the primary meaning of water for the readers of 5.6 as having reference to water baptism and Jesus' baptism in particular. Even though there is no description of Jesus' baptism by John in the Fourth Gospel, the anointing by the Spirit to which John (the Baptizer) gives testimony is clearly an allusion to this event (1.32-33). It would also be significant to the readers that John came baptizing with water in order that Jesus might be manifested to Israel (1.31). On this view, water in 5.6 has reference to the baptism of Jesus and his anointing by the Spirit. He is, after all, the one who has been given the Spirit without measure (Jn 3.34). This, then, is how Jesus came. It is not difficult to believe that the false teachers could affirm at least this part of Jesus' story in the Fourth Gospel.

However, while this shared understanding of 'water' may be accurate as far as it goes, it does not do full justice to the term, for water comes to have close associations both with the Spirit and eternal life in the Fourth Gospel. Given the remarkable similarity between 1 Jn 5.6 and Jn 19.34, it is likely that the readers of the former would have the latter in mind at this point. In point of fact, given the close associations of water with the Spirit and eternal life in the Fourth Gospel, and the specific prediction in Jn 7.37-39 that rivers of living water would come from Jesus' belly,[191] it is particularly difficult to believe that the readers would not see in this

---

190 On this cf. Thomas, *Footwashing in John 13 and the Johannine Community*, p. 88.
191 Cf. the discussion in Thomas, 'The Spirit in the Fourth Gospel: Narrative Explorations', pp. 87-104.

allusion to 19.34 a critique of an interpretation which restricts the meaning of water to a baptismal reference. For not only is Jesus anointed by the Spirit at the time of his water baptism (which might be identified at the beginning of his ministry), but the water (and the Spirit) are seen to come from him on the cross. To say that this Jesus is the one who came through water and blood is to affirm the entirety of his life and ministry, but it is also to say something about his unique role in salvation history. Thus, it adds new depth and understanding to Jesus' role as atoning sacrifice and Savior of the world.

The primary emphasis of the phrase is that Jesus is the one who came through the water (of baptism and the Spirit) and through the blood of his passion. The fact that one preposition ('through', δι') is used for both these aspects indicates that the readers are to see both elements as having reference to 'one' event, an event which includes water and blood, which receives its supreme Johnannine summary in Jn 19.34. In this way, the death of Jesus is highlighted yet again. Additional emphasis is placed upon 'this Jesus, the Son of God, the one who came through water and blood', by the appearance of the name 'Jesus Christ' in v. 6. In some ways its occurrence at this point pulls together much of that which has gone before (cf. esp. 5.1).

The next phrase alerts the readers to the fact that the theological point addressed in this sentence is one over which there is significant disagreement. The phrase in question, 'not by (in) the water alone, but by (in) the water and the blood', reveals that there are some questions as to whether or not Jesus came 'by (in) the blood'. The precise nature of the antichrists' theological understanding of Jesus is not altogether clear. It is possible that the antichrists held to a position similar to that attributed to Cerinthus. In the Cerinthian view Jesus became the Christ when the Spirit came upon him at his baptism and the Spirit departed from him when Jesus was on the cross. On this view, the reference to Jesus giving (up) the Spirit in Jn 19.30 could be seen as evidence from the Fourth Gospel for this understanding. However, as noted in the reading of 2.18-27, there are problems with this identification of the antichrists as Cerinthians. What can be known is that the attitude exhibited in 5.6 is consistent with that implied in 1 Jn 1.7-10 among those who deny that they have sin or have sinned, therefore, making unnecessary the cleansing brought by Jesus' death. It appears that the attitude of the antichrists toward Jesus was one which denied the salvific value of his death. The readers are reminded in 5.6 that proper belief in Jesus includes not only belief in and appropriation of his baptism, but also belief in and appropriation of his atoning death. Therefore, the emphasis placed upon Jesus' blood in 5.6 is not to be missed by the readers. The language of this verse is reminiscent of that found in 4.2 and may be a confessional formula of sorts.[192]

In the second half of v. 6, the confession that Jesus Christ is the one who came through the water and the blood is certified by the one who bears witness. Interestingly enough, the statement about the blood and water coming from Jesus' side in Jn 19.34 is also certified by the one who bears witness. In the Fourth Gospel the one who bears witness is the Beloved Disciple. In 1 Jn 5.6 'the Spirit is the one who bears witness, because the Spirit is the Truth'. This statement about the Spirit would not take the readers by surprise, for by this point they are well acquainted with the Spirit's identity and role. While a number of passages from the Fourth Gospel inform the readers' understanding of the Spirit's role and function, none is likely to contribute as much as Jn 15.26 at this point. In the farewell discourse Jesus says, 'When the Paraclete comes, whom I will send to you from the Father, the Spirit of Truth who comes from the Father, that one will bear witness concerning me'. Two aspects of the statement made in 1 Jn 5.6 are found in this passage from the Fourth Gospel: the Spirit is called the 'Spirit of Truth' and the Spirit is identified as the one who will bear witness to Jesus. Such similarity of thought would hardly be missed by the readers.

But not only are the readers familiar with the Spirit from the Fourth Gospel, they also know of the Spirit's work from earlier statements found in 1 John. Specifically, the readers know that they have received an 'anointing' from Jesus (2.20) and as a result know all things (2.27). They have also learned that they have been given of the Spirit (3.24) which enables them to confess 'Jesus Christ having come in the flesh' (4.2). It is not surprising then for the Spirit in 5.6 to be identified as the one who bears witness that Jesus Christ has come through the water and the blood. As with the witness of the Beloved Disciple in 19.35 ('and his testimony is true'), the witness of the Spirit may be trusted because the Spirit is Truth. Since Jesus is himself also identified as 'the Truth', the authentic nature of the Spirit's witness should be all the more apparent. The present tense verb found in 5.6 indicates that the witness of the Spirit is an ongoing reality in the community. It is not simply a past event, the Spirit's witness continues into the present. The implication is that the Spirit will continue to bear witness in the community's future as well. As in 4.2, the Spirit's activity as witness may well include prophetic speech. Therefore, if there should be any question as to the importance of Jesus having come through the blood, the Spirit, whom all in the community have received and who enables the proper confession of Jesus in

---

192 Rensberger, *1 John, 2 John, 3 John*, p. 130.

the community, acts as a witness to its significance. The witnessing activity of the Spirit now stands alongside the witness of the Beloved Disciple (in the Fourth Gospel), and those who stand with the Elder in 1 Jn 1.1-4.

Verses 7-8. The next two verses stand together and conclude the first subsection (5.6-8) of 5.6-12. That these verses stand together is indicated in part by the fact that the opening phrase and the closing one both contain reference to the fact that there are three who bear witness. Verse 7 continues the emphasis upon bearing witness begun in v. 6. However, the readers might be a bit surprised by the fact that here, as opposed to there, there is not one but there are three who bear witness. Thus the readers are told in v. 6 that the Spirit bears witness to Jesus, but they are told in v. 7 that he is not alone in his witness. The emphasis in the Greek text is upon the number three, as it stands at the beginning of the sentence. It is likely that the number three appears by means of the influence of the Torah stipulation requiring two or three witnesses in certain legal settings (Deut. 17.6; 19.15). The readers are probably aware of the way in which such ideas are utilized by Jesus in the Fourth Gospel (5.31-40; 8.17-20) and would not be taken by surprise by its influence in 1 Jn 5.7. The emphasis placed upon the number three perhaps indicates that the testimony is full in terms of numbers of witnesses. The form of the Greek phrase translated 'the ones who bear witness' in v. 7 conveys two things to the readers. First, the phrase occurs in the masculine gender (οἱ μαρτυροῦντες), despite the fact that all three witnesses that follow are neuter in gender. Such a move may underscore for the readers the personal nature of the witness being described. Second, the readers learn that the nature of the witness of these three is ongoing and continuous as this participle occurs in the present tense. Just as the readers learn of the Spirit's ongoing witnessing activity in v. 6, so they learn that the activity of these three witnesses continues even to the present. The fact that witnesses are emphasized at this point in 1 John is in accord with Johannine thought where the act of believing is grounded on the witness or testimony of others.

Before moving to consider the content of v. 8, a word should be offered about the textual problem in vv. 7-8. At this point in the text of 1 John some translations read:

> There are three witnesses in heaven, the Father, the Word, and the Holy Spirit, and these three are one. And there are three witnesses on earth, the Spirit and the water and the blood and these three are one.

Why do most modern translations omit these words? It now seems certain to most biblical scholars that these words were not originally part of

1 John. One of the main reasons for this conclusion is the fact that these words appear in no Greek manuscripts before the fourteenth century. Neither are they appealed to in the trinitarian controversies in the early Church, suggesting that they were not well known in early Christian circles. Their eventual appearance in the text appears to be the result of a marginal note mistakenly being copied into the text. It appears that a scribe mistook that written in the margin as something accidentally left out, rather than as a scribal annotation, and placed it in the text as part of the original reading.[193] Since these words were not originally part of the text of 1 John, they will not be treated as part of vv. 7-8 in this commentary.

The thought of v. 7 continues uninterrupted in v. 8 where these three witnesses are identified as the Spirit and the water and the blood. As earlier observed there is a change in gender from the masculine, 'those who bear witness', to the neuters, 'the Spirit and the water and the blood'. Normally, one would not think that such inanimate objects would serve as personal agents who bear witness. However, such an emphasis here would not likely be lost on the readers of v. 8.[194] Does this shift imply a change in meaning for the terms, the Spirit and the water and the blood, from their meaning in vv. 6-7? The readers might be inclined in this direction for a couple of reasons. First, there is an emphasis on the ongoing nature of the witness being borne. This raises the question, is it likely that the events of Jesus' life and death would be spoken of as continuing in their witness or would they be looked upon primarily as past events with enduring effects? Second, owing to their knowledge of Jn 19.34, the readers would be appreciative of the tight interplay that exists between a number of elements associated with Jesus' salvific work to include the Spirit, eternal life, water and the blood. Given the fact that certain rites have been established in the Fourth Gospel for the community to observe (e.g. the footwashing in Jn 13.1-20), it is not at all unlikely that the readers might see in v. 8 reference to such rites. In addition to the footwashing, a sign of continual cleansing from sin, it would appear that other signs were also practised by the community, including water baptism and the Eucharist. Although an allusion to the Eucharist by means of the word 'blood' is unique in the New Testament,

---

193   For the story explaining how this marginal note became part of the Textus Receptus, which underlies the KJV, see B.M. Metzger, *The Text of the New Testament* (Oxford: Oxford University Press, 1992), pp. 101-102.
194   While it is true that on occasion the neuter πνεῦμα may be referred to by the masculine ἐκεῖνος, on both occasions this change appears to be the result of the appearance of παράκλητος as the antecedent instead of πνεῦμα.

it would not be a wholly unexpected move in 1 John owing to the explicit nature of the language in Jn 6.53-56. Therefore, when the readers encounter v. 8, they are likely to be thinking of Jesus' life filled with salvific significance and his continuing presence among the community members by means of the Spirit which he sent and the signs of water and blood which continue among them. It is unlikely that the readers would see references to the Spirit and the water and the blood in exclusive terms which separate the ministry of the earthly Jesus from his continued presence among them.[195] On this reading, the Spirit and the water and the blood continue as witnesses by means of their ongoing place in the life of the community.[196] Thus the readers are likely to see a double meaning in 'the water and the blood' in this verse.[197]

Verse 8 closes with the statement 'and these three are one'. The reappearance of 'three' continues the emphasis upon the number of those who bear witness as valid and full. The unique construction of this sentence, 'and these three are one', indicates that these witnesses stand or fall together. The idea of unity in this verse is reminiscent of the unity that exists between the Father and the Son and is desired by Jesus for the disciples (17.11, 21-23). The implication is clear. One cannot separate the witness of the Spirit and the water from the witness of the blood. They all bear witness to the same one thing. Their testimony converges on the same truth: Jesus Christ, the one who came through the water and the blood, is the Son of God, the atoning sacrifice for sins, the Savior of the world.

Verses 9-12
The second subsection of 5.6-12 focuses upon the witness of God to the Son and its relationship to eternal life in the believer. In this regard it is perhaps significant that each of these verses concludes with a statement about the Son.

---

195 The close connection seen between the blood of Jesus in his death and the flesh of Jesus thought present in the Eucharist is illustrated in the writings of Ignatius. In his *Epistle to the Smyrnaeans* he describes heretics who deny the significance of Jesus' blood in his death (6.1) and consequently abstain from the Eucharist owing to their rejection of Jesus' flesh in his death and in the Eucharist (7.1-2).
196 It is also possible to see in the occurrence of 'the Spirit and the water and the blood' a reference to Jesus' continuing powers to vivify, cleanse and atone (Jn 6.63; 13.10; 1 Jn 1.7; 2.2). On this proposal cf. Brown, *The Epistles of John*, p. 582.
197 In his comment upon this text, Bede says (*Commentary on 1 John, ACCS*, XI, p. 224): 'The Spirit makes us children of God by adoption, the water of the sacred font cleanses us, and the blood of the Lord redeems us. They are invisible in themselves, but in the sacraments they are made visible for our benefit.'

Verse 9. This subsection begins with the clause 'if we receive the witness of men', an 'if' clause which does not imply doubt but assumes the certainty of the statement being made, as found in 4.11. On one level the reference to the testimony of men may be taken in a generic fashion, affirming the basic principle that properly established witnesses are to be accepted. As noted in the discussion of the three witnesses, the Torah prescribes the number and qualifications of such witnesses. However, for the readers of 1 John, 'the witness of men' may have another level of meaning owing to the fact that the readers would be familiar with a similar contrast between the witness of a man and the witness of God in the Fourth Gospel. In a passage devoted to the topic of valid witnesses (Jn 5.31-47), Jesus concedes the invalid nature of self-testimony (witness) pointing instead to a number of witnesses on his behalf. One of those identified is John, who witnessed to the Truth (5.33). But, Jesus says, 'I do not receive the witness of a man'. Rather pointedly he says, 'I have a greater witness than John...the Father who sent me has witnessed concerning me' (5.34, 37). It is likely that when the readers of 1 Jn 5.9 encounter the phrase, 'If we receive the witness of men, the witness of God is greater', they would understand this contrast in light of the contrast between the man John (who was 'sent by God'; Jn 1.6) and the Father as found in the Fourth Gospel. On this view, the testimony of men in 1 Jn 5.9 includes John's testimony regarding the anointing of Jesus by the Spirit (at his baptism) and as seen in 5.6 may represent the antichrists' understanding of Jesus and his significance. That is to say, the witness of John may have been taken as focusing exclusively upon Jesus as anointed by the Spirit and as having little or nothing to do with his death (blood), Jn 1.29 not withstanding. Clearly, the emphasis of 1 Jn 5.9-12 and Jn 5.31-47 is upon the superiority of God's witness over that of men. This should not be taken to imply that the witness of John is being denigrated. It does, however, underscore the unrivaled position of the witness of God. The God who is 'greater than our hearts' (1 Jn 3.20) offers a greater witness than any of 'us' can offer. It is greater in terms of significance and trustworthiness. Consequently, it should not be ignored.

But what, precisely, is the witness of God in v. 9? It is possible that the readers would view the three witnesses of vv. 7-8 as synonymous with the witness of God. After all, the witness of the Spirit can hardly be viewed as anything other than the witness of God. However, a couple of things suggest that the readers would not simply equate the three witnesses with the witness of God. First, the second part of v. 9 contains a formula, 'This is the witness of God', which would normally cause the readers to look forward, rather than backwards, for the content of the 'this' in question. Similar constructions occur in vv. 11 and 14 which follow. This means that the readers are less likely to look back to the three witnesses as the witness of God than they are to look forward to discover the content of the witness of God. Second, the three witnesses described in vv. 7-8 are spoken of as ongoing by means of the present tense construction, 'those who bear witness' (v. 7), whereas v. 9 uses the (perfect) past tense to describe God's witness. Consequently, the readers are not yet certain about the precise nature of the witness of God at this point in the argument of 1 John.

However, despite this uncertainty, three things may be known at this point. First, just as the witness of God is greater than the divinely inspired witnesses of Jn 5.31-47, which include John and the Scripture, so the witness of God is greater that the three divinely inspired witnesses of 1 Jn 5.7-8. Second, the witness of God, the effects of which are felt in the present, took place at a specific point in the past. For the readers, this past event is likely identified with the witness of the Father described in John 5. While any number points in the Fourth Gospel might be identified as times when the Father bore witness to the Son (cf. 12.28), the emphasis of John 5 is upon the way the works which Jesus does points to the Father and in turn testifies that the Father sent the Son. Thus, it is likely that the witness of the Father would be closely tied to those many places in the Fourth Gospel where there is an emphasis upon 'the one who sent me'. Third, the witness of God is defined in part by the fact that God has borne witness to his Son. Simply put, who knows more about the Son than the Father?[198] Therefore, the testimony of God is especially important. That the witness of God is concerned with his Son indicates that his testimony is the same as the testimony of the community. Thus, at this point in 1 John the crescendo of witnesses which began with 'we' (1.2; 4.14), and continued with the Spirit and the water and the blood (5.7-8), climaxes with the witness of God himself (5.9-12).[199]

Verse 10. In typical Johannine fashion the implications of the previous statements are spun out in the form of antithetical parallelism. As is the case in other such constructions in 1 John, the parallelism in v. 10 is not perfect. The focus of the verse is upon whether or not one believes in the Son of God, with the verb 'believe' appearing three times, once positively and twice negatively. In the opening phrase, 'The one who believes in the Son of God', the readers are reminded of the similar phrases in 5.1

---

198 Brown, *The Epistles of John*, p. 600.
199 E. Malatesta, *Interiority and Covenant: A Study of* εἶναι ἐν *and* μένειν ἐν *in the First Letter of Saint John* (Rome: Biblical Institute Press, 1978), p. 313.

and 5, where believing that 'Jesus is the Christ' and that 'Jesus is the Son of God' are signs that one has been born of God and is victorious over the world, respectively. The continuous belief, conveyed by the present tense participle, that 'Jesus is the Son of God' implies an assent to and appropriation of Jesus and his work in this verse as in the previous ones. However, on this occasion this belief also implies that the witness of God, as described in v. 9, has been received, for his witness has been given with regard to his Son. For such a believing one, this witness has been internalized, for he 'has this witness in himself'. In the Johannine orbit (Rev. 6.9; 12.17; 19.10), such an expression reveals a radical identification with and incorporation of the witness (of Jesus) on the part of the believer.[200] The expression, which appears to have a very similar meaning in v. 10 as well, is not far removed from the imagery of 'remaining' found at various points in 1 John. Specifically, the witness (of God) is manifest within the life of the one who believes. Stress is placed upon this internalization by the words 'in himself'. Such a statement reminds the readers of the Word, Truth and Spirit that are said to remain within the believer. At the same time this expression points ahead to God's gift of Eternal Life to the believer described in vv. 11-12. It goes without saying that an extremely tight interplay between believing in the Son of God and receiving the testimony of God is assumed in this verse.

The negative part of the antithetical parallelism follows in v. 10 with the words, 'the one who does not believe in God has made him a liar'. It is perhaps a bit surprising that the phrase 'the one who believes in the Son of God' is followed not by 'the one who does not believe in the Son of God' but by the phrase 'the one who does not believe in God'. The readers are not likely disoriented by this shift for they have come to appreciate the fact that 1 John's parallels are rarely perfect and that often God is the subject where one would expect reference to be made to Jesus. However, on this occasion, the shift appears to convey something else as well. By this means the extremely close connection between the witness of God and belief in Jesus is underscored. For it is impossible to believe (and receive) God('s witness) without believing in his Son. In point of fact, failure to believe God is tantamount to making him a liar. Such imagery is another part of the mirroring effect between 1.5–2.2 and this section (5.6-12). In the former passage it is said that those who claim 'we have not sinned' also 'make him a liar' (1.10). The reading of 1 Jn 1.10 reveals that making him (God) a liar entails an equation of God with the father of lies (8.44) and treating with contempt the salvific work of God. Not only would these words in 5.10 carry with them the ideas present in

---

200   Brown, *The Epistles of John*, p. 590.

1.10, but they also place into greater contrast the deception of the antichrists with the truth of the believers. Specifically, they suggest that those who claim to know God and receive his witness reveal that they stand in complete opposition to God for their lack of belief in Jesus treats the God who bears witness as a liar. One difference between the emphasis of 1.10 and 5.10 is that the former uses the present tense 'makes him a liar' while the latter uses the (perfect) past tense 'has made him a liar'. This shift in tense implies that those 'who do not believe in God' have made him a liar at a particular point in the past, the moment they rejected the witness of God.

The implicit idea that those who do not believe have rejected the witness of God is made explicit in the final part of v. 10. This is conveyed in the first instance by the word 'because' which functions to put the readers on notice that an explanation of the previous statement is being offered. The emphasis upon witness language is visible in the phrase, 'because he has not believed the witness which God has borne witness concerning his Son', in the occurrence of the term 'witness' in both noun and verb forms. With this phrase it becomes clear to the readers that the witness which the one who believes has in himself or herself is indeed the witness which God himself has offered. Conversely, it is this very witness that has not been believed. As with the verb, 'has made' so the verb 'has not believed' designates an event in the past, the effects of which continue to be felt into the present. It is not altogether clear what such moment of unbelief is in view. Perhaps the readers would understand it as the time of the false prophets' departure from the community. God's witness, which is greater than human witness, is concerned with his Son. Thus, this verse, as all those in this section, ends with a reference to God's Son. Such emphasis would not be lost on the readers.

Verse 11. A formula familiar to the readers of 1 John reappears in v. 11. On this occasion 'And this is...' is used with 'the witness'. The appearance of this formula alerts the readers to the fact that the topic under discussion is taking a new turn in what follows. This formula is sometimes used in 1 John to define a previous statement and would perhaps create in the readers an expectancy as to what follows in vv. 11-12. 'The witness' in this phrase is, no doubt, identical to the witness of God described in the previous verse. As in v. 10, the focus of 'the witness' in v. 11 is upon the Son of God. The formula 'and this is the witness' points to the following phrase, 'that God gave Eternal Life to us'. In the Greek sentence the emphasis is upon 'Eternal Life', as it stands first in this part of the phrase. God, the one who gave this witness, is also the one who 'gave' Eternal Life. The verb 'gave', which occurs in the (aorist) past tense, conveys the idea that a specific past action is in mind. It is difficult to avoid the conclusion that the readers would see in this past act a reference to the sending of Jesus into the world by God. This conclusion is based upon the fact that the sending of Jesus as an atoning sacrifice to be the Savior of the world is very much a part of his identity as Son of God and is never far from view in this section of the book. Such an understanding also fits remarkably well with the use of Eternal Life in personified form as a reference to Jesus, near the beginning of 1 John (1.2). Thus, the readers would know that in the sending of his Son, God sent Eternal Life 'to us', for the Son not only gives eternal life, he *is* Eternal Life. In this sense, it is possible to see Eternal Life as the content and result of the witness of God, for the witness of God is focused upon his Son. In addition to its close associations with Jesus, it should be observed that the term 'eternal life' is one that places emphasis upon the qualitative dimension of this life. The adjective 'eternal' serves to alert the readers to the fact that this life is the kind of life associated with God himself and is not bound by temporal limitations. As such, it is the highest kind of life possible and, remarkably, it is already the possession of the believer.

The connection between Jesus and life is made explicit in the final part of v. 11 with the statement, 'and this life is in the Son'. The words 'this life' clearly have reference to the eternal life which God 'gave to us'. While assuming the close association between the Son and Eternal Life, this statement focuses upon the fact that the eternal life the believer experiences comes from the Son. There appears to be an emphasis upon Jesus' exclusive role in this bestowal of life. Such an emphasis is at home with what the readers have come to expect with regard to the function and role of Jesus in 1 John. To underscore the fact that this eternal life is in his Son again drives home the point that those false teachers who reject the significance of Jesus and his work have cut themselves off from eternal life because they have rejected Eternal Life himself. As in all the verses in this subsection (5.9-12), this verse ends with a focus upon his (God's) Son. Clearly in this verse (and the following one) a number of Johannine themes and issues converge pushing the argument of the book forward.

Verse 12. The implications of v. 11 are made clear in v. 12, which in some ways is the finale of the entire book.[201] Again the argument takes the form of an antithetical parallelism. If God has given eternal life and this life is in the Son, then it follows that 'the one who has the Son has life'.

---

201   R.R. Williams, *The Letters of John and James* (Cambridge: Cambridge University Press, 1965), p. 58.

The words 'has the Son' remind the readers that the one who 'remains in the teaching (of Christ) has both the Father and the Son' (2 Jn 9) and 'the one who confesses the Son also has the Father' (1 Jn 2.23). On these occasions the idea of fellowship and a personal, intimate relationship with God and/or the Son is in view. In 5.12, the phrase 'the one who has the Son' not only conveys this idea but also the idea of belief in and confession of his name. The fact that the verb 'has' appears in the present tense indicates that possession of eternal life through an intimate relationship with the Son is a present and ongoing part of the believer's life. The believer is able to experience this superior form of life already in this life. Yet, the book as a whole reveals that having eternal life is not understood by the readers to be an unchangeable condition, but is viewed as a relationship which must be nurtured and developed in an ongoing way made evident in love for one another and belief in Jesus Christ.[202] Owing to the close association between the Son and eternal life, the readers might even see in the words 'has life' a reference to the believer's relationship with the Son.

The positive statement in the first part of v. 12 is followed by the negative part of the parallelism. Two aspects of this second statement merit comment. Reference to 'the Son' in the first part of the statement is changed to 'the Son of God' in the second part. The change to the fuller expression 'Son of God' underscores the unique role the Son of God has in the thought of 1 John and parallels reference to 'the Son of God' at the end of the Fourth Gospel (20.31). The position of 'life' before the verb 'has' in the Greek sentence would reveal to the readers that a certain emphasis is being placed upon this word. 'The one who does not have the Son of God does not have life', for he alone is 'the Way and the Truth and the Life' (Jn 14.6). With these words, the argument of 1 John reaches its climax.

Reflection and Response — Part Eleven

Reflection

As 1 John draws to a close, the book focuses more and more upon the witness that God has given to his Son Jesus Christ and the life that comes through belief in his name. Clearly the theme of witness dominates this section and is worthy of further reflection. 1 John tells its readers that the Spirit offers witness to the one who came through the water and the blood and the Spirit's witness is true. The Spirit's witness is joined by

---

202   Strecker, *The Johannine Letters*, p. 195.

that of the water and the blood, with all three witnesses pointing to the life and ministry of Jesus in their entirety. The greater witness of God has also been offered to his Son and is experienced in the one who believes God's witness concerning his Son. This takes the form of eternal life in the life of the believer for the one who has the Son has life. Thus, the witnesses which the believers encounter include witness given about significant past events and at the same time continue to play an ongoing role in the life of the believers.

In order to facilitate reflection upon this most significant theme, the following questions are offered. In what ways has witness been offered about Jesus to the Church and the world? How has the Spirit been active in offering such witness to Jesus? What role do the sacraments play in witnessing to Jesus? Exactly what do footwashing, water baptism and the Eucharist convey to believers about Jesus' person and work? What witness is given by the prophetic activity of the Spirit in the Church? How does the Church experience eternal life in its midst and what are its evidences and results? What position does Jesus Christ the Son of God hold in the Church today? Is it indispensable? How would you assess its significance?

What witnesses to Jesus have you personally encountered? In what ways has the witness of the Spirit been most powerfully present to you? In what ways have the sacraments served as witnesses to you about Jesus? What specific things have been conveyed to you by them? When has the prophetic activity of the Spirit offered specific testimony to Jesus? How would you describe the content and impact of this witness? In what ways have you experienced the witness of God in the form of eternal life remaining in you? How would you describe this experience? What sense of assurance do such experiences bring and in what contexts are they most likely to be experienced? How would you describe your personal relationship with Jesus Christ? Who is he to you and how have you experienced him?

Response

Obviously, there are numerous ways to respond to this important issue. Perhaps the following can encourage specific responses to this dimension of the text.

First, identify the ways in which you have experienced witness offered to Jesus Christ.

Second, in the light of the teaching of this text, assess how open you have been to the diverse ways in which God speaks concerning Jesus.

Third, identify those witnesses to which you have not paid sufficient attention and determine ways by which you can be more open to their voices.

Fourth, identify and participate in communal times of worship and fellowship where the witness of the Spirit may be manifest, experienced and responded to.

Fifth, respond to the witness of God about his Son in an intentional way by responding to the question, do I believe in Jesus Christ the Son of God.

1 John 5.13-21

The mirroring effect of 1 John continues until the end of the book, where the last section (5.13-21) echoes the opening one (1.1-4) with emphasis placed upon the theme of eternal life. There are also similarities between the way 1 John concludes and the way the Fourth Gospel concludes. Specifically, both documents appear to reach their conclusion by means of a statement of purpose (Jn 20.31; 1 Jn 5.13), only to be followed by additional materials (Jn 21; 1 Jn 5.14-21). While the additional materials in John 21 might be referred to as an epilogue, the last verses of 1 John show signs of being a conclusion of sorts, even though the arrangement at first sight appears to be somewhat episodic. Specifically, as 1 John comes to a close the readers encounter a number of themes seen earlier which reappear in new and constructive ways. The one dominant theme that tends to tie these verses together is the idea of knowledge ('we know' occurs six times in this section alone!) and/or confidence. This final section begins with a restatement of the purpose for the composition of the book (v. 13); that the readers might 'know' that they have eternal life. This gives way to an emphasis upon the 'confidence' that the believers possess, manifested by the fact that whatever they ask in accordance with the will of God will be given. The concrete example of such assurance is focused upon the intercessory prayer of a believer on behalf of a brother or sister who sins (vv. 14-17). The theme of knowledge continues in vv. 18-20, where the discussion is focused upon three 'we know' statements, which serve to reassure the readers yet again. This section and the book close with a warning in v. 21 to 'keep yourselves from idols'.

Verse 13. The final section of 1 John is introduced by a hinge verse which provides a transition from the previous section (5.6-12) to the next one. Specifically, terms such as 'believe', 'eternal life' and 'Son of God' remind the readers of the discussion in 5.6-12. At the same time, the summary nature of v. 13 points the readers to that which follows in vv. 14-21. Several things are conveyed to the readers by this verse which reads, 'These things I have written to you in order that you might know that you have eternal life, to those who believe in the name of the Son of God'. The remarkable similarity between this verse and the conclusion of the Fourth Gospel would jump out at the readers. Standing near the conclusion of the Fourth Gospel are the words, 'These things have been written in order that you might believe that Jesus is the Christ the Son of God, and in order that believing you might have life in his name'. The fact that these verses bear such a striking resemblance to one another suggests that the readers would likely be conscious of the contents of Jn 20.31 as 1 Jn 5.13 is read. In both texts there is an emphasis upon believing in the name (Jesus Christ) of the Son of God as well as an emphasis upon (eternal) life. While it appears that the conclusion of the Fourth Gospel encourages continued belief, such an emphasis in 1 John is very clear. Neither would the readers miss the similarity between this phrase and the one with which 1 John opens, for near the beginning of 1 John (1.4) the readers are told, 'And these things we write in order that our joy might be completed'. Thus, the book begins and ends with similar phrases that have reference to the purpose of the document. The occurrence of 'these things' clearly has reference not only to the preceding passage (5.6-12), but also to all that comes before in 1 John. For the first time since 2.26, the first person singular 'I have written' reappears. While the readers often encounter 'we' language throughout 1 John, the shift to first person singular language ('I have written') reminds the readers of the personal authority of the one who writes. Consistent with its occurrences since 2.14, the verb is in the (aorist) past tense; another example of the epistolary aorist.

The reason for this book's composition is made known by means of a purpose (ἵνα) clause: 'in order that you might know that you have eternal life'. On various occasions in 1 John the readers are assured of their relationship with God by means of 'knowing' vocabulary (2.13-14; 3.1-2, 14; 4.13). Therefore, it comes as no surprise to the readers that in the book's conclusion this emphasis should reappear. The fact that the readers should need such encouragement throughout the document suggests that the arguments and actions of the antichrists have had some effect upon them. In 5.13, they are assured that they have eternal life, a point made rather forcefully in the preceding verses (5.11-12). Mention of eternal life at this point not only summarizes the argument of the book to this point, but also points to this same theme in 5.20. On this occasion, the construction of the phrase in the Greek text places a certain emphasis upon the term eternal life in that the adjective ('eternal') is separated from the noun ('life') by the verb ('have'). As in v. 12 eternal life is spoken of as a current possession of the believers, as the verb 'have' occurs in the present tense. Thus, the readers are reminded that this experience is not one for which they must await the return of Jesus, but is a part of their salvation experience already.

The assurance of eternal life is given specifically 'to those who believe in the name of the Son of God'. This phrase accomplishes at least two things. First, it continues the emphasis upon the necessity of believing in Jesus Christ the Son of God, an emphasis found at various points in 1 John (3.23; 5.1, 5-6) and one closely associated with confession of Jesus (2 Jn 7; 1 Jn 4.2, 15). Second, owing to the striking similarity between this phrase and that which occurs in Jn 1.12, there is also found here a subtle reminder of the readers' status as children of God. In the Gospel text the readers are told, 'but whoever received him, he gave them authority to become children of God, to those who believe in his name'. Therefore, the one who believes in the name of the Son of God is a child of God via 'birth from above' and as a result has eternal life. The importance of believing is borne out by the fact that in both texts, the words 'to those who believe' stand in a position of emphasis.

As before, it is likely that 'believing in the name of the Son of God' conveys the idea that such life is possible only through Jesus, for he is in a unique position with regard to the readers' salvation.

Verses 14-17

In these verses the readers are encouraged with regard to the confidence they have in approaching God with a variety of requests.

Verse 14. For a third time in the last six verses the readers encounter a 'This is...' clause (5.9, 11, 14), which on this occasion is used to re-introduce the idea of 'the confidence which we have before him (God)'. The topic of confidence is not a new one to the readers as this term has appeared on at least three occasions previously in 1 John, twice with regard to Jesus' return and once with regard to prayer. The key to such confidence with regard to Jesus' return is 'remaining in him' (2.28) and being 'perfected in love' (4.17). The key with regard to prayer is 'if our heart does not condemn us' (3.21). In 5.14, such confidence grows out of the certainty (knowledge) that the readers already possess eternal life. As children of God, the believers have the confidence to speak freely with their Father. This confidence is an ongoing part of the believers' relationship with God, as is conveyed by the present tense verb ('have'). Thus, this confidence is not simply a belief but is an experience.[203] The Greek word translated 'with' or 'before' (πρός) is one that implies

---

203 Westcott, *The Epistles of St. John*, p. 189.

relationship, as it does in Jn 1.1 ('and the Word was with God'), further developing the idea that this confidence is part of the relationship between God and his children.

This confidence finds concrete expression in the fact that 'if we ask anything according to his will, he hears us'. The 'if' clause, here designating expectation, combined with the present tense verb 'ask', results in a meaning something like, 'it is always the case that whenever we ask for anything according to God's will he hears us'.[204] The language of 5.14 is not new to the readers for it reminds them of 1 Jn 3.21-22, where they are encouraged that if their heart does not condemn they may ask anything and receive it. Such language would also remind the readers of Jesus' words about prayer, for in the Fourth Gospel, he promises the disciples that whatever they ask in his name he will do for them (14.13-14; cf. also 15.6, 16; 16.24, 26). If these petitions are offered 'according to his will, he will hear us'. What would it mean to the readers to ask 'according to his will'? The one who asks according to his will is likely the same as the one who keeps his commands (3.22-24). For such a one believes 'in the name of his Son Jesus Christ', the name in which such petitions should be made. Such a one loves his or her brother or sister, a love upon which the following call for intercession is based. Such a one remains in God and God remains in this one, a oneness that implies intimacy of knowledge. 1 John 2.17 goes so far as to say that 'the one who does the will of God remains forever'. Consequently, to ask according to his will not only implies a knowledge of God and his purpose but also implies a oneness of the believer with God. When the believers make such petitions in accordance with the divine will 'we' do so with the assurance that God 'hears us'. Just as Jesus can thank God that 'you always hear me', before the tomb of Lazarus (Jn 11.42), so the believers can be assured that God hears them when they ask.

Verse 15. The emphasis of v. 14 continues in v. 15 where a shortened form of the former appears in the latter. Verse 15 opens with an 'if' clause which indicates that a consequence of the previous statement in v. 14 is being drawn in what follows. Specifically the shortened form of v. 14 reads, 'if we know that he hears us whenever we ask'. In this phrase the 'confidence' of v. 14 becomes the certainty ('we know') that one is heard in v. 15. Once again the readers are reminded of the fact that God hears 'us'. Again the present tense verb ('have') indicates that this is an ongoing reality in the believers' lives. 'If we know that he hears us... (then)...we know that we have the asked-for-things which we asked

---

204 Smalley, *1, 2, 3 John*, pp. 295-96.

from him.' The certainty that God hears 'us' results in the certainty that 'we' have what 'we' asked for. This certainty is conveyed to the readers by the second occurrence in this verse of the words 'we know'. The appearance of the words 'we have' is especially forceful at this point in v. 15, for it follows in a significant line of the occurrences of these words in 1 John. The readers have learned that 'we have God' (2.23), that 'we have eternal life' (5.11), and now that 'we have the asked-for-things which we have asked from him' (5.15). The fact that this present tense verb follows in this line escalates the assurance the readers possess with regard to their petitions. These words suggest that receiving things asked for from God is a common occurrence for the readers. It is likely that these words remind the readers of concrete experiences in which they received from God the things requested. The emphasis upon the reality of receiving answers to prayers is strengthened by construction of the Greek sentence where the same root word appears in both verb and noun forms. As indicated earlier, this construction (a cognate accusative) literally reads, 'we have the asked-for-things which we have asked from him'. Thus, in the last part of v. 15 there is an extraordinary emphasis upon God's response to believers' petitions.[205]

Verse 16. At this point in the argument of 1 John two important themes converge. On the one hand, the theme of having confidence to ask anything in accordance with the will of God finds concrete expression in this verse. On the other hand, the theme of sin and the believer re-emerges for a third time in 1 John. The convergence of these two themes not only suggests that the readers can confidently make requests with regard to brothers or sisters who sin, but also that the theme of sin and the believer is of such importance that it merits attention in the conclusion of the book.

The verse begins with the phrase, 'If anyone sees a brother sinning a sin not to death'. The 'if' clause with which this verse begins conveys the idea of something that is expected under normal circumstances. In 5.16, it is expected that in the course of the community's life, on occasion the readers will 'see' a brother or sister 'sin a sin not to death'. In this verse the term 'brother' clearly has reference to a fellow believer, as it has throughout 1 John (2.9-11; 3.14-17; 4.20-21). The situation about which the readers are alerted is seeing 'a brother sinning a sin not to death'. Among the interpretive challenges of this verse is determining what it would mean to the readers to 'see' a brother or sister 'sinning a sin to death'. Would the idea of seeing a brother or sister sin imply that one must be an eyewitness of such activity? Or would such language be

---

205 Strecker, *The Johannine Letters*, p. 202.

taken to underscore the fact that knowledge of this sinful activity must be certain, not based upon indirect evidence? Perhaps a clue as to the term's meaning for the readers is found in the fact that the ancient idea of seeing is very closely associated with the idea of knowing. On this view, the one who sees a brother or sister sinning is the one who has knowledge of such activity, which would convey the idea of first-hand knowledge, whether or not one is an eyewitness to the activity here envisioned.

If seeing conveys the idea of knowledge, how would the readers understand the words 'sinning a sin not to death'? The phrase 'sinning a sin' is unique in the New Testament, occurring only here. This construction (a cognate accusative) is similar to the phrase 'the asked-for-things for which we have asked' in the previous verse, with the same term occurring as a verb and a noun in the verse. In 5.16 the verb ('sinning') and the noun ('a sin') are from the same root word (ἁμαρτάνοντα and ἁμαρτίαν, respectively). One of the functions of this kind of construction is to emphasize a given idea or theme. In this verse, the point of emphasis is sin and the believer. Such an emphasis reminds the readers of the previous discussions of this theme in 1 John. The readers have come to learn that while sin may on occasion afflict the believer, its presence poses a very real danger to the believer. When sin is found in the believer's life, it must be confessed to and forgiven by God on the basis of the cleansing blood of Jesus, 'our advocate with the Father' (1.5-2.2). However, the readers have also come to know the provisional nature of such statements, given that those who are born of God are not able to sin (3.9). In point of fact, the readers have learned that as long as one 'remains in him' one is able to live without sin, for he himself did not sin and came to destroy sin. Therefore, as the readers encounter the idea of seeing a brother or sister sinning a sin, there is an awareness that such a situation is of no little importance. Owing to the fact that those who sin reveal that they are children of the Devil (3.10), it becomes clear that a brother or sister who sins a sin is in a very dangerous and vulnerable position. In this light, the description of this activity as 'sinning a sin not to death' would fit nicely into 1 John's dialectical view of sin and the believer. The fact that a believer might be seen sinning such a sin would not be a complete surprise, owing to the previous acknowledgment that such is the case in 1.5–2.2. At the same time, the no-nonsense approach to sin found in 3.4-10 would indicate that this sinful activity is a very serious matter indeed.

If the words 'sinning a sin' take on this meaning, how would the readers understand the words 'a sin to death'? It is possible to take reference to 'death' in this phrase as a reference to physical death. A similar phrase is found in Jesus' words about Lazarus' condition, 'This illness is not to death' (Jn 11.4). In this Fourth Gospel text, death clearly has reference to physical death. There are also certain Old Testament texts which differentiate between sins that require the physical death of the sinner (Num. 18.22; Isa. 22.14) and those that do not (Deut. 22.26). However, there are reasons to believe that the readers would see in the word 'death' a reference to spiritual death. First, the readers have already encountered the use of death to describe a spiritual state in 1 Jn 3.14. There they are told, 'We know that we have passed out of death into life, because we love the brothers; the one who does not love remains in death'. Clearly, there is a contrast between life, identified as eternal life in 3.15, and death. Second, this same contrast appears in 5.16, where death is contrasted with life, later in the verse. Third, such an understanding does not appear to be far removed from Jesus' words to his Jewish opponents in the Fourth Gospel that it is possible to 'die in your sins' (8.24) and his words in the Apocalypse to the church at Sardis that 'You are dead' (3.1). Thus, the readers are likely to see 'death' here as 'eternal death', in contrast to 'eternal life'. On this view, the phrase 'sinning a sin not to death' conveys to the readers a dire situation for such a brother or sister, but one that has not yet resulted in spiritual death.

But even in this urgent situation, the believer is instructed to ask. The context suggests that the believer is to ask with the same confidence described in vv. 14-15. In this case, it would appear to be self-evident that such asking is in accord with God's will. The present tense form of the verb 'ask' indicates that such intercession is to be an ongoing part of the community's life. Earlier in 1 John (2.2), the readers are told that Jesus is the one who functions as an advocate with the Father concerning our sins and those of the whole world. Now, the readers learn that any and every member of the community is called upon to intercede for another brother or sister. While an emphasis upon the believer's role as intercessor for a brother or sister might at first seem out of place, in point of fact it fits nicely with this theme as it emerges in the Fourth Gospel. The readers know that Jesus instructed his disciples to wash one another's feet as a sign of continual cleansing from sin (13.1-20). In that this action is to be rendered to and received from one another, there is the implication that believers play some role in this activity of cleansing. Near the close of the Fourth Gospel this role for the believer is made more explicit, even if not altogether clear. On that occasion, after Jesus breathes and says to the disciples, 'Receive the Holy Spirit', he goes on to say, 'Whatever sins you forgive they are forgiven to them, whatever things you retain, they have been retained' (20.23). Therefore, for the readers of 1 Jn 5.16 to be instructed to intercede for a brother or sister who sins would not be wholly unexpected or out of keeping with Johannine thought.

The importance of such intercession is made clear by the next words in v. 16, 'and he will give him life'. The result promised to the believer who asks is that the brother or sister who sins will be given life. There is a certain ambiguity conveyed by the words in the Greek text for the identity of the one who gives life is not altogether clear. In fact, the construction of the sentence implies that it is the believer who gives life to the brother or sister who sins. Of course, in the Johannine literature (eternal) life comes from God and his Son who is Life, and such a fact would not be forgotten by the readers at this point. However, the ambiguity of the phrase 'he will give him life' suggests that the readers would likely see the lines between God and the believer converge in the giving of life to the brother or sister who sins. In any case, the readers could not help but be impressed by the assurance they are given about the results of their asking. The implication of all this is that for the one who sins a sin not to death, such intercession results in a spiritual rejuvenation of the sinning brother or sister owing to the gift of life. Instead of experiencing spiritual death, this intercession and gift of life insure that the sinning brother or sister continues to remain in him. The first half of v. 16 concludes with the words, 'to those who sin a sin not to death'. The shift from singular ('the one who') to plural ('to those who') serves to extend the idea of such intercession and its results to include all those who may have such a need — 'to all those who sin a sin not to death'.

The first thing the readers would notice about v. 16b is the way that its content stands in such contrast to that of v. 16a. Not only does it focus on 'a sin to death', rather than 'a sin not to death', but it also appears to discourage intercession rather than encourage it. It follows rather naturally that if there is 'a sin not to death' there must be 'a sin to death'. As is the case with the former phrase, the meaning of the latter is not altogether clear, though numerous suggestions have been made as to its meaning.[206] However, if the readers are likely to take the phrase 'a sin not to death' as having reference to sinful activity that places the believer in jeopardy of 'spiritual death' (losing the 'life' which God gives), it would appear that they would take the phrase 'a sin to death' as having

---

206   Proposals include: (a) intentional sin as opposed to unintentional as described in the Old Testament and the Dead Sea Scrolls; (b) the blasphemy against the Spirit of which Jesus speaks; (c) the sin of the unrepentant, sexually immoral person in the church at Corinth for whom Paul recommends expulsion; (d) the apostasy of which Hebrews speaks; and (e) the later mortal as opposed to venial sins which the Church eventually identified.

reference to sinful activity that *has* resulted in 'spiritual death'. The meaning of death in this verse is no doubt similar to its meaning in 1 Jn 3.14, where it is a realm out of which one passes into life.[207] In 5.16, the experience of 'spiritual death' carries with it the idea of the loss of 'life'. Such an understanding of 'a sin to death' would no doubt include the kind of deception and false prophecy described in 1 John, while neither limiting the meaning of 'a sin to death' to this specific activity nor concluding that such influence is irreversible. On this latter point, it is especially significant that while Peter 'denies' Jesus in the Fourth Gospel (13.36-38; 18.15-18, 25-27), an activity attributed to the antichrists in 1 John, he is not ultimately beyond the reach of Jesus, as Jn 21.15-22 reveals. If other specific sins are to be identified in the Johannine community such a list would no doubt include the failure to keep the commands, which above all involve loving one another.

Although to this point the readers have been encouraged to ask for anything according to his will, including intercession for those who 'sin a sin not to death', at this point they are discouraged from asking, if not forbidden to do so altogether. For after a statement acknowledging the existence of 'a sin to death' they are told, 'not concerning this do I say that you should ask'. Although the Greek word here translated 'ask' is different from the term that occurs in vv. 14-16a, the readers are not likely to see any difference in meaning as these two terms (ἐρωτάω and αἰτέω, respectively) function synonymously in the Johannine literature. It is difficult to tell whether the statement discouraging intercession implies that to ask concerning 'a sin to death' would not be in accord with God's will, or if one who commits 'a sin to death' is deemed to be beyond the reach of the community. Or should these words be taken to indicate that it is not the appropriate time to offer such prayer, similar to the way in which Jesus' prayer in John 17 did not include prayer for the world (cf. 17.9)? While such options each have their strengths, on balance, this clause is not far from the warning and instruction found in 2 John 10-11, with regard to the treatment of the deceivers. These words would contain a not-so-subtle warning for the readers that it is possible for them to 'sin a sin to death' and, consequently, lose that for which they have worked (2 John 8). At any rate, it is assumed that the community is aware of the line of demarcation that exists between 'a sin to death' and 'a sin not to death' and is able to respond in an appropriate fashion.

---

207 It is difficult to determine whether this idea is associated with 'the second death', which emerges in the Apocalypse (2.11; 20.6), and could be understood as 'eternal death'.

Verse 17. At least two things are conveyed to the readers in v. 17. First, the opening statement, 'all unrighteousness is sin', serves to re-emphasize the point that sin of any sort in the believer's life is a very serious matter. The fact that this statement occurs after the distinction made between 'a sin to death' and 'a sin not to death' indicates that sin which has not yet led to death is still 'deadly'. In the Johannine literature, the Greek term translated 'unrighteousness' (ἀδικία) comes to represent any act that stands in opposition to Jesus (Jn 7.18) and is closely associated with sin (1 Jn 1.9). In fact, it appears to be the opposite of 'righteous' individuals (1 Jn 1.9; 2.2, 29; 3.7) and acts of 'righteousness' (3.12). The appearance of the word 'all' indicates that there are no exceptions to this statement. Despite the fact that a significant difference may be drawn between 'a sin to death' and 'a sin not to death', a difference that determines whether or not a believer may intercede for the one guilty of such activity, all sinful activity is a dangerous matter. For those who sin reject the Son and identify with the Devil.

A second and equally important issue addressed in this verse is the reaffirmation of the fact that 'there is a sin not to death'. This part of the verse is joined to that which precedes by the conjunction 'and', which here conveys the idea of contrast. The reappearance of the language, 'there is a sin not to death', at this point in 1 John reminds the readers of their obligation to intercede for brothers and sisters who commit such acts, and, at the same time, reassures the readers of the fact that in the event they fall into sin, all is not lost. This clause carries with it the implicit promise of forgiveness, life and remaining in him, preparing the readers for the next verse.

Verses 18-20
Appropriately enough, in a book much of which has sought to reassure the readers of their fellowship with God, 1 John closes with three statements of reassurance, each of which begins with the words 'we know'. Each of these statements focuses on an issue or theme of great importance in the document and, consequently, continues to bring together several of the major issues of 1 John in this concluding section (5.13-21).

Verse 18. The first Greek word the readers encounter in this verse, translated 'we know' (οἴδαμεν), picks up on the idea of 'knowing' in v. 13, which begins this final section of 1 John (5.13-21). In point of fact, this very verb form (οἴδαμεν) occurs twice in v. 15, offering further evidence that this theme is a significant one in the concluding section of 1 John. As before, the appearance of 'we know' language serves to assure the readers of their relationship with God. As with other occurrences of the first person plural 'we', solidarity is being expressed between the writer(s) and the readers. Not only is v. 18 connected to what precedes it by the presence of 'we know' language, but it is also intimately connected to the verses that immediately precede it which focus on sin and the believer, vv. 16-17. As noted in the reading of v. 17, there appears to be some concern that the readers not take the distinction between 'a sin not to death' and 'a sin to death' as a sign that sin is an unimportant matter. If v. 17 serves to challenge such a possibility, the first part of v. 18 functions as a frontal assault which demolishes any such notion. For here the readers encounter language familiar from 1 Jn 3.9, where the absolutely diametric opposition between the believer and sin is stressed: 'Each one who has been born of God does not sin.' These words remind the readers that they are children of God, those in whom his seed remains, those who remain in him. As such, they do not sin. Their relationship to God enables them to live without sin. In fact, it makes it impossible for them to sin, because sin reveals that the one who sins belongs to the Devil, not to God. It would not be lost on the readers of 3.6-10 that such living without sin is possible only so long as one remains in relationship with God, his Son and the Spirit. For this language to reappear near the conclusion of 1 John and on the heels of a discussion about intercession for a brother or sister who sins, underscores for the readers the importance of living lives that avoid sin at all costs. As before, the words translated 'each one who has been born of God' utilizes a (perfect) past tense verb which indicates that this birth took place at a specific point in the past, but that the effects of this birth continue into the present. The presence of the word 'each' reveals that there are no exceptions to this statement. Thus, this first phrase in v. 18 offers additional force to the statement in v. 17 that 'all unrighteousness is sin' and that all sin is dangerous.

This familiar phrase is followed by one that takes the argument in a new direction. At the same time, it presents the readers with a couple of interpretive challenges. The readers learn that 'each one who has been born of God' is not on his or her own in combating sin, 'but the one born of God keeps him'. Several things are significant about this latter phrase. First, it should be noted that the conjunction translated 'but' (ἀλλ') functions in this verse to emphasize contrast. Its adversative force could result in a translation something like 'rather'. Second, whatever the precise identity of 'the one born of God', it is clear that the readers are assured that this one 'keeps' them. Such language reminds the readers of Jesus' prayer in the Fourth Gospel where he asks the Father to 'keep' the disciples from the evil one (17.11, 15) just as Jesus has kept them by means of the name given him (17.12). In this light, there is a sense in which the statement found in this part of v. 18 would be seen by the readers as an answer to Jesus' prayer. At the same time, the dominant meaning of 'keeping' vocabulary in 1 John has reference to 'keeping his commands' and may suggest to the readers that those who keep his commands are the ones whom he keeps. Such a reciprocal 'keeping' is very much the point in the Apocalypse (3.10). At any rate, the implicit promise is that 'the one born of God' protects or guards 'each one who has been born of God'.

Third, the primary interpretive challenge of the phrase is the identity of 'the one born of God'. There would appear to be two options open for the readers of 1 John. One interpretive option is that 'the one born of God' has reference to the Son of God. Clues which suggest to the readers that this phrase has reference to Jesus are the following: (1) There is an interesting change of tense from the first construction to the second, a change from perfect past tense to aorist past tense. As the aorist has primary reference to a specific past act or series of acts, and the perfect is normally used with reference to the believer, it could very well be that this shift indicates a change of subject from the believer to Jesus. (2) While 'the one born of God' does not occur elsewhere in the Johannine literature with reference to Jesus, there is an emphasis in the Johannine literature upon the fact that he is the 'unique Son' (Jn 1.14, 18; 3.16, 18; 1 Jn 4.9). (3) The statement that 'the one born of God keeps him' is especially appropriate for Jesus in that he is described as 'keeping' the disciples in the Fourth Gospel (17.12). (4) Owing to the fact that 'the one born of God' stands in contrast to 'the evil one', mentioned in the last part of v. 18, the readers might be inclined to see a reference to the Son of God here. (5) The similarity between the constructions, 'each one who has been born of God' and 'the one born of God', conveys to the readers a sense of continuity between the children of God and the Son of God.

At the same time, there are also significant hints given to the readers that 'the one born of God' may have reference to a fellow believer. (1) One of the more significant clues is that in the move from 'each one who has been born of God' to 'the one born of God', there is no indication of a change in subject. As the believer is clearly meant in the first construction, so it would appear that the believer is in mind in the second as well. (2) In all other Johannine occurrences, 'the one who has been born of God' always has reference to the believer (Jn 1.13; 3.5; 1 Jn 3.9; 5.18a) and never to the Son of God. It follows that the readers would not expect nor follow such a radical departure on this occasion. (3) Owing to the fact that vv. 16-17 have emphasized the mutual spiritual accountability of one believer to the other, and the implication that the believer's prayer will give life to a brother or sister who sins, it follows that to say one believer 'keeps' another is not a wholly new idea. (4) Neither should it be forgotten that the believers are described in 1 Jn 2.13-14 as being victorious over the evil one.

Given these conflicting signals, how are the readers likely to understand 'the one born of God'? On balance, it appears slightly more probable that the readers would see in 'the one born of God' primary reference to the Son of God. Yet, at the same time, the remarkably ambiguous nature of the construction suggests that the readers would not exclude reference to fellow believers as well. Thus, while taking solace in the fact that the Son of God 'keeps' the believer, the readers would also see an implicit admonition and encouragement with regard to mutual accountability. The fact that the verb 'keeps' is in the present tense indicates that this 'keeping' is an ongoing part of the believer's life and journey.

The final phrase in v. 18 reveals the result of this 'keeping': 'and the evil one does not touch him'. While the identity of 'the one born of God' is not altogether clear in this verse, the identity of the evil one is certain. Earlier subtle references in 1 John to such a sinister figure come in the form of allusions to the father of lies (1.6, 10) and the malevolent force of darkness which is capable of blinding the eyes of certain individuals who claim to be in the light (2.9-11). Over this one the readers have been reminded that they are victorious (2.13-14). He is the one with whom Cain is identified (3.12). Jesus' prayer in Jn 17.15 comes very close to identifying 'the evil one' as a personal force who is otherwise known as the Devil (8.44; 13.2), the ruler of this world (12.31; 14.30; 16.11) and Satan (13.27). In 1 John 'the evil one' is one of the preferred titles for this figure, along with the Devil (3.8, 10). It is this evil one who is the subject of attention in 5.18c. As in 2.13-14, the readers are assured of victory over this nemesis, though the language describing their triumph is different in 5.18. In this verse, the readers are told that the evil one does not touch them. Here the term 'touch' conveys the idea of harm caused by the evil one 'laying hold of' a believer. However, such an ominous possibility has no chance of success owing to the protection offered by 'the one born of God'. Rather than sinning, owing to the menacing work of the evil one, the believer is assured that 'each one who has been born of God does not sin'. At this point the roles of Jesus and the believer in 'keeping' 'each one who has been born of God' appear to merge.

Verse 19. The thought of v. 18 is developed further in v. 19, with an emphasis upon the difference between believers and the world. For a second time in this short subsection (vv. 18-20) a sentence begins with 'we know'. Not only does this rhetorical device indicate a connection between these two verses, but the content of vv. 18-19 also reveals a

thematic link between them. Specifically, the first half of v. 19 develops the words of v. 18a, while the second half of v. 19 picks up on the idea expressed in v. 18c. The words of assurance, 'we know', focus on the fact that 'we are of God'. It follows that if 'one has been born of God' (v. 18) then such an individual is 'of God'. The words 'of God', which occur frequently in the Johannine Epistles (3 Jn 11; 1 Jn 3.9-10; 4.1-4, 6-7; 5.1, 4), not only says something about one's origin but also conveys something of a sense of belonging.[208] The idea of being 'children of God' is not far from this expression. The shift from the third person singular, 'each one who', to the first person plural, 'we are of God', makes the reality of the statement more personal.

While the evil one has no power to 'touch' the believer, owing to his or her being kept by 'the one born of God', 'the whole world lies in the evil one'. This statement about the world merits several observations. First, the evil one is clearly to be equated with the ruler of this world, as implied in the Fourth Gospel (12.31; 14.30; 16.11). Second, the evil one thoroughly dominates the world, with the unique expression, 'lies in the evil one', conveying the idea of the world's absolute dependence upon its ruler. While the believer is 'of God', having his or her origin in him, the world is 'in the evil one'. Third, the expression 'the whole world' reminds the readers of an earlier occurrence of these words in 1 John (2.2). There the emphasis is upon the fact that Jesus did not only die for 'our' sins, but also for the sins of 'the whole world'. It is this same world that lies in the evil one for whom Jesus serves as an atoning sacrifice. It is this same world that is characterized by its desires and lusts (2.16), that is already passing away (2.17), that refuses to believe in Jesus (Jn 16.8-10), that finds itself 'in the evil one'. However, God's love for the world, which results in Jesus' sacrificial death for the whole world, suggests that even the pessimistic reality expressed in v. 19 is not completely irreversible. The whole world is offered forgiveness through Jesus' atoning death!

The contrast between the community and the world is nowhere more starkly stated in 1 John than in this verse. Its uncompromising nature encourages the believers that they are 'of God' — that they remain in relationship with him.

Verse 20. For a third and final time in this subsection, a sentence begins with 'we know'. On this occasion the word translated 'we know' is introduced by a Greek conjunction (δὲ) which may be translated in any number of ways. In this verse the word can either function as an adversative

---

208 Brown, *The Epistles of John*, p. 622.

with a translation something like 'nevertheless', or it can mark the conclusion of a series of statements resulting in a translation like 'and', or it can even be left untranslated. It is possible that the readers would see in this term a little bit of each emphasis. On this view, the word would signal that v. 20 offers a contrast to the statement 'the whole world lies in the evil one', with which v. 19 closes, as well as indicating that this is the final 'we know' statement in this final subsection. In v. 20 the readers know that 'the Son of God comes and he has given to us an ability to understand'. This statement is the first of several found in v. 20, which draw upon the whole of the document in what may be called the book's christological and theological summary or conclusion. The first phrase reminds the reader of two extraordinarily important events in their lives. The words, 'the Son of God comes', rather clearly pick up on the idea of the manifestation of the Son of God in the Incarnation, a theme of considerable importance in 1 John (1.2; 3.5, 8; 4.9). In point of fact, this verb is used in precisely this way in the Fourth Gospel (8.42). One of the interesting things about the expression in v. 10 is the verb translated 'comes', which occurs in the present tense but has a (perfect) past tense meaning and could be rendered 'has come'. By this means the readers are encouraged to hold together the tension of this past act and the present activity of Jesus. The title 'the Son of God' would naturally convey the full meaning this term has come to have to this point in 1 John. The other thing the readers have come to know is that they 'have been given the ability to understand'. The Greek word behind this phrase (διάνοιαν) occurs only here in the Johannine literature. It does not designate 'knowledge' or 'understanding' as such, but rather the process by which such comes. In this regard, it bears a striking resemblance to the idea of 'the anointing' which the readers have received from him, an anointing that teaches them all things and makes the need for human teachers superfluous (2.20, 27).

The reason for this gift is made clear in a purpose clause which states, 'in order that we might know the one who is True'. As throughout 1 John, the idea of knowing entails more than mental assent to a set of facts, but is relational in meaning. This relational knowledge is of 'the one who is True'. While the readers might be tempted to see a reference to Jesus in these words, the following words make clear that on this occasion the phrase has reference to the Father. Reference to knowing God would not surprise the readers for they know of the heavy emphasis on this theme throughout 1 John. Mention of 'the one who is True' carries with it the idea of genuineness and authenticity, as opposed to that which is false. The relational aspect of the readers' 'knowing' is made clear by the next words, 'and we are in the one who is True'. For

1 John, knowledge leads to fellowship and mutual indwelling. In this last appearance of the 'we are in' phrase in 1 John, the readers are assured yet again of their relationship with God. They know him and are in him. In contrast to the world, which is in the evil one, the believers are in God. But just as near the beginning of 1 John, so near its conclusion, there is no fellowship with or being in the Father without fellowship with and being 'in his Son Jesus Christ'. For one cannot have the Father without having the Son (2.23). Anyone who has seen the Son has seen the Father (Jn 14.7). Reference to the full name and title, 'his Son Jesus Christ', is a clear allusion not only to all that has come before in 1 John with regard to Jesus' person and work (cf. esp. 1.3; 5.1, 5), but also to Jn 20.31, a text which lies behind the beginning of this section (5.13). Thus, the essential oneness of the Father and Son is affirmed in a way that parallels their description in the Fourth Gospel (1.1; 10.30; 20.28).

The final phrase in v. 20 contains a strikingly unrestrained declaration, 'This one is the true God and Eternal Life'. True to form, there is some ambiguity present, specifically with regard to the meaning of the pronoun 'this one'. While it is possible to take 'this one' as a reference to 'the one who is True', that is 'God', it appears that the reference is to 'his Son Jesus Christ' instead. To say that Jesus is 'the true God' is as strong a statement about Jesus being God as one finds in the Johannine literature. It not only is at home with the language of Jn 1.1, 18, but it also functions as a parallel to Thomas' confession of Jesus, 'my Lord and my God', very near the conclusion of the Fourth Gospel (20.28). In addition, the force of the statement takes on added emphasis when it is remembered that the words, 'the only true God', are used to describe the Father by Jesus in the Fourth Gospel (17.3). As with its use to describe the Father, the term 'True' here conveys the idea of something that is genuine or authentic. 'Jesus is the genuine (or authentic) God.' That both the Fourth Gospel and 1 John end with an affirmation of Jesus as God reveals something of the importance of this belief for the community. As such, the argument about the essential nature and role of Jesus found throughout 1 John culminates in this verse. No less significant is the fact that Jesus is yet again called Eternal Life. This concluding title stands in parallel to its appearance in the prologue of 1 John, where Jesus is described as 'Eternal Life which is with the Father' (1.2). By means of this title the readers are reminded of Jesus' unique role in conveying Eternal Life to the believers, a point with which this section began (5.13). For he himself is Eternal Life. Therefore, the christological argument of 1 John ends with a great climax which assures the believers of their relationship with God.

Verse 21. The final verse in 1 John begins with the seventh occurrence of the word 'children' as a form of address in this book (2.1, 12, 28; 3.7, 18; 4.4). The appearance of this term of endearment at the close of the document continues the sense of warm fellowship between the writer(s) and the readers that has been exhibited throughout the work. Following this familiar form of address are words that at first sight appear to be completely out of keeping with the emphasis of 1 John. The sentence reads, 'Children, keep (guard) yourselves from idols'. The form of the verb (aorist imperative) alerts the readers to the fact that a strict prohibition is being made. This exact phrase is found nowhere else in the New Testament. When accompanied by the pronoun 'yourselves', the verb means 'to be on guard'. The pronoun itself conveys and extends the theme of mutual accountability, which is the focus of vv. 16-18. Thus, the readers are admonished to be extremely vigilant with regard to 'the idols'. The question is, in a document in which idols have not figured at all in the argument, how would the readers likely understand appearance of the term here? The presence of the definite article 'the' indicates that specific idols are in view, but which ones? It is, of course, possible to take mention of 'the idols' as reference to the practice of idolatry (Rev. 21.8), with which at least part of the Johannine community was familiar. Such practice includes worshiping 'idols of gold, silver, bronze, stone and wood, which are not able to see nor hear nor walk' (Rev. 9.20). Apparently, such worship involved eating food sacrificed to idols (Rev. 2.14, 20). While it cannot be ruled out that the Johannine churches that would receive 1 John were susceptible to practices involving idols, there are absolutely no indications that such is the case in 1 John. Therefore, it would appear wise to look for hints within 1 John in the attempt to determine the meaning of this term for the readers.

Perhaps the most helpful clue as to the meaning of 'the idols' is the immediate context of 5.21. In v. 20, great emphasis has been placed upon the fact that the Father is 'the one who is True (or genuine)' and that his Son is 'the true God'. Such emphasis upon authenticity would stand in clear contrast to the idols that represent false gods. But who are these false gods? It follows that if Jesus is the true God and Eternal Life, if he has been sent as an atoning sacrifice to be the Savior of the world, if through his blood cleansing from sin is experienced, then those who deny Jesus, who do not confess him as the Son of God, embrace a false god and are false prophets. On this view, the readers are warned once again to keep far away from the false teaching that has divided the community. For in this deception, idolatry lurks. It is no inconsequential matter. Those who embrace this false teaching identify with the idols of this world by denying the true God. As a result, they cut themselves off from Eternal Life. Thus, this book, which has been devoted to assuring the readers of their relationship with God, concludes with a sober warning about the dangers of embracing false teaching. This somber warning is consistent with the many others that fill this document devoted to the Eternal Life that Jesus Christ the Son of God brings and is.[209]

Reflection and Response — Part Twelve

Reflection

The diverse topics found in this final section of 1 John are all related to the assurance the readers have been given throughout the book. Specifically, the readers are instructed that the purpose of the book is that they might know they have eternal life through believing in the name of the Son of God. This assurance extends to the confidence they have to speak to God and the assurance that anything they ask for in accordance with his will, they will receive. This confidence to ask even includes the intercession offered on behalf of a believer who sins a sin not to death. In addition to this assurance the readers are reminded at the close of the book of three things which 'we know'. We know that the one born of God does not sin but is kept by the one born of God so that the evil one cannot touch him or her. We know that while the whole world lies in the evil one, we are of God. We know that the Son of God is the true God and Eternal Life, and that we are in him and his Father the True One. Therefore, despite the presence of false prophets and deceivers, the believers are assured with a crescendo of encouragement that they can know the certainty of their relationship with God.

In order to facilitate further reflection on this passage the following questions are raised. What doubts currently face the Church about its relationship with God? In what specific ways are its beliefs about God challenged? How is the Church encouraged in such times of doubt? What assurances does it rely upon and how are they given? What concrete forms do these assurances take? Are you familiar with specific prayers offered by the Church that have been answered? What are some of them? How seriously does the Church take its responsibility to intercede on behalf of a sinning brother or sister? What formal means of

---

209   Bede, *Commentary on 1 John*, ACCS, XI, p. 229, astutely comments: 'You who know the true God, in whom you have eternal life, must keep yourselves away from the teachings of the heretics which lead only to eternal death. In the manner of those who made idols in the place of God, the heretics have corrupted the glory of the incorruptible God by their wicked doctrines which bear the stamp of corruptible things.'

reconciliation and forgiveness are available and utilized within the Church? In what ways is the Church distinct from the world which lies in the evil one? How does the ability to understand, given to believers, result in knowledge of the true one? How has such knowledge made a difference in the lives of individuals within the community of faith?

On a more personal level, what doubts do you experience about your relationship with God? When are these doubts felt most powerfully? What prayers have you prayed that you know, without doubt, have been answered by God? Have you ever been involved in intercession for a brother or sister who has sinned? How would you describe this experience's impact upon you and your brother or sister? Have you ever been the recipient of intercession by a brother or sister? When have you been tempted to sin but have felt yourself protected from succumbing to the temptation? What are some of the differences between you and the world? In what specific ways has the divinely given ability to understand led you to God and made clear to you the reality of Jesus Christ his Son who is Eternal Life?

Response

An appropriate response to the emphases of the conclusion of 1 John would perhaps include the following.

First, identify the things that cause you to doubt your relationship with God, perhaps making a written list.

Second, testify to someone about the concrete ways in which God has assured you of his relationship with you.

Third, purpose in your heart that when you see a brother or sister sin you will offer serious intercession on their behalf, expecting God to give life in response.

Fourth, through prayer, worship, fellowship and the reading of Scripture nurture the ability to understand so that your knowledge of God through his Son Jesus Christ will be firmly established despite any opposition you encounter.

SELECT BIBLIOGRAPHY

Brown, R.E., *The Epistles of John* (Garden City, NY: Doubleday, 1982).
Bruce, F.F., *The Epistles of John* (Grand Rapids: Eerdmans, 1970).
Bultmann, R., *The Johannine Epistles* (trans. R.P. O'Hara, L.C. McGaughy and R.W. Funk; ed. R.W. Funk; Philadelphia: Fortress Press, 1973).
Hengel, M., *The Johannine Question* (Philadelphia: Trinity Press International, 1989).
Lieu, J., *The Second and Third Epistles of John* (Edinburgh: T. & T. Clark, 1986).
Marshall, I.H., *The Epistles of John* (Grand Rapids: Eerdmans, 1978).
Rensberger, D., *1 John, 2 John, 3 John* (Nashville: Abingdon Press, 1997).
Schnackenburg, R., *The Johannine Epistles* (trans. R. Fuller and S. Fuller; New York: Crossroad, 1992).
Smalley, S.S., *1, 2, 3 John* (Waco, TX: Word Books, 1984).
Smith, D.M., *First, Second, and Third John* (Louisville, KY: John Knox Press, 1991).
Strecker, G., *The Johannine Letters* (ed. H. Attridge; trans. L.M. Maloney; Minneapolis: Fortress Press, 1996).
Thomas, J.C., 'The Literary Structure of 1 John', *NovT* 40 (1998), pp. 369-81.
—'The Order of the Composition of the Johannine Epistles', *NovT* 37 (1995), pp. 68-75.
Westcott, B.F., *The Epistles of St. John* (Grand Rapids: Eerdmans, 1966).